From the Closet to the Altar

From the Closet to the Altar

Courts, Backlash, and the Struggle for Same-Sex Marriage

MICHAEL J. KLARMAN

OXFORD
UNIVERSITY PRESS

OXFORD

UNIVERSITY PRESS

Oxford University Press is a department of the
University of Oxford. It furthers the University's objective
of excellence in research, scholarship, and education
by publishing worldwide.

Oxford   New York

Auckland   Cape Town   Dar es Salaam   Hong Kong   Karachi
Kuala Lumpur   Madrid   Melbourne   Mexico City   Nairobi
New Delhi   Shanghai   Taipei   Toronto

With offices in

Argentina   Austria   Brazil   Chile   Czech Republic   France   Greece
Guatemala   Hungary   Italy   Japan   Poland   Portugal   Singapore
South Korea   Switzerland   Thailand   Turkey   Ukraine   Vietnam

Oxford is a registered trademark of Oxford University Press
in the UK and certain other countries.

Published in the United States of America by
Oxford University Press
198 Madison Avenue, New York, NY 10016

© Oxford University Press 2013, 2014
First issued as an Oxford University Press paperback, 2014

Library of Congress Cataloging-in-Publication Data
Klarman, Michael J.
From the closet to the altar : courts, backlash, and the struggle
for same-sex marriage / Michael Klarman.
   p.   cm.
Includes bibliographical references and index.
ISBN 978-0-19-992210-9 (hardback); 978-0-19-936045-1 (pbk.)
1. Same-sex marriage—Law and legislation—United States—History.
2. Gay couples—Legal status, laws, etc.—United States—History.
3. Same-sex marriage—Law and legislation—United States—States.
4. Civil unions—Law and legislation—United States.   I. Title.
KF539.K53 2012   346.7301'68—dc23
2012023121

To my children:
Muli, Rachael, Ian, and Teymura

CONTENTS

Introduction to Paperback Edition   ix

Introduction   xix

1. World War II to Stonewall (1950s and 1960s)   3
2. Stonewall to *Bowers* (1970s and 1980s)   16
3. Hawaii and the "Defense of Marriage" (1990s)   48
4. *Baker* (Vermont) and *Lawrence* (1999–2003)   75
5. *Goodridge* (Massachusetts) and Its Backlash (2003–2008)   89
6. The Gay Marriage Spring (2009)   119
7. Backlash (Again): Maine and Iowa (2009–2010)   143
8. To the Present   156
9. Why Backlash? Part I: Courts and Public Opinion   165
10. Why Backlash? Part II: Politics and Federalism   183
11. Looking to the Future: The Inevitability of Gay Marriage   193
    Conclusion   208

Acknowledgments   221
Abbreviations Used in the Notes   225
Notes   229
Bibliography   261
Index   267

INTRODUCTION TO PAPERBACK EDITION

If anything, the pace of change on marriage equality has accelerated since February 2012, when I completed the manuscript for *From the Closet to the Altar: Courts, Backlash, and the Struggle for Same-Sex Marriage.*

In May 2012, as expected, voters in North Carolina passed a referendum amending the state constitution to bar same-sex marriage; the margin was twenty-two percentage points. Although that seems like a decisive defeat, North Carolina's neighbors, Tennessee and South Carolina, had rejected same-sex marriage in 2006 by margins of sixty-two and fifty-six percentage points, respectively. Thus, the 2012 vote in North Carolina revealed that even in the South—the region of the country most resistant to gay marriage—public opinion has been moving inexorably in its favor.

Within days of the North Carolina vote, President Barack Obama, after years of opposing gay marriage and then "evolving" on the issue, finally embraced marriage equality—something I had predicted in my book that he would not do until after the election. The timing—but almost certainly not the substance—of the president's announcement was influenced by his vice president's spilling the beans a couple of days earlier. President Obama and his strategists apparently had concluded that the political costs of endorsing marriage equality—which was still opposed by majorities in swing electoral states such as Florida, Ohio, and Virginia—were outweighed by political benefits, such as increased fund-raising in the gay community and greater enthusiasm for the president's reelection among young voters. Or, perhaps the president had simply decided that the time had arrived to do what he considered the right thing.

I am grateful to the *Harvard Law Review* for permission to reproduce in this Introduction material first published in my article "*Windsor* and *Brown*: Marriage Equality and Racial Equality," 127 *Harvard Law Review* 127–60 (2013).

At the Democratic National Convention in the summer of 2012, speaker after speaker offered rousing endorsements of marriage equality, and most Democratic U.S. senators announced support for it. On November 6, 2012, the day on which President Obama won reelection, voters in Washington, Maine, and Maryland approved gay marriage by referendum—the first time any state's voters had ever done so. In a fourth state, Minnesota, a majority of voters rejected a proposed constitutional amendment to bar gay marriage—only the second time that any state's voters had ever done so. In Iowa that day, voters retained a justice of the state supreme court who had voted in favor of same-sex marriage in a 2009 decision interpreting the state constitution; just two years previously, Iowa voters had rejected the retention of three of his colleagues. On Election Day in Wisconsin, voters elected the first openly gay U.S. senator in American history.

In December 2012, the U.S. Supreme Court granted review of lower court decisions invalidating the Defense of Marriage Act ("DOMA") and California's Proposition 8. The former was a statute defining marriage as the union of a man and a woman for purposes of federal law, and the latter was a state constitutional amendment that had overturned a state supreme court ruling in favor of marriage equality. In January 2013, President Obama strongly endorsed marriage equality in his Second Inaugural Address. Associating the struggle for gay equality with that for racial and gender equality by conjoining, alliteratively, Stonewall with Selma and Seneca Falls, the president proclaimed that "[o]ur journey is not complete until our gay brothers and sisters are treated like anyone else under the law—for if we are truly created equal, then surely the love we commit to one another must be equal as well."

Early in 2013, legislatures in Minnesota, Rhode Island, and Delaware enacted same-sex marriage. In Illinois, the senate endorsed a marriage equality bill, but it was pulled from the house at the last minute for lack of majority support. As had happened in Maryland in 2011, several black legislators representing districts with overwhelmingly African American populations declined to support the measure. (On average, African Americans are more religious than other Americans, and religiosity strongly correlates with opposition to same-sex marriage.)

By the spring of 2013, it was apparent that Republicans, too, were beginning to shift their positions on marriage equality. In the run-up to the oral argument of the marriage equality cases in the Supreme Court, three Republican U.S. senators endorsed same-sex marriage. More than a hundred prominent Republican politicians and party leaders, including the managers of the last two Republican presidential campaigns and a former chairman of the Republican National Committee, signed a Supreme Court brief supporting marriage equality. Several leading Republican fund-raisers—including, most notably, billionaire hedge fund manager Paul Singer—have endorsed gay marriage and contributed millions of dollars to Republican state legislators who have risked primary challenges by voting in favor of it. Republican superstrategist Karl Rove stated that he could imagine the Republican Party's standard bearer in 2016 supporting gay marriage. These actions and statements represented an extraordinary shift from 2004, when Republicans almost uniformly denounced gay marriage and used the issue to considerable political advantage.

On June 26, 2013, the Supreme Court in *Windsor v. United States,* by a vote of five to four, invalidated Section 3 of DOMA, which defined marriage as the union of a man and a woman for federal law purposes, such as allocating Social Security survivors' benefits or determining the immigration status of the spouse of a U.S. citizen. Under DOMA, the federal government declined to recognize gay marriages lawfully performed in the states.

Justice Kennedy's majority opinion in *Windsor* emphasizes that the federal government has traditionally deferred to state definitions of marriage: "By history and tradition the definition and regulation of marriage . . . has been treated as being within the authority and realm of the separate States." Yet *Windsor* did not ultimately invalidate DOMA on federalism grounds, perhaps because the majority appreciated the strangeness of a ruling that constrained Congress, wholly apart from any individual-rights limitations, from limiting the class of persons entitled to benefit from laws concededly within its enumerated powers. In the end, Justice Kennedy's opinion invalidates Section 3 of DOMA on the ground that Congress's motive for enacting it was to disparage and demean gays and lesbians. Justice Kennedy said nothing in response to the principal justifications proffered for the statute—most notably, honoring the choice of past Congresses to provide benefits only to couples satisfying the traditional definition of marriage and preserving geographic uniformity in the provision of federal benefits.

The same day as *Windsor,* the Court in *Hollingsworth v. Perry* dismissed an appeal from a ruling by the U.S. Court of Appeals for the Ninth Circuit invalidating California's Proposition 8. *Hollingsworth* had presented the Justices with a wide array of options. One of these was simply to reverse the lower court and reject a federal constitutional right to same-sex marriage. Another set of options was to affirm the Ninth Circuit—in an opinion that could have assumed various different breadths. The narrowest alternative, known colloquially as the "one-state" solution, was to invalidate Proposition 8, as the Ninth Circuit had done, on the ground that California had no permissible justification for leaving same-sex couples in possession of all of the rights and benefits of marriage while depriving them of the formal status, which had once been conferred upon them by state law. A broader option—the so-called eight-state solution, advocated by the Justice Department—was to require those states, including California, that had authorized civil unions for same-sex couples to permit gay marriage, based on the argument that no legitimate reason existed for granting same-sex couples all of the rights and benefits of marriage while withholding from them the formal title.

The broadest option, known as the "fifty-state" solution, was simply to identify a federal constitutional right to same-sex marriage, perhaps on the ground that marriage is a fundamental right or that classifications based on sexual orientation are entitled to strict scrutiny and the government had offered no sufficiently compelling justification for denying same-sex couples access to marriage.

Eschewing all of these options, the *Hollingsworth* Court, by a vote of five to four, declined to reach the merits of the constitutional dispute. Instead, in an opinion by Chief Justice Roberts—speaking for an ideologically mixed group that included himself and Justices Scalia, Ginsburg, Breyer, and Kagan—the Court dismissed the appeal from the Ninth Circuit on the ground that the official sponsors of Proposition 8, who had intervened at trial to defend the initiative after state elected officials had declined to do so, lacked standing to prosecute the appeal of the district court's decision invalidating the measure.

For two reasons, the four dissenters probably had the better of the standing argument, which suggests that the majority had decided to "duck" the question of whether state bans on gay marriage were constitutional. First, the California supreme court, the authoritative interpreter of that state's laws, had concluded that California law authorized an initiative's formal sponsors to assert the state's interest in defending the constitutionality of its laws once public officials had declined to do so. Dicta in a recent Supreme Court decision strongly implied that such an authorization in state law would conclusively resolve the standing issue under Article III of the federal Constitution. Even apart from that dicta, it is hard to see why a state should not be permitted to delegate to an initiative's formal sponsors—who are not simply random citizens selected off the street— the task of defending the constitutionality of their measure in federal court. It is especially difficult to fathom how ordinarily staunch defenders of the states' constitutional prerogatives such as Chief Justice Roberts and Justice Scalia could deny states the authority to determine who gets to defend the constitutionality of their laws in federal court.

Second and perhaps more important, Justice Kennedy's *Hollingsworth* dissent makes a powerful functional argument for why the official sponsors of an initiative ought to be allowed to defend its constitutionality in federal court once public officials have chosen not to do so. The reason many states embraced the mechanism of initiative early in the twentieth century was to enable citizens to circumvent elected officials who proved insufficiently responsive to their will. Empowering those same public officials to block the implementation of an enacted initiative by refusing to defend its constitutionality in court risks nullifying that mechanism. Chief Justice Roberts's opinion offers no response to this powerful functional argument in favor of recognizing the petitioners' standing in *Hollingsworth*.

Although one cannot know for sure, the Court probably chose to duck the constitutional issue in *Hollingsworth* because one or more of the five justices in the *Windsor* majority were not yet prepared to impose gay marriage on the states. Two members of the *Windsor* majority—Justices Kennedy and Sotomayor—stated at the *Hollingsworth* oral argument that they doubted whether certiorari should have been granted in that case. Kennedy wondered if review was "properly granted" given that the Court was being asked to enter "uncharted waters," while Sotomayor questioned whether now "was the time to decide the issue if states were "experiment[ing]" and further "per[colation]" might be useful. Moreover, a third member of the *Windsor* majority, Justice Ginsburg, has repeatedly stated that the Court erred in *Roe v. Wade* by intervening too quickly and too aggressively on the abortion issue, thereby preempting the political process. While all eyes were watching the marriage equality cases pending in the Supreme Court, Justice Ginsburg publicly reiterated this criticism of *Roe*. Since the Court's rulings, Justice Kennedy has publicly stated that it would have been a mistake for the Court to intervene "too soon and too broad[ly]" on gay marriage and thus risk "terminat[ing]" democratic debate on the issue.

How the justices in the *Windsor* majority would have voted if forced to resolve the constitutionality of state bans on same-sex marriage is, of course, unknowable. Yet apparently, one or more of them preferred to postpone that day of reckoning, probably because they worried that a broad constitutional ruling in favor of gay marriage in 2013 would have ignited a powerful political backlash. Many scholars and judges, including Justice Ginsburg, believe that *Roe v. Wade* fomented such a backlash, and many opponents of gay marriage explicitly warned the justices in *Hollingsworth* to avoid creating "another *Roe v. Wade*."

There is some reason to believe that the liberal justices exaggerated the backlash potential of a broad ruling in favor of gay marriage. Several factors influence whether Court decisions generate backlash, including public opinion on the underlying issue, the relative intensity of preference on the two sides of the issue, and the ease with which a particular Court ruling can be circumvented or defied. An analysis of these factors suggests that a broad marriage equality ruling in *Hollingsworth* probably would have ignited considerably less political backlash than *Brown v. Board of Education* sparked among white southerners in 1954 or that *Roe v. Wade* generated among right-to-lifers in 1973.

In 1993, when the Hawaii supreme court became the nation's first to rule tentatively in favor of gay marriage, Americans opposed that social reform by a margin of at least three to one. When the Massachusetts supreme court ruled squarely in favor of gay marriage in 2003, the country was still opposed by roughly two to one. Thus, both decisions generated potent political backlashes—the former leading directly to the enactment of DOMA in 1996 and the latter to the passage of twenty-five state constitutional amendments barring same-sex marriage.

By contrast, recent opinion polls consistently reveal majority support among Americans for gay marriage. On average, the polls suggest that supporters now outnumber opponents by roughly ten percentage points, and one recent survey showed a margin of twenty-two percentage points. Thus, a Supreme Court ruling in favor of gay marriage in *Hollingsworth* almost certainly would have generated much less political backlash than an analogous decision ten or twenty years ago would have.

In addition, Court decisions are more likely to ignite backlash when opponents of the ruling are more intensely committed about the underlying issue than supporters are. When *Brown* was decided in 1954, 70 percent of whites outside of the South agreed with it, but only 5 percent of them deemed civil rights the nation's most important issue. By contrast, in the South, where 90 percent of whites thought that *Brown* was wrong, 40 percent regarded the segregation issue as the nation's most pressing. In the mid-1950s, the whites with the strongest feelings about *Brown* generally disagreed with it the most vehemently.

Similarly, with regard to same-sex marriage in 2004, among the one-third of Americans who supported it, only 6 percent said they would be unwilling to support a political candidate with whom they disagreed on the issue. But among the two-thirds of Americans who opposed gay marriage, 34 percent said they were willing to make it a voting issue. Among evangelical Christians, that number rose to 55 percent. That large disparity in intensity of preference between the two sides of the gay marriage issue no longer exists today. Proponents of marriage equality are as strongly committed to it as opponents are resistant.

Perhaps more important, it is hard to imagine how the coming of gay marriage will affect the lives of opponents as directly and powerfully as critics of *Brown* and *Roe* believed those rulings affected theirs. For white southerners committed to the preservation of white supremacy in the mid 1950s, forced integration of their children with African Americans in grade schools was the end of the world as they knew it. Similarly, opponents of abortion regard it as murder; that critics of *Roe* are intensely committed to resisting its implementation and ultimately to overturning it is thus hardly surprising.

What is the analogous harm that gay marriage would inflict on its opponents? Concededly, expanding marriage to include same-sex couples might eventually change the meaning of marriage for religious fundamentalists who currently understand it as an institution created by God to enable a man and a woman to propagate the species. But that is an abstract and long-term effect. It is hard to see how allowing the gay partners down the street who are already living together to get married will have a direct impact on opponents of same-sex marriage that is even remotely analogous to the effects that *Brown* and *Roe* had on opponents of those decisions.

Another factor relevant to predicting backlash is the ease with which a particular Court decision can be circumvented or defied. *Brown* was easy to evade because while it barred states from segregating students by race, it left the placement of pupils primarily in the hands of local education officials, who quickly devised schemes that ostensibly eschewed racial considerations while nonetheless managing to keep schools thoroughly segregated by race. For the better part of a decade after *Brown*, virtually no school desegregation took place in the South. Similarly, abortion opponents have whittled away at the right recognized in *Roe* by devising seemingly endless regulations of abortion clinics that while ostensibly designed to protect women's health, actually have the purpose and effect of making abortions more expensive and burdensome to obtain.

By contrast, circumventing a Supreme Court ruling in favor of marriage equality would have proved nearly impossible. The public officials charged with issuing marriage licenses have no discretion over granting them to couples satisfying the legal criteria for obtaining them.

Although county clerks would have had no means of circumventing a broad marriage equality ruling, some conceivably might have resigned their positions in protest rather than complying with it, and others might have chosen simply to defy it. Resignations probably would have led to replacements rather than to any lasting impediment to gay marriage. Likewise, defiance probably would have cost resistors their jobs, unless state elected officials chose to support the clerks, thus setting themselves squarely in opposition to the Court's decision. Can one really imagine many state governors defying a marriage equality ruling in a manner analogous to southern governors' standing in the schoolhouse door to block desegregation a half century ago?

Court rulings can also be effectively nullified by discouraging beneficiaries from exercising their rights. For a full decade after *Brown*, not a single school desegregation suit was brought in Mississippi because the threat and reality of physical violence deterred prospective litigants. When the first such suit finally was filed in 1963, the lead plaintiff, Medgar Evers, was assassinated within a few months. Similarly, violence against abortion clinics and the murder of several doctors who performed abortions has deterred exercise of the constitutional right articulated in *Roe v. Wade*.

Although violence against gays and lesbians is certainly not a relic of the past, it is hard to imagine same-sex couples seeking to marry having to endure the same sort of violent intimidation that was routinely deployed against African Americans exercising their constitutional rights in the South during the civil rights era. The country is different; the issue is different; and public officials almost certainly would not slyly encourage violence in the way that extremist southern politicians such as Senator James Eastland of Mississippi and Governor Marvin Griffin of Georgia did a half century ago.

For all of these reasons, a broad marriage equality ruling by the Supreme Court in *Hollingsworth* probably would not have fomented a backlash as extreme as that ignited by *Brown* and *Roe*. Because the Court ducked the issue, however, we will never know for sure. What we do know is that invalidating the Defense of Marriage Act elicited only whimpers of protest. That decision forced no state to recognize gay marriage against its will. Moreover, opinion polls showed that by 2013, Americans favored repeal of that statute by a margin of twenty to thirty percentage points.

After *Windsor* and *Hollingsworth*, the issue of gay marriage has reverted to the states. At the time of the decisions, thirteen states and the District of Columbia recognized same-sex marriage. Action at the state level is now taking place in a variety of forums—legislatures, courts, and the battle for public opinion.

Recent developments in New Jersey illustrate how the struggle for marriage equality can proceed simultaneously in multiple forums. Early in 2012, the Democratic-controlled state legislature passed a gay marriage bill, but Republican governor Chris Christie vetoed it, perhaps partly to enhance his chances of securing the Republican presidential nomination in 2016. In the fall of 2013, gay marriage proponents were close to rounding up the legislative votes necessary to override Christie's veto. The governor, meanwhile, promoted the idea of New Jersey voters resolving the issue through a referendum. Yet many gay rights proponents strongly objected to the notion of putting civil rights up for a vote, even though opinion polls revealed that they would have been likely to win such a referendum, with as many as 60 percent of New Jerseyans now backing same-sex marriage.

Eventually, however, marriage equality came to New Jersey via a court decision. In September 2013, a trial judge ruled that civil unions, which New Jersey had provided to same-sex couples since 2006, could no longer be considered equal to marriage. This was because, after *Windsor*, the federal government, while bound to recognize same-sex marriages lawfully performed in the states, still did not recognize civil unions. When the state supreme court refused to stay that decision pending appeal, Governor Christie threw in the towel, and New Jersey became the fourteenth state to marry same-sex couples in October 2013.

In November, legislatures in Hawaii and Illinois enacted gay marriage—making them the fifteenth and sixteenth states to enjoy marriage equality. In 2014, Oregon voters will likely have an opportunity in a referendum to reconsider their 2004 vote for a constitutional amendment to ban gay marriage; polls suggest that marriage equality will win easily. Recent opinion polls conducted in Michigan, Nevada, Pennsylvania, and Virginia suggest those states may also now have majorities in favor of gay marriage.

The Supreme Court's marriage equality rulings have also unleashed a wave of litigation challenging state bans on same-sex marriage. Such lawsuits are now pending in more than a dozen states. Both sides in these suits can draw sustenance from the *Windsor* opinions. Opponents of gay marriage emphasize the federalism language in Justice Kennedy's majority opinion, which implies that gay marriage remains an issue for state resolution—a point emphasized by Chief Justice Roberts in his dissenting opinion. By contrast, supporters of gay marriage emphasize, as Justice Scalia ironically did in his *Windsor* dissent, how Justice Kennedy's emphasis on the dignity of same-sex couples and the interests of their children implies that states cannot ban gay marriage any more than the federal government can disadvantage it. Because *Windsor* provides ammunition to both sides in the struggle over same-sex marriage at the state level, lower court judges probably will resolve these challenges in line with their political ideologies, just as the Supreme Court justices did in *Windsor*. Already, a federal district judge has invalidated Ohio's refusal to recognize a same-sex marriage validly performed elsewhere, and a New Jersey state trial judge has struck down that state's ban on same-sex marriage.

Dramatic shifts in the politics of gay marriage have resulted in another important development in recent years: Democratic elected officials in the executive branch of state and federal governments are increasingly unwilling to defend lawsuits challenging the constitutionality of bans on same-sex marriage. This development accounts for the serious justiciability issues in *Windsor* and *Hollingsworth*: President Obama did not wish to defend the constitutionality of DOMA, and neither Governor Jerry Brown nor Attorney General Kamala Harris wished to defend the constitutionality of Proposition 8. Soon after the Supreme Court's rulings, the Democratic attorneys general in Pennsylvania and New Mexico announced their unwillingness to defend laws excluding same-sex couples from marriage. Indeed, such political resistance quickly seeped down to the local level. County clerks in certain liberal areas of Pennsylvania and New Mexico began issuing marriage licenses to same-sex couples on the ground that they believed their state constitutions protected same-sex marriage. In both states, Republican officials brought lawsuits to enjoin the clerks' actions.

Specific developments in particular states are highly contingent and therefore unpredictable, but the general pattern that is likely to unfold is not: Every year going forward, a few more states will embrace gay marriage. Eventually, when enough states have acted, the Supreme Court will revisit the issue and declare marriage equality a federal constitutional right.

A study by Nate Silver, the statistician whose star shone so brightly when the 2012 presidential election results precisely matched his predictions, shows what we should expect. Silver has examined state referenda on gay marriage and constructed a regression model that identifies the variables that predict the outcomes. The relevant factors include the year of the vote (that is, how distant from the present), the percentage of state residents identifying religion as an important part of their daily lives, the percentage of evangelicals in the state population, the median age of adults, and the state's general political leanings. Silver then projects those variables into the future and predicts the year in which each state will have a voting majority in favor of gay marriage.

The results are startling. According to the latest iteration of Silver's study, by 2016 thirty-two states will be likely to vote in favor of gay marriage in a referendum. By 2020, only six states—all in the Deep South—will still be likely to vote against it. By 2024, even the last holdout state, Mississippi, will have a majority in favor. Studies by other statisticians have yielded broadly similar findings.

As the number of states recognizing gay marriage grows, so do the odds of the U.S. Supreme Court's recognizing such a right as a matter of federal constitutional law. Throughout American history, the Supreme Court has frequently used constitutional law to suppress outlier practices in the states. For example, in both *Gideon v. Wainwright* (1963) and *Griswold v. Connecticut* (1965), the Court converted practices that prevailed in most states—respectively, government appointment of counsel for indigent felony defendants and the use of contraceptives by married couples in the privacy of their own bedrooms—into constitutional mandates that forced a few renegade states to conform to the consensus norm.

In cases involving the death penalty and gay rights, Justice Kennedy has been fully on board with this enterprise of using constitutional law to suppress aberrational state practices. Within the next seven years, forty-four states are projected to have voting majorities in favor of gay marriage. All of the remaining holdouts will be in the Deep South, and suppressing southern outliers is, historically, what the Supreme Court has done best.

One might object that whether the Court ultimately requires states to recognize same-sex marriage will depend on its future composition. In one sense, that observation is indisputably correct. Had there been five Antonin Scalias on the Court in 2013, *Windsor* surely would have been decided differently.

Yet even Justice Scalia is less immune to pressure to construe the Constitution in line with dominant public opinion than he admits. Scalia fiercely defends the result in *Brown v. Board of Education*, even though reconciling that decision with his commitment to textualism and originalism is nearly impossible. Scalia, like everyone else, faces enormous pressure to show that his methodological commitments can accommodate the result in *Brown*, as nobody who thinks that decision is wrong will be taken seriously today.

As public opinion shifts overwhelmingly in favor of marriage equality and resistance to it comes to seem increasingly bigoted, a majority of Supreme Court Justices will likely deem it a constitutional right. That is simply how constitutional law works in the United States.

Cambridge, Massachusetts
November 12, 2013

INTRODUCTION

Court decisions interpreting the Constitution can intersect social reform move-ments at various points in their evolution. Sometimes courts take dominant social mores, convert them into constitutional commands, and then use them to suppress outlier practices in a few recalcitrant states. When the Supreme Court declared in 1965 that the Constitution protects the right of married couples to use contraceptives in the privacy of their own bedrooms, only two states in the country—those with the largest percentages of Catholics—had laws infringing on that right. When the Court in 2003 ruled unconstitutional state laws that criminalized sodomy between consenting adult homosexuals, only thirteen states still had laws on the books criminalizing sodomy, only four of them explic-itly targeted *homosexual* sodomy, and no state actively enforced such a law. Court decisions such as these tend to be supported by public opinion and therefore are unlikely to generate much political resistance.[1]

Other judicial interpretations of the Constitution divide the nation roughly down the middle. When the Supreme Court in 1954 declared public school seg-regation unconstitutional, twenty-one of the nation's forty-eight states had laws either commanding or authorizing such segregation, and opinion polls showed that Americans were almost evenly divided in their views of the practice. Similarly, when the Court ruled in 1973 that women have a constitutional right to abortion, nearly equal numbers of Americans were on either side of the controversy.[2]

Less frequently, constitutional rulings fly in the face of dominant public opinion. When the Supreme Court ruled in the early 1960s that state-sponsored prayer in public school violates the Establishment Clause, polls showed that roughly 70 percent to 80 percent of the country disagreed. Similarly, a sizable majority of Americans differed with the Court's 1989 and 1990 rulings that the First Amendment protects the right to burn the flag in protest.[3]

Even though the Court occasionally intervenes against dominant public opinion, the justices are never truly at the vanguard of a social reform movement. They are too much a part of their culture and historical moment to interpret the Constitution in ways that would strike most Americans as bizarre.[4]

Before 1950, the Court would not have dreamed of invalidating public school segregation. A decade before *Roe v. Wade*, the justices would have thought it absurd to suggest that the Constitution protects a right of abortion. Ten years before the Court provisionally invalidated the death penalty in *Furman v. Georgia* (1972), almost nobody could have imagined a day when the Court would take seriously the argument that capital punishment is unconstitutional. On each of these issues, public opinion changed so dramatically in just a decade's time that previously inconceivable judicial rulings suddenly became possible.[5]

When the Court intervenes to defend a minority position or even to resolve an issue that divides the country down the middle, its decisions can generate political backlash, especially when the losers are intensely committed, politically organized, and geographically concentrated. In the short term, *Brown v. Board of Education* (1954) retarded racial progress in the South and radicalized southern racial politics, advancing the careers of extreme segregationists such as Bull Connor and George Wallace. In the face of rapidly rising crime rates, *Miranda v. Arizona* (1966) facilitated the election of Richard Nixon to the presidency in 1968 on a law-and-order platform. By threatening to extinguish the death penalty, *Furman* produced a dramatic resurgence in public support for it and inspired thirty-five states to enact new death penalty laws within the next four years. *Roe v. Wade* (1973) generated a politically potent right-to-life movement that helped elect Ronald Reagan president in 1980 and has significantly influenced national politics ever since.[6]

This book is about same-sex marriage litigation and the political backlash that it has produced. In the 1960s, little organized gay rights activism existed, police routinely raided gay bars, and the U.S. government would not hire open homosexuals or permit them to serve in the military. At that time, the idea of same-sex marriage would have struck most Americans as facetious. In the early 1970s, in the midst of a burst of gay activism unleashed by the Stonewall rebellion, several same-sex couples sought marriage licenses and brought lawsuits when their requests were denied. Courts did not take their arguments very seriously, casually dismissing such claims.

The gay rights movement made dramatic progress in the 1970s and 1980s on issues other than gay marriage, which itself was of little interest to most gay activists. Around 1990, partly because of the AIDS epidemic, the issue of legal recognition of same-sex relationships became more salient to the public and more important to gay activists. By the 1990s, at least a few judges, in states such as

Hawaii and Alaska, were willing to take gay marriage seriously, even though a decisive majority of Americans remained strongly opposed. A ruling by the Hawaii supreme court in 1993 that strongly implied that same-sex couples had a right to marry unleashed a powerful political backlash across the country. Within a decade, more than thirty-five states and Congress passed laws to "defend" traditional marriage.

In 1999, the Vermont supreme court ruled that same-sex couples were entitled to all the legal rights and benefits of marriage, if not the formal title. Then, in 2003, the Massachusetts supreme court became the first in the nation to squarely rule that gay marriage was constitutionally protected.

These rulings also generated political backlashes. Civil unions fast became the dominant political issue in Vermont in 2000, and many legislators who had voted in favor of them lost their jobs. After the Massachusetts ruling, more than twenty-five states passed constitutional amendments banning gay marriage, and the issue figured prominently in the 2004 elections, possibly even altering the outcome of that year's presidential contest. In 2010, three justices on the Iowa supreme court were defeated in retention elections because they had ruled in favor of gay marriage the preceding year.

Gay marriage litigation may also have distracted attention from other items on the gay rights agenda, such as federal legislation forbidding employment discrimination based on sexual orientation. In addition, by situating other gay rights reforms against the backdrop of same-sex marriage, such litigation may have rendered them more controversial than they otherwise would have been.

Yet gay marriage litigation has also had several beneficial consequences for the gay rights movement; political backlash has not been its only material effect. By making same-sex marriage a salient topic, these rulings have forced Americans to discuss and form opinions about a social reform that previously would have struck most of them as incomprehensible. Judicial rulings in favor of gay marriage also inspired gays and lesbians to greater activism and converted many of them who previously had been lukewarm on same-sex marriage into enthusiasts. By enabling thousands of gay couples to marry, such decisions also put a public face on the issue, exposed millions of Americans to married same-sex couples, and enabled gay activists to refute predictions by conservatives of the deleterious consequences that gay marriage would produce. By causing other forms of legal recognition of same-sex couples such as civil unions to seem less radical by comparison, judicial rulings in favor of gay marriage also increased public support for compromise positions.

This book explores the evolution of a movement for social reform—gay rights—and the role that courts have played in that movement. It especially examines how that movement's "last reform"—gay marriage—gradually emerged as an issue, how courts began to vindicate it at a time when public opinion remained overwhelmingly opposed, and how those judicial rulings generated political backlash. Yet it also examines how, despite that backlash, public opinion has continued to evolve in favor of gay marriage—to the point where many today regard that reform as inevitable. The book concludes with an assessment of the costs and benefits of gay marriage litigation over the last two decades and a prediction of what the future may hold—including what the U.S. Supreme Court might have to say on the subject should it get involved, as is likely to happen within the next couple of years.

This book does not criticize historical actors for failing to behave differently, nor does it seek to draw confident conclusions about how future reform movements should evaluate the trade-offs between litigation and other methods of pursuing social reform. Rather, it seeks to illuminate the complex but fascinating dynamic by which judicial intervention on the gay marriage issue has produced unexpected, wide-ranging, and conflicting consequences that continue to influence our politics today.

From the Closet to the Altar

World War II to Stonewall
(1950s and 1960s)

In the decades following World War II, a movement for gay equality faced daunting hurdles. In 1960, every state criminalized even private, consensual sex between same-sex partners. Until the 1960s, not even many civil libertarians took seriously the argument that such laws violated a constitutional right of privacy. Anti-sodomy laws, in turn, were used to justify many other forms of discrimination against homosexuals, such as police raids on gay bars, employment discrimination, and denials of child custody. Local police forces arrested thousands of homosexuals each year for alleged violations of anti-sodomy laws.[1]

The police also used laws punishing vagrancy and public lewdness to harass homosexuals. Police officers used peepholes in public restrooms to identify violators of anti-sodomy laws and acted as decoys to entrap homosexuals into illicit sexual activity. Such police harassment increased in the decades after World War II and was prevalent even in progressive cities such as New York and San Francisco. In the early 1950s, police in the District of Columbia arrested more than one thousand alleged homosexuals a year on charges such as solicitation for lewd and immoral purposes. One historian estimates that police in New York City arrested more than fifty thousand alleged homosexuals between 1923 and 1966 on charges of loitering about a public place to solicit men for the purpose of committing a crime against nature.[2]

Police targeting of homosexuals fluctuated with law enforcement priorities. Efforts to distract public attention from charges of police corruption inspired some crackdowns. A grand jury investigation of police corruption may have motivated one 1955 police crackdown in Baltimore that netted 162 gay men.[3]

Local elections could also prompt crackdowns as incumbents sought to demonstrate their toughness on vice. In 1959, the challenger in the San Francisco mayoral election charged that the incumbent had permitted the city to become "the national headquarters of the organized homosexuals in the United States," and a newspaper story reported that "the number of sex deviates in this city has soared by the thousands." Though the mayor was easily reelected, police raids on gay bars quickly followed, and the number of felony convictions of male homosexuals proceeded to skyrocket. As late as 1966, New York mayor John Lindsay approved a massive crackdown in Times Square aiming to rid the area of "honky-tonks, promenading perverts, . . . homosexuals and prostitutes."[4]

Once arrested on sodomy charges, homosexuals were often kept under constant police surveillance. Newspaper editors often printed the names, addresses, and workplaces of those arrested in police raids. Most of the gay men swept up in them simply pleaded guilty because they feared the exposure that would come with a jury trial. Homosexuals often struggled to find counsel to defend them, whether because of lawyers' personal distaste or from the lawyers' fear of being thought gay themselves.[5]

Local vice squads shared with the Federal Bureau of Investigation (FBI) the names of men arrested on homosexual morals charges. In coordination with local police departments, the FBI searched for evidence of homosexuality—and not just in connection with people it was already investigating. Its regional offices gathered data on gay bars. Friendship with a known homosexual could subject one to an FBI investigation. U.S. postal inspectors initiated correspondence with suspected homosexuals and then placed tracers on their mail in order to identify other homosexuals.[6]

State liquor authorities issued regulations prohibiting bars, restaurants, and other establishments with liquor licenses from employing or serving known homosexuals. Restaurants or bars known as homosexual hangouts faced constant police harassment as well as the risk of having their liquor license revoked. When the California supreme court refused to permit the liquor board to close a bar simply because known homosexuals gathered there, the legislature overturned the ruling and authorized revocation of liquor licenses where the premises were a resort for "panderers, or sexual perverts."[7]

In 1959 the New York State Liquor Authority announced a campaign to revoke the licenses of all bars patronized by prostitutes and homosexuals. Shortly thereafter, many New York City gay bars were shut down. Even when courts ruled in revocation cases that homosexuals had a right to congregate, they were careful to note that public displays of affection, such as holding hands or dancing together, could be prohibited as too close to the line of illicit sex. As late as 1963, a California court upheld the revocation of a liquor license where male bar patrons had been permitted to kiss and caress.[8]

The issue of homosexuality in federal government employment exploded in the early 1950s—the peak of McCarthyism. When a Truman administration official acknowledged during a congressional hearing that most of the ninety-one federal employees dismissed for moral turpitude were homosexuals,

Republicans charged that sexual perverts had infiltrated the administration and were possibly as dangerous as communists. In 1950, a Senate committee report warned that "one homosexual can pollute a Government office" because homosexuals lacked emotional stability, were morally irresolute, and were vulnerable to influence by "gangs of blackmailers." The number of alleged homosexuals dismissed from civilian posts in the executive branch increased from five a month to more than sixty.[9]

In 1953, President Dwight Eisenhower issued an executive order listing sexual perversion as sufficient grounds for exclusion from federal employment. Challenges to dismissals on such grounds were litigated all the way to the U.S. Supreme Court and failed. Well into the 1960s, the U.S. Civil Service Commission reaffirmed its policy of barring homosexuals from federal employment. In all, thousands of civilian federal employees were fired from their jobs or resigned because of alleged homosexuality. In 1952, Congress reenacted a ban on homosexual aliens entering the country.[10]

Many state and local governments also shut homosexuals out of public employment, and numerous private employers likewise treated alleged homosexuality, even without a criminal conviction, as sufficient grounds for dismissal. Homosexual acts were deemed unprofessional conduct sufficient to deny or revoke a license to practice medicine, law, or nursing. Universities sometimes expelled students for alleged homosexuality.[11]

Politicians frequently charged sexual perversion to discredit their adversaries. When Florida state senator Charley Johns, an ardent segregationist, led an investigation of homosexuality at Florida State University in 1958, sixteen faculty members and staff who had been active in the civil rights movement lost their jobs because of alleged homosexuality. Conservatives portrayed homosexuals, like communists, as capable of infiltrating themselves into the highest reaches of government and society. Homosexuals corrupted the bodies of the young, just as communists corrupted their minds.[12]

The U.S. military, which had largely overlooked homosexuality in its ranks amid the manpower shortages of World War II, cracked down with a vengeance afterward. Even soldiers who had served with distinction were dismissed and thereby disqualified from ever again holding positions of trust with the U.S. government. Military discharges based on alleged homosexuality ballooned to two thousand a year in the early 1950s and three thousand a year in the early 1960s.[13]

Service members were given less than fully honorable discharges simply for associating with known homosexuals. Military termination hearings did not require that charges be substantiated with hard facts, and service members had no right to question or even confront accusers. Service members dismissed in such fashion often had trouble securing employment in the private sector and endured "personal heartbreak" when family and friends learned of their homosexuality.[14]

The medical profession categorized homosexuality as a disease. Many states authorized judges to send homosexuals to asylums upon petition by family members. There, doctors experimented with procedures ranging from psycho-therapy to castration, lobotomy, and electroshock therapy.[15]

In the 1950s, the nation's preeminent civil liberties organization, while con-ceding that laws aimed at suppressing homosexuality might be "unenlightened and savage," did not deem them to pose any civil liberties problem. An American Civil Liberties Union (ACLU) policy statement in 1957 referred to homosex-uals as "socially heretical or deviant," pronounced laws punishing homosexual acts clearly constitutional, and expressed no objection to the government's treat-ing homosexuality as a risk factor for sensitive jobs.[16]

Responding to a desperate plea for legal assistance by a dismissed lesbian ser-vice member, an ACLU officer suggested that she "submit [her]self to medical treatment if [she] really desire[s] to abandon homosexual relations." She wrote back to express understanding that the ACLU could not help, given that "the cause of homosexuals is a decidedly unpopular one." She also observed that she was "one of the luckier ones, with an understanding family, but two of the girls discharged for homosexuality have committed suicide and one other has disap-peared completely." As late as 1963, when the ACLU prepared a list of nine items to include on its future agenda, homosexuality still did not rate as "a pressing problem in civil liberties terms."[17]

Not until after the Supreme Court in 1965 overturned a Connecticut law that criminalized a married couple's use of contraceptives in the privacy of their own home did the ACLU reconsider its position on whether a constitutional right to privacy might bear on governmental legal restrictions on homosexuality. Yet even after *Griswold v. Connecticut* persuaded the ACLU to change its policy on criminal sodomy laws, the group remained divided over the issue of police harassment of gay bars and nightclubs and continued to concede that the government could treat homosexuality as relevant to public employment.[18]

The first significant gay rights organizations were founded in the 1950s, but they operated under severe constraints, had few members, and exercised little influence. One formidable hurdle to organizing gay protest was the significant cost of being publicly identified as gay, which would often lead to police harassment and loss of employment. The Mattachine Society, the nation's first significant gay rights organization, was founded in 1951, but much as NAACP officials in the South were often forced to cloak their identity for protection before the 1960s, Mattachine members used a secretive, cell-like structure to avoid detection. Many members used aliases because they did not want their names listed on the organization's roster.[19]

Well into the 1960s, people corresponding with Mattachine Society branches asked that the organization's name not appear on return mail. Organizations receiving contributions from Mattachine branches asked that the Mattachine name be kept off checks. One sympathizer in Detroit refused to ask his Unitarian church to provide space for meetings because he was afraid of outing himself. One reason that circulation of homophile magazines such as the *Mattachine Review* remained low was that people feared receiving such materials in the mail. U.S. postmasters also occasionally suppressed such materials as obscene.[20]

Fears of persecution were well founded. After police infiltrated a Mattachine Society convention in Denver in 1959, they raided leaders' homes and arrested one of them for violating a pornography statute when they found photos of nude men. He was fired from his job, served sixty days in jail, and eventually had to leave town. Police seized the names and addresses of other Mattachine members from his home, which caused many men to scurry for cover and sever contact with the organization. The Denver chapter never recovered.[21]

Organizing protest against this severely oppressive system was difficult. Given all of the costs associated with being identified as a homosexual, gays had strong incentives to remain closeted. By contrast, few African Americans, who suffered even greater persecution under the Jim Crow system, had the option of passing as white. Because they could not hide the characteristic on which their oppression was based, blacks had little choice but to protest against the system that oppressed them. Convincing homosexuals to come out of the closet when they risked persecution for doing so was the greatest impediment to a movement for gay equality.

Another challenge confronted those who would organize a movement for gay rights: self-loathing among homosexuals. Just as black civil rights organizers had to undo the psychological damage inflicted on African Americans who had internalized some of the ideology of white supremacy, so did gay rights organizers have to cope with the corroded self-image that the ideology of heteronormativity, which treated homosexuals as immoral and depraved, instilled in many gays and lesbians.[22]

Some homosexuals thought they deserved the harassment and punishment they received. Publications by gay rights organizations such as the Mattachine Society actually printed articles that treated homosexuals as mentally ill or, worse, grouped them together with rapists and child molesters. How could society be persuaded to treat homosexuals as normal people until they regarded themselves that way?[23]

Even if homosexuals could be persuaded of the injustice of the status quo, gay rights leaders had to worry about the political backlash that aggressive lobbying for gay rights might produce. In the 1950s, Mattachine Society leaders concluded that even to lobby legislators for repeal of anti-sodomy laws would "provide an abundant source of hysterical propaganda with which to foment an ignorant, fear-inspired anti-homosexual campaign." As late as 1962, one leader of the New York Mattachine Society warned that if "a group of organized homosexuals is suddenly thrust on the guardians of public morality, the initial reaction would be indignation, horror, and a general demand to crush such a despicable monster." That same year, the *Village Voice* reported that "while other minorities militantly organize [to defend] their civil liberties, most homosexuals ask only that no one rock the boat."[24]

Instead of rocking the boat, the Mattachine Society focused on winning the support of "pillars of the community." Activists believed that gays and lesbians lacked the influence and the credibility to campaign for equality on their own behalf. Instead, they needed sympathetic professionals—doctors, lawyers, ministers—to serve as intermediaries between them and a hostile society. Such a band of "strategically placed individuals" could influence public opinion more than gay activists could. These activists also offered themselves as subjects for researchers, hoping to replace stereotypes about gays with facts. Yet the professionals were part of the problem they needed to confront.[25]

The contrast with the direct action phase of the black civil rights movement that was taking place simultaneously—the sit-in protests, Freedom Rides, and street demonstrations—could not have been starker. While ordinary black men and women were taking personal initiative to demand progressive racial change, most gays and lesbians chose to remain anonymous. Even gay activists generally sought to leverage social change through intermediaries rather than through their own personal interventions. Some of the older leaders, who had come of age at the zenith of McCarthyist repression, were especially loath to embrace anything resembling civil rights militancy.[26]

The 1960s brought small but significant changes in public attitudes toward homosexuality. As American society was rocked by dramatic change on issues such as divorce, contraception, sexual mores, and the sexual content of mass media, views about homosexuality started to become more malleable.[27]

One simple but important change was increased public discussion of homosexuality, which previously had been taboo. In 1959, the New York Mattachine Society wrote to an adult magazine to praise an article it had published on homosexuality: "Little by little, the 'curtain of silence' is being lifted, but still precious few national publications have the courage to deal with homosexuality."[28]

In earlier decades, courts had upheld suppression of homosexual novels under anti-obscenity laws, and in 1934 the Motion Picture Production Code had barred any depiction of homosexuality in movies. Official censorship of homosexuality remained prevalent in the 1950s, often at the behest of the

Catholic Church. The threat of official censorship often induced self-censorship by publishers and booksellers.[29]

Greater coverage of homosexuality in literature and film was partly a function of the Supreme Court's general deregulation of pornography, which began in 1957 and accelerated through the 1960s. These rulings revolutionized the sexual content of material—including homosexual material—available to average Americans. The Court's decision clearing male physique magazines of obscenity charges opened the door to unrestricted production.[30]

Between 1959 and 1965, the number of lesbian pulp novels being published increased tenfold. In 1966, one observer noted that lesbian literature had become so integrated into mainstream literature that it was no longer a separate category. Award-winning best sellers, such as Allen Drury's *Advise and Consent* and James Baldwin's *Another Country*, featured gay characters and subplots.[31]

After 1961, the Motion Picture Production Code permitted film portrayals of homosexuality, so long as they were done with discretion and restraint. While most depictions treated homosexuality as a perversion, they at least generated public discussion of the issue and helped foster a sense of group identity among homosexuals.[32]

Mainstream news media vastly expanded their coverage of homosexuality in the early 1960s. In 1963, the *New York Times* ran a front-page feature on New York City's flourishing male homosexual underground of bars and cruising areas. *Newsweek* then ran an article on the *New York Times* article. Much of the news coverage was less than flattering. In 1966, *Time* noted that while homosexuals deserved compassion and treatment, they suffered from "a pernicious sickness." Yet whether positive or negative, the stories forced Americans to recognize the existence of homosexuals.[33]

Gay rights activists began to garner some attention for their cause. In New York, Randy Wicker pressured a public radio station to air a program featuring eight gays discussing their sexual behavior and the prejudices they encountered after it had broadcast a discussion on homosexuality by psychiatrists. In a story headlined "Taboo Is Broken," the *New York Times* called this program the most extensive treatment of homosexuality ever heard on American radio. When a conservative newspaper columnist denounced the broadcast, the story garnered even more publicity and was picked up by *Newsweek*. Wicker also persuaded the *Village Voice* and *Harper's* to publish articles on the gay rights movement and homosexual life in New York.[34]

Presenting himself as a spokesperson for the gay rights movement, Wicker secured speaking engagements at local universities and educational societies. Publishers and broadcasters came to him for information about homosexuality. Wicker educated hundreds of thousands of Americans who previously had given little thought to homosexual issues, and he also reached thousands of gays and lesbians who had been leading isolated, guilt-ridden lives.[35]

By 1967, representatives of the New York Mattachine Society were appearing on a hundred local radio and television programs and sending speakers to hundreds of non-gay-related organizations. In 1967, Columbia University chartered the first college student homophile group in the country; similar organizations were soon founded at Cornell, Stanford, and New York University. In Greenwich Village, the Oscar Wilde Memorial Bookshop, which stocked only gay and lesbian material, became a popular meeting place where news was exchanged and gay politics discussed.[36]

In the 1960s, civil libertarians began to change their views on homosexuality. In 1962, the prestigious American Law Institute approved its Model Penal Code, which rejected criminal punishment for private sex between consenting adult homosexuals. Acting on the Wolfenden Commission report from the 1950s, Great Britain decriminalized private same-sex sodomy between consenting adults in 1967. *Newsweek* and *Time* reported on the extended debates in the British Parliament, and their coverage was far more respectful of homosexuality than their treatment of the Wolfenden report ten years earlier had been. Many American law review articles urged similar legal reforms in the United States. Some legal commentators began to compare homosexuals to persecuted racial minorities.[37]

By the mid-1960s, some ACLU branches were adjusting their policies on homosexuality, not just supporting decriminalization of same-sex sodomy but also challenging discrimination against homosexuals by government employers. In 1965, the New York Civil Liberties Union began supporting the local Mattachine Society in its protests against police raids on gay bars. After years of review inspired by the *Griswold* case, in 1967 the ACLU revised its policy on homosexuality. The right of individual privacy, the organization concluded, should extend "to all private sexual conduct, heterosexual or homosexual, of consenting adults."[38]

In addition, the ACLU objected to the enforcement of public anti-solicitation laws through entrapment or secret surveillance of public places. The ACLU also criticized the U.S. Civil Service Commission's rule treating homosexuality as an automatic disqualification for federal employment and the Immigration and Naturalization Service's ban on homosexual immigration. Securing the support of the ACLU, a prestigious organization to which many prominent lawyers and judges belonged, was a major advance for the gay rights movement.[39]

In the second half of the 1960s, some mental health professionals reconsidered their view of homosexuality as a disease. By 1967, the editors of *Psychiatric Opinion* were permitting the head of the New York Mattachine Society to participate on panels on homosexuality to offer his perspective. Sociologists who previously had viewed homosexuality as evidence of social disorganization now increasingly saw it as simply a different form of behavior—a failure to follow group rules but not something that was wrong in itself.[40]

Many of the psychiatrists and sociologists who were rethinking their views on homosexuality evolved into partisans of legal reform. When the National Institute of Mental Health in 1967 appointed a committee to investigate homosexuality, most members already had rejected the traditional view, and its final report, issued two years later, rejected the notion that homosexuals were diseased and urged a reconsideration of employment practices that discriminated against gays and lesbians.[41]

Even a few religious denominations were reconsidering their views on homosexuality. In 1964, San Francisco established a Council on Religion and the Homosexual, and other cities soon followed suit. The council's ministers provided important legitimacy to charges of police harassment when the San Francisco police broke up homosexuals' New Year's Eve ball in 1964.

In 1967, Episcopal priests in the northeastern United States urged that homosexuality be reclassified as morally neutral. Although no national religious bodies had yet repudiated the moral condemnation of homosexual behavior, some were beginning to question its criminalization. In 1968, the *Christian Century* found merit in proposals for equal employment opportunities for gays and an end to abusive police practices, although it remained dubious of the idea that homosexuality might be morally desirable.[42]

Gay rights organizations expanded rapidly in the 1960s. Membership in the New York Mattachine Society grew from under 100 in 1963 to about 445 two years later. The Society for Individual Rights, founded in San Francisco in 1964, had grown to 1,000 members by 1967, making it the largest homophile organization in the nation. The fifteen gay rights organizations that met in Kansas City in 1966 to form the North American Conference of Homophile Organizations had expanded to fifty by 1969. By the end of the decade, homophile organizations had spread to cities such as Kansas City and Seattle.[43]

In addition to growing in size, gay rights organizations also became more aggressive in their tactics. Younger gays and lesbians, who had not directly experienced the repression of McCarthyism, were more inclined to embrace their homosexuality, less fearful of the repercussions of doing so, and more willing to act aggressively. In addition, many gay rights activists had participated in the black civil rights movement, which by the early 1960s was increasingly turning to direct action protest.[44]

By the early 1960s, a more militant wing of the gay rights movement was emerging on the East Coast. This group believed in equal rights, direct action, and gay leadership of the gay rights movement, and it rejected an earlier generation's focus on assimilation, respectability, education, and deference to social scientists.[45]

One of the leaders of this movement, Franklin Kameny, argued that if the NAACP did not worry about which gene produces black skin, gay activists should not concern themselves with medical theories on the causes of homosexuality and whether it was curable. Kameny urged that gays abandon the sickness model of homosexuality, treat homosexual activity as right and good, and demand their rights, just as Jews and blacks did. At a 1968 conference of homophile organizations, activists endorsed the slogan "Gay Is Good"—an unthinkable development a decade earlier.[46]

In the first half of the 1960s, the Washington, D.C., branch of the Mattachine Society aggressively challenged the discriminatory policies of the U.S. Civil Service Commission, writing letters to politicians and Supreme Court justices and picketing in front of the commission's offices until finally extracting a meeting with officials. In 1965, demonstrators picketed outside the White House and the United Nations building in New York in response to news reports that the Cuban government was confining homosexuals to labor camps.[47]

In Philadelphia, gay activists sat in at a restaurant after the manager refused to serve several customers who he suspected were gay, and picketers demonstrated at the annual Homosexual Reminder Day on July 4. In 1967 in Los Angeles, several hundred demonstrators protested police brutality at two gay bars on New Year's Eve. In 1968, a radicalized gay rights group at Columbia University picketed a medical school forum on homosexuality because it included no homosexuals. That year, the *Advocate*, which emphasized gay pride, began publication.[48]

Gay rights organizations began to win some legal victories in the 1960s. Previously, gay rights litigation had been difficult to sustain because so few people were willing to publicly identify as homosexual. In 1966, the North American Conference of Homophile Organizations created a national legal fund, which financed litigation challenging the closing of gay bars, the exclusion of homosexual immigrants from the country, the dismissal of gay service members, and the denial of security clearances to homosexuals. The number of cases involving gay rights that reached the federal appeals courts grew from twelve in the first half of the 1960s to thirty in the second half, and gay rights claimants started to win some of those cases.[49]

Gay bar owners won significant victories in California, New York, and New Jersey, where courts refused to allow liquor authorities to revoke licenses without proof of illegal activity on the premises; allowing gays to congregate was no longer deemed sufficient grounds for revocation. Direct action protest led the New York Liquor Authority in 1966 to change its policy on openly gay bars, and the following year the New York courts ruled that two men kissing was insufficient evidence of unlawful activity to justify a license revocation. As a result, police raids on gay bars declined, and the number of such bars in New York City increased. In San Francisco, too, police largely ceased harassing gay bars by the mid-1960s, and the number of these bars increased, from fewer than twenty in 1963 to fifty-seven in 1968.[50]

In 1969, gays won an important victory in the U.S. Court of Appeals for the District of Columbia Circuit. Rejecting the federal government's blanket policy of barring employment to homosexuals, the court ruled that the civil service statute, which authorized employee dismissals for "such causes as will promote the efficiency of the service," required a showing that dismissals were related to an employee's ability to perform the job. Pressure from the ACLU played an important role in ending the United States Postal Service's practice of entrapping gay men by mailing them obscene publications and then informing their employers of their homosexuality. Gays successfully sued the New York Civil Service Commission for refusing to hire two gay men as welfare caseworkers, and the commission quietly began to hire homosexuals.[51]

By the mid-1960s, the gay community was beginning to exercise a modicum of political influence in a few cities. In San Francisco, the municipal government started sending representatives to forums arranged by homophile organizations to discuss gay concerns, and politicians such as Willie Brown and Phil Burton began courting gay voters. Local political candidates in New York City and Los Angeles also faced pressure to state their views on homosexual issues. In New York, a combination of litigation and political pressure produced meaningful changes in the city's employment practices.[52]

Curbing police harassment was a principal priority of gay activists, and their efforts began to bear fruit in some cities. In 1966, gay activists and civil liberties leaders met with Mayor John Lindsay of New York, and soon thereafter the police commissioner instructed officers to cease entrapping homosexuals. In Washington, D.C., the Mattachine Society aggressively challenged police harassment, filed charges against abusive police officers, and "forced the police into a healthy respect" for them. By the late 1960s, police entrapment of homosexuals had largely ended in the city. Curtailing police harassment was critical to the development of a protected public space for gay self-expression and political mobilization.[53]

Although the gay rights movement had made progress in the 1960s, the outlook remained bleak. A 1969 opinion poll showed that 63 percent of respondents considered homosexuals "harmful to American life." An article in *Time* observed, "Most straight Americans still regard the invert with a mixture of revulsion and apprehension."[54]

Although many legal authors in the 1960s had called for the decriminalization of same-sex sodomy between consenting adults in private, only two states had done so by 1971. An effort to repeal New York's sodomy law in the mid-1960s proved disastrous, as an aroused Catholic Church hierarchy mounted an effective lobbying campaign in response.[55]

With anti-sodomy laws remaining on the books in the overwhelming majority of states, homosexuals faced all manner of discrimination. Mothers could lose custody of their children upon divorce if fathers could prove they were lesbians. State bar associations refused admission to admitted homosexuals. Even in the Jim Crow South, blacks had never been formally barred from practicing law, and by 1917 every state admitted women to the bar. Yet lawyers who identified themselves as gay could lose their bar membership. In this environment, the incentives to remain closeted were powerful.[56]

Although police harassment of gay public life had largely ceased in San Francisco, New York, and Washington, D.C., it continued in most other cities well into the 1970s. In Chicago, after the courts made it harder to shut down gay bars on morals charges, the police adopted a new "gambit [of] plant[ing] pot in the washroom and then discover[ing] it with pretty little cries of shock and astonishment."[57]

In Atlanta, with the tacit approval of the city government and the local business community, the police waged war against "undesirables," which included hippies and homosexuals. Police officers questioned people strolling in city parks, halted cars in Piedmont Park at night and photographed the occupants, and raided a theater showing Andy Warhol's *Lonesome Cowboys*. In St. Petersburg, Florida, pervasive police harassment was producing "fear," "apathy," and "sluggishness," according to one correspondent of the New York Mattachine Society.[58]

Private violence against gays was an enormous problem as well. In Franklin County, Ohio, in 1969, a jury acquitted a man of first-degree murder for killing a homosexual. The defendant's principal defense was that the victim had made sexual advances toward him.[59]

Many jobs remained off-limits to people who were openly gay. The D.C. Circuit had put only narrow restrictions on the Civil Service Commission's policy of blanket exclusion. New York City still barred gays entirely from jobs in several professional fields, including corrections officers, policemen, firemen, and children's counselors.[60]

In 1969, a gay engineering professor who had been fired from his East Coast college because of his sexual orientation wrote to the ACLU for help. Unable to find another teaching job despite there being nothing wrong with his teaching, health, or appearance, he criticized "our sick, biased American society, [which] brutally wrecked my whole life." Although the ACLU noted that his situation was "most distressing," the organization regretfully informed him that nothing could be done. Even the ACLU's liberalized policy statement of 1967 did not deny that homosexuality was relevant to certain jobs.[61]

The American Psychiatric Association continued to regard homosexuality as a mental illness. The Immigration and Naturalization Service still barred homosexuals from entering the country because of their "psychopathic personality," and the U.S. Supreme Court rejected a challenge to that practice in 1967.[62]

Despite the progress of the 1960s, gay rights organizations had mobilized only a tiny number of people. Membership in all such groups in the United States barely exceeded five thousand. More gay rights organizations exist today in New Jersey than there were in the entire United States in the late 1960s.[63]

Although direct action protest had begun among gay rights activists, its scope was puny when compared with that generated by the black civil rights movement or the antiwar movement. The costs of being publicly identified as gay remained enormous: stigmatization, job loss, disruption of family life. Moreover, as black power, urban race riots, political assassinations, and the Vietnam War competed for national attention in the late 1960s, gay issues were at most a minor distraction for most Americans. Activists had begun to disrupt the consensus behind homophobia, but most of their journey still lay ahead.[64]

2

Stonewall to *Bowers* (1970s and 1980s)

In the early morning hours of Saturday, June 28, 1969, the New York City police raided a gay bar in the heart of Greenwich Village. New York was in the midst of a mayoral election, which was often an inauspicious time for homosexuals. The Stonewall Inn may have been an especially appealing target for the precinct's new police commander because it operated without a liquor license, reputedly had ties to organized crime, and featured scantily clad go-go boys as entertainment.[1]

Police raids of this sort had become less frequent in New York City by 1969, but they were not uncommon. What was uncommon was the resistance demonstrated by the bar's gay patrons and bystanders. Emotions may have been running particularly high because of the recent death of gay icon Judy Garland, whose funeral had taken place in New York City just one day earlier. Whatever the explanation, though, the raid unleashed tremendous pent-up resentments among the gay community.[2]

After plainclothes police had swarmed the bar and expelled about two hundred young men, a crowd of several hundred onlookers gathered in the surrounding streets. That crowd grew violent in response to officers' aggressive treatment of several bar patrons and the arrival of paddy wagons. Some bystanders threw bricks, bottles, garbage, pennies, and even a parking meter at the police officers. Others responded by "camping it up," with queens dancing in a chorus line. Eventually the police officers had to lock themselves inside the Stonewall Inn to escape the assault, and reinforcements were called in. Then a firebomb exploded inside the bar. Four police officers were wounded, and thirteen members of the crowd were arrested.[3]

The following night, large and angry crowds gathered in Sheridan Square in Greenwich Village. Graffiti on the boarded-up windows of the Stonewall Inn declared "Support Gay Power" and "Legalize Gay Bars." The police once again had to disperse a crowd that had grown to about four hundred people, some of whom were throwing bottles and lighting fires. A few nights later, police confronted a hostile crowd of about five hundred, and several more arrests were made.[4]

Similar demonstrations quickly spread to other cities. The New York Mattachine Society ran a special riot edition of its newsletter, referring to the events as "The Hairpin Drop Heard Round the World." An article in the *Village Voice* called Stonewall the first public eruption of the gay rights movement.[5]

Stonewall seemed to crystallize the incipient gay activism of the 1960s. Within weeks, gays in New York City had formed the Gay Liberation Front, a self-proclaimed revolutionary organization. Word quickly spread across networks of young radicals. Within a year, gay liberation groups had formed on college campuses and in cities across the country. These young gay activists adopted many of the tactics and some of the goals of the antiwar and black power movements. Many of them scorned the moderation and reformist politics of the homophile movement.[6]

From black power, they borrowed assertiveness and the celebration of difference rather than sameness. From the era's radical feminists, they took a rethinking of gender norms and conventional sexual ideology. From the 1960s counterculture, they absorbed a rejection of traditional middle-class values and an embrace of drug use, open displays of sexuality, and acceptance of alternative living arrangements.[7]

In August 1970, bar raids and street arrests of gay men in New York City inspired a march of several hundred protesters from Times Square to Greenwich Village. When the *Village Voice* and *Harper's* published articles perceived as hostile to gays, their offices were occupied.[8]

In 1970, Chicago Gay Liberation invaded the annual convention of the American Medical Association, while in San Francisco its counterpart disrupted the annual meeting of the American Psychiatric Association (APA). During an APA session on homosexuality at which one panelist read a paper on aversion therapy, a young bearded gay man danced around the auditorium in a red dress while other gays and lesbians scattered throughout the audience shouted "Genocide!" and "Torture!" Politicians running for office were hounded by gay militants demanding that they speak out against the oppression of homosexuals.[9]

Gay liberation transformed the meaning of "coming out," which previously had signified a private decision to accept one's own homosexuality. Some gay leaders had come out in the 1950s and 1960s through their public involvement in the movement, but rarely had they counseled others to follow their example.[10]

In the early 1970s, however, gay liberation recast "coming out" as a political act, which not only reduced individual self-loathing but also bolstered the gay rights movement. Coming out gave one an obvious stake in the success of the movement and served as an example to others. Only by coming out could gays refute prevalent stereotypes by demonstrating that they were ordinary people. As they began to seem less unusual, tolerance of them would grow, which would encourage others to come out, thus creating a powerful self-reinforcing dynamic.[11]

The number of gay activists and gay rights organizations exploded in the early 1970s. In June 1970, several thousand gays and lesbians from all over the northeastern United States commemorated the first anniversary of Stonewall with a march from Greenwich Village to Central Park to proclaim "the new strength and pride of the gay people." Between 1969 and 1973, the number of gay rights organizations in the United States grew from fifty to eight hundred. By 1976, the gay rights journal, the *Advocate*, was the twelfth-fastest-growing publication in the United States and Canada, with a circulation that had increased from nineteen thousand to sixty thousand in just two years. By the second half of the 1970s, Gay Freedom Day events were taking place in dozens of cities, with total participation exceeding half a million people.[12]

Many of today's leading gay rights organizations were founded in the 1970s. Groups such as Lambda Legal, the National Gay Task Force (later renamed the National Gay and Lesbian Task Force), Gay Rights Advocates, the Lesbian Rights Project, and the Gay and Lesbian Alliance Against Defamation educated the public and the media on homosexual issues. They documented incidents of anti-gay violence and discrimination, refuting claims that such discrimination did not exist and bolstering the case for hate crimes laws and anti-discrimination ordinances. They publicized gay rights victories including the enactment of anti-discrimination policies and the election of openly gay people to political office. By doing so, they hoped to spread the word and generate support for similar initiatives elsewhere. They policed the media, objecting to stereotyped portrayals of gays and lesbians in situation comedies, denouncing defamatory statements by public actors, and demanding that news and media programming cover issues of concern to gays and lesbians.[13]

In the heady days of gay liberation, same-sex couples sought marriage licenses for the very first time. In 1971 in Mankato, Minnesota, James Michael McConnell adopted his lover, Jack Baker, with the goal of securing tax and inheritance advantages. Later that year, they applied for and received a marriage license. A United Methodist clergyman married them in a private ceremony in September. When the state declined to recognize their marriage as valid, they filed suit in state court. The Minnesota chapter of the ACLU represented them; the national organization refused to get involved.[14]

Soon thereafter, similar lawsuits were brought in Kentucky and Washington State. Other litigation raised the issue of gay marriage in a different context:

efforts to annul a marriage on the ground that both people were of the same sex. In the early 1980s, gay couples also asserted a constitutional right to same-sex marriage in the context of federal deportation proceedings.[15]

In all of these cases, courts decisively rejected the legal arguments for gay marriage. Even where state statutes did not expressly limit marriage to a man and a woman, as was frequently the case in the early 1970s, courts nonetheless ruled that the legislature had intended to preserve the traditional understanding of marriage.[16]

Courts likewise rejected a hodgepodge of constitutional arguments that were mostly based on due process and equal protection. In response to the argument that *Loving v. Virginia* (1967), which invalidated bans on interracial marriage, had elevated marriage to the status of a fundamental right, courts distinguished *Loving* as a case involving white supremacy. Because Washington State had adopted an equal rights amendment barring sex discrimination, its supreme court also had to reject the argument that restricting marriage to opposite-sex couples constituted sex discrimination. In rejecting gay marriage claims, courts ruled that the traditional definition of marriage furthered state interests in fostering procreation and supporting child rearing.[17]

In addition to losing the cases, plaintiffs in these lawsuits suffered repercussions from their activism. McConnell, one of the Minnesota plaintiffs, lost a job offer from the University of Minnesota Library, which deemed his personal conduct "not consistent with the best interests of the University." McConnell sued the university in federal court and won at trial on the ground that a "homosexual is after all a human being, and a citizen of the United States." But that victory was overturned on appeal, as the circuit court ruled the university was justified in rescinding McConnell's job offer because of his evident interest in pursuing an "activist role in implementing his unconventional ideas concerning the societal status to be accorded homosexuals." McConnell's partner, Baker, encountered difficulties with the Minnesota bar examiners over allegations that he had fraudulently obtained the license for his same-sex marriage.[18]

One of the plaintiffs in the Washington litigation lost his job with the federal government because his lawsuit, combined with other instances of "flaunting" his homosexuality in the workplace, was deemed "immoral and notoriously disgraceful conduct" that rendered him unfit for government employment. A federal court refused to overturn his job dismissal as arbitrary and capricious.[19]

The judges who decided these early gay marriage cases did not simply reject the plaintiffs' arguments; they treated them with derision. One Minnesota justice literally turned his back on the lawyer arguing the case, just as the notoriously racist U.S. Supreme Court justice James McReynolds had turned his on prominent black lawyer Charles Hamilton Houston during a 1938 civil rights case. None of the Minnesota justices dignified the gay marriage claim by venturing a single question at oral argument, and in their opinion they invoked the book of Genesis as authority for rejecting gay marriage. The trial judge in the Kentucky case told one of the female plaintiffs that it offended the court for her to appear in a pantsuit, and he ordered her to go home and change into a dress if she wanted to attend the trial.[20]

Two of these early state gay marriage cases were appealed to the U.S. Supreme Court, which summarily rejected the appeals. Technically, these summary dismissals count as precedents that bind lower courts. However, it is not clear that courts forty years later, facing radically different circumstances, would consider themselves genuinely bound by such summary dismissals.[21]

That courts in the 1970s would so casually dismiss legal arguments in favor of gay marriage is hardly surprising. Courts almost never vindicate constitutional claims that strongly contravene public opinion. Gay marriage commanded so little support in the 1970s that pollsters did not survey public opinion on the issue. The ACLU did not formally endorse gay marriage until 1986.[22]

Recognizing how deeply rooted opposition to gay marriage was, opponents of the Equal Rights Amendment (ERA) argued that by abolishing all sex classifications, the ERA would necessarily legalize gay marriage. Making the same calculation, the Senate sponsor of the ERA, Birch Bayh, as well as many of the amendment's feminist supporters, forcefully denied that it had anything to do with gay marriage.[23]

Because the legal claims they raised seemed so implausible, these gay marriage cases attracted very little media coverage. Of the attention they did receive, most came from opponents of gay marriage. Along with other issues such as abortion, no-fault divorce, teenage pregnancy, and pornography, same-sex marriage litigation contributed to the development of a traditional values movement. Relying on the Old Testament's condemnation of homosexuality as an "abomination" and its emphasis on procreative sex, fundamentalists passionately condemned gay marriage. To many of them, the issue was even clearer than abortion was.[24]

Despite the adverse litigation results, same-sex couples in several cities continued to seek marriage licenses. In January 1975, two men in Phoenix applied for and received a marriage license. However, the county attorney quickly charged one of them with filing false documents by completing the woman's section of the license application. In March, a local court voided the marriage. The Arizona legislature eventually amended state law to clarify that marriage required a man and a woman. That same year, another same-sex couple applied for but was denied a marriage license in Plainfield, Vermont. Other unsuccessful requests for licenses were made by gay couples in Tampa, Hartford, Chicago, and Milwaukee.[25]

In March 1975, two men sought to marry in Colorado Springs. The clerk there denied them a license, explaining, "We don't do that sort of thing in El Paso County—maybe you should go to Boulder County."[26]

Heeding that advice, the two men sought out the Boulder County clerk, Clela Rorex, and found her to be more obliging. She told them she would check with the local district attorney. His opinion was that state law did not clearly prohibit same-sex couples from receiving marriage licenses and that county clerks should therefore use their discretion. After several sleepless nights mulling over the matter, Rorex decided to issue the license. She concluded that her job was not to legislate morality, that "no minorities should be discriminated against," and that the legislature should clarify the matter.[27]

The local newspaper saw Rorex's action as "a distortion of the clear intent of the law and a reckless flouting of accepted standards of our community." It also expressed concern that Boulder was receiving "unfavorable publicity," which would harm economic growth. It insisted that "deviates, weirdos, drones and revolutionaries" were not representative of Boulder's true character.[28]

Over the next few weeks, Rorex issued marriage licenses to five more gay and lesbian couples. One couple, who had traveled from Los Angeles, was married in a Unitarian church in Denver by a minister from the Metropolitan Community Church of Los Angeles. Of the forty or fifty letters and phone calls that Rorex reported receiving, supporters of her actions outnumbered opponents two to one.[29]

The gay couples were subjected to harassment and ridicule. One man was dismissed from his job. Another, from Australia, who had married to avoid deportation, was disowned and denounced by his mother. The Unitarian minister who had allowed the use of his church for a gay marriage ceremony received numerous phone calls and letters denouncing him for encouraging "unnatural alliances." To demonstrate his disgust, a Boulder retiree visited Rorex's office and requested a license to marry his horse. Rorex denied his request on the ground that the horse was too young—only eight years old.[30]

According to one report, clerks in almost every county in Colorado had been approached with similar requests for same-sex marriage licenses. Some clerks asked the legislature to enact a law clarifying that gay couples were not permitted to marry. About a month after Rorex issued her first marriage license to a gay couple, the state attorney general issued an opinion declaring that state law barred gay marriage and that marriages performed on licenses Rorex had issued to same-sex couples were invalid. Rorex immediately announced that she would comply with the attorney general's opinion.[31]

Coupled with the gay marriage lawsuits of the early 1970s, episodes such as this prompted state legislatures to take action. Gay activists in California argued that the state's repeal of its anti-sodomy law in 1975, combined with its feminist-inspired rewriting of its marriage law in 1971 to make it gender neutral—replacing "man and wife" with "persons"—legalized gay marriage in the state. In 1977, the legislature amended state marriage law to clarify that only a man and a woman could marry. State senator John Briggs explained that "the bill would restore some sense of morality to the state," and the legislature passed it by an overwhelming margin after little debate. Between 1973 and 1978, about fifteen other states likewise amended their laws to reaffirm the traditional definition of marriage.[32]

Despite these occasional efforts, most gay activists in the early 1970s were not much interested in marriage. In 1971, one activist wrote a detailed position paper for the ACLU in Washington State calling for the abolition of marriage "to protect individual freedom and the happiness which depends on it." Lesbian feminists tended to want no part of marriage, which they regarded as an oppressive institution, given the traditional rules that defined it, such as coverture and immunity from rape. An early gay manifesto denounced traditional marriage as a "rotten, oppressive institution" that is "fraught with role playing."[33]

Sex radicals tended to object to traditional marriage's insistence on monogamy. To them, gay liberation meant sexual liberation. Much of the early gay press urged men to overcome their sexual shame and experiment with multiple partners. The queer politics of the 1970s embraced slogans such as "Smash the Nuclear Family" and "Smash Monogamy." Marriage did not comfortably fit into that picture.[34]

Yet some gays and lesbians plainly preferred committed, monogamous relationships and, if obtainable, marriage. In 1968, a gay minister who had been forced out of his church because of his homosexuality founded the Metropolitan Community Church in Los Angeles, which began "marrying" same-sex couples in religious ceremonies without benefit of government documents. In its first four years, the church performed more than 150 gay marriages. By the early twenty-first century, the denomination's hundreds of churches had performed an estimated eighty-five thousand marriages.[35]

Although the state did not recognize such marriages, friends and family—and the couples themselves—did. Other gay couples, seeking the legal benefits of state-recognized relationships such as inheritance rights and medical decision-making authority, turned to the practice of adult adoptions. Many of these took place in California. In 1984, the New York Court of Appeals halted the practice in that state, which some lower courts had countenanced.[36]

Whether or not same-sex couples wanted marriage, they were not going to get it in the 1970s. This was a decade of incremental progress for gay rights, and gay marriage was a radical reform, not an incremental one. Gay rights organizations focused mainly on other issues, such as employment discrimination and building community institutions. When the ACLU of Southern California formed a homosexual rights committee in 1973, it identified six long-term priorities: protection against employment discrimination, repeal of sodomy laws, promoting the rights of institutionalized gays such as prisoners, recognition of gay student unions at universities, securing tax-exempt status for qualified gay organizations, and protecting the custody rights of lesbian mothers. Securing gay marriage—or even domestic partnerships, which would provide a few of the benefits of marriage to gay couples—was not on the list.[37]

One early accomplishment of gay liberation was pressuring the American Psychiatric Association in 1973 to remove homosexuality from its list of mental disorders. The American Psychological Association and the American Medical Association quickly followed suit. During the 1970s, roughly half of the states repealed their sodomy laws, though they did so by virtue of enacting the Model Penal Code's general reform of the criminal law; in fact, many legislators were probably unaware that they had voted to decriminalize same-sex sodomy. In other states, litigation challenged the constitutionality of sodomy laws as applied to consenting adult homosexuals. In 1975, the U.S. Civil Service Commission eliminated its blanket ban on the employment of homosexuals.[38]

In the 1970s, gays and lesbians more forcefully asserted themselves in politics. Gay bars in San Francisco played an important role in registering new voters and signing petitions to get George McGovern onto the ballot in California's Democratic presidential primary in 1972.[39]

Growing numbers of openly gay men and lesbians ran for public office. In 1973, Harvey Milk ran unsuccessfully for the San Francisco Board of Supervisors; four years later, he won a seat. In 1974, Elaine Noble, a college professor and co-founder of Boston Lesbian Feminists, was elected to the Massachusetts house of representatives, becoming the first openly gay state legislator in the country. Mayors in cities with powerful gay lobbies began appointing openly gay men and lesbians to government boards and commissions. When the predominantly gay Metropolitan Community Church in Los Angeles installed a new pastor in 1975, Mayor Tom Bradley spoke at the ceremony, and California governor Jerry Brown and both of the state's U.S. senators sent congratulatory messages.[40]

Incipient gay political power translated into concrete achievements at the local, state, and national levels. Political power was critical to curtailing police harassment. In the 1970s, several dozen localities enacted ordinances barring discrimination based on sexual orientation. Many of the first such ordinances were adopted in college towns, starting with East Lansing, Michigan, in 1972, but some cities, such as Washington, D.C., Minneapolis, and Seattle, soon followed suit.[41]

The scope of these ordinances varied widely. Some simply banned discrimination in public employment, while others extended to private employment, housing, and public accommodations. Given that most gays remained closeted, activists saw these ordinances as more important for their educational effect than for the legal protection they afforded.[42]

In the mid-1970s, school boards in cities such as San Francisco, New York, and Washington, D.C., protected teachers from discrimination based on sexual orientation. Mayors in many large cities were proclaiming Gay Pride Weeks.[43]

By the second half of the 1970s, some state politicians were taking pro-gay initiatives. In 1975, Governor Milton Shapp of Pennsylvania issued an executive order forbidding discrimination based on sexual orientation in government employment, and in 1978 he extended that ban to government contractors. By the late 1970s, Governor Jerry Brown of California had issued a similar executive order and was regularly appointing openly gay men and lesbians to judgeships and public commissions. In 1978, the Illinois Department of Insurance forbade discrimination based on sexual orientation. In 1979, Michigan prohibited discrimination based on sexual orientation in government services provided to the elderly, and in 1980 the state civil service commission barred such discrimination in government employment.[44]

Gay political clout was apparent even at the national level, though concrete victories there would prove more elusive. In 1976, twenty-five members of the House of Representatives introduced a bill to amend the 1964 Civil Rights Act to forbid discrimination based on sexual orientation. During the Democratic presidential primaries that year, candidate Jimmy Carter expressed opposition to such discrimination. Early in 1977, for the first time in American history, gay activists were invited to the White House to meet with a presidential assistant, Midge Costanza. In 1979, they returned to present petitions seeking President Carter's support for extending civil rights protections to homosexuals.[45]

Carter was the first president to appoint openly gay men or lesbians to presidential commissions, and his appointees at the Internal Revenue Service reversed a policy that prevented qualified gay organizations from receiving tax-exempt status. In 1980, the Carter administration endorsed a proposal to repeal the immigration law that had been interpreted to authorize the exclusion of homosexual aliens from the United States. Also that year, pressure from gay rights groups led the Immigration and Naturalization Service to stop harassing Canadian lesbians on their way to the Michigan Women's Music Festival and to cease questioning Cuban and Haitian refugees about their sexual orientation during interviews to determine political refugee status.[46]

In 1980, Democratic presidential candidates Edward Kennedy and Jerry Brown promised, if elected, to issue executive orders banning discrimination based on sexual orientation in the federal government. That year, for the first time ever, the Democratic Party's platform included a gay rights plank, which called for legislative and executive action to protect against discrimination based on sexual orientation. Eighty-six openly gay delegates attended the Democratic national convention that year—up from four in 1976.[47]

During his campaign for the Republican presidential nomination in 1980, Illinois congressional representative John Anderson agreed to co-sponsor the gay rights bill pending in the House. The platform of the party supporting Anderson's independent campaign in the general election condemned discrimination based on sexual orientation and encouraged Congress to grant the Civil Rights Commission power to investigate charges of such discrimination.[48]

Reflecting on such political developments, the Human Rights Campaign optimistically concluded that "support for gay rights is not the kiss of death." A political newsletter written in the District of Columbia declared, "The gay vote is now so important in national politics and some local races, that no serious politician can afford to ignore or to ridicule it." In 1980, two Washington columnists noted that the gay community "has proved to be a lode of political contributions now that it has become so much more socially acceptable for gays to surface and identify themselves."[49]

Gay rights litigation also began to win some significant victories in the 1970s. The ACLU conferred its important imprimatur on such litigation, expanding and coordinating its commitment to gay rights by launching the National Gay Rights Project in 1979. One consistent litigation winner was the First Amendment right to establish gay student organizations in universities and to support their social events, despite concerns that their activities promoted behavior forbidden by state sodomy laws. For the first time, lower courts invalidated state sodomy laws as applied to consenting adult homosexuals, though the U.S. Supreme Court indicated disagreement with those decisions.[50]

The Florida supreme court ruled that private, consensual homosexual conduct was insufficient grounds for denying someone admission to the bar. One federal district judge rejected the military's blanket exclusion of gays, while another ruled that the federal government could not bar aliens from entering the United States simply because of their homosexuality. Litigation convinced the federal Bureau of Prisons to allow prisoners access to gay-oriented materials, such as the *Advocate*.[51]

Some lower courts held that homosexuals could be dismissed from public employment based on their sexual orientation only if the government could demonstrate a rational relationship between homosexuality and one's ability to perform the job. The ACLU also earned an important victory in the D.C. Circuit, which restricted the federal government's ability to inquire into the details of private sex lives in determining whether an admitted homosexual should lose his security clearance because of potential blackmail.[52]

In the 1970s, gay activism also began to influence popular culture. Many show business celebrities—such as Valerie Harper, Cloris Leachman, Jane Fonda, Shirley Temple, and Norman Lear—publicly expressed their support for gay

rights. Activist groups made incremental progress in influencing media portrayals of homosexuality. Organizations such as the National Gay Task Force
(NGTF) demanded meetings with television network executives and, occasionally, convinced them to portray gays and lesbians in a more positive manner. In
1975, *Time* became the first major news magazine to put an openly gay man on
its cover—a decorated Vietnam veteran who had been discharged from the military because of his homosexuality.[53]

In the 1970s, Reform Judaism and some mainline Protestant denominations,
such as the Lutheran Church, the United Methodist Church, and the United
Church of Christ, began to reconsider their traditional condemnations of homosexuality and to support civil rights protections for gays and lesbians. Within
many professions, such as medicine, law, and academia, gays came out of the
closet and formed their own subgroups. Many professional organizations,
including the American Psychiatric Association, the American Federation of
Teachers, and the National Council of Churches, endorsed anti-discrimination
protections for sexual orientation.[54]

By 1980, a few large corporations, such as Ford, Xerox, and AT&T, had
adopted formal anti-discrimination policies covering sexual orientation. Gays
and lesbians formed churches, health clinics, social centers, and amateur sports
leagues. Entrepreneurs built gay publishing houses, travel agencies, and vacation
resorts. As gays became more visible, many Americans began to find homosexuality less strange and threatening.[55]

From the perspective of the twenty-first century, such changes may seem like
"a few faltering steps." Yet to gay activists at the time, they were enormous strides
forward.[56]

But gay rights progress also fomented backlash. Resistance to gay rights activism
played an important role in the mobilization of the religious right in the late
1970s. Opposition to homosexuality and the challenge it poses to traditional
patriarchal notions of social order lies at the core of fundamentalist ideology.[57]

The origins of the religious right in Florida are traceable to Anita Bryant's crusade to overturn the gay rights ordinance enacted in Dade County, Florida
(which includes the city of Miami). After an emotional, two-hour hearing in
January 1977, the country commission approved an ordinance barring
discrimination based on sexual orientation in housing, public accommodations,
and employment. The leader of the opposition was singer Anita Bryant, a former
runner-up for Miss America who was the spokesperson for Florida citrus
growers, a fervent Southern Baptist, and a thirty-seven-year-old mother of four
school-age children. Bryant argued that the ordinance "condones immorality
and discriminates against my children's rights to grow up in a healthy, decent
community."[58]

The ordinance proved to be a powerful organizing tool for the religious right. Within five weeks of its enactment, opponents had gathered six times the number of signatures needed to force a popular vote on the measure. Bryant formed an organization called Save Our Children, which ran advertisements warning that the ordinance would require schools to hire gay teachers who would proselytize for homosexuality and possibly molest children. Save Our Children raised almost $200,000 for its campaign against the ordinance.[59]

Bryant's organizing forced her opponents to do the same. The head of the principal group defending the ordinance called Bryant "the best thing that has ever happened to us." In San Francisco, gays set up a Miami Support Committee and produced bumper stickers declaring, "A Day Without Human Rights Is Like a Day Without Sunshine"—a twist on Bryant's famous orange juice commercials. A large motel in Provincetown, Massachusetts, took orange juice off its menu in protest.[60]

Fund-raisers in New York City and San Francisco generated nearly $300,000 to defend the ordinance. The executive director of a South Florida gay rights organization predicted a national "witch hunt" against homosexuals if the referendum passed. Bryant's opponents ran ads invoking the specter of Nazi-like oppression and publicized a joint statement by four psychiatrists denying that homosexuals were predisposed toward child molestation.[61]

Despite predictions of a close contest, Dade County voters turned out in unusually high numbers in June 1977 to repeal the ordinance by a whopping

Anita Bryant being led into the voting booth in Dade County, Florida, June 7, 1977. (*Associated Press/Kathy A. Willens*)

margin of 68 percent to 32 percent. Dade County would not pass another such ordinance for twenty-one years.[62]

Also in response to the Dade County ordinance, the Florida legislature banned adoptions by homosexuals and explicitly barred same-sex marriage. The state senator who sponsored the legislation explained: "They're trying to flaunt it. We're trying to send them a message telling them, 'We're really tired of you. We wish you'd go back into the closet.'"[63]

Although the referendum defeat was devastating for gay activists, the NGTF found a silver lining in the episode, which had revealed "the extent and nature of the prejudice and discrimination we face." The NGTF commenced a nationwide series of week-long open dialogues with homosexuals, entitled "We Are Your Children," the purpose of which was to introduce themselves to the American people. The organization was inundated with offers of money and help.[64]

The Dade defeat also sparked direct action protest in cities across the nation. In New York City, several thousand demonstrators gathered in Greenwich Village before marching into midtown to declare the start of a new effort to end discrimination against homosexuals. In Houston, three thousand gays and lesbians held a candlelight march to a downtown hotel to protest Bryant's appearance there at a lawyers' convention. In San Francisco, forty thousand men and women marched in a Gay Freedom Day parade, many shouting denunciations of Anita Bryant.[65]

Bryant's was not the first such effort in the country. In 1974, a similar gay rights ordinance enacted in Boulder, Colorado, had been overturned in a referendum by a margin of 64 percent to 36 percent. One of the city council members who had supported the Boulder ordinance was recalled from office soon thereafter.[66]

Yet Bryant's campaign was the first to rivet national attention on the emerging issue of gay rights. Even before the actual referendum vote in Dade County, Bryant was speaking on the topic all over the country, and she reported receiving more than twenty thousand letters on the issue. Editorializing against Bryant's "absurd as well as benighted" effort to portray homosexuals as committed to converting children, the New York Times observed that the South Florida referendum battle appeared "to have started a noisy national debate on a question that previously had been discussed mainly in muted tones."[67]

After her victory, Bryant announced that she was establishing a national committee to fight homosexuality and launching a nationwide tour to promote the repeal of similar ordinances that had been enacted elsewhere. Liberal Washington Post columnist William Raspberry, although refusing to condone homosexuality, denounced what appeared to him to be "a homosexual witch hunt in the name of religion." In the New York Times, conservative columnist William Safire, although chastising gays for seeking approval rather than mere toleration, urged Bryant to "ease up," criticized her national crusade, and warned against punishing people for their private behavior.[68]

In 1978, five municipalities repealed their gay rights ordinances in referenda. No vote was close. Wichita voters repealed their ordinance by a margin of 83 percent to 17 percent, while voters in St. Paul, Minnesota, and Eugene, Oregon, repealed their respective ordinances by a margin of 63 percent to 37 percent. Only in Seattle did a gay rights ordinance survive a referendum battle.[69]

In California, gay rights opponents went further in 1978, seeking not just to roll back local legislative gains made by gays but also to put homosexuals in an even worse position than they had traditionally occupied. An initiative sponsored by state senator John Briggs, who was running for the Republican gubernatorial nomination, would have barred gays from teaching in public schools. Briggs said the measure was necessary because most homosexuals were child molesters, which was why they became teachers. Early polling suggested the measure would pass easily.[70]

Yet even conservative former governor Ronald Reagan thought the Briggs initiative was too extreme, and he came out in opposition. California voters rejected it by a margin of 58 percent to 42 percent. At a jubilant rally in San Francisco, Mayor George Moscone called the vote "a victory over the despair which had fallen over gay people after the defeats in Miami, St. Paul, Wichita, and Eugene."[71]

Despite the defeat of the Briggs initiative, popular referenda posed a dire threat to gay rights progress. Even if local governments could sometimes be persuaded to adopt gay rights ordinances, very few cities had populations that would vote in favor of them. In addition, the religious right, with its network of churches, enjoyed significant organizing and fund-raising advantages in referendum contests.[72]

By 1978, gay activists were expressing "deep concern" about these referenda. They held a day-long "think tank" in New York City with the ACLU and the National Organization for Women—the Equal Rights Amendment was not faring well in referenda, either—to discuss legal and political options. The conference did not yield an optimistic conclusion: "We are not likely to win referenda at this early stage of our movement." Nor, thought the activists, were such referenda "seriously contestable in the courts." [73]

After the mid-1970s, the rate at which cities adopted such anti-discrimination ordinances declined, probably because of the referendum threat looming over them. In the twenty years after Anita Bryant's Save Our Children campaign, more than sixty jurisdictions held referenda on anti-gay-rights proposals; nearly three-quarters of them passed.[74]

Even aside from the backlash generated by the Dade County ordinance, progress made by the gay rights movement in the 1970s was limited. Lobbying efforts to rescind the ban on gays in the military failed, and courts generally rejected legal challenges to that policy. The Immigration and Naturalization Service continued to treat open homosexuality as sufficient grounds for excluding aliens from the United States. In 1980, Congress passed legislation forbidding the Legal Services Corporation from providing "legal assistance for any litigation which seeks to adjudicate the legalization of homosexuality."[75]

Few private employers had policies against discrimination based on sexual orientation, and even those public employers that did declined to protect public manifestations of homosexual orientation. The U.S. Civil Service Commission likewise continued to treat open manifestations of homosexuality, which it defined to include gay rights advocacy, as a sufficient basis for job dismissal. Public-school teachers were still fired because of their sexual orientation—even if not publicly manifested—and courts typically declined to intervene. Opinion polls showed that although a majority of Americans supported equal employment opportunity in general for homosexuals, 65 percent opposed permitting them to become schoolteachers.[76]

In 1975, California became the first state to specifically decriminalize same-sex sodomy between consenting adults, instead of generally implementing the Model Penal Code reform provisions that abolished a variety of little-enforced sex crimes. Religious conservatives mobilized strenuous resistance, and the bill passed only after the lieutenant governor broke a deadlock in the state senate.[77]

In 1976, the U.S. Supreme Court summarily affirmed a lower court decision rejecting a constitutional challenge to a state sodomy law that authorized punishment of up to five years in prison. The lower court had cited the Bible's condemnation of homosexuality to support its conclusion that the legislature could reasonably determine that same-sex sodomy was "likely to end in a contribution to moral delinquency." Civil libertarians and gay rights groups called the high court's decision "insensitive," "shocking," and "highly destructive."[78]

Although rarely enforced, sodomy laws created "an aura of criminality" around homosexuals and were still frequently invoked to justify other forms of discrimination against them. Virginia barred all custody awards to gay parents, while in other states that had no blanket exclusion, homophobic judges continued to deny custody based on a parent's sexual orientation.[79]

In 1985, the Massachusetts Department of Social Services allowed an openly gay couple to serve as foster parents for two young siblings. When the *Boston Globe* covered the incident, the story went viral, and the state house of representatives voted overwhelmingly to ban such placements. The social services department quickly adopted a new policy that essentially barred gays from becoming foster parents. Governor Michael Dukakis defended the new policy on the grounds that "the vast majority of people in this state and across the country" believe that the traditional family is the "best possible setting for a youngster."[80]

According to a poll taken in the late 1970s, 72 percent of Americans still thought that homosexual relations were always wrong. Even civil libertarians had qualms about affiliating with gay rights groups. In 1977, the Leadership Conference on Civil Rights was in a quandary over whether to allow the NGTF to join. Concerned that gay-bashing by ERA opponents was effective, the National Organization for Women prohibited lesbian banners at its demonstrations. Lesbians complained that feminist organizations such as NOW treated them as "lepers, like embarrassing misfits." As late as 1984, Democratic senator Tom Harkin thought it wise to return a political donation from the Human Rights Campaign.[81]

Although many of the gay rights organizations that were founded after Stonewall expanded in the 1970s, they remained severely underfunded. Lambda Legal had so little money that it mostly filed amicus briefs rather than actually representing clients. Until 1978, it could not afford a paid staff, and into the 1980s it could afford to hire only lawyers fresh out of law school. In the early 1980s, the NGTF, then the largest gay rights organization in the country, had 10,300 members and a meager annual budget of $338,000. The Moral Majority, its principal adversary, had a membership estimated at four million and an annual budget of $56 million (though, of course, not all of that was devoted to fighting against gay rights).[82]

Gay rights groups had secured access to the media to protest negative portrayals of homosexuality, but ultimately they had little to show for their efforts. Throughout the 1970s, gay media watchdogs constantly objected to references to gay characters as "fags" and "fruitcakes" and to stereotyped portrayals of gay men with limp wrists and lisped speech. When ABC responded to such protests by noting that it took "great pains not to espouse a point of view" on a controversial topic such as homosexuality, the NGTF expressed outrage and wondered what the outcry would be if the networks assumed a similar posture in response to analogous complaints by the NAACP or the Anti-Defamation League.[83]

Nicholas von Hoffman, a prominent liberal commentator on *60 Minutes* and in newspapers, repeatedly referred to gays as "fags," "fruits," and "homos" without jeopardizing his stature as a "star liberal" who was feted and honored by civil libertarians. Although conceding Von Hoffman's constitutional right "to speak and write as foolishly and tastelessly as he chooses," the NGTF thought it had the right to object to its liberal friends consorting with him, just as the NAACP would surely object to its friends palling around with extreme southern segregationists such as Bull Connor or Lester Maddox.[84]

With the gay rights movement already enduring political backlash, the election of Ronald Reagan as president in 1980 seemed to portend disaster. Reagan was elected with the strong support of religious conservatives, including the Moral

Majority, which Reverend Jerry Falwell had established in 1979 with the goal of politically organizing Christian evangelicals. For decades, these evangelicals had played a largely passive role in politics. The Moral Majority mobilized them behind a platform of supporting prayer in school and strongly opposing abortion, the Equal Rights Amendment, and the civil rights of homosexuals.[85]

Falwell's religious radio and television programming reached an estimated weekly audience of six million to fifteen million people, and his pleas for contributions elicited an estimated $56 million annually. In its first year of existence, the Moral Majority grew to four hundred thousand members nationally and raised $1.5 million. The organization sponsored rallies and seminars on how Christian evangelicals should use their political power.[86]

By the summer of 1980, the Moral Majority claimed to have registered three million new voters, most of whom were inclined to vote Republican. Falwell's group could already claim a few political victories, including ones in state politics in Florida and Alaska and the nomination of Charles Grassley as the Republican candidate for the U.S. Senate from Iowa.[87]

Falwell admitted that the positions of the Moral Majority ran counter to those stated in the Democratic Party platform. In March 1980, he noted in a speech that two months earlier he had asked President Carter why he had open homosexuals serving on his senior staff. Falwell professed to be appalled by Carter's response that "I am president of all the American people and I believe I should represent everyone."[88]

One core component of Ronald Reagan's election strategy in 1980 was to compete with President Carter, a born-again Christian, for the votes of evangelicals, a sizable percentage of whom had supported the Democrat in 1976. During the campaign, Reagan staunchly opposed abortion and ridiculed those who wanted to remove "In God We Trust" from the nation's currency.[89]

In 1980, the Republican Party embraced most of the positions of Falwell and the burgeoning family values movement. For the first time, the party's platform included a plank defending "the traditional American family." Republicans dropped their long-standing support for the ERA, endorsed a constitutional amendment to ban abortion, and adopted an anti-abortion litmus test for federal judicial nominees. Falwell was sufficiently influential to have access to Reagan's hotel suite on the day he was choosing his vice presidential candidate, though he lacked the clout to convince Reagan not to select George H. W. Bush, whose previous support for pro-choice positions made him anathema to many evangelicals.[90]

In August 1980, Reagan gave a national affairs briefing to ten thousand pastors gathering in Dallas, which prompted the *New York Times* to note that conservative evangelicals had "become a surprising and important aspect of this election." In his Dallas speech, Reagan professed shock at the argument that the

First Amendment should constrain religious people from influencing politics. A leading televangelist at the conference, James Robison, declared himself "sick and tired of hearing about all of the radicals and the perverts and the liberals...coming out of the closet." It was time, he announced, "for God's people to come out of the closet."[91]

In October, Reagan gave a speech to the National Association of Religious Broadcasters, which Falwell was hosting in Lynchburg, Virginia. This speech was Reagan's opportunity to address the religious right's concerns about his signing California's therapeutic abortion law as governor in 1967 and his opposing the anti-gay Briggs amendment in 1978. In his speech, Reagan expressed doubts about the theory of evolution, declared that the Bible contained the answers to the nation's social ills, and accused liberals of using the separation of church and state to exclude religious conservatives from politics.[92]

Late in the presidential campaign, a group called Christians for Reagan ran television advertisements in several states attacking President Carter and the Democratic Party for their support of homosexual rights—the first such ad ever run in a presidential campaign. A majority of Christian evangelicals had supported Carter in 1976, but in 1980 they voted almost two to one for Reagan.[93]

With Reagan in the White House, gay rights organizations' access to federal agencies ended. Reagan appointed Gary Bauer, a close associate of James Dobson, founder of Focus on the Family, as his domestic policy advisor. Reagan's most prominent patronage appointment for the religious right was Dr. Everett Koop, a Philadelphia physician, who was named surgeon general. Koop was an evangelical Christian who strongly opposed abortion, criticized amniocentesis as a "search and destroy mission," and declared that homosexuality was a sin.[94]

At the behest of the Moral Majority, Reagan also nominated to the U.S. Civil Rights Commission a Philadelphia minister who had stated that "the majority of Americans, particularly the godly among us, see homosexuality as sinful." A former director of the Moral Majority and several faculty members from Bob Jones University, an evangelical college in South Carolina, worked either in the Department of Education or as consultants to it.[95]

In 1981, after the District of Columbia city council voted to repeal its little-enforced sodomy law, the Moral Majority announced its top legislative priority for the year to be persuading Congress to reverse that decision. Declaring that home rule was good only so long as it was not used for "normalizing moral decadence" and warning that for Washington, D.C., to become "the gay capital of the world" would be "very terrible," Falwell launched an intensive lobbying campaign. The House of Representatives eventually voted overwhelmingly to reverse the council's decision. The D.C. sodomy law was not removed from the books for another twelve years.[96]

With a more conservative administration in office, efforts to repeal the statute authorizing the exclusion of gay aliens from the United States, which the Carter administration had endorsed, were temporarily abandoned. A gay man who had been forced to resign from the CIA because of his sexual orientation noted a government-wide campaign of discrimination during Reagan's presidency, "motivated by the worst homophobia and a warped sense of the national security, and perpetrated not by holdovers from the J. Edgar Hoover era but by a new, young cadre of neoconservatives from the hills of Lynchburg, Virginia and other sheltered bastions of bigotry."[97]

In 1982, a local offshoot of the Moral Majority tried unsuccessfully to pass a referendum in Austin, Texas, that would have affirmatively authorized housing discrimination against gays and lesbians. Gay rights organizations were forced to devote substantial resources and time to fending off the Family Protection Act, which, among other things, would have prohibited federal funding of any individual or organization that advocated or promoted homosexuality. As one gay activist observed, these were "very difficult times for the gay and lesbian community."[98]

The harsh political climate was exacerbated by the advent of the AIDS epidemic, which first attracted significant attention early in Reagan's presidency. Jerry Falwell, Reverend Pat Robertson, and other conservative religious leaders treated AIDS as "God's judgment against a nation that chooses to live immorally." A high-ranking official of the Moral Majority objected to the government's spending tax dollars on research "to allow these diseased homosexuals to go back to their perverted practices without any standards of accountability." In a fund-raising letter, Falwell accused gay men of donating blood because "they know they are going to die—and they're going to take as many people with them as they can."[99]

Initial media reports downplayed any risk that AIDS posed to the general public. But within a year or two, fear of contagion, combined with the perceived close association between AIDS and gay men, ignited widespread discrimination against gays. AIDS was invoked to deny custody and visitation rights to gay parents, to exclude gays from housing and employment, to reject anti-discrimination protections for gays, and to block the formation of a gay college students' organization.[100]

Some people were afraid to use the same public telephones or water fountains as gays. Parental protests led some schools to expel children who were infected with the virus. Conservative commentator William Buckley proposed tattooing people with the term "AIDS." William Dannemeyer, a conservative congressional representative from California, launched a bid for the Republican nomination for a U.S. Senate seat by charging that AIDS carriers emitted deadly spores and that they might be engaged in "blood terrorism." State Republican Party platforms called for barring gays and lesbians from jobs as teachers or health care workers, strict enforcement of sodomy laws, and mandatory reporting of individuals who tested positive for HIV.[101]

The percentage of Americans who deemed homosexual sex always wrong increased from 73 percent in 1980 to 78 percent in 1987, and the percentage who opposed legalization of consensual same-sex sodomy rose from 39 percent in 1982 to 55 percent in 1986. Sociologists and gay activists attributed a dramatic increase in anti-gay violence in the mid-1980s to widespread fear and anger over AIDS. At the University of Chicago, hundreds of anti-gay leaflets were distributed on campus and "Death to Faggots" bumper stickers were plastered on the doors of teachers and students who had signed a petition decrying homophobic activities on campus.[102]

President Reagan did not publicly utter a word about AIDS until a friend of his, movie star Rock Hudson, became ill with the disease in 1985. Hudson's illness finally began to draw public attention to the issue. Reagan gave his first speech on AIDS six years into the epidemic, by which time more than twenty thousand people had died.[103]

The administration also took years before requesting any congressional appropriations for AIDS research. In 1986, the Reagan Justice Department issued an opinion declaring that federal law permitted employers to discharge workers infected with AIDS in order to protect the health of other employees, despite scientific evidence that the disease could not be transmitted through casual contact.[104]

AIDS put gay activists on the defensive and forced a shift in their agenda. As the NGLTF observed, efforts to pass anti-discrimination laws "came to a screeching halt as gay political activists shifted their focus—by necessity—to AIDS issues." After Wisconsin in 1982 became the first state to enact an anti-discrimination law covering sexual orientation, not another state followed suit until 1989. In Massachusetts, where such a bill had passed the house in 1983, numerous delegates switched sides to defeat the bill in 1985, many of them invoking AIDS to explain their shift. In 1987, the New Hampshire legislature, also influenced by the AIDS epidemic, banned gay adoptions.[105]

As much as 30 percent of Lambda Legal's docket from 1983 to 1992 consisted of cases involving AIDS, which meant less attention could be paid to the rest of its agenda. In the mid-1980s, most lobbying by gay rights organizations focused on securing federal funding for AIDS-related research, blocking measures that would have discriminated against those with AIDS or those who tested HIV positive, and educating the public about the disease in order to forestall backlash.[106]

Gay activists did defeat a 1986 California ballot initiative, sponsored by conspiracy theorist and perennial presidential candidate Lyndon H. LaRouche, that would have authorized public officials to quarantine AIDS carriers and forbidden them from working in restaurants and from teaching in schools. Another proposed ballot initiative that year in Washington State would have barred homosexuals from employment in any public agency dealing with children, the disabled, or the elderly.[107]

For years, Lambda Legal's top priority had been overturning anti-sodomy laws, which it called "the bedrock of legal discrimination against gay men and lesbians." Such litigation appealed to gay rights lawyers not just because anti-sodomy laws were invoked to justify every manner of discrimination against gays, but also because such cases seemed easier to win than, for example, child custody cases. Many judges who did not believe that states had any business criminalizing private, consensual same-sex sodomy still had qualms about gay parents raising young children. The Supreme Court's landmark privacy precedent, *Griswold v. Connecticut*, also seemed more directly relevant to challenges to anti-sodomy statutes.[108]

Favorable rulings by lower courts in New York, Pennsylvania, and Texas in the early 1980s convinced Lambda Legal that the time was ripe to challenge sodomy laws in the Supreme Court. In 1983, Lambda and the ACLU convened a conference of gay rights lawyers to develop a national strategy to eradicate sodomy laws across the country.[109]

AIDS complicated their efforts. Defenders of sodomy laws used the disease to justify such statutes on public health grounds. In the mid-1980s, conservatives introduced bills to recriminalize same-sex sodomy in states that had repealed their prohibitions and to increase criminal penalties for the practice. Some judicial decisions rejecting constitutional challenges to sodomy laws explicitly invoked AIDS as a justification. When the U.S. Supreme Court in 1986 granted review in a same-sex sodomy case, an amicus brief argued that the law should be sustained because of AIDS.[110]

In 1976, the Court had summarily affirmed a lower court decision rejecting a constitutional challenge to a sodomy law. In 1986, the Court granted full review in another such case, *Bowers v. Hardwick*. Most observers predicted that the Court would be deeply divided, with Justice Lewis Powell likely to provide the decisive vote. At oral argument, both sides addressed their remarks mainly toward Justice Powell.[111]

At the justices' conference discussion of *Bowers*, Powell voted with the four liberal justices to invalidate the statute, believing that sodomy between consenting adults in private should be decriminalized. One of the liberal justices, Harry Blackmun, was surprised by Powell's statement and wondered if he would stick with that position. Indeed, Powell was troubled by the lower court decision invalidating the sodomy statute, a decision that had depicted private homosexual sex as analogous to marriage—a view that Powell certainly did not share.[112]

Not long after the conference discussion, Powell circulated a memo to his colleagues in which he reversed his tentative conference vote. Although Powell continued to believe that incarceration for private, adult consensual same-sex sodomy would constitute cruel and unusual punishment, he would not vote to create a fundamental right to same-sex sodomy. In the course of discussing the case with his (gay) law clerk, Powell volunteered that he had never known anyone who was gay.[113]

After Powell's switch, the Court rejected the constitutional challenge by a vote of 5 to 4. Justice Byron White wrote the majority opinion, which labeled "facetious" the claim that a right to engage in homosexual sodomy was "deeply rooted in this Nation's history and tradition." Chief Justice Warren Burger authored a concurring opinion, which noted that millennia of moral teaching condemned homosexuality and that the great English legal commentator William Blackstone had called homosexual sodomy an offense of "deeper malignity" than rape. Justice Powell, the critical fifth vote for the majority, wrote a separate concurrence, which publicly restated the views he had earlier expressed privately to his colleagues. Soon after retiring from the Court the following year, Powell confessed error.[114]

The gay rights community was devastated by *Bowers*. Tom Stoddard of Lambda Legal called it the gay community's *Dred Scott* (the 1857 Supreme Court decision barring Congress from acting against slavery in federal territories and ruling that even free blacks had no rights under the U.S. Constitution). His colleague Abby Rubenfeld compared it to *Plessy v. Ferguson* (the 1896 Court decision sustaining the constitutionality of state-imposed racial segregation on railroad passengers). Nobody thought that the ruling would trigger more sodomy prosecutions; its principal effect was symbolic. Stoddard explained that the Court "has expressed a certain distaste for gay men and women and suggested that they may be treated differently from other Americans." Burt Neuborne of the ACLU warned that *Bowers* would "be read as a signal by people who believe that homosexuality is sinful that they can flex their political muscles."[115]

Major metropolitan newspapers condemned *Bowers*. The *New York Times* called it "a gratuitous and petty ruling." The *Los Angeles Times* objected to the "rigid and hostile attitude woven through White's opinion." The *Atlanta Journal and Constitution* called *Bowers* "a cruelly homophobic ruling." A Gallup poll conducted a week after the decision found that more people disapproved of it than approved.[116]

Several other challenges to sodomy laws that were at various stages of litigation when *Bowers* was decided were mostly dropped. One week after *Bowers*, the Missouri supreme court relied on it to reject a challenge to the state's sodomy law. No state repealed its sodomy law between 1986 and 1991, and some amended their general sodomy statutes to specifically target same-sex conduct.[117]

Lower courts cited *Bowers* to justify all manner of discrimination against gays. In 1987, one federal circuit court relied on it to reject an equal protection claim by a lesbian who had been denied a job with the FBI because of her sexual orientation. The court ruled that government discrimination against a class of persons could not be invidious if the Supreme Court had determined that the behavior defining the class could be criminally punished.[118]

Federal circuit courts also invoked *Bowers* to reject challenges to the military's policy of excluding gays, to sustain the Defense Department's policy of applying greater scrutiny to security clearances sought by gays, and to reject a constitutional challenge to a Cincinnati charter amendment that prevented the city council from adopting anti-discrimination protections for gays. State courts got into the act as well. In 1987, the New Hampshire supreme court invoked *Bowers* in rejecting a constitutional challenge to a law forbidding gays from fostering or adopting children.[119]

Yet not all of *Bowers*'s consequences for the gay rights movement were adverse. The Court's decision made gay rights issues highly salient. Soon after the ruling, the plaintiff in *Bowers*, Michael Hardwick, appeared on *The Phil Donahue Show*, along with his ACLU lawyer and Stoddard of Lambda Legal.[120]

Moreover, conservative court decisions can produce liberal political backlashes. *Bowers* indeed galvanized the gay rights movement. An NGLTF official observed that there is "incredible anger out there—people really are prepared to come out and fight." Leaders reported that the gay community had not been so outraged since San Francisco supervisor Dan White received a mere six years in prison for murdering gay rights leader Harvey Milk.[121]

Within hours of the *Bowers* decision, small protests had erupted in several cities. The largest was in New York, where more than a thousand demonstrators marched from the federal courthouse. Gay rights groups considered organizing an economic boycott of the Coca-Cola Company, which was based in Georgia, where *Bowers* had originated. They also spoke of organizing a protest rally at Justice Sandra Day O'Connor's forthcoming appearance in San Francisco.[122]

Two months after *Bowers*, the executive director of the NGLTF reported an extraordinary outpouring of financial support, as people sent checks along with notes stating, "I can't believe the Supreme Court did this." He concluded, "Five to ten years down the line, we may thank Justice Byron White for writing that opinion."[123]

Bowers became a cornerstone of fund-raising appeals for Lambda Legal, with the first letters going out within a week of the decision. Individual contributions to Lambda increased threefold between 1985 and 1986. In 1987, three prominent New York law firms held unprecedented fund-raisers for Lambda, enabling it to open new offices and expand its litigation roster. Concerned that *Bowers* would invigorate hate campaigns against gays, the ACLU created its Lesbian and Gay

Rights Project, which would become the first national civil rights organization to endorse gay marriage.[124]

Together with the AIDS epidemic, *Bowers* was a major impetus for the 1987 National March on Washington for Lesbian and Gay Rights, which drew between two hundred thousand and three hundred thousand participants. The last such event in Washington, D.C., in 1979, had drawn between seventy thousand and eighty thousand people. The march's agenda included federal civil rights protections for gays, increased funding for AIDS research and anti-discrimination protections for AIDS victims, repeal of sodomy laws, and legal recognition of gay relationships. The march culminated in a protest by several thousand people on the steps of the Supreme Court building. Six hundred of them were arrested, including Michael Hardwick.[125]

Although *Bowers* mobilized gay rights supporters, the ruling did not clearly repulse the broad middle of the political spectrum on gay rights issues. In the mid-1980s, opinion polls continued to show strong public disapproval of homosexuality. At a time when the U.S. Supreme Court sustained state laws criminalizing same-sex sodomy among consenting adults, the notion that gay couples would one day be permitted to legally marry must have seemed a pipe dream.[126]

Although AIDS proved devastating to the gay community and debilitating to the gay rights movement in the short term, it advanced the cause of gay rights over the longer term. For one thing, the epidemic forced tens of thousands of homosexuals out of the closet. In the words of one activist, "AIDS made it so we couldn't hide anymore."[127]

By 1992, 230,000 Americans, of whom 65 percent were gay men, had been diagnosed with AIDS. One hundred fifty thousand of them had died of the disease. Most of the deceased were not public celebrities like Rock Hudson, but the friends, relatives, and co-workers of ordinary Americans. As the political director of NGLTF observed, "AIDS has increased the exposure of the gay community as human beings." The percentage of Americans who reported knowing someone who is gay doubled between 1985 and 1992.[128]

AIDS was a "call to action," which helped gay rights groups raise money and enlist new activists. Thousands of formerly apolitical gays and lesbians suddenly had a more direct stake in gay rights activism, and accordingly they volunteered to register voters and lobby policy makers. Public attitudes and government policies had now become—literally—a matter of life or death. Signs appeared in gay bars and bookstores that bluntly stated, "Voting for Our Lives." People who knew AIDS victims—some people watched dozens of their friends pass away—were spurred into action like never before.[129]

AIDS also inspired the formation of new grassroots organizations to attend to the needs of sufferers—needs not adequately addressed by government agencies.

Groups such as Gay Men's Health Crisis in New York mobilized thousands of volunteers to help AIDS sufferers, cooking their meals and cleaning their homes. Media coverage of the new AIDS activism not only gave the disease a human face but also conveyed stories about gay couples and their support groups that complicated society's stereotyped views of the gay community.[130]

In 1987, activists launched a new generation of gay militancy, reminiscent of the Gay Liberation Front of the early 1970s, by founding ACT UP, the AIDS Coalition to Unleash Power. ACT UP members shouted down public officials and religious leaders, demanding quicker government approval of anti-AIDS drugs.[131]

Mainstream foundations that were generally reluctant to support gay rights causes contributed large sums to anti-AIDS efforts. Individuals began leaving bequests to Lambda Legal, whose annual income rose dramatically in the midst of the AIDS epidemic. Largely because of AIDS, fund-raising for the Human Rights Campaign Fund doubled between 1984 and 1986. In 1986, an NGLTF official observed, "AIDS has totally transformed the way the gay political movement does business. Three years ago, the kind of access and influence we have now would have been unthinkable."[132]

AIDS forced homosexuality and gay rights to the forefront of public debate. Government officials who had previously paid minimal attention to gay people and their concerns now had little choice but to shift focus. Mayors of large cities with substantial gay populations became prominent advocates of anti-discrimination bills.[133]

Although religious and cultural conservatives sought to use AIDS to rally opposition to the "gay rights agenda," the American public generally seemed to sympathize with a community that had been afflicted with devastating losses. A Democratic-controlled House of Representatives consistently voted to raise the level of funding for AIDS treatment and research, and more than twenty states defined AIDS as a handicap entitling sufferers to civil rights protection under fair employment and fair housing legislation. Publicity surrounding instances in which someone lost housing or custody of a child after a gay partner died of AIDS influenced public opinion and government officials.[134]

By the early 1990s, the AIDS epidemic was becoming medically and legally normalized. Congress passed legislation to protect those afflicted from discrimination in spheres such as housing. In 1992, the Americans with Disabilities Act took effect, dramatically affecting the legal treatment of AIDS sufferers. Courts interpreted the statute to require employers to take reasonable steps to accommodate employees with AIDS and to bar discrimination against employees who were HIV-positive unless they posed a significant risk to others. Most judges stopped invoking AIDS as a relevant factor in lawsuits challenging sodomy statutes. Fear of AIDS had dominated American opinions of male homosexuality in the 1980s, but that fear had greatly dissipated by the early 1990s.[135]

Of course, as AIDS ceased to terrorize most Americans, its capacity to mobilize gay rights activism also diminished. As ACT UP founder Larry Kramer explained, "For activism to work, you have to be scared and you have to be angry." AIDS drugs had depleted some of that fear and anger.[136]

Despite AIDS, *Bowers,* and the hostility of the Reagan administration, the gay rights movement had made significant progress by 1990. *Bowers* was a major defeat, but gay rights litigators had won some important victories. In 1984, the Tenth Circuit invalidated a law barring public-school teachers from encouraging or promoting homosexual activity, even in their private capacities. Courts in Alaska and New York became the first to bar consideration of sexual orientation as a factor in lesbian custody cases. Although legal challenges to the military's exclusion of gays were rarely won, liberal judges were becoming supportive, speaking of gays as a group entitled to special judicial protection because historically disadvantaged and still suffering from invidious discrimination.[137]

Gay equality also achieved significant cultural progress in the 1980s. One Republican political consultant observed in 1986, "Gays are one more thing we've accepted about our political landscape, like long hair and feminists." Even President Reagan invited an openly gay couple—his interior decorator and his companion—to stay overnight in the White House.[138]

Gay pride events, once confined to large cities on the coasts, expanded into dozens of smaller cities all over the country. In the 1980s, most major public universities forbade discrimination based on sexual orientation. In 1991, *Fortune* reported that gays were "coming out of the closet in corporate America," forming gay employee associations and pushing for non-discrimination policies, diversity training, and domestic partnership benefits.[139]

Gay rights organizations broadened their size and scope. Between 1983 and 1992, Lambda Legal's annual income rose from $133,000 to $1.6 million, and its paid staff increased from three to twenty-two. The Human Rights Campaign Fund, founded in 1980 as a gay rights lobby, raised about $50,000 its first year but $1.4 million in 1986. The NGLTF's annual budget rose from $50,000 in 1973, when it was established, to $700,000 in 1987.[140]

Gay rights progress was perhaps most apparent in politics. In 1984, the U.S. Conference of Mayors became the first organization of elected officials in the United States to support civil rights protections for gays and lesbians at all levels of government. After fifteen years of trying, the New York City Council in 1986 finally adopted an ordinance forbidding discrimination based on sexual orientation. By the end of the decade, more than sixty cities, including most of the nation's largest, had enacted similar measures.[141]

In 1989, Massachusetts became the second state to pass a law barring discrimination based on sexual orientation in housing, employment, and public accommodations. By 1993, six more states had followed suit. In 1989, Vermont became the first state to enhance penalties for crimes committed with an anti-gay motive. In several other states, governors issued executive orders forbidding discrimination based on sexual orientation in government employment and establishing official liaisons for lesbian and gay issues.[142]

The number of openly gay elected officials grew—slowly but surely. By 1987, Congress had two openly gay members, both from Massachusetts. Twenty elected and appointed gay and lesbian officials appeared at that year's meeting of the National League of Cities.[143]

In 1990, gays within the Republican Party organized the Log Cabin Republicans. (Congressman Barney Frank of Massachusetts called it "Uncle Tom's Cabin Club," in light of the anti-gay influence exercised by religious conservatives within the Republican Party.) The new organization contributed to that year's victories by Republican gubernatorial candidates Pete Wilson in California and William Weld in Massachusetts. Weld promptly rewarded his gay constituency by naming an openly gay man to head the state's human rights commission.[144]

In preparation for seeking the Democratic Party's presidential nomination in 1988, Massachusetts governor Michael Dukakis endorsed a state bill to bar discrimination based on sexual orientation in employment, insurance, credit, and housing. Dukakis's stand was a stunning contrast to his decision two years earlier to bar gays in Massachusetts from becoming foster parents—a position that led some gay activists to protest his candidacy with signs proclaiming, "The Duke Is an Antigay Bigot." In the party's primary contests, Dukakis declared that anti-gay violence should be treated as a civil rights violation, opposed the consideration of sexual orientation in granting security clearances, supported immigration legislation to end the exclusion of gay aliens, and endorsed a strong party commitment to eradicating AIDS.[145]

One of Dukakis's competitors for the nomination, Jesse Jackson, courted gay voters even more aggressively. Jackson was the only Democratic presidential candidate to attend the National March on Washington for Lesbian and Gay Rights in the fall of 1987. In his speech to the 1984 Democratic National Convention, Jackson had explicitly included the gay community within his "American quilt." In 1988, Jackson promised, if elected, to issue a Harry Truman–like executive order banning discrimination against gays in federal agencies and in the U.S. military. Gays and lesbians may have accounted for nearly 50 percent of Jackson's support among whites in the 1988 Democratic primaries.[146]

Although by 1988 gay issues played a role in the campaign for the Democratic presidential nomination, Dukakis had little incentive to emphasize gay rights issues once he became his party's standard-bearer. The Republican Party's presidential nominee, Vice President George H. W. Bush, attacked Dukakis for his cultural liberalism; putting gay rights on the table would have left the Democrat even more vulnerable to such criticism. Moreover, Dukakis appeared personally uncomfortable discussing gay issues, despite his party's official commitment to supporting gay rights.[147]

The year 1992 was the first in which the principal contestants for a major party's presidential nomination aggressively courted gay and lesbian voters. Bill Clinton, who as governor of Arkansas had never taken pro-gay positions and had refused even to issue a proclamation for National Coming Out Day, became the darling of gay activists. Clinton's principal competitor for the nomination was Senator Paul Tsongas of Massachusetts, a longtime supporter of gay rights.[148]

Battling with Tsongas for the financial and political support of the gay community, Clinton promised during an appearance at Harvard University's Kennedy School of Government in October 1991 that he would, if elected president, sign an executive order barring discrimination based on sexual orientation in the United States military. All five Democratic presidential candidates eventually committed to that policy, as well as promising increased federal spending on AIDS. An article published in the *New York Times Magazine* during the 1992 presidential campaign was entitled "Gay Politics Goes Mainstream."[149]

In May 1992, Clinton told a West Hollywood fund-raiser that was attended by 650 prominent gays and lesbians not only that he would lift the military ban but also that he would support a "Manhattan Project" on AIDS, because "we don't have a person to waste." Clinton concluded, "If I could wave my arms for those of you that are H.I.V. positive and make it go away tomorrow, I would do it, so help me God, I would. If I gave up my race for the White House and everything else, I would do that." Many in the crowd were left in tears. Thousands of videotapes of Clinton's speech circulated throughout the country, quickly transforming him into the gay community's "messiah."[150]

At the 1988 Democratic National Convention, gay delegates had been instructed to maintain a low profile. By contrast, the 1992 convention in New York City was an occasion for gays to celebrate their new political clout. One hundred and thirty-three openly gay and lesbian delegates attended.[151]

Gay rights groups demanded and received an address to the convention by both an AIDS sufferer and someone who was openly gay. Bob Hattoy, an environmental lobbyist recently diagnosed as HIV positive, told the convention, "If George Bush wins again, we're all at risk. We must vote this year as if our lives depended on it. Mine does. Yours could." Roberta Achtenberg, a San Francisco supervisor and an open lesbian, told the convention that she and her partner were raising a child and defended the right of gay Americans to serve openly in the military. Fascinated by the novelty of openly gay delegates, the media in attendance rushed to profile them.[152]

The contrast with the Republican National Convention, taking place four weeks later in Houston, could not have been starker. Unlike four years earlier, representatives of gay rights organizations were not even permitted to testify before the Republican platform committee. Convention delegates waved signs proclaiming, "Family Rights Forever/Gay Rights Never." Pat Buchanan called for a "cultural war" for "the soul of America" and declared that he and President Bush stood together "against the amoral idea that gay and lesbian couples should have the same standing in law as married men and women." Reverend Pat Robertson told the convention that Bill Clinton would destroy the traditional family and cited as evidence Clinton's promises to repeal the ban on gays in the military and to appoint gays to his cabinet.[153]

The Republican Party platform called for contact tracing for those who tested positive for HIV, and it opposed non-discrimination legislation, gay adoption, and gay marriage. Phyllis Schlafly exultantly called the platform "total victory, none of this litmus test, big-tent garbage." She labeled it "one of the cleanest, clearest victories we have had." Jerry Falwell summed up: "I think it's the best convention the Republicans have had in my recollection."[154]

Moderate Republicans, such as Senators Richard Lugar of Indiana and Lincoln Chafee of Rhode Island, were appalled. While the convention met, delegates of the Log Cabin Federation, representing six thousand gay Republicans across the country, voted not to endorse President Bush for reelection.[155]

By one estimate, the gay community contributed as much as $3 million to Bill Clinton's campaign fund, roughly one out of every eight dollars raised. An exit poll revealed that 72 percent of self-identified gays voted for Clinton in the general election. When Clinton won, one official at the Human Rights Campaign Fund called it "a great day for lesbian and gay Americans." An NGLTF official declared, "For the first time in our history, we're going to be full and open partners in the Government." Gay activists had played a significant role in electing the most pro-gay president in American history. Expectations were understandably high.[156]

From the beginning of the Clinton presidency, gay activists enjoyed unprecedented access to high-ranking White House officials to discuss gay rights issues. President Clinton immediately began repaying his political debt to the gay community. He appointed Roberta Achtenberg as assistant secretary in the Department of Housing and Urban Development. Republican senator Jesse Helms of North Carolina staunchly opposed her appointment—he called her a "damn lesbian"—but Clinton stood by her, and Achtenberg became the highest-ranking gay person ever to win confirmation by the U.S. Senate. Clinton also immediately began to implement his plan to repeal the ban on gays in the military.[157]

Despite all the progress made on gay rights by the early 1990s, the idea that same-sex couples should be legally permitted to marry would have struck most Americans as ludicrous. In 1991, roughly 75 percent of Americans still thought that same-sex sodomy was morally wrong. Just 29 percent thought gays should be permitted to adopt children. Only a few states had enacted laws barring discrimination based on sexual orientation in employment, housing, and public accommodations—reform measures that were far less controversial than gay marriage.[158]

Even supporters of anti-discrimination laws often were careful to deny that such measures put the state on the slippery slope to gay marriage. Opinion polls conducted around 1990 showed support for gay marriage between 11 percent and 23 percent. Even in the countries with the most liberal policies on gay rights, same-sex marriage was not permitted at this time.[159]

Even domestic partnership legislation had made few inroads by the early 1990s. In 1982, the San Francisco Board of Supervisors passed the first domestic partnership bill in the country. It would have created a domestic partnership registry for municipal employees involved in long-term relationships—homosexual or heterosexual. Domestic partners would have been entitled to health insurance and a few other legal benefits of marriage, such as hospital visitation rights and leave to care for a sick partner. Under pressure from the Catholic Church, which called the measure "severely inimical to marriage and the family," Mayor Dianne Feinstein vetoed it.[160]

In 1984, Berkeley, California, became the first city in the United States to enact domestic partnerships. By the late 1980s, a few other progressive cities, such as West Hollywood, California, and Madison, Wisconsin, had followed suit. San Francisco finally adopted such a measure in 1990. When New York mayor David Dinkins enacted domestic partnerships through executive decree in 1993, about twenty-five cities and counties across the nation offered such benefits to municipal employees.[161]

Yet even domestic partnership benefits remained controversial to most Americans. When the city council in relatively progressive Austin, Texas, adopted such a policy in 1993, a group called Concerned Texans, Inc. gathered enough signatures to force a referendum the following year. Austin voters then rejected the council's policy by a margin of 62 percent to 38 percent.[162]

In 1993, Atlanta enacted domestic partnership benefits for city employees. Acting under pressure from a mobilized Christian Coalition Network, commissioners in neighboring Cobb County warned that "it's at our doorstep now." They passed a resolution—the first of its kind for any American county—condemning the gay lifestyle as "incompatible with the standards to which this community subscribes." Not a single state had enacted domestic partnership benefits as of the early 1990s.[163]

Only the most progressive state courts had begun—very recently—to recognize the reality of gay and lesbian partnerships. In 1989, in what ACLU lawyer Bill Rubenstein called "the most far-reaching recognition of lesbian and gay relationships ever granted by any government agency in the United States," the New York court of appeals ruled that gay partners could qualify as "family members" for purposes of inheriting a rent-controlled apartment. The court identified relevant factors in determining whether gay partners qualified: the exclusivity and longevity of the relationship, the level of emotional and financial commitment, and the ways in which the couple had conducted their everyday lives and held themselves out to society. Two years later, the Minnesota court of appeals awarded legal guardianship to the lesbian partner of a woman who had suffered brain injuries in an automobile accident.[164]

Even the most gay-friendly corporations in the country, such as Lotus and Levi Strauss, only began providing domestic partnership benefits to gay employees in 1991. The first American universities to provide such benefits to their employees—the University of Iowa, Stanford University, and the University of Chicago—did so only in 1992.[165]

The same day that Bill Clinton was elected president, Colorado voters passed a constitutional amendment that overturned gay rights ordinances adopted by several cities in the state and forbade the future enactment of such measures by state or local governments. Soon thereafter, Cincinnati voters overturned by a margin of 62 percent to 38 percent a gay rights ordinance enacted by their city council. A plethora of recent state and local referenda evidenced how difficult it was for legislatures to move in advance of public opinion on gay rights issues.[166]

President Clinton, the most pro-gay-rights president in American history to that point, had been careful during the 1992 campaign to clarify that his support for gay rights stopped short of same-sex marriage. Moreover, Clinton was forced to back down even on his signature campaign commitment to rescind the ban on gays in the military after conservatives mobilized ferocious resistance.[167]

Indeed, religious conservatives jammed phone lines at the White House and in Congress, where initial calls ran a hundred to one in favor of retaining the ban. The nation's military leadership staunchly resisted Clinton's initiative and urged him to abandon it on the ground that repealing the ban would destroy military morale, undermine recruiting, lead many religious service members to resign, and increase the risk of AIDS being transmitted to heterosexual soldiers. The chairman of the Joint Chiefs of Staff, Colin Powell, who was possibly the nation's most popular military leader since Dwight David Eisenhower, declared at the Naval Academy just before Clinton's inauguration that the presence of open homosexuals in the military would be detrimental to good order and discipline and that those service members who strongly believed that homosexuality was immoral would have to resign. Given Clinton's history as an antiwar protester and alleged draft dodger, he was disadvantaged in a public relations battle with military leaders.[168]

Congressional resistance to repealing the ban was also strong. Defense Secretary Les Aspin quickly reported to the president that a majority in Congress would block repeal. Senate minority leader Robert Dole threatened that Republicans would amend the first bill brought up by Democrats to reaffirm the existing ban. Even a leading congressional Democrat such as Sam Nunn, senator from Georgia and head of the Armed Forces Committee, strongly opposed repeal and would conduct legislative hearings on the issue in a manner supportive of retaining the ban.[169]

Both gay activists and the White House admitted to having been caught badly off guard by this extraordinary display of resistance. A headline in the *Washington Blade* asked, "Were National Gay Groups Asleep at the Switch?" Activists in the Christian right crowed that they "could not have scripted Bill Clinton's first weeks any better."[170]

Resistance to ending the ban on gay military service threatened to derail Democratic plans for quick passage of high-priority bills to reform health care and provide family and medical leave for workers. President Clinton quickly determined that he had little choice but to back down. To save face, he pledged a six-month period of "study" and then struggled to negotiate a deal with Congress and the Defense Department.[171]

The president presented "don't ask, don't tell" as a "compromise" that would end military witch hunts against gays, but it was, in fact, a thinly veiled defeat for Clinton, and gay activists regarded it as a betrayal. Even efforts to secure some protections for the private, off-duty sex lives and free speech of service members failed. The controversy greatly damaged the president, and those on both the political right and left spoke of a failure of moral leadership.[172]

In the midst of the Clinton administration's gays-in-the-military fiasco, the Hawaii supreme court issued a decision that seemed to portend the arrival of same-sex marriage.[173]

3

Hawaii and the "Defense of Marriage" (1990s)

In the early 1990s, the gay community remained deeply divided over whether to pursue gay marriage. Marriage had not been on the gay rights agenda at all in the first half of the 1980s. When gay rights leaders posed questions to leading Democratic presidential candidates Walter Mondale and John Glenn in 1983, they asked about a federal anti-discrimination law, changes in immigration law, federal funding for AIDS research, rescinding the ban on gays in the military, repealing the District of Columbia sodomy law, and ending the ban on the Legal Services Corporation's supporting gay rights litigation. They did not ask about gay marriage or even about extending some of the rights and benefits of marriage to same-sex couples.[1]

In 1989, Tom Stoddard, executive director of Lambda Legal, stated, "As far as I can tell, no gay organization of any size, local or national, has yet declared the right to marry as one of its goals." Most gay activists evinced little interest in pursuing a right to marry. Polls showed much greater concern among gays and lesbians for securing equal rights in employment, housing, and health care.[2]

In 1991, the NGLTF asked its members to rank gay rights issues in terms of importance. The survey revealed that members cared the most about, in descending order, civil rights legislation, increased funding for AIDS research, domestic partnership legislation, sodomy law reform, and the organization of college campuses. The NGLTF did not even bother to ask its members how they felt about gay marriage. When the third annual Creating Change Conference, the most significant political gathering of gay people in the country, took place in 1990, the agenda included repeal of sodomy laws, civil rights protections, hate crime reporting, and domestic partnership benefits, but not a word about gay marriage. In 1991, the two issues that dominated the legislative agenda of the Empire State Pride Agenda, New York's largest gay rights organization, were a civil rights bill and a hate crimes bill.[3]

Many gay activists at the time wanted nothing to do with marriage. Some lesbian feminists noted that marriage had long been "the focus of radical-feminist revulsion" because it was part of "a patriarchal system that looks to ownership, property, and dominance of men over women as its basis."[4]

Gay radicals also worried that securing gay marriage "would force our assimilation into the mainstream" and lead to the abandonment of the gay rights movement's goal of "transforming the very fabric of society" by "pushing the parameters of sex, sexuality, and family." These gays did not want the right to be treated the same as straights; they were different and wanted to be treated as such. They also worried that enabling gays to marry would inevitably stigmatize those who chose not to do so. Finally, some activists worried that pursuing gay marriage was to privilege the concerns of middle-class gays and divert focus from the interests of those less privileged gays for whom marriage was possibly less relevant.[5]

Gays who supported same-sex marriage conceded that marriage in its traditional form was oppressive to women. Yet expanding marriage to include gays could help "the institution divest itself of the sexist trappings of the past." Allowing same-sex couples to marry would help erode the gendered conception of the spousal roles of "husband" and "wife." As a practical matter, marriage would confer significant legal benefits—joint tax filing status, social security survivors' benefits, and spousal immunity in court testimony, to name just a few. Many of these benefits could not be duplicated outside of marriage.[6]

More important, pro-marriage activists argued that because marriage was the centerpiece of society's social structure, no other political issue more "fully tests the dedication of people who are not gay to full equality for gay people." Same-sex relationships would "continue to be accorded a subsidiary status until the day that gay couples have *exactly* the same rights as their heterosexual counterparts." Finally, some activists endorsed gay marriage as a means of discouraging the sexual libertinism of the 1970s and making gay culture more mainstream.[7]

By the late 1980s, several factors were pushing gays in the direction of pursuing legal recognition of their relationships—and even gay marriage. The AIDS epidemic had highlighted how vulnerable gay and lesbian partnerships were. By 1988, forty-six thousand people had died of AIDS, two-thirds of them gay men. The median age of the deceased was thirty-six, not typically an age at which most people are focused on end-of-life planning. Yet now an entire generation of gays had to contemplate hospital visitation, surrogate medical decision making, and estate planning.[8]

State agencies, hospitals, and funeral homes often refused to recognize same-sex relationships and privileged the decisions of even estranged family members over those of the same-sex life partners of dying AIDS sufferers. Health insurance plans rarely covered same-sex partners. Wills deeding property to same-sex partners were susceptible to challenge on the grounds of undue influence or AIDS-related dementia. Rent-controlled apartments could not legally pass to unrelated part-ners. Same-sex couples raising children were especially vulnerable. For most gays, AIDS tipped the balance in favor of legal recognition of same-sex relationships.[9]

The Sharon Kowalski case, which involved a catastrophic automobile accident rather than AIDS, also demonstrated the vulnerability of same-sex relationships. Kowalski and her partner, Karen Thompson, had lived together for four years. They jointly owned a house, had exchanged rings, and considered themselves married. Yet they had not come out as lesbians to their families, friends, or colleagues.[10]

In 1983, Kowalski was in a severe auto accident caused by a drunk driver, which left her paralyzed with brain injuries and unable to speak. On the day of the accident, Thompson was denied access to Kowalski at the hospital for two hours, and once Kowalski's father arrived, she was entirely cut out of medical decision making. The Kowalskis denied that their daughter was a lesbian. When her father was appointed guardian by a court, he denied even visitation rights to Thompson.[11]

A court battle over guardianship lasted for several years. Finally, in 1991, describing the two women as a "family of affinity, which ought to be accorded respect," the Minnesota court of appeals ruled that Kowalski was competent to make her own choice of a guardian, and she chose Thompson. The Kowalski case attracted great attention from the gay press and inspired demonstrations in twenty-one cities on National Free Sharon Kowalski Day in 1988.

Demonstrators wearing "Free Sharon Kowalski!" armbands, Aug. 7, 1988. (*Associated Press/Frankie Ziths*)

Now, for the first time, many same-sex couples prepared legal documents in anticipation of such catastrophes. Yet such documents were expensive to prepare and far from legally foolproof. Episodes such as Kowalski's underscored the need for legal recognition of same-sex relationships and fueled the campaign for domestic partnership legislation.[12]

Another important factor in the drive for legal recognition of same-sex relationships was the desire of gay and lesbian baby boomers to become parents. An earlier generation of gays and lesbians, in denial of their homosexuality, had entered opposite-sex marriages and had children. Upon divorce, they frequently had trouble maintaining custody or even securing visitation rights, particularly if they were now open about their homosexuality.[13]

By the early 1980s, with the advent of reproductive technology, a younger generation of lesbians were creating their own baby boom. By the mid-1980s, judges in some progressive states had extended the practice of second-parent adoption to include gay and lesbian partners.[14]

Gays and lesbians needed the law to adapt to the reality of their changing families. In the late 1980s, the NGLTF started its Families Project. Securing familial rights had become a top priority within the gay rights movement, even if marriage per se had not. The control of gays and lesbians over their children remained vulnerable to the discretion of homophobic judges, as illustrated by the Sharon Bottoms case from Virginia in 1993. Bottoms lost custody of her son to her mother when a judge decided that it was not in the child's best interests to be raised by an open lesbian.[15]

Additionally, as more openly gay parents raised children, volunteered at their schools, and coached their soccer teams, other Americans grew more accustomed to gay parents and less inclined to embrace traditional stereotypes of gays as "destructive pleasure seekers and child molesters." By the early 1990s, opinion polls showed growing public support for the right of gays and lesbians to adopt children. In turn, once same-sex couples were permitted to adopt children, explaining why those couples should not be permitted to marry became much harder.[16]

Another important factor in the movement to secure legal recognition of same-sex partners was demographic: younger gays and lesbians were much more supportive of gay marriage than their elders were. The younger generation had come of age at a time of gay pride and greater gay visibility. Often they had come out to their friends and family at relatively young ages. They thought of themselves as equal citizens and could not fathom why they should be denied access to traditional institutions such as marriage. One opinion poll showed that eighteen-year-old gays were 31 percentage points more likely to support gay marriage than were sixty-five-year-old gays.[17]

Changes in the meaning of marriage in most economically developed countries also facilitated expansion of the institution to include same-sex couples. As racial and religious barriers to cross-group marriages dissipated, marriage was redefined as a matter of individual choice. Falling birthrates and the rise in the average age at which people married—especially for the second or third time—weakened the connection between marriage and procreation. Moreover, one-third or more of all children were now being born outside of marriage, further severing that linkage. As marriage became less about childbearing, it became more about mutual commitment and nurturing happiness—objectives that same-sex couples could pursue as easily as opposite-sex ones.[18]

Moreover, as traditional gender norms in society have evolved and more women have assumed jobs outside the home, marriage has become less about the gendered roles of husbands and wives and more about equal partnerships. For patriarchal religious fundamentalists, one reason that same-sex marriage has proved so threatening is that it further destabilizes traditional gender roles. By contrast, those who hold more progressive gender views have found gay marriage easier to accept.[19]

At the 1987 March on Washington for Lesbian and Gay Rights, roughly two thousand same-sex couples showed their support for gay marriage by partici-pating in a mass wedding on the steps of the Internal Revenue Service building. Yet even those activists who were supportive of gay marriage did not consider it a realistic goal in the short term. Courts and legislatures were unlikely to expand marriage to include same-sex couples at a time when public opinion was over-whelmingly opposed. Moreover, even if a court or legislature could be persuaded to embrace gay marriage, the political backlash against such a reform might prove devastating. When gay rights litigator Mary Bonauto started her new job with the Gay and Lesbian Advocates and Defenders in Massachusetts in 1990, she declined to accept a gay marriage case because she thought the time for such litigation had not yet arrived.[20]

Arguments for and against gay marriage have not changed much over the past two decades. Supporters of gay marriage often manifest a libertarian bent: per-mitting gays to marry maximizes free choice in the selection of one's life partner. They deny that gay marriage causes any cognizable harm to third parties, invoking the question "How does my marriage affect yours?" Gay marriage advocates note the broad array of tangible benefits conferred by marriage and question the fairness of denying such benefits to same-sex partners. They emphasize that gay families are in fact raising children and ask what sense it makes to deny such fam-ilies the stability conferred by marriage. They invoke a proliferating body of social science evidence that suggests same-sex couples are as good at parenting as anyone else is.

Because most gay marriage supporters do not see homosexuality as a choice, they reject as absurd the argument that homosexuality should be discouraged by refusing to legitimize same-sex relationships. Gay marriage supporters note that in a society committed to the separation of church and state, religious perspectives on marriage cannot suffice to disqualify same-sex couples; secular justifications are required. Neither is tradition a sufficient basis for denying same-sex marriage, given the Supreme Court's rejection of tradition-based justifications in cases invalidating bans on same-sex sodomy and interracial marriage. Finally, gay marriage supporters argue that the institution of marriage reflects current social mores, that its meaning has changed dramatically over time, and that expanding it to same-sex couples would not be out of line with other historical shifts in its definition.

In response to the libertarian argument for gay marriage, opponents contend that the state always has and always will restrict marriage in certain ways; selecting a marriage partner has never been an entirely free choice. Even today, for example, all states bar close family members from marrying one another. Opponents also warn of a slippery slope to the libertarian argument: if free choice is the ultimate criterion, what basis does the state have for rejecting polygamy or polyamory? Opponents also deny the absence of third-party effects to gay marriage: to permit gay marriage is to denigrate the view that marriage is fundamentally about procreation. Undermining that perspective inevitably shapes how people think about marriage, which influences its future. Some gay marriage opponents also argue that allowing same-sex couples to marry will undermine marriage stability because they are inherently less committed to monogamous relationships.

Opponents also deny that children fare as well without the presence of both a father and a mother in the home. Because they tend to see homosexuality as more of a choice, they argue that legal recognition of gay marriage, by legitimizing that choice, makes it more attractive. They also invoke tradition as a justification for opposing gay marriage: if for thousands of years marriage has consisted of a man and a woman, simple risk aversion should counsel societal resistance to rapid change.

Finally, many gay marriage opponents invoke the Bible's supposed condemnation of homosexuality and God's design of marriage as an institution for a man and a woman. They argue that one can no more change the laws of God than those of nature. Even attempting to do so risks inviting God's wrath upon society. Religious opponents of gay marriage also argue that if it becomes legal, churches and religiously inspired individuals and organizations will inevitably face incursions on their religious liberty if they continue to oppose it.[21]

These are the principal policy arguments for and against gay marriage. What about the main constitutional arguments, which also have not changed greatly over the last few decades?

The constitutional case for gay marriage is two-pronged. First, proponents argue that marriage is a fundamental right under the Due Process Clause of the Fourteenth Amendment and state constitutional counterparts, which government can limit only for compelling reasons. For this proposition, they cite Supreme Court decisions invalidating bans on interracial marriage, onerous restrictions on prisoners' right to marry, and a law disallowing someone who is delinquent on child support payments to marry. If the state cannot restrict marriage in these ways, why should it be permitted to limit marriage to opposite-sex couples?[22]

Second, gay marriage proponents argue that excluding same-sex couples from marriage violates the Equal Protection Clause of the Fourteenth Amendment and its state constitutional counterparts. They argue that laws restricting marriage to opposite-sex couples constitute sex discrimination in the same way that laws restricting marriage to intra-racial couples constitute race discrimination. Under well-established precedent, sex classifications are subject to rigorous judicial scrutiny.

In addition, gay marriage supporters argue that laws restricting marriage to opposite-sex couples constitute discrimination based on sexual orientation. They argue that laws discriminating against gays should be subject to rigorous judicial scrutiny because gays share many of the group characteristics that the Court has deemed relevant in extending heightened scrutiny to race and sex classifications: immutability of the characteristic defining the group, a history of past discrimination, and a relative lack of political power.

Gay marriage advocates also argue that even if sexual orientation does not qualify for heightened judicial protection, laws restricting marriage to opposite-sex couples fail even the most relaxed standard of judicial review because they lack a rational relationship to a legitimate state interest. Supreme Court precedent, they argue, establishes that morality and tradition are not sufficient bases to support government classifications. Further, they deny that limiting marriage to opposite-sex couples rationally furthers other proffered government interests, such as providing an optimal environment for child rearing and tying procreation to marriage.

Opponents of gay marriage deny that the fundamental right to marry includes a right to marry someone of the same sex. They note that the Court's fundamental rights jurisprudence looks to tradition to define the scope of such rights, and for thousands of years marriage has generally been limited to opposite-sex couples. They also note that government restrictions on marriage—such as setting minimum age requirements and forbidding marriage between close family members—are commonplace and almost universally accepted as constitutional.

In response to the equal protection arguments, gay marriage opponents deny that laws restricting marriage to opposite-sex couples constitute sex classifications. In addition to treating men and women alike, they argue, such laws do not connote sexism in the same way that bans on interracial marriage instantiated white supremacy.

Opponents of gay marriage deny that discrimination based on sexual orientation should be subjected to the same heightened standard of judicial review as race or sex classifications. They argue that homosexuality is a choice, unlike race, and they deny that gays are lacking in political power, as evidenced by the plethora of gay rights legislation enacted by states and Congress over the last couple of decades.

Gay marriage opponents also argue that laws restricting marriage to opposite-sex couples easily satisfy the most lenient standard of judicial scrutiny. They contend that legislatures should be allowed to presume that children fare best when raised by a mother and a father until social science evidence conclusively shows otherwise. They also argue that society has a strong interest in restricting marriage to opposite-sex couples because of their procreative potential.

In December 1990, three gay couples in Hawaii applied for marriage licenses—thus commencing the modern epoch of gay marriage in the United States. Their applications were denied in April 1991, and they filed a lawsuit in May. This suit, like most other gay marriage cases brought until very recently, was filed in state court and raised claims only under the state constitution in order to keep it away from the U.S. Supreme Court, which was considered unlikely to rule in favor of same-sex marriage.[23]

A few months earlier, a gay couple had filed a similar suit in the local court in the District of Columbia. The trial judge rejected the claim in the D.C. case, and the court of appeals affirmed that decision in 1995.[24]

None of the major national gay rights organizations wanted these lawsuits filed. One of the plaintiffs later recalled, "The politically savvy thought we were nuts and didn't really want to touch us." Gay rights leaders assumed the lawsuits would lose, and they worried that simply filing them might vindicate the argument of gay rights opponents that anti-discrimination laws, then a leading priority of the gay rights movement, were simply a first step on the slippery slope to gay marriage.[25]

In Hawaii, a local ACLU lawyer brought the case without the support of his national organization. He later recalled that he had little hope of winning when he accepted the case: "In all candor, I didn't think we would get this much this soon."[26]

The Hawaii litigation began to attract attention after a loss in the trial court was appealed to the state supreme court. At that point, Evan Wolfson, a pioneer in the gay marriage movement, persuaded his colleagues at Lambda Legal to file an amicus brief—the first one that the organization had ever submitted in a marriage case. Simultaneously, Lambda urged same-sex couples elsewhere not to file gay marriage lawsuits while the Hawaii case was pending.[27]

On May 5, 1993, by a vote of 3 to 1 (with one seat on the court vacant), the Hawaii supreme court ruled in *Baehr v. Lewin* that a law restricting marriage to a man and a woman constitutes a sex classification—in the same way that a ban on interracial marriage constitutes a race classification. Under the Hawaii constitution's equal rights amendment, the law was therefore subject to the most rigorous standard of judicial scrutiny. The court remanded the case to the trial court for a hearing on whether the state could demonstrate a compelling justification for the exclusion of same-sex couples from marriage. Most commentators predicted that when the case returned to the supreme court, it would rule that Hawaii was constitutionally required to permit gay marriage.[28]

Hawaii is one of the nation's most liberal states. In 1970, it was the first state to repeal—as opposed to simply reform—its archaic abortion law, and in 1972 it was the first to ratify the Equal Rights Amendment. Hawaii also has a long tradition of diversity and tolerance, including on the issue of interracial marriage.[29]

On gay rights specifically, Hawaii has also been one of the most liberal states. Only 34 percent of Hawaiians identify as Judeo-Christian, and close male relationships are an accepted part of ancient Hawaiian culture. Hawaii repealed its sodomy law in 1973, well before most states did so. In 1991, Hawaii became only the third state to enact a ban on employment discrimination based on sexual orientation. In the 1990s, Hawaii registered the lowest percentage of people of any state who believed that homosexual relations are always wrong. In the mid-1990s, Hawaii's congressional delegation was the only one to receive a 100 percent rating from the Human Rights Campaign.[30]

Yet even in such a liberal state, gay marriage was "on the frontier" in 1993. Opinion polls revealed that between two-thirds and three-quarters of Hawaiians opposed gay marriage. The state's Democratic governor, who two years earlier had signed the anti-discrimination bill into law, now insisted that marriage was different. The Speaker of the house, a Democrat, also denounced gay marriage.[31]

Baehr provoked an enormous political backlash—both in Hawaii and on the mainland. At a prayer rally held at city hall in Honolulu soon after the decision, religious leaders expressed outrage. The Catholic Church hierarchy was "shocked and dismayed" by the ruling. The Mormon Church also expressed strong opposition.[32]

Some critics warned that the decision would turn the state into a "gay mecca," import costly AIDS cases, and kill the tourist industry. The president of an organization called Stop Promoting Homosexuality Hawaii criticized the court for shoving gay marriage down the throats of Hawaiians, something he predicted they would not stand for. Money poured in—especially from the mainland—in an effort to reverse the decision.[33]

In the spring of 1994, the Hawaii legislature denounced the court's usurpation of legislative authority and enacted a bill defining marriage as the union of a man and a woman. In response to the court's requirement of a compelling justification for excluding same-sex couples from marriage, the legislature declared that only opposite-sex marriages promoted the state's interest in fostering procreation. Even in liberal Hawaii, the bill passed the state senate by an overwhelming margin of 21 to 4. Simultaneously, the legislature created the Commission on Sexual Orientation and the Law and instructed it to produce a report describing the benefits of marriage and determining whether sound public policy justified extending some of those benefits to same-sex couples through domestic partnerships.[34]

The commission's work was delayed by a federal lawsuit challenging its membership on Establishment Clause grounds: the legislature had appointed two Catholics and two Mormons to sit on the commission as representatives of their faiths. The trial in *Baehr* was postponed until the legislature could appoint a new commission without religious quotas for its membership.[35]

The commission finally issued its report in December 1995. Over several dissents, the commission majority agreed with the state supreme court that excluding same-sex couples from marriage constituted sex discrimination without any compelling justification. It recommended either extending marriage to gay couples or creating a comprehensive regime of domestic partnerships. The trial in *Baehr* was then rescheduled for September 1996. The legislature declined to take further action until after the trial court's decision.[36]

The Hawaii supreme court's decision in *Baehr* received prominent newspaper coverage across the nation. Gay rights leaders, who were said to be "ecstatic," called the decision "a major breakthrough." Evan Wolfson of Lambda Legal predicted a "tidal wave out of Hawaii that will reach every corner of the country and affect every gay issue." The *New York Times* observed that the Hawaii court "has taken a long step toward making the state the first in the country to recognize marriages between couples of the same sex." *Newsweek* noted that marriage "may be the last frontier of the Stonewall Revolution," and *U.S. News and World Report* announced that "the next big gay controversy is here." An Associated Press article speculated that if the Hawaii court ruled in favor of gay marriage, it could "throw bombshells across America."[37]

Lambda Legal openly called for same-sex couples to travel to Hawaii to get married, should the court rule in their favor, and then seek recognition of their marriages back home. Most states recognized marriages lawfully performed elsewhere, even if those marriages could not be validly performed under their own laws. For example, even a state not permitting marriages between first cousins will ordinarily recognize such marriages as valid if performed in a jurisdiction that authorizes them. Only if a state legislature has expressly declared a certain category of marriages to be contrary to the state's public policy would that state's courts refuse to recognize them.[38]

Within months of the *Baehr* decision in 1993, Utah amended its law to clarify that marriage was between a man and a woman. A poll showed that 68 percent of Utahns opposed gay marriage.[39]

Two years later, Utah was the first state to enact a law mandating that its courts not recognize gay marriages lawfully performed elsewhere. That law was necessary, according to the legislator who introduced it, to prevent gay Utah couples from flying to Hawaii to get married once courts there approved same-sex marriage. A representative of the Gay and Lesbian Utah Democrats had boasted that his organization was lining up gay couples to fly to Hawaii to get married minutes after that state legalized gay marriage. Given that any change in Hawaii law probably would not occur for several years, the president of Utah Log Cabin called the defense-of-marriage measure a red herring intended to divert lawmakers' attention from more important matters. Nonetheless, the bill passed both houses of the Utah legislature by nearly unanimous votes.[40]

In February 1995, the South Dakota house voted overwhelmingly in favor of a bill to ban gay marriage and to reject recognition of such marriages performed elsewhere. Supporters defended the bill as necessary to protect the state from having to recognize gay marriages performed in Hawaii, once courts there legalized them, as was soon anticipated. The bill failed by one vote to get on the senate calendar, though it became law the following year. Also in 1995, a bill was introduced in the Alaska house to clarify that marriage was limited to unions between a man and woman. One assemblyman pointed to the Hawaii litigation as justification for the bill.[41]

In January 1996, San Francisco's board of supervisors passed an ordinance allowing the county clerk's office to perform same-sex wedding ceremonies for couples who registered as domestic partners. These "marriages" had no legal significance but were intended simply to confer public legitimacy upon same-sex relationships. On March 26, 1996, 165 same-sex couples publicly celebrated their domestic partnerships in a ceremony presided over by Mayor Willie Brown—the first event of its kind in the nation. Organizers portrayed these weddings as the first step toward the goal of full-fledged gay marriage.[42]

In June in New York City, openly gay city council member Tom Duane presided over a similar mass "wedding" ceremony involving two dozen gay and lesbian couples in Bryant Park. With Hawaii courts widely expected to legalize gay marriage later that year, mass gay weddings only added fuel to a growing national fire.[43]

In April 1996, the *Los Angeles Times* observed that "homosexual marriage has abruptly emerged as an emotional flashpoint in the debate about America's cultural mores." The following month the *Washington Post* declared, "Same-sex marriage has suddenly become the most visible issue in the gay rights debate." In July, an article in the *Advocate* noted, "If Americans thought gays in the military was a hot issue, then nothing can prepare them for confronting this year's most controversial gay battlefield: homosexual marriage." State legislators were inundated with letters and phone calls from panicked constituents. One poll conducted that spring showed that 68 percent of Americans opposed gay marriage.[44]

Objecting that "some radical judges in Hawaii may get to dictate the moral code for the entire nation," conservative groups provided like-minded legislators in every state with draft bills to deny recognition to gay marriages lawfully performed elsewhere. For Republicans, gay marriage was a dream issue: it both mobilized their base of religious conservatives and aligned them with most swing voters. In the spring of 1996, Republicans introduced so-called defense-of-marriage bills in thirty-four state legislatures. Supporters emphasized that the developments in Hawaii made such measures necessary.[45]

Thirteen states enacted such laws in 1996, and nine more did so in 1997. In most states, the bills passed easily, as even liberal legislators ran for cover. In Pennsylvania, the house passed a defense-of-marriage bill by 177 to 16 and the senate by 43 to 5. In Illinois, the house passed it by 87 to 13 and the senate by 42 to 9.[46]

Even most of the Democrats who voted against such measures declared their opposition to gay marriage, while calling the bills mean-spirited and unnecessary. Some of the few Democrats who embraced gay marriage paid a heavy price at the polls. In 1994, the Democratic gubernatorial candidate in Arizona, Eddie Basha, held a lead in the polls until late in the campaign, when he said he would be willing to sign legislation legalizing same-sex marriage. Basha ended up losing badly.[47]

In a few states, such as California and Nebraska, Democrats were able to block enactment of defense-of-marriage laws, only to have opponents successfully pursue popular initiatives that amended state constitutions to bar gay marriage. By 2001, thirty-five states had enacted defense-of-marriage laws or amendments.[48]

As gay marriage acquired a higher profile, in some jurisdictions it became more difficult to enact domestic partnership benefits. In 1994, Republican governor Pete Wilson of California vetoed a domestic partnership bill that had passed the legislature and would have provided very limited rights such as hospital visitation to same-sex couples. Wilson objected to what he called a foot in the door for same-sex marriage. "We need to strengthen, not weaken, the institution of marriage," the governor declared.[49]

In 1996, in the midst of coast-to-coast debate over defense-of-marriage legislation, Philadelphia mayor Ed Rendell issued an executive order extending health care benefits to the domestic partners of a small proportion of city employees. The Catholic cardinal of Philadelphia blasted Rendell's decision, which he said was likely to lead "to the deterioration of our own civilization." The president of the Black Clergy of Philadelphia objected that the mayor had put the city at risk of becoming "a modern day Sodom and Gomorrah." Rendell must have been taken aback at the ferocity of the resistance to his decision. One black pastor explained that the "fear that same-sex marriages may become a reality in other states" had provoked the backlash.[50]

Gay marriage also entered the national political arena in 1996. Two years earlier, Republicans had jolted national politics by taking control of the House of Representatives for the first time in forty years. Reverend Pat Robertson's Christian Coalition had played a critical role in that triumph, supporting nearly 60 percent of newly elected Republican congressional representatives. In an ambitious voter turnout effort, the Christian Coalition had distributed thirty-three million voter guides to churches across the nation. The coalition's newsletter, Christian America, claimed the Republican victory was "propelled by the largest surge of religious voters in history." The coalition had become one of the nation's most powerful lobbying groups, with more than one million members and a $25 million annual budget.[51]

As the 1996 presidential election approached, religious right leaders James Dobson and Gary Bauer visited leading Republican candidates and threatened to withhold support if they did not endorse the policies of Christian conservatives. The religious right also wielded enormous influence within a majority of state Republican parties. Anti-gay posturing was an easy way for Republican candidates to demonstrate support for religious conservatives. No sizable openly gay constituency existed within the party to induce Republican candidates to modulate their positions.[52]

In August 1995, Republican senator Bob Dole of Kansas returned a $1,000 check from the Log Cabin Republicans. Dick Armey, the Republican whip in the House, referred to openly gay Democratic congressman Barney Frank as "Barney Fag." Virtually every candidate for the 1996 Republican presidential nomination sought to appease the religious right. For example, Texas senator Phil Gramm, known primarily as an economic conservative, gave the commencement address at Liberty University in May 1995, where he denounced abortion and President Clinton's efforts to repeal the ban on gays in the military.[53]

As usual, the Iowa caucuses were the first opportunity in 1996 for voters to weigh in on the Republican presidential candidates. In 1988, religious conservatives had packed the caucuses, enabling Reverend Pat Robertson to defeat Vice President George H. W. Bush. In 1996, the party's front-runner for the nomination, Senator Dole, actively courted Christian conservatives, applauding the influential role that they played within the Republican Party.[54]

Just days before the caucuses, anti-gay activists, including members of the Christian Coalition, conducted a "marriage protection" rally at a Des Moines church, hosted by film actor Charlton Heston. Pat Buchanan was there to proclaim, "We've seen all the false gods of secular humanism, including the false god of gay rights." Alan Keyes was there, too, to denounce the homosexual agenda, which he said was "destroying the integrity of the marriage-based family." All of the major Republican presidential candidates except Senator Richard Lugar— that is, Bob Dole, Pat Buchanan, Phil Gramm, Lamar Alexander, Steve Forbes, and Alan Keyes—signed a "marriage protection resolution" condemning same-sex unions.[55]

In May 1996, Senator Dole co-sponsored the federal Defense of Marriage Act (DOMA). It provided that no state was required to give full faith and credit to any law or judicial decision of another state recognizing same-sex marriage. It also provided, for the first time in American history, a federal definition of marriage. For the multitude of federal benefits that turn on marriage, such as social security survivorship benefits, immigration rights, and the privilege of filing joint tax returns, only marriages between a man and a woman would qualify.[56]

Republicans defended the measure as necessary to protect states from being constitutionally required to recognize gay marriages that judges in another state had ruled constitutionally protected. Republican lawmakers repeatedly referred to developments in Hawaii to justify the measure.[57]

Although the debate over DOMA was ostensibly about gay marriage, it quickly devolved into a general attack on homosexuality. Many Republican lawmakers declared that homosexuality was morally wrong and that the state should not endorse it. Some speakers went further, denouncing homosexuality as a perversion and comparing it with polygamy and pedophilia. Representative Bob Barr of Georgia, who had sponsored the bill in the House, defended its necessity on the grounds that "the flames of hedonism, the flames of narcissism, the flames of self-centered morality are licking at the very foundation of our society: the family unit."[58]

A few Democrats offered similar sentiments. Senator Robert Byrd of West Virginia warned that "America is being weighed in the balance," that "we have lost our way with a speed that is awesome," and that traditional marriage must be defended against homosexual attack.[59]

Most Democrats who opposed DOMA did so without defending gay marriage. Marriage did not require federal protection, they argued, because individual states already had the power to deny recognition to gay marriages performed in other jurisdictions and because gay marriage did not currently exist in any state and probably would not for years. They also criticized the bill on federalism grounds, observing that in the past Congress had always left the definition of marriage up to the states.

Openly gay congressman Barney Frank of Massachusetts was one of the few Democrats to defend gay marriage on the merits. He asked whether heterosexual marriage was so fragile that a loving relationship between people of the same sex would jeopardize it.[60]

Democrats attacked the bill as a "publicity stunt," "shameless politics," and a "cynical election year gimmick" intended to help Republicans generally and presidential candidate Bob Dole specifically. Liberal columnist Frank Rich said the purpose of the bill was to turn gay marriage "into a flashpoint for a polarizing culture war in which gay people become the Willie Hortons of '96."[61]

In 1996, Republicans controlled both houses of Congress, so there was never any doubt that the bill would pass. Soon after it was introduced, Senator Dole, acting on the advice of political strategists such as William Bennett, challenged President Clinton to support the measure if he truly opposed gay marriage, as he had claimed to do during the 1992 presidential campaign.[62]

Although Clinton had run in 1992 as a pro-gay-rights candidate, the gays-in-the-military debacle at the start of his administration had led him to downplay gay rights issues since then. In 1996, the administration chose not to file a brief in the Supreme Court case challenging the constitutionality of Colorado's amendment barring gay rights ordinances.[63]

The administration decided to try to squelch the gay marriage issue by acquiescing on DOMA. One week after charging that the bill was "designed to provoke hostility towards gays and lesbians," White House press secretary Mike McCurry announced that the president would sign it if Congress passed it. Given that President Clinton vetoed the partial-birth abortion law the following week, one might surmise that the administration calculated that it had used up its quota of cultural liberalism for an election year.[64]

Although some gay activists believed that Clinton had little choice in the matter, others were furious. One of the president's most prominent gay supporters, David Mixner, a California fund-raiser and old friend of the Clintons, called the administration's decision to accept DOMA "nauseating and appalling" and "an act of political cowardice." The executive director of the Human Rights Campaign called it "a capitulation to political religious extremists," while the executive director of NGLTF said the president's action was "a slap in the face of gay and lesbian families across America." Critics wanted the president to veto the bill while reiterating his opposition to gay marriage—not the easiest of political feats to pull off.[65]

Mayor Willie Brown of San Francisco warned Clinton to expect hostile political demonstrations if he kept a scheduled appearance in San Francisco, urging him, "Don't come." When the president ignored Brown's advice and visited San Francisco, a crowd of two hundred protested Clinton's "Republicanization."[66]

In July, the House passed DOMA by a vote of 342 to 67. Only one Republican, the openly gay congressman Steve Gunderson of Wisconsin, voted against it. Even Democrats voted in favor by a margin of two to one. In September, the Senate passed DOMA by 85 to 14. Only one senator up for reelection in 1996, John Kerry of Massachusetts, voted against it. Dozens of lawmakers who usually supported gay rights voted for the measure.[67]

Although the president had left no doubt that he would approve the bill, aides reported a sharp internal debate over what he would say when signing it. In July, press secretary McCurry had called the bill "gay baiting, pure and simple."[68]

On September 21, 1996, President Clinton signed DOMA—after midnight and without public ceremony. The president chose the low profile, McCurry explained, because he believed "the motives behind this bill are dubious." In advertisements run on Christian radio stations, however, Clinton bragged about signing the bill. When gay rights groups vociferously protested, the ads were quickly pulled.[69]

Meanwhile, back in Hawaii, where all the hubbub had begun, Democrats faced a dilemma. Firmly in control of the state legislature, they were torn between wishing to accommodate gay rights supporters, who voted overwhelmingly Democratic and with whom many Democratic lawmakers genuinely empathized, and avoiding voter backlash over gay marriage, which seven out of ten Hawaiians opposed.[70]

In 1996, the state senate passed a domestic partnership bill, while the house endorsed a constitutional amendment to ban gay marriage, which would go on the ballot in 1998 if it passed the senate. Neither proposal advanced, however, as the two bodies stalemated.[71]

The trial in *Baehr* that had been ordered by the Hawaii supreme court took place over nine days in September 1996 in the courtroom of Judge Kevin Chang. It featured several expert witnesses for the state testifying that children fared better when raised by their biological parents and several experts for the plaintiffs arguing the opposite. After the trial concluded, Judge Chang took the case under advisement.[72]

Gay marriage became an issue in some state legislative races that fall. It featured prominently in the Democratic primary contest of the house Judiciary Committee chairman, Terrance Tom, a strong opponent of gay marriage. It also played a significant role in the Democratic primary race to unseat incumbent U.S. Representative Patsy Mink, who was forced to defend her vote against DOMA in Congress. The Alliance for Traditional Marriage endorsed candidates based on their opposition to gay marriage.[73]

Gay marriage also featured prominently in several general-election contests. Democrats had to explain their votes not to allow Hawaiians to decide the fate of a constitutional amendment to ban gay marriage. Incumbents generally had to defend against charges of a do-nothing legislature, for which the principal exhibit was the failure of the house and senate to take any action on gay marriage before adjournment.[74]

In the state's general election, Republicans increased their representation in the house, traditionally dominated by Democrats, from five to twelve. One twelve-year incumbent attributed his defeat entirely to his vote against putting the amendment banning gay marriage on the 1998 ballot. Republicans also picked up five seats in the senate, including that of the chairperson of the Judiciary Committee, who had blocked a vote on the gay marriage amendment. Some commentators attributed the Republican gains to the gay marriage issue, though others detected a more general anti-incumbency sentiment.[75]

In December, Judge Chang ruled that the state had no compelling justification for excluding same-sex couples from marriage. He rejected the government's arguments that children did best when raised by a man and a woman, that Hawaii had a compelling interest in ensuring that its marriages be recognized elsewhere, and that the tourist trade would suffer if the state allowed same-sex couples to marry. A banner headline in the *Honolulu Advertiser* announced, "Gay Marriage Upheld."[76]

Ninia Baehr and Genora Dancel, the lead plaintiffs in the Hawaii same-sex marriage case, after winning in the trial court, Dec. 3, 1996. (*Associated Press/ Serge J.F. Levy*)

Chang stayed his decision pending appeal. Yet, given the Hawaii supreme court's earlier decision and its generally liberal reputation, most commentators predicted that it would eventually affirm the trial court. The appeal was expected to take twelve to eighteen months to resolve. An opinion poll taken around this time showed that 74 percent of Hawaiians opposed gay marriage.[77]

Apparently cowed by the results of the 1996 elections, which they interpreted as voter frustration with the legislature's unresponsiveness to constituents' concerns, lawmakers vowed to act quickly on gay marriage when they reconvened in January 1997. Members of the House, which during the previous year had passed a marriage amendment but no partnership bill, now proposed combining the two. The amendment would authorize but not require the legislature to ban gay marriage. The reciprocal-beneficiaries law would extend benefits then available only to married couples to straight and gay couples who were prohibited from marrying under state law. Those benefits would include hospital visitation, inheritance rights, the right to make health care decisions, and the right to sue for wrongful death. The partnership law would go into effect only if voters approved the constitutional amendment.[78]

As a crowd of three thousand gay-marriage opponents rallied outside the capitol, the House passed both measures. The more liberal Senate then voted for a more generous package of benefits for reciprocal beneficiaries. Even liberal senators who opposed the marriage amendment were no longer willing to block it.[79]

In April 1997, after prolonged bargaining between the two houses, the legislature reached a compromise. It passed a constitutional amendment, to go on the ballot in November 1998, that would authorize, but not require, the legislature to limit marriage to opposite-sex couples. (The legislature phrased the amendment in this manner to reduce the chances that a federal court would invalidate it as based on animus toward gays.) The legislature also enacted a reciprocal-beneficiaries act to go into effect in July 1997, which was, by a considerable margin, the most far-reaching recognition of same-sex couples that any American legislature had approved.[80]

Most legislators and commentators assumed that Hawaiians would approve the amendment, though they also thought a federal court might then invalidate it, as the U.S. Supreme Court had recently overturned an anti-gay constitutional amendment from Colorado. It was unclear whether the Hawaii supreme court would defer its ruling on same-sex marriage in the *Baehr* appeal until after voters had an opportunity to vote on the amendment.[81]

Each side in the 1998 ballot campaign on gay marriage spent about $1.5 million, most of which came from the mainland. Mormons contributed a majority of the pro-amendment funding, though they sought to cloak their participation and urged Catholics to take the lead on the amendment instead. Catholic,

Mormon, and fundamentalist Protestant churches were the backbone of the Save Traditional Marriage '98 campaign.[82]

Pro-amendment television advertisements emphasized the effect that legalizing gay marriage would have on the education of children in public school. Amendment supporters also contended that legislatures rather than courts should decide such issues, denied that barring gay marriage was analogous to race or sex discrimination, and defended traditional opposite-sex marriage, arguing that Hawaii was at risk of becoming the first jurisdiction in the world to overhaul it.[83]

Amendment opponents compared the effort to ban gay marriage to Japanese American internment during World War II, warned that amendment supporters were the same people who wanted to deprive women of their right to abortion, protested efforts by the majority to impose its religious views on society, and warned other minority groups of the dangerous precedent that the amendment would set with regard to minority rights. But amendment opponents offered essentially no defense of gay marriage. Rather, they sought to convince Hawaiians that whatever one thought of gay marriage, the state's constitution ought not be lightly amended. One opinion poll showed that Hawaiians opposed gay marriage by 72 percent to 18 percent but supported amending the constitution to ban it by only 52 percent to 40 percent.[84]

In November 1998, Hawaiians voted by 69 percent to 31 percent to authorize the legislature to limit marriage to unions of one man and one woman. By then, the Hawaii supreme court had sat on the *Baehr* appeal for nearly two years, the justices having apparently decided not to race against the referendum. A year after passage of the amendment, the court vacated the trial judge's ruling and directed him to dismiss the lawsuit as moot in light of the change to the state constitution.[85]

The *Baehr* plaintiffs decided not to challenge the amendment under the federal constitution, apparently concluding that the U.S. Supreme Court was unlikely to prove sympathetic. By the time the Hawaii litigation had concluded, more than thirty states and Congress had enacted defense-of-marriage acts. Some gay activists in Hawaii quietly debated whether it had been a mistake to eschew incremental change and press for the legalization of gay marriage.[86]

At the same time, similar events were unfolding in Alaska. In August 1994, Jay Brause and Gene Dugan, a gay couple who had been partnered for eighteen years, applied for a marriage license. When it was denied, they filed a lawsuit in the summer of 1995. As in the Hawaii litigation, they were represented by a private attorney rather than by any of the national gay rights organizations, which learned of the litigation only after the trial court decision.[87]

A few months before the lawsuit was filed, a Republican state legislator sponsored a bill to specify that marriage in Alaska was limited to the union of a man and a woman. The legislature passed that bill in 1996. In February 1998, the trial judge in *Brause* ruled that law presumptively unconstitutional. The judge held both that the legislature's definition of marriage was a sex classification, which warranted heightened judicial scrutiny, and that the right to "choose one's life partner," of the same or opposite sex, was a fundamental one deeply rooted in tradition. Further hearings were required to determine if the state had a compelling justification for barring gay marriage.[88]

The state appealed to the Alaska supreme court, which denied review at that point in the proceedings, and the trial proceeded to discovery. Given the liberal reputation of the state supreme court, gay activists believed they were likely to win on the appeal that would presumably follow the trial.[89]

But the political process outpaced the legal process. Constitutional amendments in Alaska require a two-thirds vote of each house of the legislature followed by a referendum at the next election. The day after the trial court's decision, the senate majority leader introduced a resolution for a constitutional amendment providing that "to be valid or recognized in this state, a marriage may exist only between one man and one woman." An opinion poll showed that 65 percent of Alaskans disapproved of legalizing gay marriage. Within three months, both houses of the legislature had passed the amendment in largely partisan votes, putting it on the fall ballot.[90]

The Alaska referendum campaign did not receive the same national attention as the one in Hawaii, but it was nonetheless well financed and contentious. The state's Catholic bishops issued a pastoral letter endorsing the amendment. Gary Bauer, president of the Family Research Council, traveled to Alaska to raise funds for it. The Mormon Church in Utah contributed $500,000 to the pro-amendment campaign—the vast majority of that side's funding. By contrast, amendment opponents were able to raise only about $100,000.[91]

Amendment supporters warned that "non-elected judges, at the behest of militant activists, are seeking to undermine an understanding of marriage that societies have cherished for thousands of years." They warned that the pending litigation would invalidate Alaska's Defense of Marriage Act, encourage thousands of gay couples to travel to Alaska to get married, require grade-school sex education classes to teach that homosexual marriage was normal, impinge upon the religious liberties of churches that preached against gay marriage, and open the door to polygamy.[92]

After conducting opinion polling, amendment opponents decided not to defend gay marriage on the merits. Rather, they criticized the amendment as unnecessary because state law already barred gay marriage and because the state supreme court was unlikely to mandate it for years, if ever. Opponents urged voters not to clutter up the constitution with "the issue of the moment." The

Democratic governor opposed the amendment on that very ground after his Republican challenger accused him of supporting gay marriage.[93]

The amendment played a prominent role in the only televised debate between the candidates for lieutenant governor. The incumbent Democrat opposed the amendment as unnecessary, while the principal Republican challenger strongly supported it and denounced homosexuality as "perverted" and "disgusting."[94]

In November, Alaskans approved the amendment by 68 percent to 32 percent. The *Brause* plaintiffs decided not to bring a federal constitutional challenge against it, and their lawsuit was eventually dismissed.[95]

Even in states as liberal as Hawaii and as libertarian as Alaska, voters had overwhelmingly rejected gay marriage. A working paper prepared for the Human Rights Campaign in the fall of 1998 contemplated "declar[ing] defeat on the freedom to marry for this generation (5 yrs? 10? 20?)."[96]

At almost precisely the same time that Congress debated DOMA in response to the *Baehr* backlash, the U.S. Supreme Court struck a blow in favor of gay rights in a narrowly reasoned decision that ruffled fewer feathers.

By the early 1990s, several cities in Colorado—Aspen, Boulder, and Denver— had enacted ordinances forbidding discrimination based on sexual orientation. In 1991, gay activists made the mistake of trying to convince Colorado Springs, home of the Christian evangelical organization Focus on the Family, to pass such an ordinance. Not only was the measure overwhelmingly defeated by the city council after hundreds of conservative Christians turned up at a council meeting, but it spawned a backlash in the form of a proposed constitutional amendment to overturn existing gay rights ordinances and to forbid cities or the state from enacting similar measures in the future. To promote the amendment, supporters founded Colorado for Family Values, a coalition of leading conservative Christian organizations, including the Traditional Values Coalition, Focus on the Family, and the Eagle Forum.[97]

Supporters of the amendment argued that it would forbid only "special rights" for homosexuals, and they disparaged the idea that sexual orientation should be treated as if it were analogous to race or ethnicity. They also portrayed gays as promiscuous, emphasized the public health threat posed by AIDS, and linked homosexuality with pedophilia, just as Anita Bryant had done in her Dade County campaign in 1977. Amendment supporters ran advertisements featuring footage of gay pride parades, with an emphasis on drag queens, women in leather, and public displays of sexuality.[98]

Opponents argued that the amendment's purpose was to deny equal rights, not special rights, and to authorize discrimination against homosexuals. Polls predicted that the amendment would fail, but it passed by 53 percent to

47 percent. The following year in Cincinnati, voters adopted by 62 percent to 38 percent a city charter amendment to overturn a gay rights ordinance passed by the city council.[99]

In 1994, the Colorado supreme court struck down the state amendment on the ground that it denied gays equal participation in the political process. The following year, the Sixth Circuit rejected a similar challenge to the Cincinnati charter amendment.[100]

In 1996, the U.S. Supreme Court in *Romer v. Evans* affirmed the Colorado court's decision on the ground that the breadth of the amendment—"imposing a broad and undifferentiated disability on a single named group"—was "so discontinuous with the reasons offered for it that the amendment seems inexplicable by anything but animus toward the class that it affects." Under well-established precedent, simple animus toward a group cannot qualify as a sufficient justification for legislation. Justice Scalia vehemently dissented. He regarded the amendment as "rather a modest attempt by seemingly tolerant Coloradans to preserve traditional sexual mores against the efforts of a politically powerful minority to revise those mores through use of the laws."[101]

Suzanne Goldberg of Lambda Legal called the high court's ruling in *Romer v. Evans* "the most important victory ever for lesbian and gay rights," while Matt Coles of the ACLU's Lesbian and Gay Rights Project called it "a sea change in the struggle of lesbian and gay men for equality in America." By contrast, Colorado for Family Values thought it a "truly chilling day" when defenders of "traditional views of sexuality" were not permitted to write their values into law. Gary Bauer called *Romer* the product of "an out of control unelected judiciary."[102]

Romer probably deterred future referenda of this sort. Such measures had been all the rage in the early 1990s, and dating back to the 1970s, the gay rights movement had proved vulnerable to them. In 1991, the National Gay and Lesbian Task Force had referred to the "newest right-wing strategy" of referenda and warned that "our defensive actions on this issue have the potential of consuming all of our activist-energies for the next several years." To the extent that *Romer* interred referenda that repealed or barred gay rights ordinances, it was a significant boost to the gay rights movement.[103]

Yet, in fact, *Romer* was a narrow decision with limited implications—most definitely not the "*Roe v. Wade* for gays and lesbians," as Jay Sekulow of the American Center for Law and Justice rightly observed. Instead, *Romer* simply suppressed an outlier: no other state had passed an amendment like the one in Colorado. Indeed, voters in Idaho and Oregon had narrowly rejected similar amendments in 1994, and Maine voters had done so in 1995. Thus, *Romer* may not have been necessary to protect against any wholesale enactment of such amendments by referendum.[104]

Romer was perhaps more notable for other reasons. First, it was the high court's first defense of the civil rights of gay Americans. Thomas Stoddard declared that "gay people will feel embraced by the highest judicial court of the land." Second, *Romer* rejected moral disapproval of homosexuality as a sufficient justification for discrimination against gays. That principle might well have application outside the narrow factual context of *Romer*.[105]

Many commentators emphasized as well that the opinion had been written by one of President Reagan's appointees, Anthony Kennedy, and was joined by another, Sandra Day O'Connor. Still, the reasoning of the opinion fell far short of banning all forms of legal discrimination based on sexual orientation, such as in the contexts of military service and marriage.[106]

Despite the fierce political backlash ignited against gay marriage in the 1990s by the *Baehr* litigation, gay rights in general continued to make significant progress. The percentage of Americans who thought homosexual sex was "always wrong" remained consistently high through the 1970s and 1980s—between 70 percent and 80 percent—but then declined sharply throughout the 1990s, falling below 60 percent by decade's end. Between 1988 and 2000, the "feeling thermometer" of the National Election Study showed an increase of 20 percentage points in the number of people holding positive feelings toward gays and a decline of 23 percentage points in the number holding the most negative feelings. These changes were especially evident among younger Americans. In 1998, 77 percent of people age sixty-five and older thought homosexual sex was always wrong, while only 42 percent of those eighteen to twenty-nine agreed.[107]

Such changes in attitudes toward homosexuality were accompanied by a dramatic shift in beliefs about its nature, although the causal direction of the relationship is unclear. In 1977, only 13 percent of respondents believed that homosexuality was innate, and an additional 3 percent attributed it to a combination of genes and environment. By 2002, 40 percent thought homosexuality was genetic, and an additional 12 percent thought it was attributable to a combination of genes and environment.[108]

Once sexual orientation is seen as immutable, it becomes more difficult to justify discrimination against homosexuals as a necessary deterrent to immoral choices. Moreover, if sexual orientation is innate, parents need not worry about their children being proselytized into it—a conventional stereotype used to justify anti-gay discrimination. Changing views about the immutability of homosexuality probably help to explain the increase in support for the right of homosexuals to teach in public schools from 27 percent in 1977 to 55 percent in 1996.[109]

The size and stature of national gay rights organizations increased dramatically in the 1990s. Between 1993 and 2002, Lambda Legal, the dominant force in gay rights litigation, quadrupled its annual income, and its staff grew from twenty-two to seventy-three. Between 1991 and 1997, the Empire State Pride Agenda, New York's largest gay rights organization, increased its paid staff from two to thirteen and its annual budget from $100,000 to $1.5 million. By 1998, Parents, Families and Friends of Lesbians and Gays, founded in 1973 by twenty parents of gay children in Greenwich Village, had grown to five hundred chapters across the nation with eighty thousand members.[110]

The number of openly gay elected officials in the country increased from 52 in 1991 to 146 in 1998. The year 1994 saw the first openly gay candidates ever nominated by their parties to run for statewide offices in New York and California. That same year, the first openly gay legislators were elected in California and Arizona, and Oregon elected four openly homosexual or bisexual representatives to its sixty-seat house. Openly gay officeholders not only reflected the increased political power of the gay community but also influenced legislative debates on gay rights issues through their personal stories. In 1994 in New York, Governor Mario Cuomo appointed open lesbians for the first time to high positions in the executive branch: president of the civil service commission and commissioner of the workers' compensation board.[111]

Bill Clinton was the first American president to appoint openly gay officials to his administration—more than 150 of them. He nominated an openly gay ambassador and invited gay leaders to the oval office. In the 2000 Democratic presidential primaries, Senator Bill Bradley voiced strong support for gay rights, calling for extending the 1964 Civil Rights Act to cover sexual orientation and for repeal of "don't ask, don't tell." Vice President Al Gore endorsed domestic partnerships for same-sex couples and also endorsed repeal of "don't ask, don't tell."[112]

Greater social acceptance and political power translated into stronger public support for anti-discrimination laws. In 1977, only 56 percent of respondents thought homosexuals should have equal employment rights. By 1989, 71 percent thought so, and by 1997, 80 percent did. The number of states with laws forbidding discrimination based on sexual orientation—usually covering employment, housing, and public accommodations—grew from one in 1988 to eleven in 1998. The number of localities with such ordinances increased from eighty in 1990 to more than two hundred in 2000.[113]

On the same day in 1996 that the U.S. Senate voted overwhelmingly to pass DOMA, it failed by a single vote to pass a bill barring discrimination based on sexual orientation in employment. An opinion poll showed that 68 percent of Americans supported the bill. When President Clinton issued an executive order in May 1998 barring federal agencies from discriminating based on sexual orientation, 70 percent of Americans supported it. The number backing openly gay military service had grown to 71 percent by 2000.[114]

Between 1993 and 1999, a dozen states expanded their hate crimes laws to protect gays. Many of these were passed in response to the murder of Matthew Shepard in Wyoming in 1998. Shepard, a college student, was tortured and killed because of his sexual orientation. Demonstrators across the country protested his killing. Gay rights organizations were inundated with emails and letters expressing outrage. President Clinton denounced the murder and called for federal hate crimes legislation. The Hate Crimes Prevention Act, which would have expanded federal hate crimes laws to include sexual orientation, passed the Senate in 1999 with President Clinton's strong support before dying in committee in the House.[115]

A number of state courts invalidated sodomy laws in the 1990s, despite the Supreme Court's ruling in *Bowers* that such laws did not violate the federal constitution. Evolving attitudes toward homosexuality also influenced judges to change the law of gay adoptions. The percentage of Americans believing that gays should be legally permitted to adopt children rose from 14 percent in 1977 to 29 percent in 1992 to almost 50 percent in 2000. No state law explicitly permitted gay adoptions before Connecticut amended its law to do so in 2000. Yet the laws of very few states explicitly banned gays from adopting children, and judges increasingly permitted them to do so under the general legal standard of the "best interests of the child." In the 1990s, three state supreme courts approved the practice of gay couples using the mechanism of second-parent adoptions.[116]

Changes in the law of adoption would prove significant in the longer term for gay marriage. Once same-sex couples were permitted to adopt children, the argument for not allowing them to marry grew weaker.[117]

In child custody cases as well, appellate courts increasingly concluded that sexual orientation should not be the sole determining factor in disputes between gay and straight parents. Even courts in conservative states such as South Dakota, Alabama, and Utah made such rulings.[118]

The corporate world was also becoming more gay-friendly. In 2002, a survey of more than three hundred of the nation's largest companies found that approximately 92 percent of them prohibited workplace discrimination based on sexual orientation. In 1992, not a single Fortune 500 corporation extended benefits to the partners of gay employees. By 2000, well over one hundred of them did so. By then, 18 percent of private sector workers were employed by companies that offered domestic partnership benefits.[119]

Some religious denominations were also becoming more accepting of homosexuality. Early in 2000, the Central Conference of American Rabbis, which serves 1.5 million Reform Jews in the United States and Canada, approved a resolution declaring that gay relationships were "worthy of affirmation" and offering support to rabbis who chose to preside over gay commitment ceremonies. That summer, the top policy-making body of the Presbyterian Church came very close to approving its ministers' conducting commitment ceremonies for same-sex unions.[120]

Perhaps the largest and most significant changes were occurring in the media and in popular culture. In 1989, ABC had lost more than $1 million in advertising revenue when sponsors withdrew from an episode of *thirtysomething* because it briefly showed two gay men in bed together. In 1990 only one network television show had a regularly appearing gay character. In the early 1990s, a majority of Americans said that they would not permit their child to watch a prime-time television situation comedy with gay characters.[121]

By contrast, in the mid-1990s, the most popular situation comedies were dealing with the issue of gay marriage: *Roseanne* in 1995, *Friends* in 1996, and *Mad About You* in 1998. By 1996–97, twenty-two LGBT characters regularly appeared on television programs (albeit mostly in peripheral roles).[122]

In 1997, after months of rampant speculation, Ellen DeGeneres famously came out in a special one-hour episode of her popular television show, *Ellen*, which was watched by forty-six million viewers. It was the first time in television history that a leading prime-time character had come out as gay. *Time* put DeGeneres on its cover with the headline "Yep, I'm Gay." The accompanying feature story described her television character as like "Mary Richards [from the *Mary Tyler Moore* show], except she likes girls."[123]

After DeGeneres came out, gay characters popped up all over prime time, and they no longer generated much controversy. A year and a half later, *Will and Grace*, which featured two openly gay men as major characters, launched its run as one of television's most popular programs. The importance of changes in television portrayal of gays and lesbians should not be underestimated. Copious research shows that as people come to know others who are gay, their attitudes toward homosexuality tend to become more progressive, and many Americans feel as if they know their favorite television characters.[124]

As the political and social climate became more gay-friendly, millions of gays and lesbians made the important decision to come out to their friends, families, and colleagues. The percentage of Americans reporting someone in their family who was gay jumped from 9 percent in 1992 to 23 percent in 2000. One poll showed that the percentage of Americans who reported knowing someone who was gay increased from 25 percent in 1985 to 74 percent in 2000.[125]

The greater acceptance that for decades gays had found in large coastal cities now spread to smaller cities and towns throughout the nation. In 1996, the field director of the NGLTF, who had traveled more than a hundred thousand miles across the country, reported that "the center of gravity of the gay rights and lesbian movement is shifting" and that the largest changes were apparent in small towns. Gay nightclubs, bookstores, and film festivals spread to new parts of the country, and even smaller communities enacted anti-discrimination ordinances.

By the mid-1990s, Colorado Springs, home to Focus on the Family and the U.S. Air Force Academy and often portrayed as a hotbed of homophobia, had a gay bowling league, a lesbian bicycle club, a gay rodeo, a gay wine-tasting group, a gay newspaper, and various gay community organizations.[126]

Finally, although the 1990s had seen a massive political backlash against gay marriage at both the state and federal levels, underlying support for it continued to grow. Polls from the late 1980s showed support for gay marriage ranging from 11 percent to 23 percent. By the late 1990s, polls revealed support ranging from 29 percent to 35 percent. The Pew Research Center found an increase in support for gay marriage of 8 percentage points between 1996 and 2001. Gallup found an increase of 7 percentage points between 1996 and 2000.[127]

4

Baker (Vermont) and *Lawrence* (1999–2003)

Although gay marriage litigation in Hawaii fomented political backlash on the mainland, it also inspired gays and lesbians elsewhere to believe that their states, too, might one day recognize same-sex unions. Vermont was an especially attractive venue for a lawsuit seeking to compel such recognition. In 1990, the state legislature had passed a law enhancing penalties for crimes committed with anti-gay animus. In 1992, it passed a law forbidding discrimination based on sexual orientation in employment, public accommodations, housing, and education. In 1993, the state supreme court became the first in the country to extend second-parent adoptions to same-sex couples. In 1996, the legislature wrote that ruling into the family law code, two years after Vermont became the first state in the nation to provide benefits to domestic partners of gay state employees.[1]

Vermont was an attractive venue for gay marriage litigation for another reason: its constitution is harder to amend than that of Alaska and Hawaii. Amendments require approval by the legislature in two successive sessions plus a subsequent referendum. Thus, overturning a court decision can take years.[2]

After *Baehr*, a coalition of gay rights organizations in Vermont created a committee, the Freedom to Marry Task Force, to prepare the groundwork for a gay marriage lawsuit. According to one of the co-founding lawyers, the Hawaii supreme court decision had "showed us for the first time that we could win these cases." Yet the backlash from that decision had taught them that a litigation victory without public support to back it up was worth very little. Thus, the first aim of the task force was to educate Vermonters about gay and lesbian couples. It trained several dozen people to give talks at churches and social clubs, produced a video of unscripted interviews with same-sex couples, and set to work lobbying legislators. No lawsuit would be filed until the groundwork had been completed.[3]

By 1997, Vermont Freedom to Marry was ready. Three same-sex couples that it had recruited requested marriage licenses, which court clerks denied to them. They then filed suit—solely under the state constitution—objecting to the traditional definition of marriage as a sex classification and an abridgement of their fundamental rights.[4]

The trial judge dismissed their claims, and they appealed to the state supreme court, urging it to follow the trailblazing path set by the California supreme court fifty years earlier when it became the first in the nation to invalidate bans on interracial marriage. An opinion poll showed that Vermonters narrowly opposed gay marriage, 48 percent to 43 percent. While the litigation was pending, two of the top Democratic officeholders in the state declared their support for same-sex marriage.[5]

The plaintiffs' lawyers had expected to win in the state supreme court, and on December 20, 1999, they did. In *State v. Baker*, the court unanimously invalidated the state's exclusion of same-sex couples from marriage under the state constitutional provision guaranteeing "the common benefit, protection, and security of the people."[6]

One of the five justices would have required the state to immediately begin issuing marriage licenses to same-sex couples. The other four, however, accepted

The three plaintiff couples in the Vermont gay marriage litigation, Dec. 20, 1999. From left rear, Stacey Jolles, Nina Beck, Peter Harrigan, and Stan Baker. Seated, from left, Holly Puterbaugh and Lois Farnham. (*Associated Press/Toby Talbot*)

the state's argument that a sudden change in marriage law could prove destabiliz-ing. They gave the legislature a "reasonable period of time" to correct the discrimination inherent in denying same-sex couples the rights and benefits associated with marriage. They also gave the legislature the choice of amending the marriage law to include same-sex couples or creating a new institution for such couples that provided "the common benefits and protections that flow from marriage." In light of the recent gay marriage referenda in Hawaii and Alaska, these justices explained, to insist that Vermont extend marriage to same-sex couples was to ignore political reality and thus reduce the chances of effectu-ating the rights they sought to protect.[7]

The court's compromise ruling might also have reflected lessons learned by the justices from their 1997 decision invalidating Vermont's system of funding public education from local property taxes. That ruling had proved enormously controversial, even inspiring efforts to remove the justices responsible for it from office.[8]

Although *Baker* stopped short of mandating gay marriage, it went far beyond what any state had yet enacted. Domestic partnership legislation in California and Hawaii required that same-sex couples receive a few of the benefits of marriage, such as inheritance and hospital visitation rights. By contrast, the Vermont court seemed to suggest that gay couples should receive all of the rights and benefits of marriage.[9]

The plaintiffs expressed delight with the holding but disappointment with the remedy—a striking indication of how much opinion had changed in the pre-ceding decade. In 1990, it would have been unthinkable for gay couples to enjoy all of the rights and benefits of marriage.[10]

In an editorial, the state's leading newspaper, the *Burlington Free Press*, reiter-ated its opposition to gay marriage and praised *Baker* as a wise instance of judicial restraint. Both of the state's U.S. senators applauded the court for its flexibility on the remedy. Noting that *Baker* was consistent with the views of a majority of Vermonters, Governor Howard Dean immediately proposed the establishment of a new institution of domestic partnerships, which would duplicate the bene-fits and responsibilities of marriage. Refusing to express a personal opinion on gay marriage, Dean expressed doubt that a bill to authorize it could pass the legislature.[11]

In the first three weeks after *Baker*, the governor's office received more than eighty-six hundred phone calls, faxes, and emails about the ruling. Even though the decision had come down just ten days before the end of 1999, Vermont edi-tors and broadcasters quickly ranked *Baker* as the top news story of the year. A poll conducted immediately after the decision found that Vermonters opposed it by 52 percent to 38 percent. Nearly half of the respondents favored a constitu-tional amendment to overturn *Baker*.[12]

Some Democratic lawmakers endorsed gay marriage after the ruling. However, the Speaker of the house, a Democrat who previously had endorsed gay marriage, quickly polled his colleagues and found little enthusiasm for it. A more viable alternative, he suggested, would be domestic partnerships. Initially, even some Republicans seemed open to that idea.[13]

However, the parties' positions quickly polarized, and most Republicans announced opposition to domestic partnerships, which they said would inevitably lead to gay marriage. Some Republicans in the state senate favored amending the constitution to bar gay marriage, but that idea never gained traction in the subsequent legislative deliberations.[14]

Amid increased security, the house Judiciary Committee held hearings that lasted nearly a month. Despite a blizzard, approximately fifteen hundred people attended on January 25. On February 1, heeding a call from the Catholic bishop of Burlington, nearly two thousand opponents of the legal recognition of same-sex unions rallied outside the capitol during a second public hearing. On the other side of the debate, Vermont's Episcopalian and Methodist bishops endorsed gay marriage. In the first two months of 2000, the two sides combined to spend nearly $100,000 lobbying the legislature.[15]

The legislative hearings, broadcast by public radio across the state, afforded an opportunity for gays and lesbians to tell their stories and to demonstrate that they were ordinary people who made valuable contributions to their communities. Some commentators deemed such testimony critical to the legislature's ultimate enactment of civil unions.[16]

Encouraged by Republican lawmakers, many towns in Vermont put the question of legal recognition of same-sex couples to town meetings held in March. Across the state, legislators also held public forums so that their constituents could express their views. Some of these attracted hundreds of citizens, and emotions often ran high. Randall Terry, the anti-abortion activist who founded Operation Rescue in 1987, relocated to Vermont for three months to support opponents of legal recognition, though he was mostly shunned, even by those who shared his position. Weary of the rude gestures they received, several lawmakers turned in their specialty license plates. At least a half dozen of them saw their cars vandalized.[17]

Supporters of gay marriage conceded they did not have the legislative votes to enact it. Instead, a house committee agreed on a system of domestic partnerships (ultimately relabeled "civil unions") that provided same-sex couples the rights and obligations of marriage without the name. Even Republican committee members supported the measure. Governor Dean immediately endorsed it. The *Baker* plaintiffs announced that they would not challenge civil unions as inadequate.[18]

Through February and the first half of March, the fate of civil unions in the house remained unclear. Many Republicans opposed any legal recognition of same-sex couples, and some Democrats were undecided. Republican opposition to legal recognition intensified in early March after more than thirty town meetings resoundingly rejected gay marriage; many of them also opposed civil unions. Exit polls of Republican primary voters that month showed overwhelming opposition to any legal recognition of same-sex couples. Those lawmakers who were similarly inclined argued that legislators should listen to the voters.[19]

Lawmakers were besieged by letters, phone calls, and personal pleas. Many legislators reported that the constituent pressure was greater than any they had ever faced before. The president pro tem of the senate reported that in his decade in the legislature he had "never seen an issue that has electrified the state to [this] extent." The question of civil unions utterly dominated the legislative session.[20]

On March 15, 2000, after eight hours of impassioned and uninterrupted debate, the house voted 76 to 69 to approve a bill to establish civil unions. Many supporters drew parallels to the struggle to desegregate southern schools in the 1950s. By a vote of 125 to 22, the house defeated an amendment to legalize gay marriage. Opponents of any legal recognition failed in their efforts to secure an advisory referendum of the people. Some wavering lawmakers were persuaded to support the bill by the addition of a sentence noting that "marriage means the legally recognized union of one man and one woman." Governor Dean repeatedly denied claims that the house had passed a gay marriage bill.[21]

In April, after what one commentator called "one of the most intensely personal, deeply emotional, soul baring and heart wrenching debates ever held in the chamber," the senate passed the civil unions bill by 19 to 11. It rejected by 17 to 13 a proposed constitutional amendment to define marriage as the union of a man and a woman. On April 26, Governor Dean signed the bill—behind closed doors and without fanfare, out of deference to the thousands of Vermonters who opposed any legal recognition of same-sex unions.[22]

Even though they would have preferred marriage, gay rights groups viewed civil unions as a big victory—a cause for celebration. The state's only openly gay lawmaker declared, "Marriage, someday. But it does not feel hollow. It feels like a tremendous victory." The three same-sex couples who were plaintiffs in *Baker* dropped their lawsuit and declared themselves satisfied—for now—with civil unions. Their lawyer, Beth Robinson, explained, "Given how far we've come in a short time, and given our desire to do this in a way that doesn't divide the state, we were unanimous in our decision."[23]

Voters would have their turn to weigh in on the issue in November. Opponents of civil unions announced, "November 7 is the most important election we will ever have in Vermont." One letter to the editor of the *Burlington Free Press* encouraged voters to "keep your blood boiling. Strike back in November." Sixteen Catholic bishops from across New England issued a statement urging Vermonters to "rectify the situation that brought about the passage of the civil unions bill," which they called a stepping-stone to gay marriage.[24]

An opinion poll conducted soon after the civil unions law was enacted found that Vermonters opposed it by 52 percent to 43 percent. A poll in August showed that 49 percent of respondents said the law would affect their vote in a major way. Democrats were especially worried that their strong support for civil unions would cost them at the polls. Many lawmakers spoke of not running for reelection because of the enormous emotional toll that the debate had taken on them.[25]

Governor Dean acknowledged that public furor over civil unions might cost him his job in November. In February, before the civil unions law was enacted, 63 percent of Vermonters viewed him favorably and only 16 percent unfavorably. By late August, his favorability rating was down to 41 percent, and his unfavorability rating was up to 35 percent. Even many Democrats and independents were unhappy with the governor over civil unions. As Dean sought to divert voter attention from civil unions to his entire record compiled over nine years as governor, the Burlington Free Press declared that he faced the toughest political fight of his career.[26]

The civil unions issue galvanized conservatives, who rallied around the slogan "Take Back Vermont." Signs bearing those words appeared on cars and in yards across the state. Voter registrars reported an increase in new registrations as high as 5 percent, which they attributed to citizens' anger over civil unions. The Burlington Free Press reported, "No issue in recent Vermont history has provoked louder or more emotional debate."[27]

Legislators who had voted for civil unions but represented districts that opposed them in the advisory ballots cast on town meeting day faced severe pressure to explain their votes. A legislator who had strongly opposed civil unions created a political action committee to recruit candidates to run against legislators who had voted for the law. One prominent Republican lawmaker, who previously had been a U.S. congressman and a state cabinet member, chose to run for reelection as an independent rather than face opposition in the Republican primary because of his vote for civil unions. A Republican legislator who had helped write the civil unions law but represented a district in which voters on town meeting day had overwhelmingly opposed any legal recognition of same-sex couples faced three challengers in his primary election.[28]

In the end, of the fifteen House Republicans who had voted for the law, eight faced primary opposition, with several of their challengers noting that the civil unions law had inspired their candidacies. The Republican challenger to the incumbent secretary of state also explained that he had entered the race only because of her support for civil unions and her threat to hold court clerks personally liable if they refused to issue civil union licenses to same-sex couples.[29]

Both sides in the civil unions debate saw the Republican primary on September 12 as a referendum on the law. Amid record voter turnout, four Republican lawmakers who had voted for the civil unions bill were defeated for renomination. One Republican state senator who had supported civil unions ran eighth out of eight candidates in an at-large district that he had won two years earlier. Another Republican candidate for the state senate, who was a former lieutenant governor and a top vote-getter in her 1996 race for the senate, barely squeezed through her primary contest, finishing sixth in another multi-member district. Her support for civil unions was the only plausible explanation for the poor showing.[30]

Civil unions also played a prominent role in the 2000 gubernatorial campaign. Dean's opponent, Ruth Dwyer, criticized *Baker* and promised, if elected, to work for repeal of the civil unions law. She accused Dean of having been willing to "threaten" and "bribe" people to get the bill enacted. Her campaign theme was "Listening to Vermont," which she said the legislature and Dean had been unwilling to do on civil unions.[31]

Dwyer provoked great controversy during the campaign when she charged on a radio program that the nation's largest teachers' union was promoting a homosexual agenda in Vermont schools by supporting a program called Outright Vermont that served gay and lesbian youth who were confused about their sexuality. Dean denounced her remarks, which he called an appeal to anger and hatred. The Vermont branch of the teachers' union labeled Dwyer's comments "reckless and irresponsible." This controversy illustrated the volatility of the situation created by *Baker* and the civil unions law. When pollsters asked in August which issue would be most important to voters in determining their choice of governor, 23 percent said education and 21 percent said civil unions.[32]

Governor Dean was running for his political life. (He also had concerns for his actual life and wore a bulletproof vest much of that summer.) A leading Democratic lawmaker, who was retiring after sixteen terms in office, endorsed Dwyer. He declared that civil unions were "the only real issue" in the election, and he accused Dean of being "out of touch morally" with Vermonters and of having plotted for years to impose civil unions on the state through his appointment of Chief Justice Jeff Amestoy, who authored *Baker*, to the state supreme court in 1997.[33]

Political rallies for Dean's opponent Dwyer turned into protests against the civil unions law. Hundreds of Dwyer supporters waved "Take Back Vermont" signs. (Supporters of civil unions responded with signs saying "Take Vermont Forward.") Dwyer sought to turn unhappiness with civil unions into an anti-Dean message with the slogan "You Have to Listen to Lead." She insisted the gubernatorial race was a referendum on civil unions.[34]

In February, before the civil unions bill was enacted, Dean led Dwyer by 25 percentage points in the polls. In August, one poll had that lead down to 14 points. By mid-October, a poll conducted by the Dean campaign showed his lead down to just 5 percentage points. That poll also revealed that 28 percent of voters regarded civil unions as the most important issue in the election—a higher percentage than on any other issue.[35]

Civil unions dominated the gubernatorial debate on October 19, which Dean had sought to focus on other issues where the candidates differed, such as abortion and increasing the minimum wage. In late October, the *Burlington Free Press* reported that one subject—civil unions—"has generated a deafening emotional decibel level" in the gubernatorial race, making it impossible to carry on a conversation on other topics such as health care or education. Dean found himself under attack not just from Republicans but from blue-collar and religious Democrats. Yet Dwyer probably overplayed her hand when she compared the unrest in Vermont over civil unions to the North/South divide before the Civil War.[36]

In several legislative districts as well, the civil unions issue dominated the general election campaign. One candidate estimated that 80 percent of the people he encountered while canvassing wanted to discuss civil unions, and many Democratic candidates admitted that they encountered much anger over the issue. The president pro tem of the senate referred to a "level of tension I don't think I've ever seen in Vermont," which he found "very upsetting." The *Burlington Free Press* described the election season as "marred by rudeness, intimidation, and confrontation" and called the campaign "not just a political battle, but a moral war." Schools throughout the state reported a dramatic increase in anti-gay harassment and anti-gay graffiti. In the final week of the contest, the four members of the state's U.S. congressional delegation issued a joint call for a return to civility.[37]

In the end, Dean was reelected with 51.3 percent of the vote. Dwyer received 38.8 percent, and the Progressive Party candidate won 9.7 percent. Dean lost some towns that he had won in 1998, probably because of conservative Democratic opposition to civil unions. The lieutenant governor, who had endorsed gay marriage, was comfortably reelected. U.S. senator Jim Jeffords, a Republican who had supported the civil unions bill despite his party's opposition, was reelected in a landslide.[38]

Republicans won a twenty-one-seat majority in the lower house, which Democrats had controlled since 1984. More than a dozen pro-civil-union Democrats were defeated. Democrats lost one seat in the senate, which remained narrowly under their control. Exit polling suggested that the impact of the civil unions issue on the election was complicated. Voters indicated support for the new law by 52 percent to 46 percent. Yet the *Burlington Free Press* estimated that, through retirements and defeats, as many as thirty-six lawmakers may have lost their jobs because of their votes in favor of civil unions.[39]

In 2000, not a single jurisdiction in the world had enacted gay marriage. No jurisdiction in the United States had enacted anything like civil unions. By stopping short of requiring same-sex marriage, the Vermont court undoubtedly tempered the political backlash that its ruling ignited. Civil unions generated enormous political controversy in Vermont, but gay marriage would have produced even more. In 2000, only 15 percent to 20 percent of Vermonters favored gay marriage. A ruling in its favor probably would have had cataclysmic political ramifications.[40]

The new Republican-controlled Vermont house of representatives voted to repeal civil unions, but the bill died in the senate. Within a few years, Vermonters seemed to be generally at peace with civil unions. Republican governor James Douglas, elected in 2002, refused to challenge the law, explaining that most Vermonters had come to accept it and that the state had benefitted economically from it. Although civil unions for same-sex couples were enormously controversial in 2000, they quickly emerged as the fallback position for many opponents of gay marriage.[41]

Developments in Vermont beginning with *Baker* quickly attracted national attention. Within a week of the ruling, prominent conservatives such as Judge Robert Bork and columnist Cal Thomas were attacking it. In the *Weekly Standard,* David Frum warned that the "long-anticipated legal crisis of the American family has arrived," and he denounced domestic partnerships as an "alias" and a large and irreversible step toward gay marriage. In neighboring New Hampshire, the conservative Manchester *Union Leader* called *Baker* "Vermont's terrifying lurch towards lunacy."[42]

All ten candidates for the Republican presidential nomination in 2000 rejected not only civil unions but all forms of anti-discrimination laws protecting gays. Gary Bauer called *Baker* "in some ways worse than terrorism." Alan Keyes came to Vermont to testify against the civil unions bill, and he told an anti-gay-marriage rally that homosexuality, like pedophilia, was a perverse choice and thus government discrimination against homosexuals was desirable. Pat Buchanan also visited the state to support the Take Back Vermont campaign, and he referred to the fight over civil unions as a major skirmish in a cultural war for the soul of America.[43]

On the other side of the debate, Deb Price, author of the first nationally syndicated column on gay rights issues, congratulated Vermont lawmakers for being the most gay-friendly in the nation. At the March on Washington for Gay and Lesbian Rights in 2000, Vermont was hailed as a "beacon of hope," civil unions were viewed as a great victory, and about one thousand same-sex couples exchanged rings and vows in front of friends and families on the steps of the Lincoln Memorial. Both leading Democratic presidential candidates, Senator Bill Bradley of New Jersey and Vice President Al Gore, endorsed civil unions.[44]

Developments in Vermont "fueled the fire fanned by opponents of gay marriage." In Mississippi, supporters of a new law banning gay couples from adopting children attributed its passage partly to Vermont's embrace of civil unions.[45]

Four more states enacted defense-of-marriage laws or constitutional amendments in 2000. Advocates for these measures invoked developments in Vermont to justify them. Although some of these states were well on their way to enacting such measures before *Baker*, the Vermont ruling plainly inspired campaign organizers in some states to ban not just gay marriage but also other arrangements that offered same-sex couples some of the benefits of marriage.[46]

In California, where state law already explicitly limited marriage to unions of a man and a woman, a voter initiative called Proposition 22 sought to clarify state policy with regard to marriages lawfully performed elsewhere that would not have been permitted in California. The measure read, "Only marriage between a man and a woman is valid or recognized in California." The two sides of the campaign together spent about $16 million. The Mormon Church, the Catholic archbishops of California, and an Orange County banking magnate made sizable contributions in support of the initiative.[47]

Rather than defending gay marriage on the merits, initiative opponents warned that measures similar to Proposition 22 that had been enacted elsewhere had led to legal challenges to public and private domestic partnership policies similar to the one adopted in California in 1999. Democratic governor Gray Davis supported domestic partnerships and opposed gay marriage, but he also opposed the initiative as "wedge issue politics" that served mainly to "stir up prejudices and hostility, sometimes with tragic consequences"—an allusion to the lynching of gay college student Matthew Shepard in Wyoming in 1998. Initiative opponents ran a television advertisement that featured footage of protesters carrying signs such as "God Hates Fags" at Shepard's funeral and warned that Proposition 22 would promote more anti-gay violence.[48]

On March 7, 2000, California voters passed Proposition 22 by a margin of 61.4 percent to 38.6 percent. The losers took heart from exit polls showing that voters age forty-five and under had been closely divided on the issue. One openly gay assemblywoman said, "It's hard to be jubilant today but the time will come."[49]

That same year in Nebraska, opponents of gay marriage easily collected the 105,000 petition signatures needed to put a constitutional amendment banning it on the November ballot. It provided that "the uniting of two persons of the same sex in a civil union, domestic partnership or other similar same-sex relationship shall not be valid or recognized in Nebraska." This initiative was among the broadest anti-gay-marriage measures in the country and was drafted directly in response to developments in Vermont.[50]

Supporters raised three-quarters of a million dollars, most of it coming from national Catholic, Mormon, and evangelical groups. Their adversaries raised only about $150,000. Rather than defending gay marriage, amendment opponents warned that enacting the measure might dissuade employers and insurers from offering health care benefits for same-sex couples and prevent gays from entering into legal agreements for adopting partners' children or authorizing health care proxies, which was how some state courts elsewhere had interpreted measures containing similarly broad language.[51]

Polls left no doubt that the measure would pass, though, as usual, they underestimated the amount of support for barring gay marriage. In November, Nebraskans passed the amendment by 70 percent to 30 percent.[52]

Although gay marriage and civil unions remained enormously controversial early in the twenty-first century, the right of consenting adults to engage in same-sex sodomy in private was becoming much less so. Since *Bowers* was decided in 1986, not a single state had recriminalized homosexual sodomy, and efforts to eradicate sodomy laws had gained traction.[53]

After *Bowers*, gay rights litigators had shifted their focus to state courts. In 1990, a Michigan appellate court invalidated that state's sodomy law under state constitutional provisions concerning privacy and equality. In 1992, the Kentucky supreme court followed suit, calling "outrageous" the state's attempt to justify criminalizing same-sex sodomy on the grounds that homosexuals were more promiscuous, more likely to prey on children, and more prone to engage in public sex acts. Although some state courts continued to uphold such laws, many others followed Kentucky's lead. Gay rights groups also lobbied state legislatures to repeal sodomy laws, and several did so in the 1990s.[54]

As a result of this litigation and lobbying, by 2003 only thirteen states still criminalized sodomy between consenting adults, and only four of them explicitly targeted homosexual sex. By contrast, in 1960 every state criminalized same-sex sodomy, and at the time of *Bowers* in 1986, half the states still did so.[55]

Moreover, by 2003, many more gays and lesbians were in stable relationships, which often involved raising children. Their claim to fitting within the sort of privacy interest that the Supreme Court had traditionally acknowledged in familial relationships had grown more robust. Although opinion polls still showed that roughly half of Americans thought homosexual sex was wrong, very few people any longer seemed to support criminal prosecution of it.[56]

"Very few" is not "none," however. In September 1998, police in Houston burst into the apartment of John Lawrence based on a report, which turned out to be false, that an armed gunman was present. Instead, they found two men engaging in sodomy. The men were arrested, charged, and prosecuted. In response to the sodomy charge, they pleaded no contest and were fined $200.

Lawrence was the isolated case in which police had actually arrested and prosecuted someone for private, adult, consensual same-sex sodomy. In Harris County, Texas, the prosecutor could recall no other instance during his twenty-two-year tenure in which such a case had been prosecuted. Because Lawrence had been charged and convicted, he clearly had legal standing to challenge the statute, which eliminated the principal obstacle that had frustrated gay rights litigators in their efforts to get courts to invalidate sodomy laws.[57]

In June 2003, the U.S. Supreme Court invalidated the Texas law by a vote of 6 to 3. Writing for a majority consisting of himself and the four most liberal justices, Anthony Kennedy noted that the liberty protected by the Due Process Clause of the Fourteenth Amendment "presumes an autonomy of self that includes freedom of thought, belief, expression, and certain intimate conduct." In a concurring opinion, Justice Sandra Day O'Connor both portrayed the Texas statute as motivated by animus toward gays and rejected "moral disapproval" as a sufficient justification for the law. Even Justice Clarence Thomas's dissenting opinion, which called the Texas law "uncommonly silly" while declining to rule it unconstitutional, reflected the dramatic changes in social mores regarding homosexuality that had occurred since *Bowers*.[58]

In the seventeen years between *Bowers* and *Lawrence*, opinion polls showed that Americans had gone from opposing the legalization of homosexual relations by 55 percent to 33 percent to supporting legalization by 60 percent to 35 percent. As one religious conservative put it after *Lawrence*, "Even most Christians believe that what is done in the privacy of one's home is not the government's business." *Lawrence* was an easy decision for the Court, in the sense that it simply involved translating into constitutional law a social norm that already commanded overwhelming popular support.[59]

Lawrence probably would have been an uncontroversial ruling were it not for the extent to which gay marriage was emerging as a salient issue by 2003. Yet the connection between *Lawrence* and gay marriage could not be ignored, despite the best efforts of the justices in the majority to deny it. Justice Kennedy emphasized that *Lawrence* involved "the most private human conduct, sexual behavior, and in the most private of places, the home." He carefully noted that the case did not "involve whether the government must give formal recognition to any relationship that homosexual persons seek to enter."[60]

Justice O'Connor's concurrence similarly stressed that simply because "this law as applied to private, consensual conduct is unconstitutional under the Equal Protection Clause does not mean that other laws distinguishing between heterosexuals and homosexuals would similarly fail under rational basis review." Further, she noted that in defense of its ban on same-sex sodomy, Texas had failed to assert a legitimate interest, "such as national security or preserving the traditional institution of marriage." O'Connor even went so far as to stipulate, without explication, that "other reasons exist to promote the institution of marriage beyond mere moral disapproval of an excluded group."[61]

Despite such protestations, Justice Scalia's powerful dissent charged that "only if one entertains the belief that principle and logic have nothing to do with the decisions of this Court" could one believe that *Lawrence* had no implications for gay marriage. Scalia was far from alone in making that connection. The executive director of Basic Rights Oregon reported that the day after *Lawrence*, a reporter called him and asked whether gay marriage was next. He told the reporter, "That's just what Justice Scalia is saying" and "That's a smoke screen." The reporter replied, "No, actually that's what gay rights activists are saying on the national level," and read him a couple of quotes to that effect. Indeed, one lawyer for Lambda Legal declared that *Lawrence* "makes it much harder for society to continue banning gay marriage." Another Lambda lawyer said after *Lawrence* that marriage was "inevitable now," though he added, "In what time frame, we don't know."[62]

Around the time of *Lawrence*, well-publicized judicial rulings and political developments in Canada, which promised soon to make it the third nation in the world—after the Netherlands and Belgium—to legalize gay marriage, further increased the visibility of that issue. One day after *Lawrence*, a state judge in New Jersey heard arguments in a gay marriage case. Another gay marriage case had been argued before the Massachusetts supreme court in March 2003 and was still awaiting decision. In September, New York's Democratic Party became the third in the nation to endorse gay marriage.[63]

Because of its obvious relevance to gay marriage, *Lawrence* provoked an angry response from religious conservatives, who were described as "outraged" and "apoplectic." Lou Sheldon of the Traditional Values Coalition compared *Lawrence* to the September 11 terrorist attacks and referred to it as a wake-up call "that the enemy is at our doorsteps." James Dobson of Focus on the Family warned that "the homosexual activist movement . . . is poised to administer a devastating and potentially fatal blow to the traditional family." Religious conservatives organized a Marriage Protection Week, for which they prepared model sermons that called homosexuality the greatest extant threat to American society and portrayed it as a fate worse than the death of a child. Jerry Falwell, Tony Perkins, and the U.S. Conference of Catholic Bishops all announced support for a federal constitutional amendment to define marriage as the union of a man and a woman.[64]

Many Republicans in Congress denounced *Lawrence* and called for passage of the federal marriage amendment. President Bush had rarely mentioned the gay marriage issue during his first three years in office. After *Lawrence*, however, his press secretary, Ari Fleischer, reiterated the president's belief "that marriage is an institution between a man and a woman." In addition to proclaiming Marriage Protection Week, Bush signaled his support for the federal marriage amendment, which he finally explicitly endorsed in February 2004.[65]

Support for gay marriage declined in all ideological groups in the period immediately after *Lawrence*. Indeed, *Lawrence* temporarily reversed what had been a consistently upward trend in public support for the decriminalization of same-sex sodomy.[66]

5

Goodridge (Massachusetts) and Its Backlash (2003–2008)

Less than five months after *Lawrence*, the Massachusetts supreme court confirmed the worst fears of Justice Scalia and religious conservatives. Like Vermont a few years earlier, Massachusetts was fertile ground for gay marriage litigation. In 1989, it had become just the second state to forbid discrimination on the basis of sexual orientation in employment and public accommodations. In 1993, the state supreme court had become only the second to authorize second-parent adoptions by same-sex couples. In 1999, that court had become among the first in the nation to grant visitation rights to a lesbian who had helped raise her former partner's biological child. Massachusetts was also one of the relatively few states to have resisted the lure of defense-of-marriage acts in the 1990s.[1]

Inspired by developments in Vermont, Gay and Lesbian Advocates and Defenders (GLAD) filed a gay marriage lawsuit in Massachusetts in April 2001. Lambda Legal filed a similar suit in New Jersey in 2002, and gay activists in Indiana and Arizona initiated such litigation as well. In its lawsuit, GLAD rejected civil unions as an inadequate remedy (though, of course, courts are not bound to respect the remedial requests of litigators).[2]

Even in liberal Massachusetts, gay marriage was an unorthodox notion in 2001. The Massachusetts Family Institute had been pursuing a state defense-of-marriage act since 1998 and a state marriage amendment since 1999. In response to the filing of *Goodridge v. Department of Public Health,* a citizens' group, Massachusetts Citizens for Marriage, quickly launched a ballot initiative to ban gay marriage.[3]

The Massachusetts constitution specifies two different routes to amendment. First, two consecutive sessions of the legislature, sitting as a constitutional convention, can pass an amendment by simple majority vote, which the people can then ratify in a referendum. Second, initiative petitions signed by citizens numbering at least 3 percent of the vote cast for governor in the preceding election—which would mean at least 57,100 citizens after the 1998 gubernatorial election—can force a vote on an amendment by the legislature sitting in convention. If 25 percent of the legislators in convention approve the amendment in two consecutive sessions, it goes on the ballot for popular approval. The president of the state senate has absolute authority over calling a constitutional convention and its agenda.[4]

Starting the petition process in September 2001, within three months the Massachusetts Citizens for Marriage had collected about twice the number of signatures needed to place the marriage initiative on the agenda of the next constitutional convention. After the legislature declined to adopt the measure as its own, the initiative went before the state constitutional convention in 2002.[5]

In May, senate president Thomas Birmingham, who may have wished to demonstrate his liberal bona fides before launching a bid for the Democratic gubernatorial nomination, used his authority as presiding officer of the convention to block consideration of the marriage amendment. The following month, he adjourned the convention after just a few minutes, explaining that lawmakers needed additional time before considering the amendment. Two hundred gay marriage opponents seated in the House gallery erupted into deafening jeers and chanted, "We want a vote! We want a vote!"[6]

When the convention met again in July, Birmingham again blocked a vote, calling the marriage amendment hateful and mean-spirited. Even some legislators who opposed the amendment were dismayed by the methods Birmingham had used to kill it.[7]

Had the convention voted on the marriage amendment in 2002, gay rights advocates assumed that they would have lost. Had the amendment gotten on the ballot, they expected to suffer an overwhelming defeat. In 2002, the Massachusetts legislature would not even have adopted civil unions. A bill to provide domestic partnership benefits for gay and lesbian state employees had failed to get out of committee in the house after passing the senate in 1998, 1999, and 2001.[8]

In June 2002, former labor secretary Robert Reich, running for the Democratic gubernatorial nomination in Massachusetts, had made a big splash by endorsing gay marriage. Gay rights advocates could not name a single prominent national politician who supported Reich's position. That fall, Shannon O'Brien, who had defeated Reich for the nomination, saw her campaign battered when she unexpectedly and awkwardly endorsed gay marriage two weeks before the election, after campaigning for months on a platform of supporting only civil unions.[9]

In November 2003, the Massachusetts supreme court ruled that the state constitutional provision declaring that all persons are born "free and equal" barred the state from excluding same-sex couples from marriage. Massachusetts thus became only the fifth jurisdiction in the world to allow gay marriage. The others—Ontario, British Columbia, Belgium, and the Netherlands—had all enacted gay marriage only within the last two years. The court delayed implementation of its order for 180 days "to permit the Legislature to take such action as it may deem appropriate in light of this opinion." One gay rights lawyer described the ruling as "the Berlin Wall coming down" for the gay community.[10]

By contrast, for the Catholic bishops of Massachusetts, the decision was a "national tragedy." They distributed literature to a million Catholic households in the state urging people to mobilize in support of a state constitutional amendment to overturn *Goodridge*. The Catholic Action League of Massachusetts went further and suggested impeaching the justices. Focus on the Family sent letters to more than four thousand Massachusetts clergy—mostly evangelical Protestants—inviting them to meetings across the state in January to rally in defense of traditional marriage.[11]

In 2002, victorious Republican gubernatorial candidate Mitt Romney had campaigned in support of domestic partnerships that would provide health benefits, survivorship rights, and adoption rights to same-sex couples. In November 2003, possibly eyeing a future bid for the Republican presidential nomination, Romney denounced *Goodridge* and called for a state constitutional amendment to overturn it.[12]

Romney also requested that the state attorney general ask the court to stay implementation of its order until the people of Massachusetts had had an opportunity to vote on such an amendment—which would be 2006 at the earliest. Democratic attorney general Thomas Reilly refused even to transmit the governor's request to the court. Romney then invoked a 1913 law, which had been enacted to prevent interracial couples' coming to Massachusetts to get married in circumvention of their home states' laws, to forbid municipal clerks to issue marriage licenses to out-of-state gay couples.[13]

Goodridge was slightly ambiguous on whether civil unions might satisfy the court. Governor Romney, Attorney General Reilly, and Democratic Speaker of the house Thomas Finneran opined that the court would accept civil unions, while Harvard Law School professor Laurence Tribe, former governor William Weld, two former state attorneys general, and three state and local bar associations strongly rejected that notion.[14]

A poll of legislators taken about ten days after *Goodridge* found significant opposition to a constitutional amendment containing language broad enough to be interpreted as barring civil unions, and the *Boston Globe* reported that lawmakers seemed to be gravitating toward a compromise that would authorize civil unions while barring gay marriage. The state senate quickly framed a civil unions bill and sent it to the court for an advisory opinion on whether it satisfied *Goodridge*.[15]

On February 3, 2004, the court replied that civil unions were insufficient because they would relegate gays and lesbians to "second-class citizen status." As of May 17, 2004 (the fiftieth anniversary of *Brown v. Board of Education*), the justices proclaimed, the commonwealth of Massachusetts must begin granting marriage licenses to same-sex couples. Even many gay rights enthusiasts expressed shock that the court had not accepted civil unions as a compromise, as the Vermont court had done four years earlier. Polling conducted around this time showed that 50 percent of gays and lesbians regarded civil unions as essentially the equivalent of marriage.[16]

An opinion poll conducted by the *Boston Globe* six months before *Goodridge* showed Bay Staters supporting gay marriage by 50 percent to 44 percent. A poll conducted just days after the decision found them approving *Goodridge* by 50 percent to 38 percent. Another poll taken a couple of weeks later showed support for *Goodridge* at 59 percent to 37 percent.[17]

Yet, within a couple of months, opinion polls were telling a rather different story. In January, a Zogby poll found that 50 percent of Massachusetts residents believed the court had overstepped its bounds, 52 percent thought that marriage should be between a man and a woman, and 69 percent favored giving voters an opportunity to resolve the issue. Another poll conducted about ten days later revealed that 54 percent of Bay Staters favored a marriage amendment—an increase of 8 percentage points from the previous month. A poll in February showed voters opposing gay marriage by 53 percent to 35 percent, while 71 percent favored allowing the voters to decide. However, 60 percent of respondents supported civil unions for same-sex couples.[18]

In anticipation of the constitutional convention to meet in February, both sides of the gay marriage debate commenced a statewide political campaign. In what one state senator called the "most intense outreach" by the Catholic Church he had ever seen, the four Catholic bishops of Massachusetts sought to mobilize the state's three million Catholics in support of a marriage amendment. Archbishop Sean Patrick O'Malley denounced *Goodridge* as a usurpation of legislative power, and the newspaper of the Boston archdiocese devoted twelve stories to marriage in the week before the convention. The Church's aggressive lobbying campaign apparently had some effect, as polls showed the percentage of Massachusetts Catholics opposed to gay marriage increasing from 47 percent to 66 percent.[19]

In late January, two thousand opponents of gay marriage assembled at three large rallies across the state. The week the convention met, prominent religious leaders—representing African American clergy, the Catholic Church, and Orthodox Jews—issued coordinated statements calling on the convention to defend traditional marriage. Tony Perkins of the Family Research Council came to Massachusetts and told a press conference that gay marriage would open the door to polygamy.[20]

On the other side of the debate, labor unions representing nearly two hundred thousand workers across the state endorsed same-sex marriage. State

Democratic leaders, ignoring deep divisions within party ranks, also resolved to support gay marriage.[21]

The court's advisory opinion rejecting civil unions as inadequate was issued the week before the convention met, thus eliminating the compromise position toward which many legislators had seemed to be gravitating. Opponents of gay marriage, including Romney and Finneran, continued to search for ways to block or at least delay implementation of *Goodridge*, but these efforts began to look increasingly hopeless.[22]

When the convention met on February 11, 2004, four thousand people crammed into the statehouse, with thousands more milling around outside. Seeking to avoid a reprise of the 2002 convention at which gay marriage opponents had packed the galleries, MassEquality turned out hordes of gay marriage supporters, who waved American flags and sang "God Bless America." Many legislators had never before seen gays and lesbians demonstrating for their rights. Their presence in the statehouse enabled lawmakers to better understand how their decisions would impact the lives of their next-door neighbors, not some "bunch of wild eyed, crazy people out in the street protesting."[23]

In turn, the Catholic Church mobilized thousands of gay marriage opponents, including in their ranks abortion foes from Massachusetts Citizens for Life. Besieged by letters and lobbyists, legislators reported that "there has been nothing like this" in all their years on Beacon Hill.[24]

Legislators were initially divided into three main blocs. The largest group favored a constitutional amendment to limit marriage to opposite-sex couples while implicitly authorizing the legislature to establish civil unions by failing to forbid same-sex couples from forming relationships that were the legal equivalent of marriage. A second bloc favored straightforward implementation of *Goodridge*. The third group supported an amendment to ban gay marriage while *mandating* the creation of civil unions. This last option was widely regarded as the most helpful to the presidential candidacy of U.S. senator John Kerry of Massachusetts, because it mirrored his position of opposing gay marriage while supporting civil unions. The Democratic National Convention was scheduled to meet in Boston that summer, and Kerry's many friends in the state legislature wanted to avoid any action that might damage his candidacy.[25]

The compromise amendment—the third option—appeared to be rapidly gaining support among legislators as the state constitutional convention drew near. Yet both gay activists and social conservatives opposed it. Governor Romney endorsed the first option, possibly influenced by his ambitions for a future Republican presidential nomination.[26]

A substantial majority of legislators—as many as 137 of the 199 who participated in the convention—wished to overturn *Goodridge* and constitutionally ban gay marriage. Yet this group could not agree on how to treat civil unions. The first option came the closest to passing, falling just two votes shy of the 101 required to pass the amendment and send it on to the next year's convention for a second vote. The third option—an amendment to bar gay marriage but require the legislature to recognize civil unions—then failed by 104 to 94. Many gay marriage supporters voted for it, fearing that something worse might pass, though they hoped to kill it in the end.[27]

Yet another proposal, which would have defined marriage as the union of a man and a woman and provided that nothing in the amendment either required or prohibited civil unions, was also defeated by 103 to 94. Gay marriage supporters, who were perfectly content with the status quo of *Goodridge*, then filibustered the remainder of this two-day session of the convention.[28]

The defeat of the conservatives' amendment seemed to shift the convention's momentum in the direction of the compromise amendment that would ban gay marriage but require civil unions, even though that amendment, too, had failed to receive majority support. After the convention's first session had adjourned, house Speaker Finneran announced his support for the compromise amendment. For years, Finneran had blocked the house from even considering domestic partnership benefits, but now he endorsed a constitutional mandate of civil unions.[29]

Democratic senate president Robert Travaglini also endorsed the compromise, which generated additional momentum in its favor. Democratic leaders lobbied their caucus to support it. In late March, at a subsequent session of the constitutional convention, it passed by 105 to 92. Critical support came both from liberals who preferred gay marriage but feared not getting even civil unions and from conservatives who wished to bar civil unions but were determined at least to give the people an opportunity to vote on banning gay marriage.[30]

For the compromise amendment to become part of the state constitution, it still had to pass another constitutional convention during the legislature's 2005–6 term and then be endorsed by Massachusetts voters. Gay marriage supporters, who had seen their ranks grow over the course of the convention, were confident that they could block the amendment at the next convention.[31]

Immediately after the convention passed the compromise amendment, Governor Romney vowed to ask the state supreme court to delay implementation of *Goodridge* until after a referendum on the amendment could be held. However, state law required the governor to make such a request through the attorney general, and Tom Reilly, a possible Democratic gubernatorial candidate in 2006, refused to cooperate. An opinion poll conducted around this time showed Bay Staters evenly divided on the compromise amendment.[32]

Cognizant of the backlash that *Baker* had ignited in Vermont in 2000 and aware of Governor Romney's energetic efforts to recruit more Republican candidates for the state legislature in 2004, commentators and politicians predicted possible retaliation at the polls against those legislators who had supported gay marriage at the convention. The Massachusetts Catholic Conference launched its first-ever voter registration drive to oust such lawmakers, and an editorial in the newspaper of the Boston archdiocese warned of "a backlash in November."[33]

A special election in March 2004 was widely viewed as a harbinger of how gay marriage would play out in the fall elections. In the race to succeed state senator Cheryl Jacques, who had resigned to take up a leadership post at the Human Rights Campaign, Republican representative Scott Brown strongly opposed gay marriage and Democrat Angus McQuilken strongly supported it. Governor Romney campaigned aggressively for Brown and raised money for him, hoping to send a message to gay marriage supporters in the legislature. Brown narrowly prevailed.[34]

Gay rights organizations worked hard to prevent political backlash from materializing in the fall elections. MassEquality devoted $700,000 to the campaign and supplied hundreds of volunteers to help legislators who had supported gay marriage. In the September primaries, all seven gay marriage supporters who faced challenges emerged victorious.[35]

Moreover, two Democratic incumbents who had opposed gay marriage lost their primaries to opponents who favored it. In what the *Boston Globe* called a "stunning upset," a sixteen-year incumbent, Vincent Ciampa, who had been a lieutenant to the Speaker of the house and enjoyed the support of his district's political establishment, was narrowly defeated in his primary by a twenty-seven-year-old gay man, Carl Sciortino, who had never before held political office. To be sure, Sciortino did not emphasize gay marriage on the hustings. Yet gay marriage was the issue that galvanized young activists to volunteer for Sciortino, inspired Congressman Barney Frank to co-host an August fund-raiser for him, and secured him the financial support of MassEquality.[36]

Two weeks after the primaries, the marriage amendment suffered another major setback. Marking a "seismic shift on Beacon Hill," Speaker Finneran, a vocal critic of *Goodridge* and prominent supporter of the compromise amendment, announced his resignation from the house. His replacement, Salvatore DiMasi, was a strong supporter of gay marriage.[37]

Senate minority leader Brian Lees, another key supporter of the compromise amendment, now declared that the battle to overturn *Goodridge* was "pretty much over." Several lawmakers who had voted for the compromise amendment in March now stated privately that they might switch their positions. Thousands of gay couples had married since May without causing any significant disruptions, and the controversy over gay marriage had largely faded from public view.[38]

As the general election approached, polls showed that gay marriage was not a pressing issue for most voters, and Governor Romney's staff announced that he would not highlight it in the election campaign despite his continuing strong opposition. By contrast, the Catholic Church continued to press the issue, reminding voters that the next legislature would decide whether the people of Massachusetts would have a say on gay marriage. In a handful of hotly contested legislative races, gay marriage was a defining issue.[39]

In the general election in November, all fifty incumbent legislators who had supported gay marriage at the convention and now faced challengers won their contests. In four open seats, departing lawmakers who had supported gay marriage were replaced with like-minded successors. In another three open seats, legislators who had opposed gay marriage were replaced with supporters. A *Boston Globe* analysis of the election results concluded that supporters of gay marriage had made a net gain of two or three legislative seats.[40]

By March 2005, a poll in the *Boston Globe* showed that 56 percent of respondents supported gay marriage. In three special legislative elections held that spring, legislators who opposed gay marriage were replaced by supporters.[41]

By refuting widespread predictions of political backlash, this series of election results seemed to significantly influence Massachusetts legislators. Several of them now privately stated that they knew of colleagues who would have endorsed *Goodridge* the previous year had they not feared electoral reprisals. In May 2005, the Massachusetts Democratic Party voted overwhelmingly to endorse gay marriage in its platform.[42]

The legislature was next scheduled to meet in constitutional convention in September 2005. In August, Speaker DiMasi, reflecting a growing consensus on Beacon Hill, predicted that the compromise amendment would now be rejected. Not only had some amendment supporters been replaced by opponents and others been publicly quoted as rethinking their positions, but also some conservatives were abandoning the amendment in favor of a separate ballot measure intended for 2008 that would outlaw gay marriage without mandating civil unions.[43]

In September, the convention rejected the compromise amendment by 157 to 39—an extraordinary shift in eighteen months. Even Republican minority leader Lees, who had co-sponsored the amendment in 2004, now voted against it. He explained, "Gay marriage has begun, and life has not changed for the citizens of the Commonwealth, with the exception of those who can marry." Other legislators who switched their votes likewise explained that gay marriage had begun without causing any "earthquakes."[44]

The convention's defeat of the compromise amendment still left open the possibility of a citizens' initiative, which could place an amendment on the ballot in 2008 if it could secure the requisite number of signatures and then win support from 25 percent of the delegates attending constitutional conventions conducted over two successive legislative sessions. (If all two hundred legislators attended a convention, the support of fifty would be required to pass the amendment.) Even after the compromise amendment was overwhelmingly defeated in September 2005, opponents of gay marriage continued to express confidence that at least sixty legislators supported their position.[45]

The Massachusetts Family Institute immediately launched a petition drive and by December had secured twice the required sixty-six thousand signatures. The proposed amendment, supported by Governor Romney and the Catholic Church, would ban same-sex marriage without mentioning civil unions. In order to avoid inviting a challenge under the state constitutional provision barring reversal of court rulings by citizens' initiatives, the proposed amendment left in place the sixty-five hundred gay marriages that had already occurred. An opinion poll conducted in September 2005 suggested that initiative proponents faced an uphill battle even if they could get their proposal onto the ballot: registered voters opposed the measure by 56 percent to 40 percent.[46]

On the final day of the 2006 legislative session, after the state supreme court had ruled that lawmakers had a duty to vote on the citizens' initiative, the amendment secured sixty-two votes in convention, enough to advance it to the next legislative session. But in June 2007, with recently elected governor Deval Patrick and Speaker DiMasi lobbying hard in opposition, amendment supporters could secure only forty-five votes in convention, effectively killing the amendment.[47]

In the five years after *Goodridge*, twelve thousand gay couples married in Massachusetts—4 percent of all the marriages that took place during that period. By 2011, polls showed that Bay Staters supported gay marriage by 60 percent to 30 percent. Indicative of how far opinion in Massachusetts had moved, when Republican Scott Brown in 2010 competed in the special election to fill Ted Kennedy's U.S. Senate seat, he declared that "gay marriage is settled law" and that "people have moved on." By contrast, in 2001 Brown had criticized as "not normal" state legislator Cheryl Jacques's raising children in a lesbian relationship, and in 2004 he had run for the state senate on an anti-gay-marriage platform.[48]

Although *Goodridge* did not generate much political backlash in Massachusetts, it did across the rest of the country. The Massachusetts court's decision received vastly greater media attention than had *Baehr* or *Baker*, and it brought gay marriage to the forefront of political debate in 2004. That year, the number of newspaper articles on gay marriage was ten times what it had been in 2000. By March 2004, two-thirds of respondents in a national survey reported that they were following the issue, and 29 percent said they were following it very closely.[49]

National polls conducted in the months after *Goodridge* showed opponents of gay marriage outnumbering supporters by a margin of roughly two to one. For example, a poll conducted by the Pew Study Center in November 2003 revealed 62 percent opposed to gay marriage and 30 percent in favor. Four other Pew polls taken over the course of 2004 found roughly similar margins of opposition: 65 to 28, 60 to 29, 59 to 32, and 56 to 32.[50]

In the five states that had conducted referenda on gay marriage between 1998 and 2002—Alaska, Hawaii, California, Nebraska, and Nevada (twice)—opposition had ranged from 61 percent to 70 percent. Not a single state likely would have approved gay marriage by referendum in 2004. Not a single state legislature had endorsed gay marriage yet, and only two had enacted civil unions—one of them (Vermont) acting pursuant to court order.[51]

Some evidence suggests that *Goodridge* temporarily halted or even reversed a liberalizing trend in favor of gay marriage; support did not rebound to previous levels until the summer of 2005. For example, Pew Study Center polling found the following trend in public opinion on gay marriage: In January 2000, opponents outnumbered supporters by 18 percentage points and in July 2003 by 15 percentage points. *Goodridge* was decided in November 2003. In August 2004, opponents of gay marriage outnumbered supporters by 31 percentage points and in December 2004 by 29 percentage points.[52]

Indeed, *Goodridge* may have caused a temporary resurgence in anti-gay sentiment generally. Positive responses to the question whether homosexuality was "morally acceptable" fell by 6 percentage points in the months after the decision.[53]

Not only did most Americans reject gay marriage in 2003–4, but those who opposed it generally felt more passionate than did those who supported it. A survey by the Pew Study Center in November 2003 found that of the 30 percent of Americans who supported gay marriage, only one-third strongly favored it, while of the 62 percent who opposed it, two-thirds felt strongly.

Given such strong opposition to gay marriage across the nation, *Goodridge* was bound to ignite a backlash if voters in other states considered a Massachusetts court decision relevant to their lives, either practically or symbolically. Although the federal Defense of Marriage Act purported to free states from any obligation to respect other state's gay marriages under the Full Faith and Credit Clause, the constitutionality of that statute remained uncertain. Critics of *Goodridge* were quick to warn that "activist judges" in other states were just "waiting for their chance to be creative, too," and invalidate the federal statute and its state counterparts. Tony Perkins, president of the Family Research Council, warned, "If same-sex couples 'marry' in Massachusetts and move to other states, the Defense of Marriage Act will be left vulnerable to the same federal courts that have banned the Pledge of Allegiance and sanctioned partial-birth abortion."[54]

Religious conservatives vehemently denounced *Goodridge*. James Dobson wrote that the fight against gay marriage would be "our D-day, or Gettysburg or Stalingrad." Within a week of the decision, representatives of several conservative organizations met in Washington, D.C., to plan a national strategy to counter it, including demands for a federal marriage amendment. The president of Concerned Women for America, Sandy Rios, declared that her group would use the amendment "as a litmus test for offices from president to street sweeper," and she warned that religious conservatives would withhold their votes from President Bush in 2004 if he did not back the federal marriage amendment. The Traditional Values Coalition began sending 1.5 million mailings a month to prospective voters to rally support for the amendment.[55]

On a state visit to London when *Goodridge* was decided, President Bush immediately announced that he would work with Congress to defend traditional marriage. Many Republican lawmakers called for passage of the federal marriage amendment, which had been introduced in Congress that spring. The press reported that White House aides were divided over whether the president should try to exploit gay marriage as a wedge issue. In his State of the Union address on January 20, 2004, Bush warned that a federal marriage amendment would be "the only alternative left" if "activist judges," who "have begun redefining marriage by court order," persisted in their efforts.[56]

On February 12, the recently elected mayor of San Francisco, Gavin Newsom, claiming to be upset about the president's efforts to divide the nation over gay marriage, instructed city officials to begin issuing marriage licenses to same-sex couples. Newsom's action was largely symbolic, as experts were certain that the state would not recognize such licenses. His action was also very popular in a city where public support for gay marriage ran strong.[57]

Some gay activists were enthusiastic about opening a "western front" on gay marriage, while others feared the possibility of inciting a political backlash. Congressman Barney Frank telephoned Newsom to urge him to stop the marriages.[58]

Conservatives were aghast. Matthew Staver, president of the Liberty Counsel, denounced Newsom for "essentially setting himself up as king." Declaring that California law was clear and same-sex marriage was not permitted, California governor Arnold Schwarzenegger ordered the state attorney general to intervene to stop the same-sex weddings in San Francisco. Facing pressure from conservatives to take more forceful action, Schwarzenegger then went on *Meet the Press*, warned of serious civil unrest if the gay marriages continued, and predicted that people might die.[59]

Within ten days of Newsom's order, three thousand same-sex couples, including many from all around the country and overseas, had married in San Francisco. Newsom himself presided over the weddings of his gay chief of staff and his lesbian policy director.[60]

One participant in a same-sex wedding called his marriage ceremony "one of the highlights of my life" and predicted that even gay marriage doubters would get caught up in the emotion and joy of such occasions. One person who witnessed same-sex couples lining up in nasty weather with fussing children to become the first in the country to marry called the experience "just amazing." Supporters from across the nation used the Internet to send the newlyweds "flowers from the heartland." Accompanying notes carried greetings such as "To a happy couple, with love from Minneapolis."[61]

Conservative groups immediately filed lawsuits to stop the city from issuing marriage licenses to same-sex couples, but trial judges refused to hastily grant temporary restraining orders. By the time the California supreme court on March 11 ordered the city to cease and desist, more than four thousand same-sex couples had received marriage licenses. (In August, the California high court voided these licenses.) San Francisco's gay marriages attracted enormous attention from the national media and "put the first public face on married lesbian and gay couples."[62]

Same-sex marriage quickly spread to other parts of the country. In Sandoval County, New Mexico, county clerk Victoria Dunlap began issuing marriage licenses to same-sex couples on February 20. Her motives were unclear. Unlike Mayor Newsom in San Francisco, she had not consulted with gay rights leaders, who were unhappy with her action. Critics later noted that Dunlap had a history of friction with the county commissioners and that "when she gets bored, she has a media event." Her own explanation was very different: "There's nothing in the law that I can find that would prohibit issuing same-sex marriage licenses." Unable to quickly secure guidance from the county attorney, Dunlap recounted, she simply chose to err on the side of not infringing upon anyone's rights.[63]

As news spread on the radio that Sandoval County was issuing same-sex marriage licenses, gay and lesbian couples, some of whom had previously entertained no thoughts of marriage, began rushing to the county courthouse. Sixty-six gay couples received marriage licenses before 4:00 p.m., when county officials ordered a halt, stranding more than a hundred people still in line. During the day, two preachers performed impromptu wedding ceremonies outside the courthouse.[64]

Dunlap, a Republican, was quickly denounced by state party leaders, who called on the governor to convene a special legislative session to consider a constitutional amendment to ban gay marriage. An opinion poll showed that New Mexicans opposed same-sex marriage by 61 percent to 29 percent. The county attorney and the state attorney general quickly filed for a temporary restraining order against Dunlap, which was immediately granted.[65]

Dunlap complied with the order, though over the next few weeks she periodically threatened to resume the process, which raised the hopes of gay couples, who lined up outside the courthouse hoping to receive marriage licenses. The Sandoval County Republican central committee formally censured Dunlap for "bringing disgrace to the party as a whole." That spring Dunlap chose not to run

Sandoval County clerk Victoria Dunlap, June 14, 2004. (*Associated Press/Susan Montoya Bryan*)

for reelection as county clerk, deciding instead to run for a seat on the county commission; she lost her primary election by 75 percent to 25 percent.[66]

In Oregon, the leading gay rights organization, Basic Rights Oregon, began strategizing about gay marriage soon after *Goodridge*. The group concluded that the most direct path to marriage equality in Oregon was for gay couples to start getting married, regardless of any political backlash this might produce. National gay rights organizations supported that decision, deeming Multnomah County, which includes Portland, a fertile environment in which to pursue the experiment.[67]

Facing increased pressure from gay marriage supporters after San Francisco began marrying thousands of gay couples, the Multnomah County Commission on March 3 followed suit. The process by which the new policy was adopted, however, outraged opponents. Concerned that a court might shut down gay marriage before it got started, the four county commissioners who supported it conspired to exclude from meetings at which the issue was discussed the fifth commissioner, who was known to be a strong opponent.[68]

In the seven weeks following March 3, more than three thousand gay couples married in Multnomah. Counties containing the University of Oregon and Oregon State University also felt pressure to marry gay couples, though the governor managed to dissuade them from doing so.[69]

In the small village of New Paltz, New York, twenty-six-year-old mayor Jason West, elected the previous year as the Green Party candidate, had asked the village attorney soon after his election whether New York mayors had the power to preside over same-sex marriages. New York law was ambiguous, the attorney had replied, and the mayor was free to follow his own judgment. West then concluded that New York law clearly did not forbid gay marriage, and he planned to conduct one by the summer of 2004.[70]

Pressured by developments across the country and concerned that a court might preempt his action, in February 2004 West asked the town clerk to begin issuing marriage licenses to same-sex couples. She refused on the ground that she had received contrary orders from the state department of health. Proclaiming himself willing to go to jail, on February 27 Mayor West began officiating at weddings of same-sex couples, even though no marriage licenses had been issued. On the first day, he presided over twenty-one same-sex marriages. Crowds of several hundred people celebrated the weddings. Within a few days, the list of same-sex couples from around the country that had signed up to marry in New Paltz had grown to four hundred.[71]

Republican governor George Pataki quickly asked the state attorney general to halt the New Paltz weddings. But Democratic attorney general Eliot Spitzer, at that point a likely gubernatorial candidate in 2006, refused to seek an injunction. Less than a week later, the local district attorney charged Mayor West with multiple counts of solemnizing marriages without a license. (These charges were dropped in July.)[72]

New Paltz mayor Jason West preparing to marry a gay couple, Feb. 27, 2004. (*Associated Press/Jim McKnight*)

For two years, gay rights groups had unsuccessfully sought a ruling from Spitzer on whether state law permitted gay marriage. Now, within days, Spitzer issued an opinion declaring that New York law did not allow such marriages and thus the New Paltz "marriages" were void. Yet he also opined that New York law would recognize gay marriages that had been lawfully performed in other jurisdictions—making New York the first state to do so. With Mayor West barred by court order from performing more gay marriages, a couple of ministers stepped in, defying threats of prosecution.[73]

On March 8, 2004, the city clerk of Asbury Park, New Jersey, issued marriage licenses to seven same-sex couples after concluding that state law did not forbid such marriages and that the state and federal constitutions required that they be permitted. The city's deputy mayor then presided over these couples' weddings. After a threat of criminal prosecution by the state attorney general, the Asbury Park city council quickly voted to end the issuance of marriage licenses to same-sex couples. Altogether, more than seven thousand gay marriages took place in California, New Mexico, Oregon, New York, and New Jersey between February and April 2004.[74]

Then, on May 17, 2004, Massachusetts began marrying same-sex couples in pursuance of *Goodridge*. Unlike the gay marriages performed elsewhere, the Massachusetts ones were unquestionably lawful. In Cambridge, Massachusetts, officials opened city offices at one minute past midnight so their city could be the first in the state to issue gay marriage licenses. Two hundred and fifty couples were waiting in line, along with a crowd of ten thousand to cheer them on. About six thousand gay marriages took place in Massachusetts over the following year.[75]

The same-sex marriages performed in San Francisco prompted President Bush to finally endorse a federal constitutional amendment limiting marriage to opposite-sex couples, which for months he had been resisting pressure from conservatives to do. The president explained: "After more than two centuries of American jurisprudence, and millennia of human experience, a few judges and local authorities are presuming to change the most fundamental institution of civilization." With regard to legal arrangements other than marriage, such as civil unions, Bush declared that state legislatures should be free to "make their own choices."[76]

Some of Bush's political advisors believed that he had lost the popular vote in the 2000 presidential election because millions of evangelical Christians had chosen to stay home. Endorsing the federal marriage amendment could be seen as part of a strategy to ensure that this did not happen again. Supporting the amendment seemed to carry little political risk at a time when polls showed that 59 percent of Americans favored it. Forty-one percent of respondents called same-sex marriage an important issue in the 2004 election, and 24 percent said

Julie and Hillary Goodridge receiving their marriage license, Boston, May 17, 2004. (*Associated Press/Charles Krupa*)

they would vote only for candidates who shared their view on that subject. A national survey conducted that spring suggested that gay marriage was a more potent issue for voters than either abortion or gun control.[77]

The issue was a boon for Republicans. Americans rejected gay marriage by a margin of two to one in 2004. Religious conservatives are a vital constituency within the Republican Party. For example, between 70 percent and 80 percent of self-identified evangelical Protestants have voted Republican in recent presidential elections. In 2004, religious conservatives were both overwhelmingly opposed to gay marriage and highly motivated to make it a major issue in that year's election campaigns. One official of the Southern Baptist Convention declared, "I have never seen anything that has energized and provoked our grass roots like this issue [same-sex marriage], including *Roe v. Wade*."[78]

Moreover, unlike on many other issues about which religious conservatives felt strongly—opposition to no-fault divorce, the teaching of evolution in public schools, human embryo research, and abortion—a clear majority of Americans agreed with them on gay marriage. On other gay rights issues, such as partnership benefits, hate crimes legislation, and anti-discrimination laws, this was no longer the case.[79]

For Democrats, by contrast, gay marriage was a vexing issue. Approximately 70 percent of self-identified gays vote Democratic, which helps explain why most Democratic politicians generally support gay rights. Yet some traditionally Democratic-leaning constituencies, such as the elderly, working-class Catholics, and African Americans, tend to strongly oppose gay marriage. Thus the issue was a perfect wedge with which Republicans could pry apart the Democratic coalition.[80]

In 2004, most Democratic politicians adopted a nuanced position on gay marriage: they supported conferring all or many of the legal benefits of marriage on same-sex couples, opposed gay marriage itself, but also opposed a federal marriage amendment—usually on states' rights grounds that are not commonly associated with the Democratic Party. For most voters who opposed gay marriage, the Democrats' position was harder to understand and support than the Republicans' much simpler condemnation of it.[81]

In 2004, Republicans controlled both houses of Congress. The party's platform endorsed the federal marriage amendment, and Republican leaders were determined to force Democrats in Congress to vote on it, even though the amendment stood no chance of securing the two-thirds majority in each house of Congress that is required before amendments can be transmitted to the states for ratification.[82]

The marriage amendment reached the floor of the Senate in July. Senator Wayne Allard of Colorado, the main sponsor of the amendment, declared, "There is a master plan out there from those who want to destroy the institution of marriage." Senator Rick Santorum asked, "Isn't that the ultimate homeland security, standing up and defending marriage?" Democratic senators accused Republicans of playing politics by forcing a roll call vote that they knew they would lose.[83]

In the end, only forty-eight senators voted to cloture the Democrats' filibuster against the amendment—far short of the sixty votes required to end debate and the sixty-seven votes required to approve the amendment. In September, House Republicans similarly forced a vote on the marriage amendment. The tally was 227 to 186 in favor—again far short of the two-thirds majority required for passage. Republican representatives voted seven to one in favor, while Democrats voted four to one against.[84]

Meanwhile, more legally efficacious action against gay marriage was taking place in the states. Before *Goodridge*, only three states—Alaska, Nebraska, and Nevada—had adopted constitutional amendments barring gay marriage. Within five years of the Massachusetts court's decision, more than twenty-five additional states had enacted such measures.

Republicans had strong incentives to put marriage referenda on the ballot, especially in states that were considered potentially pivotal in the 2004 presidential election. One poll conducted late in 2003 found that respondents favored Bush over the (as yet undetermined) Democratic nominee for president by 46 percent to 42 percent before being informed of their respective positions on gay marriage and civil unions, but they preferred Bush by 51 percent to 35 percent after being so informed. Gay marriage referenda would inspire religious conservatives to vote, make gay marriage more salient in voter choices between political candidates, and put Democrat politicians on the defensive. As one gay activist observed about the state marriage referenda, "This is about politics. Maybe we can't draw a direct line linking this to Karl Rove, but we can connect the dots."[85]

In 2004 alone, thirteen states passed referenda barring same-sex marriage—a "resounding, coast-to-coast rejection of gay marriage," as one newspaper put it. In total, opponents of gay marriage spent approximately $6.8 million and supporters $6.6 million.[86]

Amendment backers insisted that *Goodridge* had forced their hand: statutory bans on gay marriage, which thirty-nine states had enacted by 2004, were no longer sufficient. One sponsor of Missouri's amendment explained, "As we've seen happen in Massachusetts, if the will of the people is not clearly spelled out in the constitution, then all it takes is a few activist, renegade judges to circumvent [it]." Rather than defending gay marriage on the merits, amendment opponents tended to object only to the principle of writing discrimination into constitutions.[87]

The first gay marriage referendum in 2004 took place in Missouri in early August. Amid heavy voter turnout, more than 70 percent of Missouri voters supported the amendment, despite a campaign in which opponents vastly outspent proponents. The vice president of Focus on the Family rightly predicted that Missouri would be "the first of many dominos to fall." In Mississippi, the marriage amendment won 86 percent of the vote. Even states with relatively progressive records on gay rights, such as Michigan, Ohio, and Oregon, passed marriage amendments by handy margins. In only two states did the amendments secure less than 60 percent of the vote.[88]

Ohio's referendum may have been the most consequential because the state proved critical to the outcome of the presidential election in 2004. Early that year, in response to *Goodridge*, the Ohio legislature rushed through a defense-of-marriage statute. Yet when the legislature declined to approve a constitutional amendment to ban gay marriage, a group called Citizens for Community Values collected signatures to put such an amendment on the fall ballot.[89]

The leading force behind this measure was Phil Burress, an anti-pornography activist in Cincinnati since the early 1990s. After the Hawaii supreme court decision in *Baehr* in 1993, Burress had expanded his targets to include gay marriage, founding the Ohio Campaign to Protect Marriage, which became a state affiliate of Focus on the Family and the Family Research Council.[90]

In gathering petition signatures to place the marriage amendment on the ballot, Burress's group reached out to religious organizations, including a large mosque in Cincinnati and black churches throughout the state. Ministers made announcements from their pulpits reminding parishioners to sign petitions after services concluded. The twelve Catholic bishops of Ohio jointly issued a public statement supporting the amendment. In less than ninety days, the Ohio Campaign to Protect Marriage gathered 550,000 signatures—only 323,000 were required to qualify the amendment for the fall ballot—and it registered 54,000 new voters in the process.[91]

During the fall election campaign, referendum supporters again focused on churches, urging pastors to discuss the issue with their congregations and sending two and a half million bulletin inserts to seventeen thousand churches. Amendment backers denied that their motivation was to help President Bush carry Ohio, though they admitted the measure was likely to do so by energizing socially conservative voters. The two sides together spent nearly $1.5 million on the amendment campaign.[92]

Ohio's amendment would prohibit not only gay marriage but also any legal status "that intends to approximate the design, qualities, significance or effect of marriage." That language would have pretty clearly barred government agencies and public universities from offering domestic partnership benefits to same-sex couples. Amendment opponents further alleged—though supporters denied— that the measure would bar private companies involved in contracting with the state from providing such benefits and thus possibly would deter corporate relocations to Ohio.[93]

Amendment opponents barely mentioned the word "gay" in their advertisements. The chairperson of the coalition opposing the amendment declared, "It's not a gay issue." Several leading Republican politicians in the state, including Governor Robert Taft and both of Ohio's U.S. senators, insisted that the amendment was overly broad, potentially harmful to the state's economy, and unnecessary in light of the state's recently enacted defense-of-marriage law. Still, it passed easily, by 62 percent to 38 percent.[94]

The most heavily contested and lavishly funded contest over gay marriage in 2004 took place in Oregon. The day after the Multnomah County Commission in March voted to issue marriage licenses to same-sex couples, a group called the Defense of Marriage Coalition launched a petition drive for a voter initiative to amend the state constitution. Gay marriage supporters doubted that the 130,000 signatures required could be gathered in the five and a half weeks that remained before the ballot deadline.[95]

Yet even without paying signature gatherers, the Defense of Marriage Coalition collected 240,000 signatures. One opponent of gay marriage reported that in twenty-five years in Oregon politics, he had never seen anything like this response. Sixty-five thousand signatures came directly from churches, many of which evinced far greater enthusiasm in opposing gay marriage than they had in recent campaigns against pornography and abortion. One church played a DVD produced by the Defense of Marriage Coalition at its services and registered 375 new voters while collecting petition signatures. Other churches donated money and put up lawn signs.[96]

One advertisement run by amendment supporters featured a deputy superintendent of public instruction discussing how gay marriage would lead to teaching about homosexuality in kindergarten. This ad capitalized on the fear of many parents who might have been willing to accept their children as gay if they turned out to be so but nonetheless preferred that they be straight and thus opposed schools' possibly influencing the children's choice by treating homosexuality as acceptable. Amendment backers also emphasized that if Oregon adopted gay marriage, Catholic schools would be forced to admit the children of gay couples. Learning from previous defeats in Oregon referenda, amendment supporters tried to avoid overtly homophobic messages.[97]

Although polls in other states showed that marriage amendments were likely to run the table, polls in Oregon indicated a dead heat. Oregon had defeated anti-gay-rights referenda in 1992, 1994, and 2000. Deeming Oregon their best chance at a victory, national gay rights organizations devoted hundreds of thousands of dollars to defeating the marriage amendment there. The Oregon campaign was by far the most expensive in the country in 2004: gay marriage supporters outspent their opponents by $2.8 million to $2.2 million. They lost anyway, by 57 percent to 43 percent.[98]

None of the thirteen states that enacted constitutional amendments barring gay marriage in 2004 actually permitted same-sex couples to marry at the time, so the referenda deprived nobody of marriage rights that already existed. However, these amendments did make it harder for those states to adopt gay marriage in the future, as legislatures would be powerless to act by statute. Either the state constitutions would have to be amended again or else courts would have to invalidate the state constitutional bans under the federal constitution.[99]

Moreover, nine of the thirteen state marriage amendments adopted in 2004 contained language broad enough to be interpreted to forbid civil unions and even domestic partnership benefits for gay couples. In some of these states, domestic partnership benefits were already available to at least some gay and lesbian public employees. After the marriage amendments were enacted, those benefits had to cease. In Ohio, judges went so far as to interpret the marriage amendment to forbid enforcement of domestic violence laws in the case of unmarried couples.[100]

Same-sex marriage also became an issue in many congressional races in 2004. Most Republican candidates expressed opposition to gay marriage and support for the federal marriage amendment. Most Democrats expressed support for civil unions and opposition to gay marriage but also opposition to the federal amendment. Republicans questioned the commitment of Democrats to traditional marriage in light of their opposition to the federal amendment and frequently ran advertisements accusing Democrats of supporting gay marriage.[101]

This pattern repeated itself in several U.S. Senate races in 2004: in Illinois, where Barack Obama faced off against Alan Keyes; in Washington, where Patty Murray ran against George Nethercutt; in Wisconsin, where Russ Feingold was challenged by Tim Michels; and in Nevada, where Harry Reid faced challenger Richard Zeiser. Democrats won each of these contests, so the gay marriage issue was, at most, a minor nuisance to them.[102]

In other Senate races, however, the issue loomed larger and almost certainly cost Democratic candidates votes. In two states, it probably cost them the election.[103]

In Arkansas, polls showed that voters overwhelmingly favored incumbent U.S. Democratic senator Blanche Lincoln over her challenger, Republican state senator Jim Holt. Yet Arkansans also strongly supported the federal marriage amendment. Holt declared the amendment the "overwhelmingly large" issue in the Senate race. Lincoln sought to focus the election on other issues while defending her vote against the federal marriage amendment on federalism grounds. She insisted that she supported the state marriage amendment that was on the ballot that fall.[104]

Holt called it "mind boggling" that Lincoln would defend traditional marriage based on her Christian values while voting against the federal amendment. Despite spending only about $100,000 to Lincoln's $6 million, Holt won 44 percent of the vote—a surprisingly strong showing that some experts attributed to the gay marriage issue. The same day that they reelected Lincoln, Arkansans approved a state constitutional ban on gay marriage by 74 percent to 26 percent.[105]

In Oklahoma, Republican Tom Coburn and Democrat Brad Carson competed for the Senate seat being vacated by Republican Don Nickles. James Dobson, founder of Focus on the Family, came to Oklahoma to campaign for Coburn and to attack Carson for his position on gay marriage, even though Carson had voted for the federal marriage amendment in Congress. Dobson warned that homosexuals "want to destroy the institution of marriage" and observed that in Norway, which permitted gay marriage, 80 percent of children were born out of wedlock.[106]

A Washington-based group headed by Gary Bauer ran an advertisement that, distorting a year-old story from the *Washington Blade*, suggested that Carson supported gay marriage and that gays had been instructed to keep his support secret to enhance his political prospects in Oklahoma. Coburn won the election handily. His margin of victory was likely enhanced by the gay marriage ban on the ballot, which mobilized conservatives to turn out and passed by 76 percent to 24 percent.[107]

In the U.S. Senate race in Kentucky, the gay marriage issue probably proved decisive. Incumbent Republican senator Jim Bunning was running for reelection against an underfunded, relatively unknown opponent, Dr. Daniel Mongiardo. A series of missteps during the campaign, however, rendered Bunning suddenly vulnerable. In February, he startled civic leaders in Louisville by stating that a new bridge that had been promised to the city would be delayed indefinitely because northern Kentucky, where Bunning lived, needed a new bridge to Cincinnati. Bunning subsequently denied making the remarks, which, unfortunately for him, had been tape-recorded.[108]

In March, Bunning declared that Mongiardo, the olive-skinned son of Italian immigrants, resembled the recently killed sons of former Iraqi dictator Saddam Hussein. Mongiardo demanded an apology, but Bunning's campaign denied that the senator had made the remarks. After eyewitnesses publicly confirmed that he had made them, Bunning's lieutenants insisted that he had been joking. As some critics began questioning the seventy-two-year-old Bunning's judgment and even his mental soundness, campaign aides steered him away from public speeches.

Kentucky had a marriage amendment on the ballot that fall, and Bunning began attacking gay marriage to rescue his floundering campaign. Mongiardo had co-sponsored that amendment in the state legislature, but he opposed the federal marriage amendment. With the contest unexpectedly tight in its final weeks, state Republican leaders campaigning with Bunning called Mongiardo, a forty-four-year-old bachelor, "limp-wristed" and a "switch hitter." Republican state senator Elizabeth Tori declared that Mongiardo "is not a gentleman. I'm not even sure the word 'man' applies to him."[109]

Bunning refused to apologize for statements made by Republicans who were not on his staff. Reporters began asking Mongiardo if he was gay. (He firmly denied that he was.) Just before Election Day, Republicans ran commercials that featured the sound of wedding bells and hinted that Mongiardo was weak on the gay marriage issue.[110]

In November, Bunning defeated Mongiardo by 50.7 percent to 49.3 percent. The state marriage amendment passed by 75 percent to 25 percent. Some analysts attributed Bunning's victory to a large turnout of rural conservatives who had been mobilized to vote against gay marriage. Because President Bush enjoyed a commanding lead in Kentucky opinion polls, many conservatives might have stayed home were it not for the marriage amendment.[111]

In the U.S. Senate race in South Dakota, Republican John Thune, an evangelical Christian, challenged Democratic Senate minority leader Tom Daschle. Blaming "runaway" courts for making gay marriage a political issue, Thune turned it into the centerpiece of his campaign. He crisscrossed the state, warning that "the institution of marriage is under attack from extremist groups. They have done it in Massachusetts and they can do it here." Prominent religious conservatives James Dobson, Tony Perkins, and Gary Bauer came to Sioux Falls and told a crowd of five thousand that if the institution of marriage was not defended from homosexual attack, "it's going to be gone."[112]

Like most Democratic candidates for national office in 2004, Daschle opposed both gay marriage and the federal marriage amendment. Thune and Republican governor Mike Rounds pressed Daschle to explain why he opposed a constitutional amendment that most South Dakotans supported. The director of the state branch of Concerned Women for America warned that Daschle "has promised the homosexual lobby that he would ensure the defeat of the federal marriage amendment." After Daschle blocked a Senate vote on the amendment, Focus on the Family Action ran a full-page advertisement in South Dakota newspapers, proclaiming, "Shame on You, Senator Daschle."[113]

In the November balloting, Thune defeated Daschle by 51 percent to 49 percent; it was the first defeat of a Senate party leader in more than fifty years. Across the border in North Dakota, a state marriage amendment passed by 73 percent to 27 percent. The gay marriage issue likely mobilized enough religious conservatives and/or influenced enough swing voters to cost Daschle reelection.[114]

Gay marriage also played a role in the 2004 presidential election. Among competitors for the Democratic presidential nomination, only those with the slimmest chances of success—Al Sharpton, Carol Moseley-Braun, and Dennis Kucinich—endorsed same-sex marriage. Front-runners Howard Dean, John Kerry, and John Edwards supported civil unions and opposed gay marriage. Yet they were also reluctant to criticize *Goodridge*, a decision warmly embraced by the liberal base of their party, and they condemned the federal marriage amendment. In 1996, Kerry had been the only senator running for reelection that year to vote against the Defense of Marriage Act. Yet in 2004, he reiterated his opposition to gay marriage and, when pushed, indicated that he would support a state constitutional amendment to ban it in Massachusetts.[115]

During the general election campaign, President Bush regularly called for passage of the federal marriage amendment and repeatedly reminded voters that Kerry hailed from Massachusetts, where *Goodridge* had been decided. Bush warned, "Activist judges and local officials in some parts of the country are not letting up in their efforts to redefine marriage for the rest of America." In the summer of 2004, political analysts reported that the president's campaign strategists had "hit on the issue they think may save them in the 2 November election: same-sex marriage."[116]

The most salient issues in the 2004 presidential campaign were the war in Iraq, terrorism, and the economy, and such issues undoubtedly influenced the candidate preferences of most swing voters. Yet the outcome of the election quite possibly turned on gay marriage.[117]

Many pundits had predicted that the election would come down to Ohio, and it did. Had President Bush not received Ohio's electoral votes, he would not have won a second term. His margin of victory in Ohio was about 119,000 votes, just over 2 percent of the total vote. The gay marriage ban on the Ohio ballot passed by 62 percent to 38 percent. If the marriage amendment mobilized enough conservatives who otherwise might have stayed home to turn out or if it induced enough swing voters who opposed gay marriage to vote for Bush, then it may have determined the outcome of the presidential election. (Gay marriage may also have enabled Bush to win Iowa and New Mexico, both of which he won by well under 1 percent of the vote, but he would have been reelected president even without the electoral votes of either state.)[118]

Among four key groups of voters, Bush's increased share of the popular vote in 2004 over what it had been in 2000 was higher in Ohio than it was among those same groups nationally. Each of those groups disproportionately opposes gay marriage, which was an especially salient issue in Ohio in 2004.

Among voters over sixty years old, Bush's share of the vote in Ohio in 2004 increased by 10 percentage points from what it had been in 2000; among such voters at the national level, his share increased by 7 percentage points. Among voters with only a high school education, Bush's share of the vote increased by 12 percentage points in Ohio, as compared with 10 percentage points nationally. Among frequent church-goers, which is the group most likely to oppose gay marriage, the increase in Bush's share of the popular vote was 17 percentage points in Ohio, as compared with just 1 percentage point nationally. Many commentators remarked upon the extraordinary mobilization of evangelical Christians in Ohio in 2004.[119]

Blacks turned out in record numbers in Ohio in 2004—partly in response to the widespread perception among African Americans that many black votes had not been counted in the contested 2000 presidential election in Florida. In 2004, Republicans quietly targeted black churches across Ohio, with a heavy emphasis on the gay marriage issue. For example, in Columbus, the Ohio Campaign to Protect Marriage contacted 70 percent of the city's black pastors during the election campaign.[120]

Bush's share of the black vote in Ohio increased from 9 percent in 2000 to 16 percent in 2004—an increase of 7 percentage points. By contrast, at the national level, Bush's share of the black vote increased by only 2 percentage points in 2004. Had John Kerry won the same share of the black vote in Ohio that Al Gore had won in 2000, the state would have been a virtual dead heat.[121]

The marriage amendment may also have spurred Republican voter turnout in the rural, socially conservative western and southern portions of Ohio, thus offsetting the unusually high Democratic turnout in cities such as Cleveland and Columbus. During the campaign, Ohio secretary of state Ken Blackwell taped a message urging support of the amendment that was played in over three million telephone calls.[122]

On the Sunday before Election Day, the Ohio Campaign to Protect Marriage distributed 2.5 million church bulletin inserts supporting the amendment. On the final weekend of the campaign, Bush volunteers in southern Ohio distributed fliers asking "Who shares your values?" and quoting the president's promise to defend the sanctity of marriage from activist judges. The referendum banning gay marriage polled better in southern Appalachian counties than in any other part of the state. In one such county, voters approved the ban on gay marriage by 10,590 to 2,658. Bush's vote totals and margins of victory in 2004 soared in the southern and western parts of Ohio over what they had been in 2000.[123]

Scholars have reached mixed conclusions on whether gay marriage was a contributing factor to Bush's narrow victory in Ohio. At the very least, a plausible case can be made that a Massachusetts court decision on gay marriage influenced the outcome of a presidential election.[124]

Most gay activists were despondent on the morning of November 3, 2004. Not only had President Bush been reelected, but the eleven states conducting referenda on gay marriage the previous day had unanimously rejected it—mostly by overwhelming margins. One commentator called this "as resounding a defeat as any social group is likely to experience in American politics."[125]

Gay activists hurriedly convened to discuss future strategy and tactics. Even strong supporters of gay marriage conceded that perhaps they had pressed the issue too far and too fast. An openly gay officeholder in California questioned "the strategic wisdom of pushing forward an issue that draws vehement opposition from nearly two-thirds of voters." Matt Foreman, the executive director of the NGLTF, declared, "Our legal strategy is at least 10 years ahead of our political and legislative strategy." The nation's largest gay rights organization, the Human Rights Campaign, accepted the resignation of its executive director, Cheryl Jacques, and announced a more measured political strategy with a diminished focus on gay marriage.[126]

In politics, perception can be as important as reality. Whether or not gay marriage had been decisive in Bush's reelection—and nobody can possibly know for sure—many people believed that to have been the case. Republicans were thus certain to press again for enactment of the federal marriage amendment, and as many as fifteen additional states were poised to consider their own bans on gay marriage. Once those measures had been adopted, perhaps initiatives against gay adoption and foster parenting would follow.[127]

One commentator concluded that "we are likely witnessing the beginning of what may be a long period of defeat for gay and lesbian causes." Another observed, "The short term reality is that the American political landscape, especially at the national level, will be dominated by conservative ideologues who have little patience for challenges to heteronormativity such as same-sex marriage."[128]

Two weeks after the election, the president's chief political strategist, Karl Rove, said on Fox News that President Bush would "absolutely" push for a federal marriage amendment in his second term because without it "we are at the mercy of activist federal judges." A few weeks later, the Bush administration, evidently rewarding religious conservatives for their electoral contributions, announced that it would be renominating ten of the most controversial federal judicial candidates from Bush's first term, whose confirmation Democratic senators had blocked through filibusters. Alluding to Senator Daschle's fate in South Dakota, James Dobson threatened to put "in the bull's eye" six Democratic senators from red states who faced reelection in 2006 if they continued to block Bush's conservative judicial nominees.[129]

In 2005–6, President Bush appointed John Roberts and Samuel Alito to the U.S. Supreme Court. Both are staunch conservatives who are exceedingly unlikely to interpret the Constitution to protect gay marriage. Thus, the political backlash ignited by *Goodridge* possibly helped to reelect a president whose judicial appointments may delay the legal recognition of same-sex marriage.[130]

Still, despite the backlash against gay marriage, the country had continued to become more progressive on gay rights issues generally. In 2004, Cincinnati residents voted to repeal the anti-gay-rights amendment they had added to their city charter eleven years earlier. Voters in North Carolina and Idaho elected their first openly gay state legislators, and in Dallas, Texas, they elected an open lesbian as sheriff.[131]

The number of Americans who supported allowing gays and lesbians to serve openly in the military increased from 56 percent in 1992 to 81 percent in 2004. The number who favored expanding anti-discrimination laws to cover sexual orientation rose from 48 percent in 1988 to 75 percent in 2004. In 1992, only 27 percent of Americans thought that gay couples should be permitted to adopt children; that number had increased to 50 percent by 2004. The number of Americans who supported granting same-sex couples the legal rights and benefits of marriage increased from 23 percent in 1989 to 56 percent in 2004.[132]

Civil unions for same-sex couples had generated formidable political backlash in Vermont in 2000. Yet, late in the 2004 presidential campaign, President Bush clarified that "I don't think we should deny people rights to a civil union, a legal arrangement, if that's what a state chooses to do." Also in 2004, even though conservative religious organizations such as Focus on the Family and the Family Research Council wanted to forbid civil unions as well as gay marriage, Republicans omitted a bar on civil unions from the federal marriage amendment they sponsored in order to make it more politically palatable.[133]

In 2004–5, several state legislatures took actions that reflected the shift in public opinion in favor of legal recognition of same-sex relationships. Maine adopted domestic partnership legislation that extended rights such as medical decision making and funeral arrangements to same-sex couples. The Maryland legislature passed a similar measure, but the Republican governor vetoed it. Connecticut became the third state—after Vermont and California—to adopt civil unions. The Oregon senate, though not the house, passed a similar bill. Moreover, the trend in public opinion toward greater support for gay marriage seemed likely to continue, as polls showed that roughly 60 percent of respondents age eighteen to twenty-nine already supported it.[134]

Despite such long-term trends, religious conservatives and Republicans stood to benefit in the short term by keeping public attention focused on gay marriage. State legislatures continued to vote by lopsided margins to put marriage amendments on the ballot, and voters continued to pass them handily. In 2005, two more states enacted marriage amendments, and in 2006, eight more states did so. In 2006, Wisconsin passed such a measure by a margin of 19 percentage points and Virginia did so by a margin of 14 percentage points. In South Carolina and Tennessee, such amendments passed by margins of 56 and 62 percentage points, respectively.[135]

Amendment opponents still rarely sought to defend gay marriage on the merits. Rather, they focused on broad language in some of the amendments that would forbid legal recognition to relationships of "unmarried individuals." Such language, they argued, could be construed to encompass heterosexual couples and to forbid, for example, judicial protective orders for the benefit of unmarried victims of domestic violence. Even in Virginia, where amendment opponents outspent supporters by a margin of more than three to one, the ban on gay marriage passed easily. As the *Washington Post* observed in 2006, "The safest bet in American politics in recent years has been a state ban on same-sex marriage."[136]

In 2006, Arizona voters became the first to reject a marriage amendment, but they did so only because the amendment's language was broad enough to be interpreted as forbidding domestic partnership benefits for gay and straight couples. Such benefits were already available to many elderly cohabiting heterosexual couples under a Tucson law and to many private and public employees under corporate and state and local government health care plans. At least some voters did not want those benefits taken away. In 2008, Arizona voters passed a stripped-down measure that barred only gay marriage. That year, two other states also passed marriage amendments.[137]

Even though nobody thought the federal marriage amendment could pass, Republicans, who still controlled Congress in 2006, forced another vote on it. Before the Senate vote, President Bush again defended the amendment as necessary because "activist judges and some local officials have made an aggressive attempt to redefine marriage in recent years." Democrats accused the president of playing politics.[138]

After two days of emotional speeches in the Senate, Republicans were able to muster only forty-nine votes to end debate and bring the amendment to the floor. Later, the House voted 237 to 187 in favor of the amendment—also far short of the two-thirds majority required to send the amendment to the states for ratification. In many congressional election campaigns, Republicans denounced Democrats who had voted against the amendment.[139]

Goodridge and the flurry of gay marriages that followed early in 2004 inspired gay marriage litigation in several other states. In 2004–5, such suits were filed in Connecticut, Florida, Iowa, Maryland, New York, Oregon, and Washington. (A similar lawsuit had already been filed in New Jersey in 2002.)[140]

Trial judges in several cities with extremely gay-friendly populations—Seattle, Baltimore, New York, San Francisco—ruled that gay marriage was protected under state constitutions. Liberal newspaper editors applauded such decisions. After a Seattle trial judge had ruled in favor of gay marriage, the *Seattle Post-Intelligencer* encouraged the state supreme court to "demonstrate similar wisdom—and valor" by quickly affirming the decision.[141]

Yet for several years after the *Goodridge*-inspired backlash of 2004, not a single state high court followed the path charted by the Massachusetts justices. In 2006–7, state supreme courts in Georgia, Maryland, New Jersey, New York, and Washington ruled against gay marriage under their state constitutions. The U.S. Court of Appeals for the Eighth Circuit also rejected gay marriage under the federal constitution. These courts refused to treat gay marriage as a fundamental right or sexual orientation as a suspect classification (either holding would have triggered the most rigorous standard of judicial scrutiny). Applying a more relaxed standard of judicial review instead, these courts held that laws excluding same-sex couples from marriage plausibly furthered government interests in linking procreation to marriage and providing an optimal environment for child rearing.[142]

Whether these courts were influenced in their decisions by the post-*Goodridge* political backlash is impossible to know for sure. *Goodridge* remained an aberrational legal ruling in 2006–7, so perhaps these state courts would have rejected its reasoning even had the decision not generated a massive political backlash. Moreover, most of these state court rulings were divided. Dissenting judges apparently had not been intimidated from endorsing gay marriage by the political backlash ignited by *Goodridge*.

As one would expect, none of these state courts admitted that its ruling against gay marriage had been influenced by concerns about possible political repercussions. Yet by the time these cases were decided, conventional wisdom held that *Goodridge* had ignited a potent political backlash in 2004, which had been harmful both to gay rights and to Democrats.[143]

Most of the judges deciding these cases were elected, and gay-marriage opponents were not shy about threatening to raise the issue in judicial reelection campaigns. In 2006 in Washington State, the Faith and Freedom Network targeted dissenting justices who had supported gay marriage in their retention elections. In Maryland, a Republican legislator threatened to commence impeachment proceedings against the Baltimore trial judge who had ruled in favor of gay marriage.[144]

Perhaps tellingly, even high courts with reputations for liberal activism, such as those in New Jersey and Washington, ruled against gay marriage in 2006–7. Several of these court decisions emphasized judges' obligation to defer to legislative decision making. The New York court noted, "We believe the present generation should have a chance to decide the issue through its elected representatives." Similarly, the New Jersey court observed, "We will not short-circuit the democratic process from running its course." This was an unusual statement coming from a court that had earned one of the most aggressively activist reputations in the country by ordering equalization of educational funding across school districts and forcing low-cost housing into resistant municipalities.[145]

Although denying that gay marriage was constitutionally protected, the New Jersey court ordered that same-sex couples be allowed to form civil unions that afforded them all the rights and obligations of marriage. How to reconcile this holding with the court's professed deference to legislative decision making the justices did not say.

The New Jersey court's compromise decision, which followed in the path blazed by the Vermont court in 1999, elicited a collective "Huh?" from the courtroom audience. Denying same-sex couples the formal title of "marriage" did not violate the state constitution, the majority explained, because the court would not "presume that a difference in name alone is of constitutional magnitude." By contrast, the dissenters, who insisted that gay marriage was constitutionally protected, cautioned that "we must not underestimate the power of language."[146]

The New Jersey court's compromise ruling seemed to perfectly reflect public opinion in the state. An opinion poll conducted soon after the decision showed that New Jerseyans supported it by 54 percent to 37 percent, while only 29 percent favored gay marriage.[147]

Although many gay activists expressed disappointment with what they called "separate but equal" status, which "took us from the back of the bus to only the middle of the bus," many commentators praised the ruling as a wise compromise. Nate Persily, a professor at Columbia Law School, applauded the justices for "an incredibly smart and politically astute opinion."[148]

Both Democrats and some gay activists saw the advantage of settling for civil unions just two weeks before Election Day. That fall, eight states were conducting referenda on gay marriage, and New Jersey featured a hotly contested U.S. Senate race in which the Democratic incumbent supported civil unions but not gay marriage. Interestingly, three of the four New Jersey justices who mandated civil unions but not gay marriage were appointed by Democratic governors, while all three of the justices insisting that gay marriage was constitutionally required were Republican appointees.[149]

Within two days of the New Jersey court's decision, Richard Land of the Southern Baptist Convention declared that supporters of traditional marriage "ought to give a distinguished service award to the New Jersey supreme court." Land predicted that the ruling would boost voter turnout among social conservatives, especially in those states conducting marriage referenda. Across the nation, Republicans sought to use the New Jersey decision to rally dispirited conservatives in opposition to judicial activism. President Bush, who had not mentioned gay marriage for weeks, denounced the decision at fund-raisers in Iowa and Michigan and called marriage a "sacred institution that is critical to the health of our society."[150]

In Virginia, the struggling incumbent senator, Republican George Allen, used the New Jersey ruling to remind voters of the state ballot measure on marriage and of challenger Jim Webb's opposition to it. In Pennsylvania, Republican senator Rick Santorum, struggling for his political life, called the ruling "an affront to democratic process" and warned that gay couples would travel from Pennsylvania to New Jersey to obtain civil unions, return home, and sue for legal recognition. Despite such efforts to capitalize on the New Jersey decision, Republicans suffered a massive defeat in the fall congressional elections.[151]

The New Jersey court had required that civil unions be allowed for same-sex couples, and gay marriage litigation was alive in California, Connecticut, and Iowa. Still, the multiple rejections of gay marriage by state supreme courts in 2006–7 seemed to represent the "nail in the coffin for the litigation strategy."[152]

Law professor Carl Tobias observed that it did not appear these issues were "going to be resolved favorably to the plaintiffs in the courts." Gay rights activist and scholar John D'Emilio went further, pronouncing the gay-marriage litigation campaign "a disaster." Indeed, D'Emilio wondered if the gay rights movement might not be further from securing marriage in 2006 than it had been in 1993. Other gay activists who had been predicting rapid advancement toward gay marriage now wondered whether reaching their goal might not take decades. Yet within a mere two years such gloomy predictions would look like "ancient history."[153]

6

The Gay Marriage Spring (2009)

Gay marriage suffered political and legal setbacks between 2004 and 2007, yet Americans continued to become more progressive in their attitudes toward gay rights. More and more religious denominations supported larger and larger chunks of the gay rights agenda. By 2006, 263 Fortune 500 companies offered health care plans that included benefits for same-sex domestic partners.[1]

The number of states providing health care benefits to the same-sex partners of public employees rose from zero in 1993 to fifteen in 2008. The number of states authorizing additional punishment for hate crimes motivated by anti-gay animus increased from eleven in 1993 to thirty-two in 2008. The number of states with anti-discrimination laws covering sexual orientation rose from eight in 1993 to twenty in 2008.[2]

In 2007, the Democratic-controlled U.S. House of Representatives finally passed the Employment Nondiscrimination Act to forbid job discrimination based on sexual orientation. The measure had first been proposed on the fifth anniversary of Stonewall in 1974 by New York representatives Ed Koch and Bella Abzug. Also in 2007, Oregon and Washington enacted domestic partnership laws, while New Jersey and New Hampshire adopted civil unions.[3]

Opinion polls showed that support for gay marriage was growing again. By 2006, moderates and conservatives had returned to their pre-*Lawrence* levels of support, while liberal backing had increased 25 percentage points from its 2001 level. Polls by the Pew Study Center showed that opponents of gay marriage outnumbered supporters by 29 percentage points in late 2004, 17 percentage points in 2007, and just 12 percentage points in 2008. A Gallup poll conducted in 2007 showed that Americans opposed gay marriage by only 53 percent to 46 percent. Polls by CBS News revealed that public support for either gay marriage or civil unions increased from 53 percent in 2004 to 57 percent in 2006, 61 percent in 2007, and 65 percent in 2008.[4]

In Massachusetts, the only state in which gay marriage was legal during these years, public support grew so rapidly that Republicans stopped mentioning the issue. For the first time, significant numbers of Democratic officeholders in many states began openly advocating gay marriage.[5]

As support for gay marriage grew and memories of the political backlash ignited by *Goodridge* faded, two more state supreme courts found a right to same-sex marriage in their constitutions in 2008. In May, the California supreme court—a moderately conservative, Republican-dominated court that legal scholars described as "cautious"—ruled in favor of gay marriage by a margin of 4 to 3. The ruling was to take effect in thirty days. Because California has no residency requirement for marriage, the decision had important consequences for other states as well. Seventeen thousand gay and lesbian couples married in California during the summer and fall of 2008.[6]

In October, by the same 4-to-3 margin, the Connecticut supreme court in *Kerrigan v. Commissioner of Public Health* reached the same result under its state constitution. In contrast to other courts ruling on gay marriage since *Goodridge*, the California and Connecticut courts found no evidence that children fared worse when raised by same-sex couples, rejected as irrational the states' argument that limiting marriage to opposite-sex couples furthered a public interest in linking procreation to marriage, and determined that gays and lesbians were entitled to heightened judicial protection because sexual orientation was an immutable characteristic and because gays both had suffered from a history of rampant discrimination and currently lacked political power.[7]

Both states were fertile ground for judicial rulings in favor of gay marriage. In 1999, California had adopted a domestic partnership registry that conferred hospital visitation rights and health care benefits on the domestic partners— same-sex and opposite-sex—of state employees. That law was expanded in 2003 to include most of the rights and benefits of marriage. In 2005, a Democratic-controlled legislature passed a gay marriage bill, but Republican governor Arnold Schwarzenegger vetoed it on the debatable ground that the state's 2000 voter initiative, which the legislature was powerless to overturn, had not only barred recognition of other states' gay marriages but also forbidden such marriages in California.[8]

An opinion poll in 2007 found Californians evenly divided on gay marriage, with 46 percent in favor and 46 percent opposed. By contrast, in 2000, Californians had passed Proposition 22, which provided that "only marriage between a man and a woman is valid or recognized in California," by a margin of 61 percent to 39 percent. Moreover, the California supreme court sits in San Francisco, directly across the street from city hall, where thousands of same-sex couples had euphorically celebrated their marriages in February and March 2004. Justices on the court have openly gay law clerks, their decisions are covered by openly gay reporters, and they have daily interactions with gay lawyers and litigants.[9]

In Connecticut, the state legislature, unprompted by judicial decree, had adopted civil unions in 2005. Public support for gay marriage had also increased dramatically. In 2008, Connecticut residents supported *Kerrigan* by 52 percent to 39 percent and opposed amending the constitution to overturn it by 61 percent to 33 percent. Fully 82 percent of Connecticuters supported either gay marriage or civil unions, while just 12 percent opposed any legal recognition of same-sex relationships.[10]

Vis-à-vis public opinion in Connecticut, *Kerrigan* is an example of a court intervening relatively far along the curve of social reform and thus generating little opposition. Just months after the ruling, the Connecticut senate easily reconfirmed for an additional term in office three of the justices who had joined *Kerrigan*.[11]

Although public opinion on gay marriage had progressed enough to embolden the California supreme court to find it constitutionally protected, sufficient opposition remained to ensure a formidable effort to overturn the decision. Even before the court's ruling, opponents of gay marriage had secured enough petition signatures to place a marriage amendment on the fall ballot. An epic battle in the saga of same-sex marriage ensued.[12]

Protect Marriage, a broad coalition of gay marriage opponents that included the Mormon Church, the California Catholic Conference, and many evangelical churches, ran the campaign to qualify a marriage amendment for the ballot and then to pass it. A network of seventeen hundred pastors worked with Protect Marriage in support of the amendment, known as Proposition 8, which provided simply, "Only marriage between a man and a woman is valid or recognized in California."[13]

Amendment supporters conducted focus groups, which revealed that even people who doubted the claim that allowing gay marriage would affect marriage for heterosexuals were concerned that legalizing it would influence what their children were taught in public school. Proposition 8 backers ran advertisements showing a couple from Massachusetts, the only state where gay marriage was legal, describing how their seven-year-old son had returned from school one day to explain that a man could marry a man.[14]

In response, Proposition 8 opponents persuaded the California superintendent of public instruction to declare that the public school curriculum would not be influenced by the fate of gay marriage. However, when a public school in San Francisco took a class of first graders to city hall to witness the same-sex wedding of their lesbian teacher and brought along the media, gay marriage opponents had the video footage to prove their point.[15]

The decision of Proposition 8 strategists to focus on the impact that gay marriage would have on children's education apparently proved very effective. Californians with children under the age of eighteen living at home voted in favor of Proposition 8 by a margin of nearly two to one. Indeed, ever since the days of Anita Bryant's Save Our Children campaign, opponents of gay rights have often enjoyed political success by emphasizing the threat that homosexuality poses to children—usually with more or less explicit references to homosexuals as child predators.[16]

Proposition 8 backers also argued that religious liberty would suffer from the legalization of gay marriage, as churches inevitably would be forced either to recognize such marriages or else to be vilified as bigoted. Amendment supporters were careful not to publicly denigrate homosexuality or to oppose civil unions or other legal recognition of the rights of same-sex couples. One political consultant described this strategy as putting "the fire-eating Christians under a porch somewhere."[17]

Based on the advice of their own political consultants, Proposition 8 opponents ran a campaign that rendered gay and lesbian couples largely invisible. The public face of the opposition to Proposition 8 was Mayor Gavin Newsom of San Francisco—a heterosexual. Rather than defending gay marriage on the merits, Proposition 8 opponents analogized banning it to Japanese American internment during World War II and to the southern system of Jim Crow.[18]

It was the most expensive ballot contest in American history, the two sides together spending roughly $85 million. In a letter to be read from church pulpits, the president of the Mormon Church urged members to donate "means and time" to promote the amendment, and church elders visited Mormon families to instruct them on how much money to give. Thousands of Mormons contributed a total of $15 million to $20 million to the campaign in support of Proposition 8— roughly half of its funding. Other congregations used church databases to organize financial and logistical support for Proposition 8. On the other side of the campaign, gay rights groups, the California teachers' unions, Hollywood celebrities, and large technology companies such as Apple and Google provided most of the financial support.[19]

Opinion polls consistently predicted that Proposition 8 would fail, perhaps by a substantial margin. Yet, on November 4, 2008, California voters passed the amendment by 52.2 percent to 47.8 percent.[20]

That same day, Florida voters also passed a constitutional amendment barring gay marriage by 62 percent to 38 percent. Arizona, the only state ever to have rejected a referendum to ban gay marriage (in 2006), passed a stripped-down version of the amendment, which no longer covered civil unions or domestic partnerships, by 56 percent to 44 percent. All thirty states to have conducted referenda on the issue had now banned gay marriage. Responding to a decision of their own state supreme court, Arkansans passed a voter initiative by 57 percent to 43 percent that barred individuals cohabiting outside of a valid marriage from adopting or providing foster care to minors. Though the language of the initiative was broader, its purpose was to target same-sex couples.

Perhaps ironically, the presence of African American presidential candidate Barack Obama on the ballot facilitated the passage of Proposition 8. Blacks in California turned out in extraordinary numbers to help elect Obama. Normally constituting 6 percent to 7 percent of the state's electorate, African Americans were 10 percent of California's voters in 2008. Studies have found that 58 percent to 70 percent of blacks voted in favor of Proposition 8, even though Obama himself opposed the amendment in recorded messages played in telephone calls directed at black voters in California (in his speeches, however, he also opposed gay marriage). On average, African Americans are more religious than are whites, and religiosity highly correlates with opposition to gay marriage.[21]

Opponents immediately challenged Proposition 8 in court. Omitting a federal constitutional challenge in order to keep the case away from the U.S. Supreme Court, they argued that Proposition 8 was a constitutional "revision" rather than an "amendment" because it prevented the judiciary from playing its traditional role of protecting minority rights. Under the California constitution, "revisions" must originate in the legislature; they cannot be voter initiatives, as was Proposition 8.

California precedent on distinguishing "revisions" from "amendments" is thin, as the state supreme court had only twice previously rejected initiatives as "revisions." Supporters of Proposition 8 threatened to launch a recall campaign against any justice who dared to invalidate it. Indeed, California has a history of recall campaigns against state supreme court justices. In 1986, three of them lost their jobs over perceived refusals to follow the will of the voters on the death penalty. In 1997, two others were forced to mount serious election campaigns to survive a recall effort after they voted to invalidate a state law requiring parental consent before minors could obtain abortions.[22]

Justices facing upcoming retention elections would have been reckless to set aside the will of the people as registered in Proposition 8. One cannot know whether political calculations played any role in their decision, but in May 2009, the justices rejected by a vote of six to one the "revision" challenge to Proposition 8. In the same decision, however, the court refused to interpret ambiguous language in the amendment in such a manner as to expunge the roughly eighteen thousand gay marriages that had already taken place in California.[23]

Although gay marriage did not quite enjoy majority approval in California in 2008, support for it had grown from 38.6 percent in 2000 to 47.8 percent in 2008—a rate of increase of roughly 1 percentage point per year. Given that exit polls showed that 61 percent of those between ages eighteen and twenty-nine voted against Proposition 8, the final word on the subject probably had not been spoken. Indeed, had nobody over the age of sixty-five participated in the balloting, gay marriage would have survived in California.[24]

Although the passage of Proposition 8 was a devastating disappointment to gay rights advocates, the defeat seemed to mobilize their movement. One activist observed that it "took a catastrophe like this to really wake people up," and another credited Proposition 8 with forcing the gay community "out of our stupor." An op-ed in the *Washington Post* referred to Proposition 8 as "this generation's Stonewall," while a gay activist in Los Angeles called the defeat "the greatest thing that could have happened" to the gay rights movement.[25]

The passage of Proposition 8 produced—almost overnight—a "major explosion of protest and activism" for gay equality. Daily demonstrations expressing anger and disappointment erupted across California. On November 15, 2008, demonstrations took place in more than one hundred cities across the nation and even in some cities in Canada, England, and Australia. Ten thousand protestors gathered in San Francisco, nine thousand in Los Angeles, four thousand in New York City, and two thousand in Salt Lake City. In Boston, one of the speakers declared, "We are the American family, we live next door to you, we teach your children, we take care of your elderly."[26]

These protests were organized not by traditional gay rights organizations but via the Internet and cell phones. A twenty-six-year-old Seattle blogger, Amy Balliett, orchestrated much of the protest.[27]

Across California, new gay rights organizations formed. Angered by the measured approaches of established gay rights groups, which they blamed for the

Demonstrators protesting the passage of Proposition 8 in front of San Francisco's city hall, Nov. 15, 2008. (*Associated Press/Darryl Bush*)

passage of Proposition 8, young activists embraced more confrontational tactics, such as mass demonstrations and direct action protest. They criticized Proposition 8 opponents for working harder to reassure straight people that gay marriage would not affect them than to mobilize gay rights supporters.[28]

In December, they planned a demonstration called Day Without a Gay, in which gay rights supporters stayed home from work, called in "gay," and spent their day volunteering for the movement. Determined to win back marriage equality in California, the young activists began canvassing the state door-to-door, telling residents the stories of gay couples. Noting that the "scale and tempo of the movement has been remarkable," one reporter called the demonstrations "the greatest resurgence of LGBT activism in decades."[29]

One form that the protests against Proposition 8 took was boycotts of the Mormon Church and other supporters of the amendment. Less than a week after Election Day, more than three thousand demonstrators in Salt Lake City marched past the Mormon temple to protest the church's support for Proposition 8. In New York City, a crowd estimated at ten thousand demonstrated outside the Mormon temple on the Upper West Side, chanting, "Shame on you," while carrying signs declaring "Love Not H8" and "Did You Cast a Ballot or a Stone?" Two Mormon temples, one in Los Angeles and one in Salt Lake City, received envelopes containing white powder—later determined by the FBI to be non-toxic.[30]

In San Diego, gay rights groups boycotted the Manchester Grand Hyatt, whose owner had donated $125,000 in support of Proposition 8. Sixty gay demonstrators conducted a "kiss-in" outside the hotel. In Salt Lake City, a similar kiss-in led to clashes between anti-gay onlookers and pro-gay kissers who were protesting the Mormon Church's recent eviction of two gay men from its property for kissing. In the summer of 2009, kiss-in demonstrations spread to more than fifty cities.[31]

Dissension also erupted within the Mormon Church, as some members protested the church's prominent role in support of Proposition 8, while others quit the church entirely. In 2009, the Mormon Church, probably seeking to defuse some of the criticism it had endured over its role in Proposition 8, supported a Salt Lake City ordinance barring discrimination based on sexual orientation in employment, housing, and public accommodations. This was the first time the church had ever supported such a measure, occasioning criticism from conservative religious organizations such as the Family Research Council.[32]

Other supporters of Proposition 8 were also targeted for protests and boycotts after the Human Rights Campaign published a list of donors to the Yes on 8 campaign. A Palo Alto dentist who had contributed $1,000 was prominently featured on a website targeting donors and lost patients as a result. A Sacramento theater director resigned from the California Musical Theatre in response to the controversy ignited by his $100,000 donation in support of Proposition 8.[33]

In November 2008, the nation elected not just its first black president but also its most gay-friendly one. Although Obama insisted that he opposed gay marriage, he supported every other major legal reform on the gay rights agenda: repeal of "don't ask, don't tell" and the Defense of Marriage Act and enactment of federal hate crimes legislation and the Employment Nondiscrimination Act.[34]

Moreover, although gay marriage had been constitutionally barred in three more states in 2008, that year's election was widely deemed "an unmitigated disaster" for the Republican Party—the party identified with an anti-gay agenda. For the first time in fourteen years, Republicans controlled neither house of Congress nor the presidency. Only 21 percent of voters self-identified as Republican—the lowest percentage registered since polling on this question began in 1983.[35]

As the *Washington Post* observed in the election's immediate aftermath, the Republican party faced a "considerable rebuilding task" with "no obvious leader and no clear path back to power." This seemed like good news for gay marriage, which was rapidly gaining support among Democrats and independents, while backing among Republicans was stagnant.[36]

As 2009 began, gay marriage bills were in the hopper in Maine, Vermont, New Hampshire, Rhode Island, New York, and New Jersey, and a ruling on gay marriage was expected soon from the Iowa supreme court. By that spring, just six months after Proposition 8 had seemed to hobble the movement for marriage equality, it suddenly sprang forward.[37]

In 2005, after years of carefully canvassing the state, gay rights litigators in Iowa selected six representative same-sex couples to serve as plaintiffs in a gay marriage lawsuit to be filed in state court. In 2007, they won their case at the trial level. On April 3, 2009, the Iowa supreme court in *Varnum v. Brien* affirmed that decision by a vote of 7 to 0.[38]

The justices interpreted state constitutional provisions declaring that all people are born "free and equal" and are entitled to equal "privileges and immunities" to confer the right of marriage upon same-sex couples. The court applied a heightened level of scrutiny to what it deemed to be a classification based on sexual orientation and rejected as inadequate or as too remotely served the government's proffered interests: tradition, providing an optimal environment for child rearing, connecting procreation to marriage, and protecting the traditional institution of opposite-sex marriage.[39]

Varnum emphasized the obligation of judges to defend individual rights against majoritarian oppression. The court also proudly referred to the vanguard role that the Iowa judiciary had played on issues such as slavery, racial segregation, and women's rights. Finally, the court noted the unspoken religious justification for barring gay marriage, which it rejected on Establishment Clause grounds. Deeming civil unions to be separate and unequal, the court gave the state just three weeks to begin issuing marriage licenses to same-sex couples.[40]

Gay marriage supporters were euphoric, especially in light of their devastating defeat on Proposition 8 just six months earlier. The *Washington Blade* declared that there is "a rainbow over Iowa today." The national media treated the ruling as immensely important. Unlike courts in Massachusetts, California, and Connecticut, which had ruled in favor of gay marriage by margins of 4 to 3, the Iowa decision was unanimous, and its author had been appointed by a conservative Republican governor.[41]

Moreover, Iowa is part of the nation's heartland, not on one of its politically left-of-center coasts, meaning that gay marriage could no longer be dismissed as "just a coastal thing." Richard Socarides, who had been President Clinton's principal advisor on gay rights, declared that *Varnum* "represents the mainstreaming of gay marriage" because "there's nothing more American than Iowa." "If it can happen in Iowa, it can happen anywhere," warned Maggie Gallagher, co-founder and chairperson of the board of the National Organization for Marriage (NOM).[42]

Yet in 2009 a clear majority of Iowans still opposed gay marriage. When the *Christian Science Monitor* interviewed people in Davenport soon after the decision, most of them expressed shock. Iowa, they pointed out, was not San Francisco. An average of eight opinion polls conducted in Iowa between 2003 and 2008 showed that opponents of gay marriage outnumbered supporters by 57.5 percent to 33.8 percent. A poll conducted by the *Des Moines Register* in 2008 found that Iowans opposed gay marriage by 62 percent to 32 percent.[43]

Led by Catholic bishops and a conservative family group representing mostly evangelical Protestants, gay marriage opponents denounced *Varnum* for rejecting the wisdom of thousands of years of human history, and they demanded that Iowans be allowed to vote on a constitutional amendment to overturn the decision. Yet amending the Iowa constitution is much more difficult than amending that of California: an amendment must pass the legislature in consecutive two-year sessions and then be approved in a referendum. An alternative route, not used since 1857, would have permitted Iowa voters in 2010 to call for a constitutional convention to meet in 2011.[44]

Democrats had taken control of both houses of the Iowa legislature in 2006, and they had expanded their majorities in 2008. The day *Varnum* was decided, Democratic leaders in both legislative houses praised it and said they were "exceedingly unlikely" to permit legislative votes to begin the amendment process. When state Republican leaders tried to force a vote on a resolution supporting a marriage amendment, the Democrats blocked it.[45]

Varnum put Democratic governor Chet Culver in a difficult position. On several previous occasions, he had unambiguously opposed gay marriage. In January

2008, Culver had told reporters, "We'll do whatever it takes to protect marriage between a man and a woman," and he had promised a swift legislative response if the state supreme court ever ruled in favor of gay marriage.[46]

After *Varnum*, however, Culver initially ducked the media and then equivocated, observing that both sides of the debate felt strongly and he needed to study the decision before reacting. A few days later, he said that while he disagreed with the decision as a matter of religious conviction, he would be reluctant to amend the state constitution in ways that the court had called discriminatory. Government attention, he added, was better focused on the economy.[47]

Republicans disparaged the governor for reneging on his promises and demanded that the people of Iowa be given an opportunity to vote on the issue. Bob Vander Plaats, a leader among Iowa's evangelical Christians, declared that if he were governor, he would issue an executive order blocking implementation of the court's decision—a statement reminiscent of efforts by Arkansas's segregationist governor Orval Faubus to impede execution of a federal court desegregation order in Little Rock in 1957. Vander Plaats also encouraged county recorders to refuse to issue marriage licenses to same-sex couples, and he called for the impeachment of the entire state supreme court.[48]

Meanwhile, in New England, opinion polls showed support for gay marriage approaching majority status. Vermont and New Hampshire had already adopted civil unions, but many gay rights advocates regarded them as inadequate. The Vermont Commission on Family Recognition and Protection, which had been boycotted by conservatives who considered it stacked with supporters of gay marriage, held hearings across the state in 2007–8 and issued a report to lawmakers declaring that civil unions fell short of providing equality.[49]

In 2009, Democrats controlled both houses of the Vermont legislature, and most of them supported gay marriage. An opinion poll conducted in January showed that Vermonters favored gay marriage by 58 percent to 39 percent. Yet many Democratic legislators were skittish about tackling an issue that generally was thought to have cost them control of the state house in 2000. In addition, Republican governor Jim Douglas strongly disapproved of the legislature's taking up gay marriage at a time of economic crisis.[50]

However, an aggressive lobbying campaign by Vermont Freedom to Marry may have persuaded Democrats to press the issue. In March, the legislature held raucous hearings on gay marriage, which were attended by as many as a thousand people. Legislative leaders now predicted that a gay marriage bill would pass, though whether the governor would sign it was uncertain. Republican opponents decried the speed with which the legislature was acting and demanded—unsuccessfully—a non-binding public referendum on gay marriage.[51]

Eventually Governor Douglas indicated that he would veto the gay marriage bill, and last-minute drama unfolded as Democrats scrambled to secure the votes necessary to overturn his veto. On April 7, 2009, just four days after *Varnum*, Vermont became the first state to enact gay marriage through the legislative process—a fact whose significance was highlighted by many commentators. (The California legislature had passed a gay marriage bill in 2005, but Governor Schwarzenegger had vetoed it.)[52]

Vermont's neighbor, New Hampshire, had adopted civil unions in 2007, and some Democratic legislators were reluctant to consider gay marriage just two years later. Democrats had not campaigned on the issue in 2008, and Democratic governor John Lynch had explicitly opposed gay marriage during his gubernatorial campaigns in 2006 and 2008.[53]

Yet the momentum generated by developments in Iowa and Vermont proved irresistible to New Hampshire Democrats. A gay marriage bill narrowly passed both houses, mostly along party lines—186 to 179 in the house and 13 to 11 in the senate. Republican legislators asked for a non-binding voter referendum, which Democrats rejected.

Whether Governor Lynch would sign the bill was uncertain. Phone lines to his office were jammed by thousands of calls, and both sides of the debate aired television advertisements aimed at pressuring the governor. Lynch eventually announced that he would sign the bill, provided that certain amendments were added to protect religious objectors. Republicans denounced the governor as a flip-flopper and a liar. The legislature accepted the religious accommodations demanded by Lynch, who then signed the bill on June 3. Republicans promised to make gay marriage an issue in the 2010 state elections. A couple of opinion polls suggested that New Hampshirites narrowly opposed the law.[54]

While Governor Lynch was deliberating in New Hampshire, Maine acted. An opinion poll conducted in April showed that Mainers were narrowly divided on gay marriage: 49.5 percent opposed and 47.3 percent in favor. That month, nearly four thousand of them packed a legislative hearing, at which two hundred speakers representing both sides of the debate gave ten hours of passionate testimony.[55]

After weeks of great uncertainty, the Maine senate passed the gay marriage bill by 21 to 13 and the house by 89 to 57. Democrats controlled both houses, and just a handful of Republicans voted in favor. As elsewhere in New England, Democrats blocked a Republican proposal for a referendum on the issue. Democratic governor John Baldacci signed the bill, explaining that his conversion on gay marriage reflected the changing times. He also noted that Mainers were free to overrule him at the polls.[56]

The legislative debates over gay marriage in New England brought to a head the issue of religious exemptions. Virtually nobody believes that the Free Exercise

Clause of the Constitution would permit governments to compel churches to perform gay marriages. The real debate is over how broadly to exempt from anti-discrimination laws religious organizations and religiously inspired businesses and individuals who do not wish to provide goods, services, accommodations, or facilities to same-sex weddings. For example, should a wedding photographer or a florist who opposes gay marriage on religious grounds be exempted from a state law barring discrimination based on sexual orientation in public accommodations? About twenty states had such anti-discrimination laws by 2009.[57]

One opinion poll revealed that support for gay marriage increased 14 percentage points when people were asked about a law that guaranteed that no church or congregation would be forced to perform such marriages against its wishes. Democrats such as Governor Lynch of New Hampshire may have demanded broader religious exemptions partly to reduce public opposition to gay marriage.[58]

By June 2009, Rhode Island was the only state in New England without gay marriage. Opinion polls showed support there as high as 60 percent—the second-highest percentage of any state. Yet opposition from the Republican governor and some Democratic leaders in the legislature blocked gay marriage. Strenuous resistance from the Catholic Church, which regarded same-sex unions as a "perversion of natural law," probably helped stem the tide toward gay marriage in the state with the highest percentage of Catholics of any in the nation.[59]

By the spring of 2009, it also appeared possible—perhaps even likely—that New Jersey and New York would enact gay marriage later that year. In 2007, the New Jersey legislature had enacted civil unions in response to its state supreme court decision and established a Civil Union Review Commission. After conducting extensive public hearings and gathering evidence, that commission concluded in December 2008 that civil unions were inherently unequal and should be replaced with gay marriage.[60]

An opinion poll conducted in April 2009 found that New Jerseyans supported gay marriage by a margin of 49 percent to 43 percent. Democratic governor Jon Corzine announced that he would support a bill to legalize gay marriage, and Democratic leaders in the legislature declared that they would back such a bill if convinced it had a good chance of passing. Late that summer, both the governor and state legislative leaders seemed to be contemplating enactment of gay marriage during the lame-duck legislative session to be held after the November elections.[61]

In New York, a gay marriage bill had failed to reach the floor of the senate after passing the General Assembly in 2007. Then, in November 2008, Democrats took control of both houses of the legislature for the first time in four decades. The Democrats' majority in the senate was slim, however, and they had trouble electing a majority leader. Three Latino Democrats balked at supporting the

party's heir apparent, Malcolm Smith. One of the three, Ruben Diaz, emphasized that he could not support anyone for the senate leadership who favored gay
marriage. Smith had already indicated that he would permit a floor vote on a gay
marriage bill if he became majority leader.

The deal that ultimately enabled Smith to ascend to the leadership position
with the support of the three dissident Democrats was not publicly disclosed,
though Diaz insisted that gay marriage had been discussed and that he was comfortable with how the issue had been resolved. Early in 2009, the *New York Times*
reported that no legislative vote on gay marriage was imminent, as several
Democratic senators remained opposed.[62]

Developments in New England that spring, however, inspired louder calls in
Albany for gay marriage. Governor David Paterson led the chorus. As senate
minority leader in 2002, Paterson had helped secure the votes necessary to add
sexual orientation to New York's public accommodations law. As governor in
2008, he had ordered state agencies to recognize gay marriages lawfully performed in other jurisdictions.[63]

On April 16, 2009, Paterson introduced a bill to legalize gay marriage in
New York and pledged to throw the weight of his office behind it. One opinion
poll showed New Yorkers supporting gay marriage by 53 percent to 39 percent.
A second poll showed the state evenly divided, with 46 percent supporting gay
marriage and 46 percent opposed. On May 12, the general assembly passed the
gay marriage bill by 89 to 52.[64]

The bill's test would come in the state senate. The majority leader, Smith, was
a strong supporter. But the Democratic majority was only 32 to 30, and Smith
announced that he would permit a floor vote only if the bill was virtually certain
to pass. However, as many as four Democratic senators were likely to oppose it.
The most prominent of them was Diaz, a Pentecostal minister from the Bronx
who years earlier had lost his seat on the city's Civilian Complaint Review Board
over controversial statements he had made about homosexuality.[65]

In 2009, Diaz remained implacable in his opposition to gay marriage. Thus,
the gay marriage bill was likely to pass only if some Republicans supported it.
Several Republican senators from swing districts, mostly on Long Island,
declared their minds to be open, and the senate minority leader announced that
he would not invoke party discipline on gay marriage.[66]

Intense lobbying took place on both sides of the issue. The Conservative Party
threatened to strip its party affiliation and ballot line—worth several thousand votes
per district—from any Republican who supported gay marriage. The National
Organization for Marriage likewise threatened to spend considerable sums in
support of primary challenges to Republicans who "sell out marriage voters."[67]

On the other side, Mayor Michael Bloomberg and New York's two Democratic
U.S. senators supported the gay marriage bill. Governor Paterson pushed hard

for it, promising to personally lobby state senators, although his abysmal approval ratings sapped his political influence. Paterson repeatedly compared the battle for gay marriage to the anti-slavery crusade of the nineteenth century. Many African American ministers strongly protested the comparison, noting that blacks had no choice over their skin color, while gays chose to engage in homosexual sex. Gay rights organizations commissioned polls in the districts of uncommitted senators, hired lobbyists, and urged sympathetic constituents to put their political connections to work.[68]

The outcome of the gay marriage debate remained in doubt as the legislature's spring session wound to a close. Several Republican senators were reluctant to be the first in their party to publicly commit to supporting the bill, and Smith continued to insist that he would not bring the measure to the floor unless assured that it would pass. In May, thousands of people demonstrated in competing rallies in New York City. In early June, Smith stated that he did not have enough votes to enact the bill. When openly gay senator Thomas Duane contradicted him, Senator Diaz demanded that Duane release the names of the committed senators or else "shut up."[69]

On June 8, two weeks before the legislative session was scheduled to end, the senate erupted in confusion. Disaffected with the Democratic Party, which he had helped to put in power in Albany in 2008, mercurial billionaire Tom Golisano orchestrated the defection of two Latino Democrats from New York City—state senators Pedro Espada Jr. and Hiram Monserrate. The senators' motives for defecting were unclear, though both of them were under legal investigation—one for alleged embezzlement of federal funds and the other for a felony assault charge against his girlfriend. Their defections cost Smith his position as majority leader; he was replaced with another Democrat who supported a power-sharing arrangement with Republicans.[70]

The leadership controversy brought all senate business, including the gay marriage bill, to a halt. Governor Paterson had previously promised to force a senate vote on gay marriage before the summer adjournment. But as the leadership controversy dragged on for weeks, he reluctantly agreed to delay a vote. When Democrats eventually regained tenuous control of the senate, Diaz, who was critical to their majority, enjoyed an effective veto over gay marriage.[71]

By the spring of 2009, opinion polls in several other states registered near-majority support for gay marriage, and legislatures began to take action accordingly. In April, the Washington legislature passed a bill known as the Everything but Marriage Act. This measure expanded the rights conferred by domestic partnerships, which had first been authorized by the legislature in 2007 and covered hospital visitation, inheritance rights without a will, and the ability to authorize autopsies and organ donations. In 2008, the legislature had expanded domestic partnership rights to include community property and powers of attorney. Now, in 2009, the legislature added all of the remaining rights available to married couples, minus the term "marriage." Gay rights advocates accepted the measure as a compromise that might forestall a voter referendum.[72]

In the spring of 2009, Nevada approved a domestic partnerships bill, which provided many of the rights and benefits of marriage to same-sex couples. Colorado approved a narrower measure that allowed same-sex couples to enter into "designated beneficiary agreements" to facilitate estate planning, medical decision making, and joint insurance coverage.[73]

That summer, Wisconsin became the first midwestern state to enact a broad domestic partnerships bill, which provided rights of inheritance, hospital visitation, and medical leave to domestic partners, who could be gay or straight. Conservatives challenged the law as inconsistent with the state's defense-of-marriage amendment, adopted in 2006, which forbade state recognition of "a legal status identical or substantially similar to that of marriage for unmarried individuals." Democrats insisted that the domestic partnerships law was constitutional because it made available only forty-three of the two hundred or more benefits of marriage conferred by state law.[74]

Inspired by legislative action elsewhere in the nation and emboldened by the recent Democratic takeovers of Congress and the presidency, the city council of the District of Columbia voted in May 2009 to recognize gay marriages lawfully performed in other jurisdictions. Council members clearly signaled that if Congress did not block the measure (it had thirty days in which to do so), they would soon take up a bill to legalize gay marriage in the District. When Congress failed to block the recognition bill, the D.C. city council in December legalized gay marriage.[75]

Both of these measures were controversial in the black community. African American ministers and former mayor Marion Barry led the opposition to gay marriage in Washington, D.C. One poll showed that 92 percent of whites in the city supported gay marriage, but only 41 percent of African Americans did so. On average, blacks living in the District were older, more religious, and less well educated than whites.[76]

Republicans in Congress sought to block the council's gay marriage measures, but Democratic leaders would not permit floor votes. Same-sex couples began marrying in Washington, D.C., in March 2010.

Even in states where gay marriage was not yet on the political horizon, opinion polls registered dramatic increases in support by 2009. A poll conducted in Michigan that spring found that support for gay marriage had increased from 24 percent in 2004 to 46.5 percent in 2009, while backing for civil unions had expanded from 42 percent to 63.7 percent. Even in Pennsylvania, which has the third-oldest population in the country, support for gay marriage had increased from 35 percent in 2004 to 42 percent in 2009.[77]

The spring's heady developments on gay marriage even led some commentators to wonder whether justices on the California supreme court might be influenced in their ruling on the constitutionality of Proposition 8. They were not, however, and on May 26, 2009, they upheld the amendment by a vote of 6 to 1. That decision sparked the largest gay rights demonstrations in California since Proposition 8 passed in November. Thirty-five hundred protestors marched through downtown San Diego, sitting in at a clerk's office to demand marriage licenses for gay couples, chanting and singing, and reading aloud from Martin Luther King Jr.'s "Letter from a Birmingham Jail."[78]

Gains made by the gay marriage movement across the country in the spring of 2009 also invigorated debate among gay activists in California over whether to wage a new referendum campaign to overturn Proposition 8 in 2010 or wait until 2012. Noting "an enormous and unprecedented sea change in both public opinion and momentum on the issue of marriage equality," Kate Kendell of the National Center for Lesbian Rights in San Francisco observed that California "is a different place when it comes to marriage equality than it was six months ago."[79]

In town hall meetings across the state, gay activists debated the timing question. Those preferring to wait noted the difficulty of financing another costly referendum battle in the midst of a deep recession, polls continuing to show a state divided down the middle, and the significantly reduced turnout of young voters to be expected in an off-year election such as 2010. Polls also revealed that 60 percent of Californians wished not to revisit the issue so quickly.[80]

Despite near-unanimous recommendations from political consultants to wait until 2012, the grassroots groups formed after Proposition 8, which consisted mostly of younger activists, pressed for a new referendum campaign in 2010. Regarding Proposition 8 as a deep injustice, these activists were less concerned with opinion polls and more with changing people's attitudes through protest.[81]

Arguments for trying again in 2010 included not having to compete with the Obama reelection campaign for funds and the likely presence on the ballot that year of a Democratic gubernatorial nominee who supported gay marriage—probably either Gavin Newsom or Jerry Brown. Sixty-nine percent of the members of Equality California, a statewide group backing gay marriage, preferred 2010 over 2012, as did 82 percent of the Courage Campaign, a multi-issue progressive organizing group in California. A straw poll of gay marriage activists in California taken at a July summit, during which tempers flared over the timing issue, favored returning to the ballot in 2010 by a margin of two to one.[82]

For gay marriage advocates, the tide seemed to be turning in the spring of 2009. In early April, the National Marriage Project director of Lambda Legal predicted that people would look back and identify this "as a moment when our entire country turned a corner." One week later, syndicated columnist Ellen Goodman observed, "In the glacial scheme of social change, attitudes are evolving at white-water speed." In May, one reporter noted, "Instead of states dragging their feet, it's now almost a race to legalize same-sex marriage." Another commentator called the shift in public opinion from 2004 to 2009 "nothing short of a political tsunami" and predicted that Proposition 8 would quickly "be seen as the swan song of the old order."[83]

National opinion polls seemed to confirm these anecdotal observations of transformative change. A CBS News/*New York Times* poll conducted in April found that 42 percent of Americans favored gay marriage—the highest level of support ever recorded by this poll and an increase of 9 percentage points from the previous month. A CNN poll showed support at 44 percent—an increase of 10 percentage points in five years. An ABC News/*Washington Post* poll conducted in April found that Americans backed gay marriage by 49 percent to 46 percent.[84]

In the spring and summer of 2009, stories about gay marriage seemed to be everywhere. For several weeks in April and May, gay marriage was the first or second most frequently covered story on the Internet.[85]

In April, the eventual runner-up in the Miss America beauty pageant, Carrie Prejean of California, caused a hullabaloo when she declared, in response to a judge's question, that same-sex marriage was contrary to the values according to which she had been raised. A co-director of the pageant expressed sadness at her remark, while the judge who had asked her the question later called Prejean a "dumb bitch" on a YouTube video.[86]

Religious conservatives rallied around Prejean, insisting that her controversial views on gay marriage had cost her the Miss America crown, defending her free speech rights, and criticizing gay rights advocates for demonizing their opponents as bigots. That fall, Prejean spoke at the Values Voters Summit sponsored by the Family Research Council. When she explained how God had chosen her to lead the fight against gay marriage, the audience erupted into thunderous applause.[87]

Also in April, Baltimore Ravens linebacker Brendon Ayanbadejo, a three-time NFL Pro Bowl choice, endorsed gay marriage and ridiculed the notion that Britney Spears could get married after a one-night stand while a gay couple could not despite a ten-year loving relationship. In May, with President Obama poised to make his first nomination to the U.S. Supreme Court, speculation abounded on what that nominee's position on gay marriage might be and indeed whether the president might appoint the first openly gay justice in American history. Two lesbian law professors from Stanford University, Kathleen Sullivan and Pam Karlan, were prominently mentioned as possibilities. Conservative Christians such as Senator John Thune of South Dakota warned the administration not to nominate an openly gay candidate, as this would be "a bridge too far right now." In July, the Episcopal Church voted overwhelmingly to authorize wedding rites for same-sex couples.[88]

This extraordinary progress on gay marriage in the spring of 2009 did not elicit from Republicans anything like the tremendous uproar that *Goodridge* had produced in 2003–4. Executive orders by President Obama on abortion and stem cell research, combined with gay marriage developments, dealt religious conservatives setbacks the likes of which had not been seen in decades. Yet, as one Republican pollster noted, the political silence was "deafening." One journalist observed, "The lack of outrage is striking." Not only had there been no Armageddon, but there had "hardly been a press conference."[89]

The severity of the economic collapse in 2008–9 may partially explain the Republicans' muted response to developments on gay marriage. Former Republican presidential candidate Rudy Giuliani declared that "people are not concerned about issues like gay marriage because they are concerned about the economy."[90]

Reverend Rick Warren, the famed evangelist and gay marriage opponent whose selection by Obama to give the invocation at his inauguration aroused great ire among gay activists, stated on *Larry King Live* in April that gay marriage was a "very low" priority for him. This was a dramatic shift from 2004, when Warren had called it one of five "nonnegotiable" issues in a letter to his Saddleback Church congregation. When King asked Warren to comment on the recent Iowa court decision, Warren replied, "That's not even my agenda." Instead, Warren was focused on remembering the Rwanda genocide on its fifteenth anniversary and responding to the debilitating impact of the recession on the nation's spiritual climate.[91]

Even some prominent Republicans were beginning to express doubts whether their party would benefit from continuing to harp on gay marriage—a huge reversal from five years earlier, when the issue was largely viewed as a political godsend to Republicans. Former vice president Dick Cheney, father of a lesbian, now defended gay marriage on libertarian grounds. With one opinion poll showing that 57 percent of Americans under the age of forty supported gay marriage, Steve Schmidt, the thirty-eight-year-old manager of John McCain's 2008 presidential campaign, urged Republicans to reconsider their position or else risk becoming a perpetual minority party. Ted Olson, who had been George W. Bush's Supreme Court lawyer during the Florida election controversy in 2000, explained to Larry King that gay marriage was not a Republican issue or a Democratic issue but one of individual rights. Utah's Republican governor, Jon Huntsman Jr., who was frequently mentioned as a possible presidential candidate in 2012, endorsed civil unions.[92]

Despite such calls for reconsidering its position, the Republican Party was not about to endorse gay marriage anytime soon. Polls showed that, at most, one in five Republicans favored gay marriage. The party's base, dominated by religious and other social conservatives, strongly opposed not only gay marriage but also any legal recognition of same-sex couples.[93]

Among Democrats and independents, the increase in support for gay marriage over the previous two decades was stunning. Democrats went from opposing gay marriage by a margin of two to one to supporting it by two to one. Independents went from opposing it by five to three to supporting it by that same margin. By contrast, Republicans had hardly moved at all. Socially moderate Republicans had simply abandoned the party.[94]

As public opinion on gay marriage changed rapidly while the Republican Party seemed immovable, many Democrats sensed a political opportunity to exploit the divide that was opening between the Republican base and independent voters. As recently as 2008, major contenders for the Democratic presidential nomination had stood united in opposition to gay marriage. Yet with polls now showing 62 percent of Democrats and a majority of independents in favor of gay marriage, many leading Democrats began to come out in support.[95]

Howard Dean, a front-runner for the Democratic presidential nomination in 2004, announced that had he still been governor of Vermont in 2009, he would have signed the state's gay marriage bill. Running for reelection in New Jersey in 2009, Governor Jon Corzine made gay marriage an important part of his campaign platform. Both U.S. senators from New York, Charles Schumer and the newly appointed Kirsten Gillibrand, announced their support for gay marriage early in 2009, as did Senator Christopher Dodd of Connecticut and Senator Patrick Leahy of Vermont a few months later. Senator Tom Harkin of Iowa, one of many Democrats who had voted for the Defense of Marriage Act in 1996, came out for repeal in the spring of 2009. When Senator Arlen Specter of Pennsylvania switched parties to become a Democrat in October, he likewise embraced repeal of DOMA. In July, former president Bill Clinton became the highest-profile political convert on gay marriage.[96]

Amid these political developments, a gay marriage lawsuit was filed in federal court for the first time in two decades. Brought in May 2009 in the northern district of California, *Perry v. Schwarzenegger* refocused national attention on San Francisco, where five years earlier thousands of gay marriages had jolted the nation. *Perry*, which challenged Proposition 8 under the federal constitution, garnered attention as much for its lawyers as for the legal issues it raised.[97]

Those lawyers were David Boies and Ted Olson, who had been on opposite sides of *Bush v. Gore*, the Supreme Court case that had terminated the vote recount in Florida in the 2000 presidential election. That Olson, a leading

Attorneys Ted Olson and David Boies with plaintiffs Sandy Stier and Kris Perry, June 15, 2010. (*Associated Press/Ben Margot*)

Republican lawyer who had served in the administrations of Ronald Reagan and George W. Bush, supported gay marriage was seen as symbolically important.[98]

Olson explained now that he had personally opposed the federal marriage amendment endorsed by the Bush administration while he was working for it. The time was long overdue, he proclaimed, for American society to rectify the grave injustice of denying equality to gays and lesbians. To social conservatives such as Ed Whelan, president of the Ethics and Public Policy Center, the *Perry* litigation was "a betrayal of everything Ted Olson has purported to stand for." The new organization that had hired Boies and Olson, the American Foundation for Equal Rights, had received millions of dollars from gay rights donors and used it to hire twenty lawyers to work on the litigation. Olson predicted that the case would eventually reach the U.S. Supreme Court.[99]

A joint statement by the ACLU and eight national gay rights organizations condemned the filing of a federal lawsuit as premature. One Lambda Legal officer called the litigation "risky" and warned that a loss in the Supreme Court could take decades to undo; it had taken seventeen years to overturn *Bowers v. Hardwick* in *Lawrence v. Texas*. She also expressed annoyance that eminent lawyers not affiliated with the gay rights movement felt free to ignore the gay activists' carefully developed strategy of keeping gay marriage cases out of federal court.[100]

Professor Laurence Tribe of Harvard Law School likewise warned that pressing the issue before a conservative Supreme Court was "not necessarily the wisest thing to do." Nan Hunter of Georgetown Law School observed that the Supreme Court rarely invalidates a law, such as the ban on same-sex marriage that is still on the books in roughly forty-five states. Perhaps even worse than losing in federal court, other commentators warned, would be winning, which might ignite a severe political backlash in those parts of the country where public opinion still strongly opposed gay marriage.[101]

To such criticism, Olson responded, "We think we know what we are doing." The lawsuit was not premature, Olson argued, because he believed he could count five votes on the current Court in favor of gay marriage. Friendly enough with Justice Anthony Kennedy to invite the jurist to his wedding three years earlier, Olson cited Kennedy's opinions in *Romer* and *Lawrence* as the basis for his confidence. Olson also noted that if he and Boies did not file the federal lawsuit, someone else would do so soon, and at least they had the advantages of tremendous resources at their disposal and vast experience arguing cases in the Supreme Court.[102]

Indicative of changing public opinion on gay marriage in California, state officials chose not to defend the lawsuit. Governor Schwarzenegger professed neutrality, while Attorney General Jerry Brown, at that time a likely candidate for the Democratic gubernatorial nomination in 2010, argued that Proposition 8 was unconstitutional. The federal district judge to whom the case had been assigned, Vaughn Walker, approved the intervention of Proposition 8's sponsors to defend the amendment in court.[103]

Unable to prevent the lawsuit from proceeding, national gay rights groups sought to file a brief supporting the challenge to Proposition 8 but on narrow grounds that would not apply much beyond the facts of this case. Boies and Olson opposed their motion to intervene and Judge Walker denied it, though these organizations did ultimately cooperate with the plaintiffs, suggesting expert witnesses and sharing briefs from past cases. The trial in *Perry* was scheduled to begin in January 2010.[104]

Perry was the most visible federal court litigation involving gay marriage in 2009, but it was not the only one. In March, the Gay and Lesbian Advocates and Defenders brought suit in federal court in Boston against DOMA, and the Massachusetts attorney general filed a similar suit that summer. Another lawsuit in California—initially filed in state court but then removed by the U.S. government to federal court—challenged DOMA on the ground that it interfered with the right of married same-sex couples to travel across state lines.[105]

Gay marriage developments in the spring of 2009 put the Obama administration in a difficult position: as Republicans such as Dick Cheney, Ted Olson, and Steve Schmidt endorsed gay marriage, it became harder for Democrats such as President Obama and Secretary of State Hillary Clinton to explain why they did not.

Exit polls showed that 70 percent of self-identified gays and lesbians had voted for Obama in the 2008 presidential election. Obama's deputy campaign manager was gay, as were several of the president's key advisors. He included gay rights issues in most of his stump speeches. Obama supported almost all of the gay rights political agenda, such as repeal of "don't ask, don't tell" and DOMA.[106]

Yet in the spring of 2009, President Obama had plenty of reasons to resist growing pressure from the gay community to switch his position and come out in support of gay marriage. His administration had its hands full with an economic stimulus package, health care reform, and environmental legislation. In addition, Democrats retained vivid memories of how President Clinton's first six months in office in 1993 had been consumed by his abortive effort to repeal the ban on gays in the military. Furthermore, many newly elected Democrats in Congress represented fairly conservative districts, which would not have supported gay marriage.[107]

Instead of endorsing gay marriage, the administration invited families headed by gay and lesbian couples to the White House for the annual Easter Egg Roll. It also appointed gays to prominent positions in the federal government, issued an executive order extending limited benefits to same-sex partners of federal employees, lifted visa restrictions on people with HIV, reversed Bush administration policy on allowing same-sex couples to identify themselves as married in the census, approved regulations protecting gays and lesbians from discrimination in the sale and rental of housing, and declared June to be Gay Pride Month in commemoration of Stonewall's fortieth anniversary.[108]

With Democrats in control of both Congress and the presidency for the first time since 1994, liberals had high expectations for progress on gay rights legislation. The hate crimes bill passed the House in April and the Senate in July and was signed into law in October. The prospects for Congress enacting the Employment Nondiscrimination Act were better than ever before.[109]

Yet with the tide on gay marriage seeming to turn in the spring of 2009, the Obama administration continued to act cautiously, defending in court the constitutionality of both "don't ask, don't tell" and DOMA. The administration committed only to repealing "don't ask, don't tell" in a "sensible way" and gave no indication that the president was rethinking his position on gay marriage.[110]

Although some gay activists counseled patience, newspapers and the Internet were awash with stories describing growing irritation with the president. One group of frustrated but still hopeful gay activists started a website featuring a ticking clock and observing that five months into the Obama administration, "zero percent equality" had been achieved. Richard Socarides, President Clinton's gay rights advisor, asked in early May 2009, "Where is our fierce advocate?"—a reference to Obama's promise to be a "fierce advocate of equality for gay and lesbian Americans," which the president-elect had made in response to the furor sparked by his inviting Rick Warren to give the invocation at his inauguration. Conceding that the president had his hands full dealing with an economy in turmoil, activists nonetheless wondered how he had managed to issue executive orders on abortion and stem cell research but, during this "change moment" on gay marriage, could do nothing substantial on gay rights.[111]

The relationship between the president and the gay community deteriorated in mid-June when the administration filed its brief defending DOMA from constitutional challenge in federal court in California. Congressman Barney Frank slammed the brief as a "big mistake," for appearing to equate gay marriage with incest, and he demanded an explanation from the president. Jared Polis, another openly gay congressional representative, declared himself "shocked and disappointed" by the brief, which yet another critic said could have been written by Reverend Pat Robertson. Socarides denied that the administration was legally obliged to defend DOMA in the most offensive way possible, and he urged gays to loudly protest in order to avoid being sacrificed on the altar of political expediency.[112]

On June 12, 2009, the same day the administration filed its brief in the DOMA case, Campbell Brown of CNN ran a segment asking, "Is President Obama selling out the gay community?" Dan Savage, a gay syndicated columnist, wrote: "I'm sick of hearing about the President's commitment. I want to see action from the White House.... The President has sold us out in California today"—a reference to the administration's DOMA brief, which Savage called "insanely bigoted." The mayors of both San Francisco and Los Angeles criticized the brief as well. The administration dispatched its highest-ranking openly gay official to explain that it could not cherry-pick which laws to defend in court but also to promise that DOMA would be repealed "before the sun sets on this administration."[113]

On June 17, when the administration announced that some benefits—though not health care coverage—would be extended to the same-sex partners of federal employees, a gay radio host wrote on his blog, "The Obama administration is throwing us a pathetic bone: benefits for federal workers. Wow. Give me a break!" On June 19, when invitations went out to gay rights leaders to come and talk with the president, followed by a White House reception to commemorate the fortieth anniversary of Stonewall, one activist responded: "Is the president playing us stupid? It is going to take more than lip service and a party for us to believe we've got a friend in the White House." For fifteen minutes in the Oval Office, one of the president's top campaign lieutenants, Steve Hildebrand, told Obama of the "hurt, anxiety and anger" that he and other gay supporters felt at the administration's slow pace of engagement with gay rights issues. Some prominent gay political donors were so fed up with the administration that they pulled out of a late June fund-raiser for the Democratic National Committee.[114]

Still, more than two hundred gay activists joined the president in the White House on June 28 to commemorate the fortieth anniversary of the Stonewall riots. History was in the making as the president and First Lady entered the event to the tune of ABBA's "Dancing Queen." This was a huge contrast to the first time gay activists ever visited the White House, in March 1977, to meet with mid-level aides to President Jimmy Carter on a Saturday when the press and the president were not around.[115]

Obama acknowledged the impatience of the gay community, insisted that progress had been made and that more would follow, and reiterated his promises regarding hate crimes legislation, a federal ban on employment discrimination with regard to sexual orientation, and repeal of DOMA and "don't ask, don't tell." Reminding his audience that he had been in office for only six months, the president declared, "By the time this administration is over, I think you guys will have pretty good feelings about [it]."[116]

On gay marriage, though, the administration would not budge. The president refused to comment after the Iowa court decision in April. When reporters asked White House press secretary Robert Gibbs about gay marriage amid the stunning developments in New England, he curtly replied that the president's position had not changed: he favored civil unions but not gay marriage. During a two-hour NBC News special, *Inside the Obama White House*, the president evinced his greatest unease when asked about gay marriage, responding with a non sequitur about why DOMA should be repealed.[117]

Focused primarily on health care reform, the administration was determined not to give social conservatives an issue around which to rally opposition. Yet as one critic observed, "At this rate, Obama is in danger of being outpaced on gay rights not just by the American people but by the non-suicidal wing of the Republican Party."[118]

Backlash (Again): Maine and Iowa (2009–2010)

Although legislatures in New England and courts in California, Connecticut, and Iowa were approving gay marriage, it remained unclear whether a majority of voters did so. The astonishing poll results of April and May 2009 were quickly revealed as temporary blips. By June, support for gay marriage had returned to what it had been before the events of that spring—roughly 33 percent, according to a CBS News/*New York Times* poll.[1]

The spring's developments also served as a powerful rallying cry for religious conservatives. In April, the National Organization for Marriage ran a television advertisement warning, against a backdrop of dark clouds and lightning bolts, of a storm on the horizon: gay marriage. The ad featured a New Jersey church group that had been charged with discrimination for opposing gay marriage and parents complaining about what their children were being taught in school on the subject. NOM announced plans for a $1.5 million campaign against gay marriage in key states including New York and New Jersey.[2]

Political backlash against the Iowa court decision developed gradually through 2009. An opinion poll in September showed that Iowans opposed the ruling by 43 percent to 26 percent. Moreover, the percentage of those strongly opposed was nearly double the percentage of those strongly in favor. Another poll showed that 67 percent of Iowans wanted an opportunity to vote on the issue.[3]

Given such poll numbers, Iowa Republicans had little incentive to drop the matter. Especially in the upcoming Republican gubernatorial primary, an election typically dominated by conservatives, opposition to gay marriage was virtually a prerequisite for any candidate. Polls showed that even though most Iowa voters were focused on jobs and the economy, one-third of Republicans deemed gay marriage a very important issue.[4]

Immediately after *Varnum*, Representative Steven King of Iowa, one of Congress's most conservative members, threatened to run in the 2010 gubernatorial race if Democratic governor Chet Culver did not "step up and be very definitive" against gay marriage. Two weeks later, King reported that he had conducted eleven town hall meetings across the state since the ruling, almost all of them packed, and that gay marriage had been the first question on most people's minds. Bob Vander Plaats, a likely candidate for the Republican gubernatorial nomination, challenged Culver to issue an executive order staying implementation of *Varnum* until Iowans were given an opportunity to vote on gay marriage. The Iowa Family Policy Center urged county recorders to refuse to issue marriage licenses to same-sex couples, but the state attorney general promptly warned local officials that they must abide by the court's ruling, which all of them did.[5]

By the summer of 2009, it was clear that gay marriage would play a prominent role in the following year's gubernatorial election. All five candidates for the Republican nomination opposed gay marriage, and four of them called for a state constitutional amendment to ban it. Vander Plaats, one of the front-runners, repeatedly promised that, if elected governor, he would halt such marriages by executive order. Another candidate advocated evicting from office the three supreme court justices who faced retention elections in 2010.[6]

That summer, gay marriage became an issue in a special election for the Iowa house. In April, the Republican candidate, Stephen Burgmeier, then a Jefferson County commissioner, had called for a resolution to forbid county officials from issuing marriage licenses to gay couples and had promised to stage a George Wallace–style stand in the courthouse door on the first day that gay marriage became legal. Burgmeier backed down only after the state attorney general threatened to remove from office county officials who defied *Varnum*. When he announced his candidacy for the house seat, Burgmeier pledged to work to end gay marriage in Iowa.[7]

Although Burgmeier downplayed gay marriage during his campaign, the National Organization for Marriage spent more than $85,000 for advertising on his behalf—more money than either candidate raised himself. Burgmeier's Democratic opponent, who tried to neutralize the issue by supporting a marriage referendum, won by just over a hundred votes. Yet NOM and the state Republican Party claimed a "moral" victory on the ground that President Obama had won this district, controlled by Democrats for the previous thirteen years, by fourteen hundred votes.[8]

In Maine, where the legislature had enacted gay marriage in May, opinion polls showed the state narrowly divided—49.5 percent opposing gay marriage and 47.3 percent supporting it. Unlike Vermont and New Hampshire, however, Maine has a constitutional provision authorizing popular recall of legislation— the so-called people's veto. The day after the governor signed the gay marriage bill, a coalition that included the Catholic archdiocese of Portland and evangelical Christians from the Maine Family Policy Council began circulating petitions to recall the law. To get Amendment 1 on the ballot, fifty-five thousand signatures had to be obtained by August 1. In less than three months, gay marriage opponents gathered an impressive one hundred thousand signatures.[9]

The anti-gay-marriage coalition hired the same public relations firm used by Proposition 8 proponents in California and employed the same strategy of emphasizing the effect that gay marriage would have on the public school curriculum. The coalition's fund-raising appeals solicited contributions "to keep homosexual education out of Maine's classrooms." Amendment backers even hired the same Mormon couple from Massachusetts who had been featured in television advertisements in California expressing anger at the public schools' teaching their seven-year-old about two princes getting married. Amendment 1 supporters also warned of lawsuits being filed against religious opponents of gay marriage and of churches being deprived of their tax-exempt status. The National Organization for Marriage, derided by opponents as a front group for the Mormon Church, spent over $1.5 million on the campaign. The Catholic Church contributed another $500,000.[10]

Gay marriage supporters were desperate for a victory to prove that they could win a popular vote somewhere. In an off-year election, the eyes of the political nation were on Maine. Gay marriage supporters outspent their opponents by roughly $5.8 million to $3.8 million. Because they were defending legislation rather than a court decision, they entered the contest better organized at the grassroots level than their compatriots in California had been. Their organization was impressive. They arranged swaps of frequent flyer miles and car pools for out-of-staters wishing to help with the campaign, and they encouraged sympathizers to combine their summer vacations in Maine with organizing to support gay marriage.[11]

Seeking to rectify perceived flaws in the campaign against Proposition 8 in California, gay marriage supporters in Maine ran television ads featuring schoolteachers denying that gay marriage would influence the public school curriculum. They even convinced Maine's governor and attorney general to denounce the charge as a red herring. Amendment opponents tried to humanize gay marriage in a way that the campaign against Proposition 8 had eschewed. Rather than hiding gays and lesbians, supporters of gay marriage showed them incorporated into ordinary families and highlighted the pain they would suffer if the recall measure passed.[12]

Maine is the third-least-religious state in the country, and religiosity strongly correlates with opposition to gay marriage. Statistician Nate Silver's sophisticated model calculated the odds of the amendment passing at one in four. Opinion polls also initially suggested that Amendment 1 would fail, though by the end of the campaign, polls revealed a race that was too close to call.[13]

In the end, Maine followed the path taken by every other state to vote on gay marriage: Amendment 1 passed by 52.8 percent to 47.2 percent. In Portland, the state's largest city, voters rejected the amendment by three to one. Yet in smaller cities the amendment won majority support, and rural voters were overwhelmingly in favor. Voter turnout was much higher than anticipated. But youth turnout was down in an off-year election, undoubtedly facilitating passage of the amendment.[14]

The *New York Times* called the result in Maine a "crushing loss" for the gay marriage movement, which had made "remarkable progress nationally" in 2009. An editorial in the *Los Angeles Times* asked, "If not in Maine, then where?" and concluded that the fight for gay equality "will be more difficult, more complicated and probably will take a good while longer than it should." Maggie Gallagher of NOM insisted that the Maine result disproved "the story line that is being manufactured that suggests the culture has shifted on gay marriage and the fight is over."[15]

Yet, had resolution of the issue been left up to students at the University of Maine, gay marriage would have prevailed by 81 percent to 19 percent— suggesting that the final word on the subject had not yet been heard. Noting that opinion polls showed a large majority of Mainers in favor of civil unions, some gay activists wondered whether marriage should not be temporarily relegated to the back burner and attention focused instead on securing some of its tangible legal benefits through domestic partnerships or civil unions.[16]

The same day that Mainers rejected gay marriage, Washingtonians voted on a measure to overturn the Everything but Marriage Act. After the legislature enacted it in May 2009, the Washington Values Alliance, objecting to what it called gay marriage in disguise, had secured the necessary 120,000 petition signatures to put the measure on the November ballot. Some conservatives wondered if resources should not be conserved for the gay marriage fight certain to come, especially as polls showed a substantial majority of Washingtonians favoring either gay marriage or civil unions. Business interests in Washington strongly opposed the repeal effort.[17]

In August, a federal judge temporarily blocked efforts by gay activists to secure from the state the names of people who had signed the referendum petitions. Their intention was to post the names online, ostensibly to enable supporters of Everything but Marriage to discuss the issue with petition signers whom they knew. The judge ordered the state not to make the names public, ruling that the First Amendment entitled petition signers to a hearing at which they would have the opportunity to show that publishing their names might result in harassment and intimidation. The U.S. Court of Appeals for the Ninth Circuit reversed that decision, but the Supreme Court stayed the ruling until it could hear the case, which did not happen until after the election.[18]

In November, voters sustained the Everything but Marriage Act by 53 percent to 47 percent. Given that an opinion poll that spring had showed Washingtonians opposed to gay marriage by 50 percent to 43 percent, the willingness of gay activists to accept a compromise short of marriage almost certainly was critical to their victory in November. Indeed, one study has found that gay marriage bans score 5 or 6 percentage points lower when they are written broadly enough to bar civil unions.[19]

The defeat of gay marriage in Maine seemed to influence the decision in California on whether to revisit Proposition 8 in 2010 or wait until 2012. One source reported a "strong consensus" that a win for gay marriage in Maine would have made it difficult to restrain gay activists in California from forging ahead in 2010. A couple of weeks after Maine passed Amendment 1, however, the Courage Campaign in California announced that it lacked the financial support, leadership, and public opinion backing to try to overturn Proposition 8 in 2010. The *Perry* litigators treated the defeat of gay marriage in Maine as a vindication of their decision to challenge Proposition 8 in federal court: constitutional rights must not be left to the electorate to defend.[20]

The defeat of gay marriage in Maine also raised the stakes in New York. As we have seen, the road to gay marriage in New York, which had seemed promising in the spring of 2009, took a detour that summer when Democratic control of the state senate imploded. After Democrats were restored to power, Governor Paterson announced that he would bring the gay marriage bill before a special legislative session scheduled for after the November election. An opinion poll showed that registered voters in New York supported gay marriage by 51 percent to 42 percent. Just before the election, the *New York Times* declared that New York was "tantalizingly close" to approving gay marriage.[21]

Governor Paterson lobbied hard for gay marriage that fall, as did other prominent state Democrats, including Senator Charles Schumer and state attorney general Andrew Cuomo. Mayor Michael Bloomberg also made phone calls to undecided state senators. Yet gay marriage became a harder sell in New York after voters in Maine rejected it, Governor Jon Corzine lost his reelection bid in New Jersey, and outraged conservatives in upstate New York forced the Republican candidate out of a special congressional election partly because of her support for gay marriage.[22]

New York Democrats still thought they had a chance to enact gay marriage or at least to lose on a close vote. However, in early December, the state senate defeated gay marriage by the lopsided margin of 38 to 24. In the end, neither moderate Republicans from Long Island nor swing-district Democrats from New York City or upstate supported the measure; eight Democrats voted against it. One senate supporter of gay marriage called the vote "the worst example of political cowardice I have ever seen," alleging that several senators who had privately promised support capitulated to political pressure in the end and voted against gay marriage. An opinion poll offered a ray of hope for the future to gay-marriage backers: New Yorkers between the ages of eighteen and thirty-four favored gay marriage by 71 percent to 20 percent.[23]

High hopes for gay marriage in New Jersey had crashed when Governor Corzine was narrowly defeated for reelection in November. Expressing strong support for gay marriage, Corzine had promised to bring the issue before the lame-duck legislative session scheduled for after the election. Just before the election, legislative backers predicted that gay marriage would pass if Corzine was reelected. By contrast, Corzine's opponent, Chris Christie, strongly opposed gay marriage—though not civil unions—even to the point of supporting a state constitutional amendment to block it, if necessary.[24]

After Corzine lost, gay marriage advocates figured that if they did not force a vote in the legislature's lame-duck session, then Christie would block gay marriage for at least the next four years. Gay marriage opponents hoped that the rejection of gay marriage in Maine would influence the votes of New Jersey legislators.[25]

Both sides lobbied aggressively. The National Organization for Marriage spent $250,000 on advertising, warning that children would be taught about gay marriage in school. Catholic bishops had priests distribute petitions against gay marriage to parishioners, of whom at least 150,000 signed. On the other side, the Human Rights Campaign and the National Gay and Lesbian Task Force donated staff members to Garden State Equality as it made a last-minute push for gay marriage, which opinion polls suggested a narrow majority of New Jerseyans supported.[26]

Within weeks of the election, support for gay marriage was draining away from the legislature. Corzine's loss apparently had rattled New Jersey Democrats, as had the defeat of gay marriage in Maine. Democrats had majorities in both houses of the legislature, but some of them now announced their opposition, leaving gay rights activists feeling betrayed. Almost no Republicans were willing to support gay marriage after the election. Not even an intervention by Bruce Springsteen could save gay marriage in New Jersey.[27]

After delaying the vote for lack of support, the senate finally killed the measure in January by a margin of 20 to 14. Corzine would have signed the bill had it passed. With Christie promising to veto any such legislation during his governorship, gay marriage supporters immediately vowed to return to the state supreme court. In the summer of 2010, the court told them that they must file a new lawsuit in trial court, which they did. That case is now proceeding to trial.[28]

Amid such defeats, gay marriage supporters admitted that they had misread public opinion in the spring and had allowed their optimism to outpace reality. Their one silver lining in the fall of 2009 was the enactment of gay marriage legislation by the D.C. city council. Councilors were not deterred by the strong opposition of the Catholic archbishop, who threatened that the Church would cut off social service programs involving adoption, homelessness, and health care rather than provide benefits to the spouses of gay employees.[29]

The District of Columbia Board of Elections and Ethics refused to permit a referendum on the city council's gay marriage law, ruling that to do so would violate the city charter, which does not permit referenda on matters of discrimination against minority groups. A local judge sustained the board, and Congress declined to overturn the council's action. Same-sex couples started marrying in the District of Columbia in March 2010.[30]

Defeats for gay marriage in Maine, New York, and New Jersey bolstered efforts to undo it in Iowa and New Hampshire. In the Granite State, gay marriage opponents prepared petitions to be delivered to town hall meetings in March 2010, asking them to instruct state legislators to schedule a non-binding referendum on gay marriage. In addition, some candidates for the Republican gubernatorial nomination in 2010 promised to work for repeal of gay marriage.[31]

In February, the New Hampshire legislature voted overwhelmingly against both a bill to repeal gay marriage and a constitutional amendment to forbid it. (Constitutional amendments are especially difficult to obtain in New Hampshire; they require support by 60 percent of both legislative houses, followed by voter approval of at least 66 percent in a referendum.) By April, 58 percent of town meetings that expressed a view declined to support a non-binding referendum on gay marriage.[32]

Unable to convince the Democratic-controlled legislature to repeal gay marriage, NOM ran a $1.5 million advertising campaign entitled "Lynch Lied," which accused Governor Lynch of breaking promises to voters on gay marriage and other issues. Although Lynch won reelection in 2010, Republicans scored huge victories in state legislative races, mostly on the basis of campaigns emphasizing job creation and deficit reduction.[33]

Now possessing legislative majorities large enough to override the governor's veto, Republicans introduced both a bill and a constitutional amendment to overturn gay marriage. Yet, early in 2011, Republican legislative leaders announced that repeal of the marriage equality law would not be a party priority in a year when all attention should be focused on the economy. Crying betrayal, NOM promptly mailed literature to voters in the house majority leader's district, criticizing him for standing with Governor Lynch in opposition to traditional family values.[34]

Despite a poll showing that New Hampshirites opposed repeal by an overwhelming margin of 62 percent to 29 percent, a Republican-controlled house committee approved a bill to repeal gay marriage in September 2011. The house was supposed to consider it early in 2012, though that vote has been delayed repeatedly. Some New Hampshire conservatives even pressed to make gay marriage a principal issue in the state's Republican presidential primary in January.

Yet, indicative of how far opinion has evolved even among New Hampshire Republicans, the marriage repeal bill would replace gay marriages with civil unions and would not interfere with the roughly eighteen hundred same-sex marriages that have taken place since the law went into effect. Governor Lynch's decision not to seek reelection in 2012 may improve the chances of the bill eventually becoming law because, depending on his successor, the bill's backers may no longer need the two-thirds majorities in both houses required to override a gubernatorial veto.[35]

The backlash against gay marriage in Iowa was formidable. In 2009, local groups opposing gay marriage and calling themselves Let Us Vote participated in parades and conducted public meetings. As many as a thousand Iowans, mobilized by the political action committee of the Iowa Family Policy Center, rallied at the statehouse, chanting "Let us vote," as the legislative session opened in 2010. However, Democratic leaders continued to block a legislative vote on a state constitutional amendment to ban gay marriage.[36]

Gay marriage was a prominent issue in Iowa's Republican gubernatorial primary, which was actively contested through the first half of 2010. Bob Vander Plaats, who had been the state chairman for Mike Huckabee's presidential campaign in Iowa in 2008, which won a surprise victory in the caucuses, tried to use gay marriage to mobilize his evangelical Christian base and catapult him to victory. Endorsed by Huckabee, the Iowa Family Policy Center, and James Dobson of Focus on the Family, Vander Plaats not only supported a state constitutional amendment to ban gay marriage but also reiterated his pledge to halt such marriages by executive order. A second Republican candidate, Rod Roberts, promised that, if elected, he would refuse to approve a budget until the legislature permitted a vote on the gay marriage amendment.[37]

The front-runner in the gubernatorial primary, former governor Terry Branstad, called Vander Plaats's idea for an executive order "ill-advised" and likely to elicit a citation for contempt of court. Instead, Branstad counseled patience: gay marriage opponents should elect enough Republicans to the state legislature that Democrats could no longer block a vote on the marriage amendment, which Branstad supported. Yet Branstad also emphasized his opposition to discrimination based on sexual orientation and his support of rights such as hospital visitation and adoption for same-sex couples. Such declarations sharply distinguished him from the other Republican candidates in the field.[38]

Vander Plaats not only criticized Branstad for disparaging his proposed executive order but also blamed the former governor for appointing two of the

justices who had joined the unanimous decision in *Varnum*. At a spring
fund-raiser for the Iowa Christian Alliance, Vander Plaats's call for an executive
order to block gay marriages elicited raucous applause and whistles of support
from the crowd. Though his proposal was pretty clearly unconstitutional, it
nonetheless mobilized conservative Christians behind his candidacy.[39]

Vander Plaats and Roberts promised, if elected, to appoint as judges only
opponents of gay marriage. Branstad replied that under Iowa's merit selection
system, the governor was required to appoint one of the three candidates recommended by a non-partisan commission. Branstad's opponents also announced
that they would encourage Iowa voters to reject the three supreme court justices
who were up for retention that fall. By contrast, Branstad promised only to
encourage voters to decide on the judges based on their own convictions. In
May, a former political director of the Iowa Republican Party declared marriage
to be the defining issue in the gubernatorial primary.[40]

Polls suggested that Branstad would win easily. Yet, largely on the strength of
the gay marriage issue, Vander Plaats managed to win 40.7 percent of the vote to
Branstad's 50.4 percent. Although he lost the primary, Vander Plaats had succeeded in focusing public attention on gay marriage and pushing Branstad to a
more conservative position on that issue. Soon after the primary, when Branstad's
running mate for lieutenant governor declared support for allowing Iowans to
vote on civil unions as well as gay marriage, Branstad rushed to distance himself
from her remarks, noting that he opposed civil unions, too.[41]

Meanwhile, Vander Plaats turned his attention to the judges responsible for
Varnum. Although it could take years to get a marriage amendment on the ballot,
political retaliation against the judges who decided *Varnum* was a more immediate
possibility. In Iowa, judicial appointees are nominated by a merit selection panel
consisting of fifteen members, most of whom are appointed by the governor and
the state bar association. As noted earlier, the governor's judicial appointments
must come from a list of three candidates proposed by the merit selection
committee. Once appointed, judges must face the voters periodically in non-
partisan retention elections.[42]

Since Iowa adopted merit selection in 1962, only four judges had ever been
defeated for retention. All of them had suffered from "some kind of personal
weirdness problems," according to a local political analyst. Not a single state
supreme court justice had ever lost a retention election. On average, they had
been retained with 75 percent of the vote. A judge in northwest Iowa who in
2003 divorced a couple who he did not realize were lesbians faced a recall
campaign led by Representative Steven King. He held on to his seat with just
59 percent of the vote. In 2007, religious conservatives had called for the
impeachment of the Polk County trial judge who ruled in favor of gay marriage
in *Varnum*.[43]

As early as November 2009, Republican gubernatorial candidate Roberts had suggested targeting the three state supreme court justices who would be up for retention elections in 2010. After running a close second in the gubernatorial primary, Vander Plaats announced the formation of Iowa for Freedom, which hired six full-time staff members to plan a political campaign against the justices' retention. Pastors at conservative churches coordinated the effort. When Americans United for the Separation of Church and State threatened to push for revocation of the tax-exempt status of these churches, more than two hundred of the pastors pledged to violate federal law and preach against retention from the pulpit.[44]

Backed by the American Family Association, a Mississippi-based non-profit that promotes conservative Christian values, Iowa for Freedom funded robo-calls that announced, "We are taking back control of our government from political activist judges." NOM and the Family Research Council sponsored a forty-five-county tour with a purple bus emblazoned with the faces of the three justices up for retention. Speakers such as Representative King and Republican presidential candidate Rick Santorum argued that the justices should be evicted from office because their ruling on gay marriage ignored millennia of tradition and the views of a majority of Iowans.[45]

A justice on the Alabama supreme court who was himself facing a contested reelection race published an op-ed in the *Des Moines Register* urging voters to punish the justices for their gay marriage ruling. Several Republican presidential hopefuls for 2012—Tim Pawlenty and Newt Gingrich, in addition

Protestor standing in front of the bus used in the campaign against retention of the three Iowa supreme court justices, Oct. 25, 2010. (*Associated Press/Charlie Neibergall*)

to Santorum—endorsed the anti-retention campaign. For a state judicial retention election to receive this sort of national attention and money was virtually
unprecedented.[46]

The three justices vowed not to formally campaign, granted no media interviews, and refused even to form a committee to raise money and fend off the
challenge, which they legally were entitled to do. However, one of them, Chief
Justice Marsha Ternus, conducted a statewide speaking tour in which she warned
that subjecting judges to political pressure would compromise their impartiality.[47]

The Iowa Bar Association created an organization called Iowans for Fair and
Impartial Courts to educate citizens on judicial selection without taking a position on the retention votes. Two former lieutenant governors, one from each
major political party, formed a coalition called Justice, Not Politics to fight to
preserve merit selection. Neither group specifically defended *Varnum*. Retired
U.S. Supreme Court justice Sandra Day O'Connor traveled to Des Moines to
defend merit selection. Two retired Iowa supreme court justices debated Vander
Plaats at a public forum, touting the role of courts as guardians of the rights of
unpopular minorities.[48]

Polls indicated that the retention votes were likely to be close. Groups
opposing retention spent $948,000, with $635,000 of that coming from NOM.
A pro-retention group, the Fair Courts for Us Committee, spent $366,000.[49]

In the end, the two associate justices were rejected by 54 percent to 46 percent, while the chief justice was defeated by 55 percent to 45 percent. Gay
marriage was the only issue in the retention campaign. Polls showed that the
same demographic groups that tend to oppose gay marriage—senior citizens,
men, Republicans, lower income earners, those who did not graduate from
college, and evangelical Christians—tended to oppose retention. In all five of
the state's major metropolitan areas, the justices won majorities for retention. In
some rural areas, however, voters rejected retention by margins as large as eight
to one.[50]

The same day that the justices were defeated, Republicans seized control of
the state house and pulled almost even in the senate. Vander Plaats immediately
called on the four remaining justices to resign. Governor-elect Branstad blamed
the justices' defeat on the Democratic senate majority leader, who had refused to
permit a legislative vote on the marriage amendment. Branstad also warned the
state's judicial nominating commission to propose only candidates "who respect
Iowa voters' rejection of last year's same-sex marriage ruling."[51]

The Iowa retention elections had ramifications for state judges throughout
the country. Conservative activists were emboldened to threaten more such
efforts in the future. Brian Brown, executive director of NOM, announced that
his group might try to organize future campaigns to remove the other four Iowa
justices. The executive director of the American Family Association, which had

contributed $100,000 to the Iowa retention campaign, warned "those who impose what we perceive as an amoral agenda, we're going to take [you] out." The president of Operation Rescue opined that the Iowa campaign could serve as a model for judicial challenges across the nation.[52]

Taking advantage of their new majority status in the Iowa house, Republicans quickly passed a resolution to place a marriage amendment on the ballot in 2013. Yet Democrats retained a slender majority of twenty-six to twenty-four in the senate, and majority leader Mike Gronstal persisted in blocking a floor vote. Several Democratic senators had indicated that they were likely to support the amendment if forced to vote on it.[53]

In November 2011, Democratic control of the state senate was put in jeopardy when Governor Branstad appointed a Democratic senator to the state utilities commission, necessitating a special election in a Republican-leaning district. If Republicans could win this seat, the senate would be evenly divided between the parties, and Gronstal's ability to continue to block a vote on the marriage amendment might be undermined.[54]

Together, the two sides spent nearly a million dollars on the race and bombarded district residents with phone calls and letters about gay marriage. In the end, the Democratic candidate narrowly prevailed. With Democrats maintaining tenuous control of the senate and Gronstal seemingly immovable in his opposition to allowing a vote on the marriage amendment, the earliest it can get on the ballot is 2014. By that date, a majority of Iowans may well support gay marriage.[55]

Still, given the prominent role that the Iowa caucuses play in presidential nominating contests, the gay marriage issue could not disappear from state politics. As many as 60 percent of Republican caucus-goers describe themselves as evangelical Christians. These voters provided Arkansas governor Mike Huckabee with a surprise victory in the 2008 caucuses.[56]

An opinion poll conducted by the *Des Moines Register* showed that 84 percent of Iowa Republicans believe that marriage should be between a man and a woman. Nearly 60 percent of likely Republican caucus-goers said that for a candidate to support civil unions would be a "deal killer" for them. Such voters were unlikely to be receptive to calls from some Republicans that the party declare a truce over social issues in order to focus on the economy in 2012.[57]

Accordingly, Republican presidential hopefuls came under enormous pressure in Iowa to oppose gay marriage. In 2009, Mitt Romney was quick to denounce *Varnum*. As we have seen, in 2010 several of the Republican presidential candidates endorsed the campaign against retention of the Iowa justices. Indeed, when launching his presidential bid, one way that former Speaker of the U.S. House of Representatives Newt Gingrich sought to allay evangelicals' concerns about his two divorces and recent conversion to Catholicism was to secure

$200,000 in funding from an anonymous donor to jump-start the anti-retention campaign. Likewise in New Hampshire, which held the first of the presidential primaries in January 2012, efforts by Republican state legislators to repeal gay marriage forced Republican presidential candidates to firmly reiterate their opposition to gay marriage.[58]

All of the major Republican contenders except Jon Huntsman and Ron Paul signed the NOM pledge, which requires candidates to support the federal marriage amendment, defend DOMA in court, and appoint only judges and an attorney general who oppose gay marriage. By signing the pledge, Rick Perry and Michele Bachmann seemed to contradict statements they had made earlier in 2011—when New York enacted gay marriage—that states should decide this issue for themselves. Apparently they preferred contradicting themselves to risking the ire of social conservatives by refusing to take the pledge.[59]

Just days before the Iowa caucuses, NOM ran a television ad criticizing Ron Paul for failing to support the federal marriage amendment. During a Republican presidential debate in Iowa, Santorum attacked Romney for permitting gay marriages on his watch as governor of Massachusetts. After winning the endorsement of Vander Plaats, Santorum rode a last-minute surge of evangelical support to a narrow victory in the caucuses. After that, he won the endorsement of NOM's Maggie Gallagher and of leading evangelicals such as Gary Bauer, based largely on his strenuous opposition to same-sex marriage.[60]

8

To the Present

Despite the backlash against gay marriage in Maine and Iowa in 2009–10, the overall social trend toward liberalization of attitudes and policies on gay rights issues remained unmistakable. The same day that Mainers rejected gay marriage, voters in Kalamazoo, Michigan, approved an ordinance forbidding discrimination based on sexual orientation. Residents of Chapel Hill, North Carolina, elected their first openly gay mayor. In Atlanta, Detroit, and St. Petersburg, Florida, voters elected their first openly gay city councilors. One month later, Houston, the nation's fourth-largest city, elected a lesbian mayor. An opinion poll showed that 76.5 percent of respondents deemed her sexual orientation irrelevant. In April 2010, President Obama nominated the first openly gay candidate for a judgeship on a federal court of appeals.[1]

In May 2010, a Gallup poll found for the first time ever that a majority of Americans—52 percent—believed that sex between same-sex partners was morally acceptable. In July, NBC announced that it would permit same-sex couples to participate in its Modern Wedding Contest on the *Today* show. That same month, a movie featuring a lesbian couple raising two children became a smash hit. *The Kids Are All Right* treated a same-sex couple and their parenthood as simple facts of American life. A reviewer in *Entertainment Weekly* wrote that the movie "erases the boundaries between specialized 'gay content' and universal 'family content.'"[2]

Also in July, Rush Limbaugh came out in support of civil unions for same-sex couples. Soon thereafter, conservative commentator Glenn Beck declared that "same-sex marriage isn't hurting anybody. Honestly, I think we have bigger fish to fry."[3]

In 2010, with health care reform legislation enacted, the Obama administration announced that repeal of "don't ask, don't tell" would be an administration priority. The president got no objection from his defense secretary or the chairman of the Joint Chiefs of Staff, though both requested that Congress put off action for a year, during which time the Pentagon could study the impact of changing the policy. Soon thereafter, Secretary of Defense Robert Gates announced that the Pentagon would begin easing enforcement while the study was pending. In the meantime, the administration continued to defend the constitutionality of "don't ask, don't tell" in court, eliciting much criticism from gay activists.[4]

Since "don't ask, don't tell" was adopted in 1993, about thirteen thousand service members had been discharged because of their sexual orientation, including eight hundred who were deemed "mission-critical" troops, such as fifty-nine Arabic-speaking linguists. A Gallup poll conducted in 2009 showed that 69 percent of Americans believed that gays should be permitted to serve openly in the military, up from 43 percent in 1993. Even among three voting blocs that traditionally have been the least supportive of gay rights— conservatives, Republicans, and weekly church-goers—about six in ten now supported permitting gays to serve openly in the military. Most of the military experts who had previously defended the policy had either changed course or died by 2010.[5]

Twenty-five countries—including many of America's staunchest allies, such as Israel, Canada, Australia, and the United Kingdom—had already lifted their own bans on openly gay members of the military, and expert studies had found no deleterious impact on military efficiency. Most nations that in 2010 still barred gays from the military were not ones with which the United States ordinarily likes to compare itself: China, Cuba, Iran, North Korea, and Pakistan. Yet some leading Republican congressional representatives, such as John Boehner and Mike Pence, objected to President Obama's undertaking "some social experiment" while the nation was fighting two wars.[6]

In May, the House passed a bill to authorize the Defense Department to repeal "don't ask, don't tell" sixty days after receiving the military's report on implementation. In September, however, Senate Republicans blocked a similar measure by threatening a filibuster, which left the prospects of repeal in 2010 uncertain. Some gay activists blamed the defeat on the president's "lack of leadership."[7]

That summer, after a federal district judge in California struck down Proposition 8, an administration spokesperson reiterated President Obama's opposition to gay marriage. Criticism from gay activists came fast and furious. Deploring the president's lack of "moral leadership," one commentator noted the irony that "America's first black president will be remembered as shirking the last great civil rights struggle."[8]

The administration also found itself in the uncomfortable position of defending in court two statutes—"don't ask, don't tell" and DOMA—that it wanted repealed and which lower courts were starting to invalidate. In the fall of 2010, when gay activists denounced as "indefensible" the administration's decision to appeal lower court rulings invalidating "don't ask, don't tell," the White House released a statement promising that the president would intensify his efforts to persuade the Senate to join the House in supporting repeal.[9]

In late October, Obama told a group of liberal bloggers that while he was still "unwilling to sign onto same-sex marriage," his views were "evolving," he thought about the issue "a lot," and "the trend lines" looked "pretty clear." Activists believed that the president was laying the groundwork for an eventual change in position. Just before Christmas, the Senate passed, and President Obama signed, the bill repealing "don't ask, don't tell." In January 2011, White House press secretary Robert Gibbs, pressed for an answer about the president's views on gay marriage, reiterated that Obama "thinks a lot" about the issue.[10]

The federal lawsuit challenging the constitutionality of Proposition 8, filed in the spring of 2009, was assigned to Judge Vaughn Walker, an appointee of President George H. W. Bush. Walker had a reputation for being smart, unpredictable, and somewhat libertarian. Gay rights groups had opposed his appointment to the bench because, as a private lawyer, he had represented the U.S. Olympic Committee in its successful lawsuit to prevent San Francisco's Gay Olympic Games from infringing on its name. During that litigation, Walker had been harshly criticized for putting a lien on the home of a gay-games leader who was

President Obama signing repeal of "don't ask, don't tell," Dec. 22, 2010. (*Associated Press/Evan Vucci*)

dying of AIDS. It took two years and two renominations to consummate his appointment.[11]

Before *Perry*, few gay marriage cases had actually gone to trial; lower courts usually resolved them based solely on the legal arguments. But Judge Walker wanted testimony on factual issues such as the effect of same-sex parenting on children and the history of discrimination against gays. Walker decided to make the trial accessible on YouTube pursuant to a Ninth Circuit pilot program, approved the preceding month, to permit cameras at selected civil trials. Defenders of Proposition 8 objected to televised proceedings on the ground that their witnesses feared retaliation. The U.S. Supreme Court quickly reversed Judge Walker's decision, holding that he had not allowed adequate opportunity for public comment on the proposed rule change that would have permitted live streaming of the proceedings.[12]

The twelve-day trial in *Perry* took place in January 2010. The challengers to Proposition 8 called a series of academic experts, including psychiatrists, sociologists, historians, economists, and political scientists—many of them affiliated with the nation's most elite universities, such as Harvard and Stanford. These experts testified that gay couples were as good at parenting as straight couples, that gay couples would benefit from marriage, that homosexuality was not a choice, that the definition of marriage has evolved historically, that gays have suffered from a history of discrimination, that gay marriage would boost the state's economy, that gays were politically disadvantaged in California, and that civil unions and domestic partnerships for same-sex couples were stigmatizing and unequal.[13]

Proposition 8 challengers also called as a witness William Tam, a San Francisco chemical engineer who had been one of the five official proponents of the amendment. Tam had compared gay marriage to pedophilia and polygamy, claimed that gays were twelve times as likely as straights to be child molesters, and warned that California would fall into the hands of Satan if gay couples were permitted to marry. The plaintiffs sought to use Tam's testimony to show that Proposition 8 was motivated by discriminatory animus toward gays, which might incline Judge Walker to invalidate it under *Romer v. Evans*, the Supreme Court's 1996 decision striking down Colorado's amendment barring local gay rights ordinances.[14]

The intervenors in *Perry*, who defended Proposition 8 because California officials declined to do so, denied that Tam had played any significant role in the amendment campaign. In the end, they called only two witnesses. One was a political scientist who testified that gays had ample political power in California. The other was David Blankenhorn, founder and president of the Institute for American Values, who testified that allowing same-sex couples to marry would discourage heterosexuals from doing so and might eventually lead to the legalization of polygamy. When the trial concluded, Proposition 8 defenders criticized Judge Walker for allowing "a spectacular show trial of irrelevant evidence."[15]

In August, Judge Walker struck down Proposition 8. Although he noted that aspects of the Proposition 8 campaign demonstrated animus toward gays, Walker also ruled in favor of gay marriage on broader grounds. He held that Proposition 8 interfered with the fundamental right to marry, the core of which involved two people choosing to form a committed relationship. In addition, he ruled that Proposition 8, though it warranted rigorous judicial scrutiny as discrimination based both on sex and sexual orientation, failed even to satisfy the more relaxed standard of minimum rationality review under the Equal Protection Clause. *Lawrence* had ruled that tradition was an insufficient justification for sustaining legislation, and Walker found that the other proffered state objectives of encouraging straight couples to marry and promoting an optimal environment for child rearing were not even remotely served by excluding gay couples from marriage. Judge Walker's ruling was immediately appealed to the Ninth Circuit, the most liberal federal appeals court in the nation, which stayed his decision pending the outcome of the appeal.[16]

Conservatives denounced Walker's ruling as "extreme judicial activism" and "judicial tyranny," and they declared that the judge had "contempt for the rule of law." NOM, the American Family Association, and Pat Buchanan now assailed Walker for having refused to recuse himself from the case even though he was gay.[17]

Walker's sexual orientation had been an open secret in San Francisco for years; he neither advertised it nor tried to hide it. Not long after his decision, Walker announced his retirement from the bench and came out openly as gay. Gay marriage opponents challenged his ruling on the ground that as a gay man involved in a long-term relationship, Walker possessed a direct interest in the outcome of the litigation and thus should have disqualified himself from presiding. That challenge was later rejected by a different federal district judge, whose decision was then affirmed by the Ninth Circuit.[18]

Also in the summer of 2010, a federal district court in Boston invalidated for the first time the section of DOMA defining marriage as the union of a man and a woman for federal purposes, such as filing a joint tax return or qualifying for social security survivors' benefits. Judge Joseph Tauro, a seventy-nine-year-old appointee of President Richard Nixon, found this statutory provision unconstitutional on two grounds. First, for Congress to deny federal benefits to same-sex couples who were married under state law was an invasion of state sovereignty. Second, Congress had no rational basis for denying recognition to gay marriages that had been recognized by states. Judge Tauro denied that the statute rationally furthered proffered state interests, such as encouraging procreation, providing an optimal environment for child rearing, and bolstering the institution of marriage.[19]

In the fall of 2010, new lawsuits were filed in federal courts in New York and Connecticut challenging this same section of DOMA. Early in 2011, a federal district judge in California indicated that she was likely to follow Judge Tauro in striking down this provision. In February, the Obama administration announced that the president had determined DOMA to be unconstitutional and that the Justice Department would no longer defend the law in court—though it would continue to enforce the statute until repealed or invalidated by a definitive court decision. Some commentators observed that the administration ran little political risk in shifting its position on DOMA in light of the dramatic changes sweeping the nation on gay marriage.[20]

Republicans promptly criticized President Obama for subverting the democratic process by unilaterally repealing a statute. A spokesperson for House majority leader John Boehner wondered why the president "thinks now is the appropriate time to stir up a controversial issue that sharply divides the nation" when most Americans were worried about jobs and government spending. Former Reagan administration solicitor general Charles Fried insisted that the administration was obliged to defend the statute in court even if it believed the law was unconstitutional. Republican presidential hopeful Newt Gingrich accused the president of violating his oath of office. Boehner announced that the House of Representatives would hire a private lawyer to defend DOMA in court, and former Bush administration solicitor general Paul Clement was quickly hired to do so. Still, the overall Republican response to the administration's change of position on DOMA was far more muted than it likely would have been just a couple of years earlier.[21]

The repeal of "don't ask, don't tell," together with the administration's shift on DOMA, produced a noticeable change in gay activists' sentiments toward the administration. Richard Socarides, a frequent critic of the president on gay rights issues, said there is "no question the president delivered in a major way for his gay supporters." One gay Democratic fund-raiser reported, "People who haven't given in a long, long time emailed me their credit card numbers."[22]

In March 2011, a bill to repeal DOMA was introduced for the first time in the U.S. Senate. One poll showed that Americans now opposed DOMA by 51 percent to 34 percent. An ABC News/*Washington Post* poll revealed, for the first time ever, that a majority of Americans—53 percent—supported the legalization of gay marriage. In May, a Gallup poll confirmed that finding. Six opinion polls conducted within a year showed national support for gay marriage ranging from 51 percent to 53 percent.[23]

Reacting to the federal court decisions invalidating DOMA and the shift in the administration's litigation posture, immigration judges began to adjourn deportation proceedings against gays and lesbians whose same-sex marriages were recognized by state law but not by the federal government. In June 2011, a federal bankruptcy judge in the Central District of California ruled DOMA unconstitutional, and twenty of his twenty-four colleagues took the unusual step of signing on to his opinion.[24]

Also in June, the Immigration and Customs Enforcement director issued new guidelines clarifying that one of the factors to be considered in prosecuting deportation cases was whether the defendant—gay or straight— was married to a U.S. citizen. Later that summer, Secretary of Homeland Security Janet Napolitano announced that her department would be under- taking a case-by-case review of pending deportation proceedings—which resulted in the suspension of some cases. In July, the Justice Department urged the Ninth Circuit to invalidate DOMA in a case challenging that court's decision to provide employment benefits to the same-sex spouses of court employees. In November, the Senate Judiciary Committee approved the Respect for Marriage Act, which would repeal DOMA, by a party-line vote of 10 to 8.[25]

As 2011 began, the Maryland legislature appeared poised to enact gay marriage. Democrats had gained two senate seats in November 2010 to increase their majority in the upper chamber to thirty-five to twelve. The senate president, who previously had opposed gay marriage, approved a committee realignment that virtually guaranteed that a marriage equality bill would reach the senate floor. Democratic governor Martin O'Malley announced that he would sign such a bill if it passed the legislature.[26]

An opinion poll taken in 2010 showed that Marylanders supported gay marriage by 46 percent to 44 percent. Given the proximity of Maryland to the District of Columbia and the state attorney general's 2010 opinion declaring that Maryland would recognize as valid gay marriages lawfully performed elsewhere, the state already effectively had gay marriage. In February 2011, the leader of the state senate rated the chances of the gay marriage bill's passing at 60 percent to 70 percent. When the state senate, traditionally the more conservative of the two chambers, narrowly approved the bill in February, the deal seemed done.[27]

Yet, in the end, "defeat was snatched out of the jaws of expected victory." African American ministers from Prince George's County, home to some of the largest and most influential black churches in the country, preached against gay marriage, which they saw as a violation of God's law, and urged their parishioners to pressure legislators to vote against it.[28]

Blacks are approximately 30 percent of Maryland's population. Although they tend to be more liberal than whites on economic issues, they also tend to be more religious, which correlates with opposition to gay marriage. For example, one poll found that 71 percent of white Marylanders supported gay marriage, while only 41 percent of black Marylanders did so.[29]

Under pressure from their constituents, several black delegates from Prince George's County who had been thought likely to support the bill decided to oppose it, which left the measure one or two votes short of a majority in the lower house. Backers decided to table the measure rather than see it defeated. One delegate from Prince George's County explained, "The power of the black churches was a big part of the problem."[30]

Gay marriage supporters insisted that they would try again in Maryland in 2012. Some gay marriage opponents admitted that they would have been prepared to accept civil unions. The *Washington Post* concluded, "The direction of the debate seems clear enough; the pace is frustrating."[31]

Several state legislatures enacted civil unions in 2011: Hawaii, Delaware, Illinois, and Rhode Island. In Rhode Island, lawmakers held hearings on gay marriage, which newly elected governor Lincoln Chafee supported. But the Democratic president of the state senate opposed it, and the openly gay Speaker of the house ultimately abandoned the marriage bill, leading the legislature to compromise on civil unions. Governor Chafee signed that measure, though many gay activists urged him to veto it, partly because it was not marriage and partly because it contained a broad religious exemption. With the rest of New England allowing gay couples to marry, and Rhode Island recognizing the validity of gay marriages lawfully performed elsewhere, few gay couples in Rhode Island took advantage of the civil unions law.[32]

In 2011, gay marriage finally triumphed in New York through the legislative process. By 2010, most Democrats running for state office in New York supported gay marriage—a dramatic shift from just a few years earlier. Wealthy donors who supported gay marriage successfully targeted incumbent state legislators who opposed it in three districts. They spent nearly $800,000 in negative television advertising, which did not mention the marriage issue. Newly elected Democratic governor Andrew Cuomo called for gay marriage in his State of the State address, and a poll taken early in 2011 showed that New Yorkers supported gay marriage by a margin of 56 percent to 37 percent.[33]

The Human Rights Campaign financed an advertising barrage, which included video testimonials supporting gay marriage by celebrities such as actress Whoopi Goldberg and New York Rangers hockey star Sean Avery. Several prominent Republican fund-raisers, including billionaire financial executive Paul Singer, provided financial support to the lobbying campaign.[34]

On the other side, Catholic archbishop Timothy Dolan proclaimed gay marriage a radical assertion of government power comparable to that exercised by totalitarian regimes such as North Korea. Dolan also argued—perhaps surprisingly for a Catholic prelate committed to natural law principles—that New York should conduct a referendum on gay marriage.[35]

Democrats had lost their senate majority in New York in 2010, so gay marriage could pass only if it attracted some Republican support. The Conservative Party again threatened to deny its ballot line to any Republican legislator voting in favor of gay marriage. After a week of high drama in which newspapers reported that the bill remained one vote shy of a senate majority, it finally passed that body on June 25, 2011, by a margin of 33 to 29. Only one Democrat, Ruben Diaz, voted against the bill, while four Republican senators voted in favor.[36]

Evan Wolfson, president of Freedom to Marry, called the result "an immense win that brings giant momentum to the movement to end marriage discrimination in the U.S." The number of Americans living in states that allowed gay couples to marry had doubled overnight. Moreover, for the first time ever, a state legislative chamber controlled by Republicans had voted in favor of gay marriage.[37]

In the second half of 2011, gay activists contributed hundreds of thousands of dollars to the campaign coffers of each of the four Republican senators who had voted for gay marriage, both in gratitude for their votes and to protect them against future Conservative Party primary challengers. Mayor Bloomberg held a fund-raiser for the four senators and contributed $10,000 himself to each senator's reelection campaign. Gay activists also made substantial donations to the New York senate Republican leadership to acknowledge its having permitted the gay marriage vote to take place.[38]

In other states as well, a few Republicans were beginning to break party ranks and endorse gay marriage. In Iowa, a former Republican state senator, Jeff Angelo, launched Iowa Republicans for Freedom, which defended gay marriage on libertarian grounds. Republicans in Colorado formed Coloradans for Freedom, which supported a civil unions bill that Republican legislators killed in 2011.[39]

After New York enacted gay marriage, prominent conservative commentator David Frum recanted his opposition, observing that he and other conservatives were "strangely untroubled" by New York's action and denying that gay marriage was responsible for the declining stability of the American family. Leading Republicans on Capitol Hill were conspicuously silent in response to New York's action.[40]

By contrast, NOM announced a $2 million political campaign to punish those "turncoat" senate Republicans who had made gay marriage possible in New York. In September, it spent more than $50,000 to oppose the Democratic candidate in a special congressional election, David Weprin, who was the first Albany lawmaker to appear on the ballot since the legislature approved gay marriage. Weprin lost his race. Although economic issues dominated the brief campaign, constituents repeatedly asked Weprin about gay marriage, and the issue apparently resonated with many in the district's large Orthodox Jewish community.[41]

9

Why Backlash? Part I: Courts and Public Opinion

Most court decisions are not highly salient events, but there are some notable exceptions, such as *Brown v. Board of Education* (1954) and *Roe v. Wade* (1973). Prominent Court decisions can direct public attention to previously ignored issues. Americans were not preoccupied with flag burning until the Supreme Court issued two controversial rulings on the subject in 1989 and 1990. Within six months of a 1990 Supreme Court decision involving the right to die, half a million Americans drafted living wills.[1]

Gay marriage received virtually no media coverage until the Hawaii supreme court decision in *Baehr* in 1993. That ruling was noted by newspapers across the country. In 1996, both the trial of *Baehr* on remand and the court's decision received prominent national news coverage. Announced just ten days before the end of 1999, the Vermont supreme court's decision in *Baker* was quickly ranked by editors and broadcasters as the state's top news story of the year. In 2000, the civil unions issue was the nearly unanimous choice as top news story in Vermont.[2]

To an even greater degree, the Massachusetts supreme court's ruling in *Goodridge* raised the visibility of gay marriage. For the following year, gay marriage stories captured front-page newspaper headlines, and the issue played a prominent role in the 2004 elections, including the presidential contest. An opinion poll conducted by the *Boston Globe* just days after the decision found that more than 90 percent of Bay Staters were aware of it.[3]

Court decisions not only made gay marriage salient but also made people aware of how much change had recently occurred on other gay rights issues. Other legal reforms—such as state laws forbidding discrimination based on sexual orientation, court decisions permitting gays to adopt children, and local government ordinances providing partnership benefits to gay couples—did not attract the same media attention as did judicial decisions on gay marriage. For many religious conservatives, therefore, *Goodridge* served as a slap in the face, forcing them to acknowledge the dramatic changes in attitudes and legal practices regarding sexual orientation that had occurred in recent decades.[4]

Furthermore, in much the same way that *Brown* had forced the hand of many southern politicians who had not previously taken a public position on school desegregation and would have preferred not to discuss it, *Goodridge* compelled sometimes reluctant politicians to articulate their views on gay marriage. For the two years before *Goodridge*, gay activists had unsuccessfully demanded that New York attorney general Eliot Spitzer provide an opinion on whether state law permitted gay marriage. Within a week of Mayor West's marrying gay couples in New Paltz in 2004, Spitzer issued an opinion declaring that New York law did not permit gay marriages within the state but did require that such marriages be recognized if lawfully performed elsewhere.[5]

Similarly, Mayor Michael Bloomberg had refused to express an opinion on gay marriage during his first two years in office. Within a week of the New Paltz marriages, he seemed to indicate in remarks made at a private dinner for gay and lesbian journalists that he supported changing New York law to legalize gay marriage. A year later, when a trial judge in New York City declared that same-sex couples had a constitutional right to marry, Bloomberg accompanied his announcement that the city would appeal the ruling with his first clear public statement of support for changing state law to permit gay marriage. In Santa Fe, New Mexico, candidates for county clerk were asked for the first time about their positions on gay marriage months after the Sandoval County clerk had sparked great controversy by issuing marriage licenses to same-sex couples.[6]

Not only do court decisions make people aware of previously unnoticed social change and force politicians to take positions on issues that they have previously ducked, but they also impose substantive resolutions of policy issues that may be very different from those supported by most voters. It is this aspect of judicial decisions that is the most important cause of backlash.

On equality issues, such as those involving race and sexual orientation, public opinion often varies widely across a spectrum of sub-issues. Under Jim Crow, for example, whites were generally more opposed to interracial marriage and the desegregation of grade schools than they were to desegregating public transportation or permitting African Americans to vote. Similarly, in the twenty-first century, public opinion has been much more opposed to gay marriage than to civil unions, and it has been even less resistant to laws forbidding employment discrimination based on sexual orientation or to the decriminalization of same-sex sodomy.[7]

With regard to both race and sexual orientation, marriage was the item on the reform agenda that generated the greatest public resistance—"politically the toughest issue," as Congressman Barney Frank called gay marriage in 1996. In 1954, polls showed that a narrow majority of Americans supported *Brown v. Board of Education,* while 90 percent of them still opposed interracial marriage. Similarly, in 1996, 84 percent of Americans supported equal rights for gays in employment, but only 33 percent favored gay marriage.[8]

Furthermore, parties on the opposite sides of social reform debates sometimes have rank orderings of priorities that are inversely related. When this happens, political compromise becomes possible, and social reform can occur without generating intense backlash.

Thus, for example, under Jim Crow, whites most strenuously opposed interracial marriage and grade school desegregation, as previously mentioned, while most blacks cared less about those issues than about securing equal funding for black schools, protection from white violence, and the right to vote. Before *Brown* made school desegregation salient and non-negotiable, blacks and whites in the Jim Crow South had room to bargain (although widespread disenfranchisement of blacks dramatically reduced their bargaining power).[9]

Likewise, on issues of sexual orientation in recent decades, gay rights advocates have tended to prioritize objectives such as securing legal protection from workplace discrimination and hate crimes. In 1994, a *Newsweek* poll of self-identified gays and lesbians found that 91 percent thought equal rights in the workplace were very important and 77 percent identified health care and social security benefits as very important, but only 42 percent said that legally sanctioned gay marriage was very important. Notably, public opinion was most strongly supportive on the issues that gays cared the most about. Gay marriage, which most gays did not prioritize, generated the strongest opposition from most Americans.[10]

In other countries, where courts typically play a less central role on issues of social reform, gay rights progress has occurred more incrementally through legislatures and has generated less political backlash. (The lesser religiosity of those countries' populations is undoubtedly also a relevant factor in explaining the relative absence of backlash resulting from gay rights progress.) First legislatures decriminalized same-sex sodomy. Then they permitted gays to serve in the military, enacted laws forbidding employment discrimination based on sexual orientation, and adopted some form of domestic partnership benefits. Gay marriage came later, if at all. More incremental change enabled public opinion and politicians to gradually adjust to gay equality, abated some of the tangible harms suffered by gay couples, and allayed concerns of those troubled by the prospect of gay marriage.[11]

Court decisions can shift the order in which social reform occurs and advance to the forefront of debate issues that remain intensely controversial. The point is not that court decisions generate greater backlash than identical legislative policy resolutions would have, but rather that courts may issue unpopular decisions that legislatures, confronting the same issue at the same time, would have avoided.[12]

Court rulings such as *Baehr* and *Goodridge* generated enormous political backlash because they endorsed gay marriage at a time when public opinion, which had been growing more progressive on other gay rights issues, remained strongly opposed to it. When *Baehr* was decided in 1993, not a single jurisdiction in the world had embraced gay marriage. The most progressive cities in the United States were just beginning to adopt domestic partnerships, and the Clinton administration was suffering a devastating defeat in its effort to allow gays to serve openly in the military—which roughly half of all Americans supported. Even in Hawaii, one of the most gay-friendly states in the nation, more than 70 percent of the population opposed gay marriage. Only six states, mostly in New England, registered even 30 percent support for gay marriage at the time.[13]

When *Goodridge* was decided ten years later, no state legislature had yet come close to adopting gay marriage. Only two states had enacted domestic partnerships for same-sex couples, and Massachusetts was not one of them. Although public opinion in Massachusetts was closely divided on gay marriage in 2003, the country as a whole remained opposed to it by roughly two to one. Even Massachusetts legislators sympathetic to gay rights were shocked that the court had refused to compromise by accepting civil unions, as the Vermont supreme court had done four years earlier. When the Iowa supreme court ruled in favor of gay marriage in 2009, opinion polls suggested that Iowans still opposed it by a margin of more than 20 percentage points.[14]

Had the Hawaii legislature enacted gay marriage in 1993 or the Massachusetts legislature done so in 2003, they likely would have ignited political backlashes similar in scope to what transpired after *Baehr* and *Goodridge*. To be sure, conservative opponents of gay marriage denounce as judicial tyranny those court decisions that proclaim it to be a constitutional right. For example, in 2003, former solicitor general Ken Starr decried *Goodridge* as "a terrible judicial usurpation of the power of the people through their elected representatives to fashion social policy."[15]

Yet that rhetoric is hard to take seriously. When gay marriage opponents lose in court, they argue that legislatures are the appropriate forum in which to resolve the issue. But when they lose in legislatures, as they began to do in several New England states in the spring of 2009, they insist that gay marriage ought to be resolved through a vote of the people, as if some principle inherent in democracy requires that certain important issues be resolved only by popular referendum. Moreover, opponents of gay marriage plainly do not subscribe in general to any such principle of direct democracy: they would strongly oppose putting up for a vote their own right to the free exercise of religion.[16]

When the legislative or executive branches of government have advanced beyond public opinion on gay rights issues, political backlash has ensued. In 1977, Anita Bryant mobilized a potent backlash against the gay rights ordinance adopted by the Dade County Commission. In 1993, Colorado voters adopted a constitutional amendment to overturn the gay rights ordinances enacted by several cities in the state. That same year, President Clinton's effort to remove the ban on gay military service generated a firestorm of political resistance, which forced him to back down. In 2009, Maine voters repealed the gay marriage law enacted by their state legislature earlier that year.[17]

Yet legislatures are less likely than courts to stray far from public opinion. After several local referenda orchestrated by Bryant repealed gay rights ordinances in 1977–78, city councils became far more cautious about enacting them until public opinion had shifted in their favor. Although the Maine legislature in 2009 miscalculated public opinion on gay marriage, it did not miss its mark by much. An opinion poll conducted soon after the legislature enacted gay marriage showed that Mainers opposed it by just 49.5 percent to 47.3 percent, and in November they rejected it by only 52.5 percent to 47.5 percent.[18]

By contrast, when courts in Hawaii and Alaska protected gay marriage in the 1990s, voters in those states overturned the decisions by margins of roughly 70 percent to 30 percent. No state legislature was even close to enacting gay marriage in the 1990s.

Political backlash results from government action that strongly contravenes public opinion. Whether that action derives from legislatures or courts seems relatively unimportant. Yet courts are more likely than legislatures to take action that is sufficiently deviant from public opinion to generate powerful backlash.

Throughout American history, constitutional interpretation by courts has been constrained by public opinion. The Supreme Court did not dream of protecting women under the Fourteenth Amendment before the women's movement. The justices did not question the constitutionality of the death penalty or abortion restrictions until public opinion on these issues began to shift dramatically in the 1960s. The Court did not even question the constitutionality of racial segregation and black disenfranchisement until after World War II ignited various economic, social, and political forces for progressive racial change.[19]

How did courts such as those in Hawaii in 1993, Alaska in 1998, Vermont in 1999, Massachusetts in 2003, and Iowa in 2009 advance so far beyond public opinion on the issue of legal recognition of same-sex relationships? For starters, even though judges are part of contemporary culture and thus not impervious to public opinion, they are more insulated than legislators from its influence because they live a more cloistered existence and are less politically accountable. Elected judges stand for reelection less frequently than do legislators, and appointed judges are even more insulated from public opinion than elected ones. To say that judges are constrained by dominant public opinion is not to deny that they enjoy more leeway to depart from it than do more directly accountable legislators.[20]

Even more important, judges may occasionally misread public opinion because they are better educated and more affluent than the average American. Their elite socioeconomic status predisposes judges to hold views on certain cultural issues that are more liberal than those of the mainstream. Judges are part not only of the cultural elite but of a distinctive subculture—the legal elite— which tends to be even more liberal than the general public on issues such as gender equality and gay equality.[21]

The socioeconomic elite are as much as 40 percentage points more likely to be pro-choice on abortion issues than are people at the other end of the socio- economic spectrum. Only 43 percent of those with a college education disap- proved of the Supreme Court's decisions barring government-sponsored prayer in public schools, while 72 percent of those with less than a college education disapproved. People possessing an advanced degree were 51 percentage points less likely to support a constitutional amendment permitting the government to ban flag burning than were people who had not finished high school.[22]

On gay rights issues as well, the socioeconomic elite are generally more liberal than are average Americans. One Roper poll found that 74 percent of respon- dents with postgraduate education would be willing to vote for a well-qualified homosexual for president, while only 46 percent of those lacking a high school diploma would do so. A 1998 opinion poll found that among those lacking a high school degree, 51 percent thought that high school sex education courses should teach that homosexuality is immoral, while only 23 percent of those with a college degree agreed.[23]

Education levels are inversely correlated with religiosity, which strongly pre- dicts views about gay marriage. Exit polls from Michigan's marriage referendum in 2004 revealed that 82 percent of respondents who reported attending church more than once a week voted against gay marriage, while only 35 percent of those who never attended church did so. Exit polls on Proposition 8 in California in 2008 showed that 84 percent of those attending church at least once a week voted to ban gay marriage, while 83 percent of those never attending church voted against the ban. In 2009, polls showed New Yorkers divided down the middle on gay marriage—46 percent in favor and 46 percent opposed. However, those attending religious services at least once a week opposed gay marriage by 66 percent to 26 percent, while those infrequently attending church services supported it by 56 percent to 36 percent.[24]

To be sure, the culturally elite bias of judges on gay rights issues is partially offset by another demographic variable: age. Judges are much older than the average American, and age is inversely correlated with support for gay marriage. For example, a Vermont poll conducted in 1999 found that 73 percent of respondents between the ages of eighteen and twenty-four supported gay marriage, while only 20 percent of those sixty-five and above did so. A team of political scientists who examined multiple opinion polls on gay marriage found a gap of 44 percentage points in support between the youngest and oldest survey respondents. For many judges, however, the culturally elite bias in favor of gay marriage apparently has trumped the age bias against it.[25]

The elite bias of judges probably helps explain an otherwise puzzling phenomenon—why so many of the landmark judicial decisions on gay marriage have been authored by Republicans (Judge Joseph Tauro in the Massachusetts DOMA cases, Judge Vaughn Walker in *Perry*, Chief Justice Margaret Marshall in Massachusetts, Chief Justice Ronald George in California, Justice Mark Cady in Iowa, and Justice Richard Palmer in Connecticut). Even the conservative component of the lawyerly elite apparently is more supportive of gay marriage than is the average American.[26]

Judges may advance beyond public opinion on issues such as gay marriage not simply because they possess different values than ordinary Americans do but also because they function within an institution that operates according to different norms than the political system does. Even liberal politicians such as President Bill Clinton or Senator John Kerry have defended the traditional definition of marriage on the grounds that their constituents support it or that tradition commands it. Likewise, voters participating in referenda on gay marriage may oppose it because of visceral revulsion or because of their understandings of the Bible.[27]

For example, when asked to explain their reasons for voting in favor of Proposition 8 in California, 48 percent of respondents identified the preservation of traditional values and 33 percent singled out their religious beliefs. When speaking candidly before a Maine rally organized by NOM, one gay marriage opponent declared, "We must understand that the enemy will never accept defeat in their efforts to destroy the family as God designed." As the Iowa supreme court observed in *Varnum*, the principal (though often unspoken) reason for excluding same-sex couples from marriage has been the perception that the Bible commanded it.[28]

However, judges and the constitutional norms they have developed under the Establishment Clause and the Equal Protection Clause require that government policies serve secular objectives, and they have deemed tradition and morality to be insufficient justifications for legislation. Therefore, lawyers defending gay marriage bans in court have been forced to articulate other government interests that are said to be served by excluding gay couples from marriage. Yet because these proffered justifications are generally not the real reasons for banning gay marriage, they usually appear unpersuasive, even disingenuous.[29]

Thus, for example, lawyers have often defended bans on gay marriage as serving the government interest in promoting procreation within marriage. Yet allowing only opposite-sex couples to marry is wildly over- and under-inclusive to that government objective. In the *Perry* case, when lawyer Charles Cooper offered this justification for Proposition 8, Judge Walker made fun of him, noting that the last marriage he had performed was between a ninety-five-year-old man and an eighty-three-year-old woman.[30]

Similarly absurd is the argument that, because opposite-sex couples can become pregnant through accident, marriage is necessary to provide stability to their relationship with their children. By contrast, same-sex couples are said not to require government-backed stability in their relationships with their children because they can become parents only through deliberative and arduous processes such as adoption and artificial insemination. Could anyone really believe that these are the sorts of reasons for so many Americans' passionate opposition to gay marriage?[31]

Political backlash is especially likely when a court decision not only contravenes public opinion but has supporters who are less intensely committed than are its opponents—at least those supporters who are less immediately impacted by the decision. Massive resistance to *Brown v. Board of Education* was so potent partly because whites who opposed the decision cared so much more than did whites who supported it. African Americans, who for the most part strongly endorsed the ruling, had little political influence in the 1950s, especially in the South, where they were still largely disenfranchised.

In 1954, more than 70 percent of whites outside of the South agreed with *Brown*, but only about 6 percent of them viewed civil rights as the nation's most important political issue. These lukewarm defenders of *Brown* generally opposed aggressive enforcement measures, such as cutting off federal education money to segregated school districts. By contrast, in the South, where more than 85 percent of whites thought *Brown* was wrong, 40 percent of respondents identified civil rights as the country's most important political issue. Only the civil rights movement of the 1960s would equalize the intensity of commitment of those whites who opposed segregation and those who supported it.[32]

Over the last quarter century, the same disparity in intensity of preference has existed on gay rights issues generally and on same-sex marriage specifically. (Gays, likely to care the most about gay rights issues, are only 5 percent to 10 percent of the population and thus are in need of allies with similarly strong commitments.) One opinion poll in 1986 found that three times as many Americans were very unsympathetic to homosexuals as were very sympathetic.

In 1993, Americans were divided down the middle over the ban on gays in the military, but many more opponents of gays' serving openly felt strongly than did supporters. Thus opponents were better able to generate letters to Congress and phone calls to radio programs condemning President Clinton's effort to repeal the ban.[33]

Disparate intensity of preference on gay marriage has been enormous. In 2004, Americans opposed gay marriage by a margin of roughly two to one. But among the third who favored it, only 6 percent said they would refuse to vote for a political candidate who opposed that position. Among the two-thirds who rejected gay marriage, however, 34 percent said they would refuse to support a candidate who did not share their views. Among evangelical Christians, 55 percent said they would refuse to do so. Likewise, one trio of political scientists reported that between 30 percent and 40 percent of Americans said they strongly opposed gay marriage, while only 8 percent to 14 percent considered themselves strong supporters.[34]

One Presbyterian minister whose views on gay marriage evolved over time tells a story that nicely captures this phenomenon. For him to continue publicly opposing gay marriage, despite his shifting views, was easier because his congregants who supported gay marriage would never leave the church simply because it maintained its traditional stance of opposition. By contrast, those congregants who felt that homosexuality was a sin "would bolt in a heartbeat if we ever allowed gay clergy or gay marriage," and they would take with them half the church's budget. Given such extreme disparities in intensity of commitment, it is small wonder that gay marriage rulings have generated such political backlash.[35]

Disparate intensity of preference on gay rights issues can exist within voters as well as across them. Exit polls conducted on Election Day in 2004 revealed that more than 60 percent of Americans supported either gay marriage or civil unions. Yet eight of the eleven state ballot initiatives passed that day prohibited both. Why didn't more voters who supported civil unions while opposing gay marriage vote against amendments that prohibited both? Similarly, in North Carolina, pollsters found that 40 percent of those who supported civil unions for same-sex couples nonetheless said they were planning to vote in 2012 for a constitutional amendment barring both gay marriage and civil unions. Apparently those voters occupying the middle of the spectrum on gay rights issues have opposed gay marriage more vehemently than they have supported civil unions.[36]

Opponents of gay marriage not only have tended to care more about the issue than their opponents but also have been better organized. Because opposition to gay rights is often grounded in religiosity, opponents of gay rights measures can capitalize on preexisting church networks, media outlets, and national coordinating committees. These are the same sorts of organizational advantages that the civil rights movement, growing out of black churches, enjoyed in the 1960s.[37]

In 1982, the largest gay rights organization in the country, the National Gay Task Force, had 10,300 members and a budget of $338,000. Its main opponent on gay rights issues, the Moral Majority, had four million members and a budget of $56 million. In virtually every marriage referendum held over the last fifteen years, the opposition to gay marriage has been led by organizations composed of evangelical churches and, usually, the Catholic and Mormon Churches. Petition signatures were gathered in churches. Ministers denounced gay marriage from the pulpit and urged their congregants to vote against it. Special collection plates were passed to raise funds for the opposition campaigns. Gay marriage advocates have had to struggle to match such organizational prowess.[38]

As we have seen, court decisions can enact policy positions that deviate significantly from the preferences of the average voter and alienate those with the strongest opinions. Another important effect of court decisions is shaping the policy agenda of both litigation winners and losers. One mechanism by which court decisions influence policy agendas is by encouraging beneficiaries of a ruling to take concrete steps to implement it.[39]

After *Brown v. Board of Education,* the NAACP urged southern blacks to petition school boards for immediate desegregation on threat of litigation. Blacks filed such petitions in hundreds of southern localities, including in the Deep South. In a few cities, such as Baton Rouge and Montgomery, blacks even showed up in person to try to register their children at white schools.[40]

The petition campaign by African Americans to implement *Brown* stimulated more resistance than had the decision itself. Southern whites in droves joined Citizens' Councils—organizations pledged to maintaining white supremacy by all means short of violence—as southern blacks began filing desegregation petitions with local school boards. These whites reasoned that "we must make certain that Negroes are not allowed to force their demands on us." As the *Jackson Daily News* editorialized, "There is only one way to meet the attack of the NAACP. Organized aggression must be met by organized resistance."[41]

Gay marriage rulings had a similar implementation effect. In 2000, same-sex couples flocked to Vermont from out of state to secure civil unions even though their own states did not recognize such an institution. Similarly inspired by *Goodridge,* thousands of same-sex couples applied for marriage licenses in San Francisco and Portland early in 2004. Smaller numbers did so in Sandoval County, New Mexico; New Paltz, New York; and Asbury Park, New Jersey. More than one thousand gay couples married in Massachusetts on May 17, 2004, the day that *Goodridge* went into effect.[42]

Keith Maynard and Chip McLaughlin receive applause from the crowd as they walk down the front steps of city hall in Cambridge, Massachusetts, after being among the first same-sex couples to apply for a marriage license in the early morning hours of May 17, 2004. (*Associated Press/Josh Reynolds*)

Scenes of gay and lesbian couples celebrating their marriages on the steps of city halls appeared on the front pages of newspapers and on nightly television news programs. Such images enabled conservatives to mobilize support for state and federal constitutional amendments to bar gay marriage. Even at a time when polls showed a majority of Americans supporting civil unions, focus groups still evidenced great discomfort with the idea of homosexuality and visceral revulsion toward an advertisement showing gays or lesbians kissing.[43]

The weddings inspired by *Goodridge* elicited the same reaction as that advertisement. Though these weddings were paid for by gay rights supporters, they did the work of opponents. Such marriages both made the implications of *Goodridge* concrete and increased the visibility of gay marriage to the rest of the country.[44]

Observing that "there are millions of Americans angry and disgusted by" the gay weddings they saw on television, the executive director of the Campaign for California Families labeled gay marriage "the new Civil War in America." Only after these weddings did President George W. Bush unequivocally announce his support for a federal marriage amendment. In Cincinnati, Ohio, a group called Citizens for Community Values began mobilizing to put a marriage amendment on the state ballot on the same day that gay couples began legally marrying in Massachusetts.[45] After the 2004 elections, a lawyer for the Alliance Defense

Fund, a Christian group that sued to block gay marriages in California, observed that while *Goodridge* had been the "trigger" for the political backlash over gay marriage, the weddings in San Francisco had "definitely accelerated the reaction" by providing images of same-sex couples embracing and celebrating their marriages.[46]

Court victories inspired same-sex couples who had long hoped to marry to finally do so. They also influenced the preferences of many gay couples who had not previously given much thought to marriage. Before *Baehr*, marriage had elicited relatively little interest among gays and lesbians, perhaps mainly because the prospect of its ever becoming available seemed so slim.[47]

Within a few months of *Baehr*, however, the *Advocate* declared that gay marriage is the "new hot issue in the nation's gay and lesbian community." The following year, a survey of gay men conducted by the *Advocate* found that 85 percent would marry a same-sex partner if legally permitted to do so. Gay men now identified marriage as a higher priority than securing a federal antidiscrimination law or ending the ban on gays in the military.[48]

Baehr influenced the agenda of gay rights organizations. Before *Baehr*, the leadership of Lambda Legal had been divided over whether to pursue same-sex marriage. *Baehr* effectively ended that debate, as Lambda added marriage to its list of priorities and, in 1994, established its marriage project. Only after *Baehr* did the Equality Federation, a national coalition of gay rights organizations, begin meeting regularly to discuss marriage strategy. The Hawaii litigation also inspired similar lawsuits in Alaska and Vermont a few years later.[49]

Some gay activists were unhappy that three same-sex couples in Hawaii and their lawyer had been able to influence the focus of the gay rights movement. Agenda control is critical to success in politics. Any interest group wants to focus public attention on issues that give it an advantage over its adversaries. In the 1990s, gay rights opponents were delighted to shift attention away from issues on which they were rapidly losing public support, such as anti-discrimination protections for gays and lesbians, and to focus instead on gay marriage, which 70 percent or more of the country opposed. As one gay rights lobbyist observed in 1996, "It's a mark of how far we've come that the religious right feels compelled to shift its attention to the last frontier."[50]

Baehr and the subsequent embrace of same-sex marriage by gay activists enabled religious conservatives and the Republican Party to put the gay rights movement on the defensive. In both state legislatures and Congress, conservatives introduced bills to defend traditional marriage. In response to charges that they were manipulating the issue for political advantage, they noted that Hawaii judges had forced the matter upon them. For example, Bob Barr, sponsor of the Defense of Marriage Act in the U.S. House of Representatives, denied that anyone in Congress had "invented" the issue. Rather, "homosexual extremists" such as Lambda Legal had "forced" the issue through litigation, leaving Hawaii poised to adopt gay marriage through judicial decision.[51]

Similarly, after *Goodridge*, supporters of constitutional amendments banning gay marriage responded to the charge "that the issue is being forced upon the nation by fundamentalist Christians" by observing that the issue had arisen only "because of a dozen or so judges in Vermont and Massachusetts." In 2004, the Republican secretary of state of Ohio, Ken Blackwell, insisted that it was "an activist court in Massachusetts," not Republican campaign committees, that had set the stage for a national debate on gay marriage.[52]

As defense-of-marriage acts began to sweep the states and Congress in the mid-1990s, liberal columnist Ellen Goodman observed, "I am still not sure how gay marriage came to dominate the gay rights issue. No strategist could pick a hotter button to push." Evan Wolfson, one of the nation's earliest advocates of marriage equality, observed in 1996, "We knew the backlash would be strong and ferocious, but the backlash is happening before we have even won anything."[53]

Within the gay rights movement, some activists concluded that they had little choice but to defend against the conservatives' attack upon gay marriage. Evan Wolfson observed, "We're doing this now because it happened now." Noting that "we are now fighting for our political life," the legal director of the National Center for Lesbian Rights declared that "the luxury of deliberation and reflection" did not exist.[54]

Other activists, however, considered this approach "disastrous." They were playing "into conservative hands," as they lacked public support on marriage and must learn to "get to A and B before we can get to E." Defending same-sex marriage against the conservative onslaught also diverted scarce resources from other objectives such as fighting AIDS and securing anti-discrimination laws and hate crimes protection.[55]

In the mid-1990s, more than 80 percent of Americans believed that gays should enjoy the same job opportunities as everyone else, but fewer than a third supported gay marriage. One lesbian couple writing in the *Washington Post* warned, "If the movement's chances of achieving more basic legal protections end up being forfeited because gay marriage has taken center court, we have only ourselves to blame." In July 1996, the *Advocate* observed, "Some gays and lesbians wonder how marriage came to dominate gay rights in the first place and whether the backlash to it is jeopardizing other gains."[56]

In New York, for years the principal objective of the state's largest gay rights organization, the Empire State Pride Agenda (ESPA), had been the enactment of a general anti-discrimination law protecting gays. In 1993, the lower house of the legislature passed such a bill for the first time. In succeeding years, the assembly repeatedly passed the measure, but it could not make it to the senate floor.[57]

In 1996, however, ESPA had to shift focus away from securing the civil rights bill to fending off defense-of-marriage measures that Republicans introduced in both legislative houses. Paula Ettelbrick, legislative counsel of ESPA, explained, "Knowing that we needed to use all of our chits to stave off an anti-gay-marriage bill…, we did not heavily push [the civil rights] bill in the Senate this year." In such a political environment, preserving the status quo suddenly seemed like a significant victory. ESPA was expecting the "bruising fight" over gay marriage to continue in the legislature the following year.[58]

No gay marriages actually occurred in the 1990s, and the potent political backlash ignited by *Baehr* must have raised significant doubts as to whether any ever would. *Goodridge* changed that. By making gay marriage a reality, *Goodridge* converted many gays and lesbians into marriage enthusiasts and soured them on legal arrangements that fell short of marriage.

Before *Goodridge* put marriage squarely on the table, many gays and lesbians were ambivalent about it, and polls showed that roughly half of them regarded civil unions as the equivalent of marriage. By making gay marriage seem possible, *Goodridge* also made it seem more desirable.[59]

Within twenty-four hours of *Goodridge*, marriage proposals and engagements were taking place among same-sex couples across Massachusetts. The marriages in San Francisco and Portland early in 2004, which ignited political backlash among conservatives, were hugely emotional events for many gays and lesbians. Fully appreciating for the first time what they previously had been denied, many gays and lesbians began to desire marriage very strongly. Same-sex couples who had been partnered for decades without seriously contemplating marriage now dropped everything to race off to San Francisco to get married before courts could shut down the weddings. Even many gays were surprised by how much demand for marriage existed among them now that it had become legally available.[60]

Goodridge inspired gays not only to marry but also to litigate for gay marriage in other states. Marriage lawsuits were quickly filed in California, Connecticut, Florida, Iowa, Maryland, New York, Oregon, and Washington. In Seattle, where a gay marriage lawsuit had been in the works for years, the marriages in San Francisco and Portland spurred Lambda Legal and the ACLU finally to act. According to one Lambda official, "The train was leaving the station and we could either be on it, or be chasing it." In California, *Goodridge* inspired a state legislator to introduce a gay marriage bill, which passed a house committee in April 2004—the first time any legislative body in the United States had endorsed gay marriage.[61]

As in the 1990s, the focus on gay marriage after *Goodridge* necessarily diverted some attention away from other gay rights issues on which public opinion was far more supportive. By 2004, 81 percent of Americans favored permitting gays to serve openly in the military, and 75 percent supported laws banning discrimination based on sexual orientation in employment, public accommodations, and housing. Yet only 34 percent favored gay marriage. One wonders whether the federal Employment Nondiscrimination Act might not have been enacted by now had gay marriage not become such a dominant issue on the gay rights agenda after *Goodridge*.[62]

Moreover, the focus of the gay rights movement on securing marriage in certain relatively liberal states diverted resources away from the gay rights struggle in more conservative states, where gays lacked even basic legal protections against violence and discrimination in employment, housing, and public accommodations. One gay activist in Oklahoma observed, "I'm not sure that a lot of Gays and Lesbians in Oklahoma would have put [same-sex marriage] at the top of their list," because they were struggling for "things that are somewhat more basic than that." When gay activists went door-to-door in Cincinnati in 2004 to gather signatures for repealing the 1993 charter amendment forbidding gay rights ordinances, the first questions they invariably received were about gay marriage, which had been rendered salient by *Goodridge* and the West Coast weddings.[63]

This agenda-setting effect of *Goodridge* was especially significant on the issue of legal benefits for same-sex couples. By the early twenty-first century, although most Americans still opposed gay marriage, they supported legal benefits for same-sex partners, such as hospital visitation, inheritance rights, and social security benefits. A Gallup poll conducted just six months before *Goodridge* showed that Americans supported such benefits by 62 percent to 35 percent. By 2009, Gallup found that 67 percent of Americans believed that same-sex couples should enjoy health insurance and other employment benefits, while 73 percent favored inheritance rights. As one woman interviewed in 2009 in a Walmart in Davenport, Iowa, explained when asked about *Varnum*, gay marriage was contrary to her Christian beliefs, but she thought that gay couples ought to enjoy equal rights and she supported finding some middle ground.[64]

Civil unions were the most comprehensive form of legal benefits for same-sex couples short of marriage. *Goodridge* diverted attention from civil unions and focused it squarely on gay marriage. That shift was important because by early 2004, a plurality or slender majority of Americans supported civil unions. (To be sure, growing support for civil unions was almost certainly in part a function of gay marriage becoming more realistic.) Within a few years, a substantial majority supported them. In 2009, a Quinnipiac poll found that while Americans opposed gay marriage by 55 percent to 38 percent, they supported civil unions by 57 percent to 38 percent.[65]

In the years after *Goodridge*, voters in state after state were asked to express their views on gay marriage, and they rejected it. Polls suggest a very different outcome if these voters had been asked instead about civil unions. In 2006, when Virginians rejected gay marriage by 57 percent to 43 percent, polls showed that 59 percent of them backed civil unions. In 2009, when Maine voters rejected gay marriage by 53 percent to 47 percent, polls showed that they supported civil unions by 74 percent to 23 percent. That same year, when the New York legislature narrowly rejected gay marriage, polls showed that New Yorkers favored civil unions by 65 percent to 27 percent. Thus, in many states over several years, the singular focus of gay activists on marriage probably cost same-sex couples the tangible legal benefits that civil unions would have afforded.[66]

One reason that gay activists had deemphasized civil unions was because *Goodridge*, by placing gay marriage on the table, had made them seem less attractive. Before *Goodridge*, many same-sex couples had cared more about the package of legal protections that accompany marriage than about the formal status. Yet, after *Goodridge*, anything less than marriage seemed like "second-class citizenship" and "tepid half measures." Civil unions, which only a few years earlier had appeared to be an enormous advance, had now come to seem "separate and unequal"—like telling Rosa Parks that she could move to "the middle of the bus."[67]

In 2005, when the Connecticut legislature took up a civil unions bill, the largest gay rights group in the state initially opposed it as inadequate. When the legislature enacted the measure, far fewer same-sex couples entered into civil unions than had done so under the Vermont law in 2000. Marriage equality in Massachusetts apparently had tarnished the appeal of civil unions elsewhere.[68]

The agenda-setting effect of *Goodridge* not only cost gay activists concrete gains on issues such as civil unions but also undermined the ability of Democrats— whose party was more supportive of gay rights—to take maximum advantage of the extremist views on gay rights issues of the religious conservatives who constitute much of the base of the Republican Party. Gay marriage unified Republicans in opposition. Other gay rights issues increasingly divided them and left the party politically vulnerable as public opinion came to reject the anti-gay views of religious conservatives.[69]

In the early 1990s, Christian conservatives in the California Republican Party successfully pressured Governor Pete Wilson to veto a bill forbidding discrimination based on sexual orientation—a measure that opinion polls showed two-thirds of Californians supported. As state Republican parties came to be increasingly dominated by conservative Christians in the early 1990s, they adopted platform planks calling for stringent enforcement of anti-sodomy laws and demanding that gays be barred from employment as schoolteachers and health care workers. The religious right criticized the administration of George H. W. Bush for even meeting with gay activists or funding workshops on AIDS education.[70]

In 2000, all ten candidates participating in the Republican Party presidential primaries, which traditionally are dominated by conservatives, rejected all forms of legal protection for gays, including anti-discrimination laws. Indeed, most religious conservatives have opposed hate crimes legislation protecting gays and lesbians, which most Americans support. Religious conservatives have even opposed measures aimed at stopping the harassment of gay schoolchildren, on the ground that such laws are a Trojan horse for recruiting children into the homosexual lifestyle.[71]

Specifically on the issue of legal recognition of same-sex partnerships, the base of the Republican Party has become increasingly estranged from dominant public opinion, which supports granting various legal benefits to such couples. The leading anti-gay marriage groups even tried to prevent gay and lesbian partners of those killed in the September 11 attacks from receiving benefits from the victim compensation fund.[72]

In April 2010, in response to stories such as that of Janice Langbehn, who was denied access to her dying lesbian partner in a Miami hospital, President Obama issued an order requiring American hospitals participating in the Medicare or Medicaid programs to allow full visitation rights for same-sex partners. The Family Research Council promptly denounced Obama as "pandering to a radical special interest group" and "undermining the definition of marriage." One liberal commentator wondered whether Republicans would garner much political support on the platform of "vote for the GOP and we'll promise to let gay people die horrible, miserable deaths in complete isolation."[73]

The widening gap between the views of religious conservatives and those of average Americans on partnership rights for same-sex couples has created dilemmas for Republican politicians. In 2004, President George W. Bush had to decide whether to condemn civil unions as well as gay marriage. Doing so would have pleased his base but possibly alienated independent voters, most of whom believed that same-sex couples should enjoy some of the rights of marriage. Bush waited until just before the election to announce that he had no objection to states' adoption of civil unions.[74]

In 2008 in California, Proposition 8 supporters were deeply divided between those who wanted to ban only gay marriage and those who also wanted to deprive same-sex couples of other legal rights they enjoyed, such as adoption, hospital visitation, and insurance coverage. When the Republican candidate for lieutenant governor in Iowa in 2010 told a newspaper that she favored allowing Iowans an opportunity to vote on civil unions, not just gay marriage, religious conservatives in the party created such a furor that gubernatorial candidate Terry Branstad had to distance himself from her remarks. By 2010, the Republican Party was increasingly divided between modernizers such as Jon Huntsman Jr., who supported civil unions, and the conservative religious base, which opposed them as simply gay marriage's "mischievous twin."[75]

Because public debate in the first decade of the twenty-first century mainly focused on gay marriage, Republicans were able to maintain a united front of opposition. Putting the spotlight on civil unions or domestic partnerships instead would have divided Republicans. Moreover, to the extent that religious conservatives might have had their way on such issues, the party would have been badly out of step with the direction in which public opinion was trending.

Focusing on the most radical item on the gay rights agenda—same-sex marriage—also diverted attention from some of the more extreme condemnations of homosexuality emanating from the religious right. As the American public became more accepting of homosexuality in the 1990s, gay rights opponents had to be careful not to use arguments that demonized gays. Yet the hard core of the gay rights opposition believes that homosexuality is a sin and is sorely tempted to say so.[76]

In 1998, appearing on a conservative talk show, Republican Senate majority leader Trent Lott called homosexuals sinners and compared them to alcoholics and kleptomaniacs. Objecting to the decision of officials in Orlando, Florida, in 1998 to permit gay rights groups to put rainbow flags on city light poles, Reverend Pat Robertson predicted that it would "bring about terrorist bombs,... earthquakes, tornados and possibly a meteor." In the Republican Party primaries in 2000, Gary Bauer referred to Vermont's *Baker* decision as "in some ways worse than terrorism." As Californians debated an initiative to ban gay marriage in 2000, the *Los Angeles Times* reported that religious leaders at a prayer breakfast held during the state's Republican Party convention "caused a stir by calling gay marriage an evil akin to Nazi Germany, and homosexuality evidence of a nation on the brink of collapse."[77]

Moderates tend to reject such harsh characterizations of homosexuality, which is why supporters of anti-gay initiatives always emphasize that they are not anti-gay and do not support discrimination. The strident anti-gay rhetoric of the 1992 Republican Party convention was widely deemed to have hurt the party with independent voters, who tend to be uncomfortable with overt homophobia. When religious conservatives in Oregon in 1992 promoted a ballot measure deeming homosexuality—along with pedophilia, sadism, and masochism—as "abnormal, wrong, unnatural, and perverse," voters decisively rejected it. Yet as the gay rights agenda became increasingly focused on gay marriage, which most Americans opposed, it became harder for Democrats and gay activists to take advantage of such extremist rhetoric.[78]

10

Why Backlash? Part II: Politics and Federalism

For the most part, political backlash emanating from court decisions does not arise spontaneously. Judicial rulings may provide the occasion for backlash, but politicians seize the opportunity to stoke backlash for political advantage.[1]

Gay rights became a valuable issue for religious and social conservatives in the 1970s and 1980s partly because more Americans agreed with them on it than on abortion. By the 1980s, the agenda of religious conservatives had been largely absorbed into that of the Republican Party. As public attitudes toward gay rights became more progressive in the late 1980s and 1990s, the traditional items on the gay rights agenda—the repeal of sodomy laws and the enactment of hate crimes legislation and anti-discrimination laws—no longer frightened most Americans.[2]

From this perspective, gay marriage litigation proved a godsend to religious conservatives and Republicans. Ballot measures to bar gay marriage diverted attention from other gay rights issues, primed voters to consider gay marriage as they chose between political candidates, thrust a wedge into the Democratic Party's political coalition, and mobilized the Republican Party's base in a way that few other issues could.[3]

For the national Republican Party, *Goodridge* was an early Christmas gift. Opinion polls conducted in 2003–4 showed that Americans opposed gay marriage by roughly two to one. Among Republican-leaning voters, the margin of opposition was more than five to one.[4]

Opposition to gay marriage may have mobilized white evangelical Christians—a core component of the Republican Party's base—even more than the abortion issue did. In 2004, Republican strategists were especially keen to energize Christian evangelicals, whose turnout in 2000 had been significantly lower than it was in 1996. During the campaign, Bush political strategist Karl Rove held weekly telephone conference calls with prominent evangelicals such as James Dobson of Focus on the Family. For people such as Dobson, gay marriage threatened "the future of western civilization" by attacking the under-pinnings of the traditional family.[5]

One political analyst noted that gay marriage was "a real gift" to the religious right because "it's revitalized their base and revitalized their fund-raising." In 2004, gay marriage played a prominent role in the fund-raising of religious right organizations, after playing almost no role in 2003. Focus on the Family distrib-uted special mailings to pastors in states where marriage amendments were on the ballot, encouraging them to preach against gay marriage, outlining sample sermons, and urging their involvement in grassroots organizing in support of those amendments.[6]

In 2004, Ohio's Republican secretary of state, Ken Blackwell, sent a letter to fifteen hundred state party leaders announcing that the gay marriage issue might determine the winner of Ohio's electoral votes. At a gathering of prominent con-servatives held just before the Republican National Convention, the agenda included a session titled "Using Conservative Issues in Swing States." The fea-tured speaker, on the topic of gay marriage referenda, was Phil Burress, whose group had put the marriage amendment on the ballot in Ohio.[7]

At the Republican convention, Karl Rove admitted to Ohio reporters that to the extent the state ballot initiative on marriage "energizes people who might not otherwise vote, it tends to help us." The leader of the Georgia legislature's black caucus predicted that if a marriage amendment got on the state ballot that year, which it did, Republicans might take over the state house of representatives in November—which they did, for the first time since Reconstruction.[8]

Democrats thought it no coincidence that marriage amendments appeared on the ballot in potential swing states in the presidential election, such as Ohio, Michigan, and Oregon. In 2011, in remarks that were unintentionally made public, a Republican state legislator in North Carolina told a closed-door meet-ing of the Republican legislative caucus that a ballot initiative on gay marriage was needed to help conservative groups "get their ground game working."[9]

Gay marriage not only mobilized Republicans but was also, in the words of Republican pollster Richard Wirthlin, "an ideal wedge issue" to use against Democrats. While Republican voters overwhelmingly oppose gay marriage, Democrats have been pretty much split down the middle until very recently. Although gay rights supporters vote heavily Democratic, so do certain con-stituencies that disproportionately oppose gay marriage: the elderly, African Americans, and the working class.[10]

For example, in 2006, African Americans in Virginia voted 81 percent to 11 percent in favor of the Democratic candidate for the U.S. Senate, Jim Webb, while they supported the state constitutional amendment banning gay marriage by 61 percent to 34 percent. In 2009, an opinion poll conducted by the *Los Angeles*

Times found that 68 percent of whites in California supported gay marriage, but only 37 percent of blacks did so.[11]

For this reason, *Goodridge* was a nightmare for most Democratic politicians. One top advisor to a Democratic presidential candidate in 2004 admitted, "I got a bad case of acid reflux as soon as I heard about it." Democratic politicians did not wish to anger their liberal base, which supported *Goodridge*, but neither did they wish to alienate those Democratic constituencies that opposed it or the majority of independent voters, who also rejected it.[12]

Those Democrats who could do so tried simply to duck the issue. Christine Gregoire, running for governor of Washington in 2004, refused to take a public position on gay marriage, conveniently noting that, as state attorney general, she might have to defend the state's defense-of-marriage law in court. Most Democratic politicians decided to embrace civil unions, which polls showed that Democratic voters supported by 55 percent to 40 percent, while opposing gay marriage but also opposing the federal marriage amendment.[13]

However, the Democrats' compromise position proved difficult to sell, especially when contrasted with the typical Republican position of strong opposition to gay marriage and strong support for a federal constitutional amendment to ban it. Both because supporters of gay rights exercise significant influence within the Democratic Party and because many Democratic politicians in their hearts had no problem with gay marriage, many of them were more comfortable emphasizing their support for civil unions than their opposition to gay marriage.[14]

In 2004, however, those Americans who occupied the middle of the spectrum on gay rights issues were, on average, more strongly opposed to gay marriage than they were supportive of civil unions. One poll found that respondents favored by 55 percent to 33 percent a Republican statement of opposition to gay marriage over a Democratic statement of support for civil unions. Some voters were simply confused by the Democrats' position of opposing gay marriage while also resisting a federal constitutional amendment to bar it. As one African American woman in Cleveland who identified herself as a born-again Christian explained her decision to vote for President Bush in 2004, she knew exactly where he stood on gay marriage, while she was not sure precisely what John Kerry believed.[15]

Republicans had a field day with the issue in 2004, forcing Democrats to discuss gay marriage, cast legislative votes on state and federal marriage amendments, and explain to voters why state and federal constitutions should not reflect the preferences of a clear majority of Americans. State marriage initiatives proved so effective at mobilizing religious conservatives and winning over independents and crossover Democrats that Republicans put them on the ballot in more than twenty-five states in the five years after *Goodridge*, winning every referendum but one (and that one defeat was quickly reversed). Marriage amendments did not magically appear on state ballots; Republican legislators and conservative interest groups closely aligned with the Republican Party put them there. As one Virginia Democrat explained, the marriage amendment in that state was a "contrived initiative straight from Karl Rove's playbook."[16]

Politicians frequently have the incentive to foment backlash, but their capacity to do so is not unlimited. Efforts by conservatives to use gay rights progress to fuel backlash have not been uniformly successful.

In 1976, conservatives in California tried to place a referendum on the ballot to reverse the legislature's recent repeal of the sodomy law, but they were unsuccessful because most Californians no longer believed that the state should be criminalizing sex between consenting adult homosexuals. In 1992, Republican efforts to demonize Bill Clinton as the pro-gay candidate were not notably successful, partly because economic concerns dominated the election but also because Clinton had emphasized that his commitment to gay rights ended short of marriage. In 2006, Republican candidates around the country tried to foment backlash against the New Jersey court's ruling in favor of civil unions but had little success in doing so, probably because most Americans supported civil unions by then.[17]

By contrast, gay marriage rulings such as *Baehr* and *Goodridge* teed up an issue ripe for political exploitation. At the time of these decisions, Americans overwhelmingly rejected gay marriage, and opponents were often quite passionate in their convictions. The Republican Party was unified in opposition and its base highly mobilized. Democrats were deeply divided, and many of their leaders were personally conflicted. The issue offered great political benefits and few costs to Republicans, who took full advantage.

When public opinion on judicial rulings divides heavily along regional or geographic lines, political backlash becomes more likely. The combination of geographically segmented opinion and the incentives that a federal political system creates for local politicians to respond to that opinion establishes a dynamic that not only ignites backlash but then repeatedly exacerbates it.

For example, in 1954, Americans were split almost precisely down the middle on whether *Brown v. Board of Education* was rightly decided, but opinion among whites was divided largely along regional lines. Roughly 85 percent of white southerners thought that *Brown* was not just wrong but egregiously so. Outside of the South, however, approximately 70 percent of whites supported *Brown*. African Americans mostly backed the decision, but in the South they were still largely disenfranchised and thus exercised relatively little political influence.[18]

In such an environment, southern politicians had obvious incentives to aggressively oppose the enforcement of *Brown*. The more extreme their rhetoric, the better voters liked it. Standing in the schoolhouse door to defy federal court desegregation orders made governors such as Orval Faubus and George Wallace practically invincible in southern politics.[19]

Yet northern voters were largely appalled by such antics. Governor Theodore McKeldin of Maryland called Faubus "the sputtering Sputnik from the Ozarks." Roy Wilkins of the NAACP recognized that Faubus was "a valuable enemy, [who] has aided in many ways in clarifying the issue of segregation" and "aroused and educated to our point of view millions of people in America." When President Eisenhower dispatched federal troops to rescue the Little Rock Nine from possible violence and to ensure their safe matriculation at Central High School, northerners overwhelmingly supported the president.[20]

By contrast, in the South, denunciations of Eisenhower's intervention were fast and furious. Several southern politicians compared the use of federal troops at Little Rock to the Soviet Union's invasion of Hungary in 1956. Governor George Timmerman of South Carolina criticized the president for "trying to set himself up as a dictator." Senator Richard Russell of Georgia condemned the use of "storm troopers." Alabama circuit judge George Wallace compared Eisenhower to Hitler and accused the president of substituting "military dictatorship for the Constitution of the United States."[21]

Governor Faubus's futile resistance to federal authority made him a southern political hero. He won four more gubernatorial elections in Arkansas and attracted enormous and hugely enthusiastic crowds as he traveled throughout the South. Attentive politicians elsewhere in the region observed and then mimicked Faubus's tactics. Political candidates made wildly irresponsible promises to preserve white supremacy regardless of the costs.[22]

Some of the southern politicians elected in this frenzied environment deliberately used police brutality against civil rights demonstrators, calculating that southern voters would reward such behavior. Others simply used incendiary rhetoric that probably encouraged white vigilantes to brutalize civil rights "agitators." Such violence, in turn, mobilized northern whites, who had been lukewarm in their support of *Brown* in the 1950s, to demand federal legislative intervention to end Jim Crow.[23]

A similar phenomenon unfolded after *Goodridge* with regard to gay marriage. Opinion on gay rights also tends to divide along regional lines: urban versus rural, and the West Coast and the Northeast versus most of the rest of the country. Gays and lesbians are much more likely to be out of the closet in big cities than in smaller towns and rural areas. Urban dwellers are thus much more likely to encounter gay parents at their children's school or soccer games, and greater familiarity tends to make people more comfortable with same-sex relationships.[24]

By the beginning of the twenty-first century, many American cities already had majorities or near-majorities in favor of gay marriage. However, in most small towns and rural areas, and even in some larger cities not situated along the East or West Coast, opposition remained strong.

In Oregon's 2004 marriage referendum, voters in Multnomah County (Portland and environs) voted against banning gay marriage by three to two, while in many rural counties the margin in favor of the ban was as high as three to one. In Missouri's 2004 referendum, voters in St. Louis rejected the ban on gay marriage by 53.2 percent to 46.8 percent, and in Kansas City they supported it by only 50.7 percent to 49.3 percent. By contrast, in twenty-two rural Missouri counties, voters favored the ban by margins of more than 85 percent to 15 percent. In Maine's 2009 referendum, voters in Portland, the state's largest city, opposed the repeal of gay marriage by a margin of 47 percentage points, while in some small towns, the margins in favor of repeal ran as high as 37 to 44 percentage points.[25]

Under the American system of federalism, marriage law is made at the state level, and marriage licenses are distributed at the local level. Combining a federal political system with geographic segmentation of opinion heightens the possibility of political backlash. Moreover, marriages are mostly portable—that is, marriages in one jurisdiction are usually recognized as legally valid in others. Therefore, a state court ruling that expands the definition of marriage is seen as potentially relevant to other jurisdictions in a way that most state court decisions would not be.[26]

Politicians have incentives to respond to voter sentiment within their jurisdictions. Officeholders in places where support for gay marriage is strong are likely to endorse it—perhaps even to try to implement it—regardless of whether voters elsewhere remain strongly opposed.

As early as 1995, the mayor of Ithaca, New York, unanimously supported by an all-Democratic city council, agreed to grant a marriage license to a gay couple. Fearing that news would travel quickly to Albany, the Empire State Pride Agenda began planning for the political fallout that a gay marriage would likely produce. Similarly concerned, national gay rights organizations urged the couple to desist until public opinion could be educated on the issue.[27]

In 1996, while concerns that Hawaii was about to legalize gay marriage led dozens of states to consider defense-of-marriage acts, the San Francisco board of supervisors adopted an ordinance allowing the county clerk's office to perform same-sex "wedding" ceremonies for couples who registered as domestic partners. In 2003, the left-leaning city council of Cambridge, Massachusetts, was so exultant over *Goodridge* that councilors lined up to co-sponsor a measure to authorize the city clerk to issue marriage licenses to same-sex couples immediately rather than waiting for the decision's implementation date. The gay rights group that had litigated *Goodridge* urged the councilors to restrain their enthusiasm, which they did, eventually contenting themselves with a resolution endorsing the decision. In each of these instances, local politicians took actions that were popular in their jurisdictions, although threatening to foment backlash elsewhere.[28]

As we have seen, the gay marriage ceremonies conducted (mainly) in San Francisco and Portland early in 2004 generated at least as much backlash against gay marriage as had *Goodridge* itself. The San Francisco marriages were largely the work of one man, Mayor Gavin Newsom. A mere two months before issuing the order to grant marriage licenses to same-sex couples, Newsom had been narrowly elected mayor, winning just 53 percent of the vote against a Green Party candidate whom he had outspent by roughly eight to one. Newsom's opponent had outflanked him on the political left and warned after his concession speech, "When Mayor Newsom is wrong, we'll be there to oppose him."[29]

According to Newsom's subsequent account, the immediate catalyst for his decision to grant marriage licenses to same-sex couples was President Bush's State of the Union address, in which he threatened to support a federal marriage amendment if activist judges continued to redefine marriage. Newsom may well have believed that marrying gay couples was simply the right thing to do; many of his senior advisors, including his chief of staff, were gay. Yet Newsom cannot possibly have failed to notice that engaging in civil disobedience by violating California's marriage law was also the politically savvy thing to do.[30]

Mayor Gavin Newsom speaking with Pali Cooper and Jeanne Rizzo moments after the California supreme court halted the issuance of marriage licenses to same-sex couples in San Francisco, March 11, 2004. (*Associated Press/Noah Berger*)

On February 12, 2004, Newsom ordered city clerks to grant marriage licenses to same-sex couples. A spokesperson of the Green Party promptly declared, "Gavin Newsom's stand on gay marriage made us real proud." A local Democratic pollster observed, "Newsom has earned the respect of many progressives and liberals." An opinion poll showed that in the San Francisco Bay area, people supported gay marriage by 58 percent to 37 percent. Reflecting that opinion, most other local elected officials backed the mayor.[31]

Newsom's approval ratings immediately shot up to 69 percent, and by the summer of 2004, they hit 85 percent—unprecedented numbers for a San Francisco mayor. Newsom quickly became a national celebrity, appearing on television programs such as *Good Morning America*, *Larry King Live*, and *Nightline*. He was also profiled in the *New York Times*, *USA Today*, and *Time*. *Newsweek* ranked him, along with Barack Obama and Mark Warner, high in the "galaxy of bright Democratic lights."[32]

Newsom's actions made him a political icon in San Francisco as well as a plausible future candidate for state office, given that public opinion in California was trending gradually but ineluctably in favor of gay marriage. One observer noted, "By the time this guy is ready to be a United States Senator, in a decade, will this have been Rosa Parks on the bus that the people of California are willing to accept?" In later years, gay couples would name their children after Newsom. In 2010, he was elected lieutenant governor of California.[33]

In a federal system, policy initiatives undertaken in one jurisdiction often pressure public officials elsewhere to follow suit. During the white South's massive resistance to *Brown*, southern politicians had a hard time explaining to constituents why they had to desegregate their schools when neighboring states had not yet done so. This dynamic exacerbated Governor Faubus's dilemma over school desegregation in Little Rock in 1957. Alabama and Texas had successfully flouted federal court desegregation orders the previous year. Moreover, the segregationist governor of Georgia, Marvin Griffin, visited Little Rock two weeks before schools were scheduled to desegregate and expressed shock that any governor with troops at his disposal would allow racial integration. Arkansans approached Faubus on the street, demanding to know, "If Georgia doesn't have integration, why does Arkansas?"[34]

Similarly, once Mayor Newsom had blazed a new trail by ordering city officials to grant marriage licenses to same-sex couples, public officials in other very liberal jurisdictions felt pressure to follow suit. In New Paltz, New York, Mayor Jason West may have made political calculations similar to those of Newsom. New Paltz is a village of six thousand residents, 75 percent of whom are under the age of thirty-five. In 2004, local opinion was overwhelmingly supportive of gay marriage. More than five hundred people turned out to celebrate the same-sex weddings conducted by Mayor West, and he was mobbed like a rock star when he appeared at a local nightclub frequented by gays. West addressed political rallies, gave speeches reminiscent of the 1960s civil rights movement, and declared himself willing to go to jail for the cause of gay marriage. When he was arraigned in court for marrying couples without a valid marriage license, more than a thousand people rallied in his support. Messages that West received ran ten to one in favor of his actions. Like Newsom, West appeared on national television programs.[35]

Elsewhere in the state, Mayor Michael Bloomberg also came under pressure to issue marriage licenses to same-sex couples in March 2004. Although he resisted that pressure then, in February 2005, as he prepared for his reelection bid, Bloomberg declared his support for gay marriage.[36]

In March 2004 in King County, Washington (which includes Seattle), demonstrators marched on the office of county executive Ron Sims to demand that he issue marriage licenses to same-sex couples, as Portland and San Francisco had begun to do. Although Sims announced that state law barred him from doing so, he was careful to note that he did not personally support the law.[37]

Seattle's mayor, Greg Nickels, noting that cities in Washington were not permitted by law to issue marriage licenses, declared that he would applaud a decision by county executive Sims to authorize such licenses to same-sex couples. Eager to somehow demonstrate support for gay marriage, Mayor Nickels issued an executive order directing all city departments and public contractors to recognize their employees' out-of-state same-sex marriages.[38]

Given strong support for gay marriage among their constituents, the decisions of local officials such as Mayors Newsom and West to issue marriage licenses to same-sex couples were politically shrewd. The political repercussions of their actions elsewhere, however, were rather different. San Francisco and New Paltz may have been ready for gay marriage in 2004, but most of the country was not.

Images of same-sex couples celebrating their marriages outside of city hall in San Francisco were quickly broadcast by national media across the country and enabled conservatives to mobilize grassroots campaigns for state constitutional amendments to bar gay marriage. The same-sex couples who traveled to California from other states to get married returned home to more conservative communities and found themselves a hot topic of conversation at work and in their hometown newspapers. A lesbian couple from Durham, North Carolina, traveled to San Francisco to marry, then ended up on NBC's *Today*, as well as being interviewed by the local newspaper and a statewide public radio program. One resident of Albuquerque, New Mexico, explained how the gay marriage licenses issued in Sandoval County proved a powerful mobilizing force for conservative Christians throughout the state: gay marriage in Massachusetts or San Francisco might seem largely irrelevant to New Mexicans, "but when it happens right next door, you can't ignore it."[39]

The West Coast marriages, more than the *Goodridge* decision that inspired them, ignited the powerful political backlash of 2004. Republican politicians in jurisdictions where people overwhelmingly rejected gay marriage had strong incentives to keep the issue salient in voters' minds.

After the 2004 elections, many prominent Democrats blamed Mayor Newsom for providing conservatives with an issue around which they could rally supporters. One of California's Democratic U.S. senators, Dianne Feinstein, observed that the thousands of gay weddings in San Francisco "energized a conservative vote" and that the "whole issue has been too much, too fast, too soon. And people aren't ready for it." President Bush's senior political advisor Karl Rove had to stifle a grin when asked after the election whether he was indebted to Mayor Newsom for opening city hall to same-sex marriages.[40]

Unless Mayor Newsom had short-term national political ambitions, he had little reason to care what voters in states such as Ohio or Missouri thought about gay marriages in San Francisco. His actions made him a political hero at home and laid the groundwork for a future campaign for statewide office in California. Yet the sharp geographic segmentation of opinion on gay marriage ensured that his actions would generate a dramatic political backlash elsewhere in the country.

11

Looking to the Future:
The Inevitability of Gay Marriage

Constitutional amendments to bar gay marriage will appear on at least two more state ballots in 2012, as Republicans took control of many state legislatures in 2010, after campaigns mainly fought over the issues of unemployment, budget deficits, and the Obama administration's health care reform. In Minnesota, conservatives had been trying unsuccessfully for years to get such an amendment on the ballot. In 2010, the National Organization for Marriage ran television advertisements on behalf of the Republican candidate for governor (who lost), and the Catholic archbishop of St. Paul and Minneapolis sent out an anti-gay-marriage DVD just before Election Day. After Republicans took control of the state legislature, they quickly passed a marriage amendment and put it on the 2012 ballot. In January 2012, a Minnesota appellate court revived a gay marriage lawsuit that had been dismissed by a trial judge. Supporters of the marriage amendment then cited that decision as a reason to pass the amendment.[1]

Polls show Minnesotans split roughly down the middle on gay marriage. Historically, such polling tends to underestimate opposition to gay marriage. However, cutting in the opposite direction, Minnesota law requires that for an amendment to pass, a majority of the voters who cast election ballots must support it. Voters who return ballots but choose not to vote on the amendment are counted as voting against it. All said, the outcome in Minnesota is probably too close to call with any confidence.[2]

North Carolina is the only southern state not yet to have passed a constitutional ban on gay marriage. Republicans had tried for a decade to get such an amendment on the ballot, but Democrats had blocked it. After Republicans took control of the state legislature in 2010—the first time they controlled both chambers in North Carolina in more than a century—they quickly proposed a marriage amendment for 2012.[3]

However, before constitutional amendments can appear on the ballot in North Carolina, they must pass both houses of the legislature by a 60 percent majority. Securing such a supermajority on the marriage amendment would have been impossible without some Democratic support. The price extracted by swing-vote Democrats was that the amendment appear on the primary ballot in May rather than on the general election ballot in November. Thus, the marriage amendment cannot affect the presidential contest in North Carolina, which in 2008 was one of the closest of any state in the nation. Opinion polls suggest that the North Carolina amendment is almost certain to pass, even though it contains broad language that would forbid civil unions as well as gay marriage. As of January 2012, Public Policy Polling had the amendment winning by a margin of 22 percentage points.[4]

In 2010, Republicans also seized control of the New Hampshire legislature, and many of them were determined to repeal the gay marriage law. Given the economic crisis, gay marriage opponents were unable to prompt the legislature to act in 2011, but it will probably vote on a bill to repeal gay marriage in 2012. Assuming the legislature passes that bill, Democratic governor John Lynch will almost certainly veto it. Republicans have the supermajorities in both chambers to override a gubernatorial veto, but it is not certain all of them would vote to do so on a repeal of gay marriage. Some Republican legislators are social libertarians who are on record opposing the repeal bill.[5]

Opinion in New Hampshire has shifted so heavily in favor of gay marriage in recent years that voters would be very unlikely to repeal gay marriage if such a measure were to appear on the ballot, which probably explains why Republicans have preferred a statutory repeal to a constitutional amendment. One recent poll shows that New Hampshirites oppose repeal of gay marriage by 62 percent to 27 percent.[6]

Early in 2012, three more state legislatures passed gay marriage bills. On February 13, Washington became the seventh state in the nation to enact gay marriage, with the strong support of Governor Christine Gregoire, who embraced it for the first time in her eighth and final year in office. Democrats control both houses of the state legislature, though without the support of four Republicans in the senate, the measure would not have passed. Gay marriage opponents need to gather 120,000 signatures by early June to secure a fall referendum on the new law, which they are very likely to be able to do. The referendum vote may well be close, even though one recent poll found that Washingtonians support legalizing gay marriage by 55 percent to 38 percent.[7]

Just a few days after Washington State acted, the New Jersey legislature passed a gay marriage bill. Indicative of rapidly changing public opinion in the state, twenty-four out of forty senators voted for the measure, compared with just fourteen the last time the chamber considered it—in 2010. An all-out lobbying campaign by public sector unions, the state bar association, and civil rights icon Congressman John Lewis apparently influenced the votes of swing legislators. However, Governor Christie quickly delivered on his promise to veto the bill. Democrats would need more Republican support than they are likely to get to override his veto.

In its stead, Christie has proposed a popular referendum on gay marriage in the fall of 2012. Such a referendum would have a good chance of succeeding, given that one poll conducted late in 2011 revealed New Jerseyans in favor of legalizing gay marriage by 52 percent to 36 percent, while another taken early in 2012 showed them supporting gay marriage by 52 percent to 42 percent. Yet gay activists and leading Democratic lawmakers have rejected the idea of a popular vote on what they consider an issue of civil rights. Litigation challenging the exclusion of same-sex couples from marriage is still pending in the New Jersey court system and could reach the state supreme court later this year.[8]

Just one week after New Jersey lawmakers acted, the Maryland legislature enacted gay marriage. In 2011, a gay marriage bill narrowly failed in the House of Delegates, despite having passed in the senate, when African American ministers in Prince George's County and Baltimore encouraged their congregations to lobby lawmakers against it.

In 2012, Governor Martin O'Malley aggressively supported the measure, which he had not done the preceding year. In addition, gay activists ran a well-funded media campaign in support of gay marriage that targeted the black community. It featured prominent African Americans, such as civil rights hero Julian Bond, Newark mayor Cory Booker, and Reverend Al Sharpton, supporting gay marriage. The Maryland AFL-CIO also backed the bill, and its endorsement may have influenced swing-vote delegates.

Maryland's new gay marriage law likely will face a tough referendum challenge in the fall. A poll conducted by the *Washington Post* in late January 2012 found Marylanders narrowly supporting gay marriage by 50 percent to 44 percent.[9]

Legislators in Illinois also introduced a gay marriage bill in 2012, after the state enacted civil unions the preceding year. Chicago mayor Rahm Emanuel has pledged to aggressively lobby for the measure with state legislators. Pundits consider the bill a longshot to pass this year.[10]

A marriage initiative sponsored by *supporters* of gay marriage will appear on the ballot for the first time ever in 2012 in Maine, which rejected gay marriage by about 6 percentage points in a 2009 referendum. Given that a recent poll shows 54 percent of Mainers favoring gay marriage, the amendment has a good chance of passing.[11]

Indeed, such a measure probably could pass in California as well in 2012, though gay marriage supporters have decided not to launch another expensive referendum campaign while the *Perry* litigation winds its way through the federal courts. Statistician Nate Silver's sophisticated model predicts that in 2012 at least 54 percent of Californians would vote to overturn Proposition 8.[12]

Gay marriage supporters are likely to promote referenda soon in other states that currently bar gay marriage by constitutional amendment. Polls in several such states—Colorado, Hawaii, Nevada, Oregon—now show support for gay marriage at or very near 50 percent. One study shows that legislatures usually do not enact gay marriage until public support is nearer to 60 percent. Thus, in those states where constitutional amendments can be put on the ballot without legislative approval, gay marriage supporters may choose to go directly to the people.[13]

When might President Obama be expected to shift his position on gay marriage? In the midst of New York's enactment of gay marriage in June 2011, the president attended a "gay gala" in Manhattan. Quoting an unnamed Democratic strategist close to the White House, the New York Times reported that presidential advisors were calculating the political costs of the president's coming out in favor of gay marriage. In November, one of his cabinet members endorsed gay marriage. Moreover, President Obama has stated several times that his views on the subject were "evolving."[14]

Yet Obama is unlikely to endorse gay marriage before the 2012 election. To be sure, for the president to embrace gay marriage would invigorate the party's liberal base and younger voters. However, as rapidly as public opinion is shifting on the issue, support for gay marriage could still cost the president much-needed votes in swing states such as Ohio, Pennsylvania, Virginia, North Carolina, and Florida. Especially given how vulnerable the president appears to be on the economy, embracing gay marriage before the election seems unlikely. Still, one wonders how long President Obama will remain willing to stand on the losing side of history. Should he win a second term in November 2012, the odds of his embracing gay marriage early in it seem pretty high.[15]

If any social change seems inevitable, it is the growing acceptance of gay equality generally and gay marriage specifically. In the years since Goodridge alone, the pace of change has been extraordinary. In 2003–4, Americans opposed gay marriage by roughly two to one. In the summer of 2010, for the first time ever, a national poll showed a majority of Americans supporting gay marriage, by 52 percent to 46 percent. Several subsequent polls corroborated this finding. In 2011, the Human Rights Campaign issued a report showing that seventeen states had popular majorities in favor of gay marriage, up from zero in 2004 and just three in 2008.[16]

The trend in favor of gay marriage has accelerated dramatically in just the last three years. Before 2009, the annual rate of increase in support for gay marriage was about 1.5 percentage points, but since then it has been closer to 4 percentage points. That rate of change suggests a basic cultural shift rather than just demographic replacement. Indeed, the percentage of senior citizens supporting gay marriage has increased by 15 percentage points over the last five years.[17]

For several reasons, this potent trend in favor of gay marriage is unlikely to be reversed. First, the basic insight of the gay rights movement over the past four decades has proved powerfully correct: as more gays and lesbians have come out of the closet, the social environment has become more gay-friendly. In turn, as the social environment has become more hospitable, more gays and lesbians have felt free to come out of the closet. This social dynamic is powerfully reinforcing. How it could be reversed is difficult to imagine.[18]

Having more gays be open about their sexuality has influenced public attitudes and policies in several ways. Simply revealing how many people are homosexual increases the political power of the gay rights movement. Exit polls in 2000 showed that 4 percent of voters self-identify as gay, but that probably understates the percentage of homosexuals in the population. In addition, simply identifying more people as openly gay is empowering for gays and lesbians because it diminishes the sense of isolation and abnormality from which many of them have suffered. Moreover, gays' coming out of the closet enables the compilation of a record to document discrimination based on sexual orientation, which lays the foundation for anti-discrimination laws. Demonstrating the existence of discrimination against a group when many of that group's members understandably chose to remain invisible has proven difficult.[19]

Perhaps most important, gays coming out of the closet significantly influences the views of other people on gay rights issues. One of the factors that most strongly predicts support for gay equality is knowing someone who is gay. As more gays and lesbians openly embrace their sexuality, more parents, children, siblings, friends, neighbors, and co-workers know and love someone who is openly gay. Because few people favor discrimination against those whom they know and love, every gay person coming out of the closet creates more supporters of gay equality. In addition, anti-gay stereotyping—one classic example being gays as child molesters—becomes less effective as people grow more familiar with gays.[20]

In 1985, only a quarter of Americans reported that a friend, relative, or co-worker had told them that he or she was gay. More than half of all Americans believed that they did not know anyone who was gay. As noted earlier, when Supreme Court justice Lewis Powell was deliberating in 1986 over his vote in *Bowers v. Hardwick*, he told his (gay) law clerk that he had never known a gay person. In 1987, speaking against a bill to ban discrimination based on sexual orientation, a Massachusetts legislator declared, "There are no gay people in my district."[21]

By 2000, the number of Americans reporting that they knew somebody who was openly gay had tripled to 75 percent. The percentage who reported having a gay friend or close acquaintance increased from 22 percent in 1985 to 43 percent in 1994 to 56 percent in 2000. Membership in the organization Parents, Families and Friends of Lesbians and Gays had grown to eighty thousand by 1998. Polls indicate that these numbers have continued to rise dramatically over the last decade. In Michigan, the number of respondents reporting that they know someone who is gay increased from 56 percent in 2004 to 80 percent in 2009.[22]

Personally knowing gay people strongly correlates with having progressive views on issues of gay equality. In a 2003 survey, only 13 percent of those who reported having close friends or family members who are gay agreed with the statement that permitting gay marriage would undermine the morals of the country. By contrast, 63 percent of those who reported not having any close friends or family members who are gay agreed with this statement. Another study in 2004 found that among those who reported knowing someone who is gay, 65 percent favored either gay marriage or civil unions, while only 35 percent of those who reported not knowing any gay people supported them.[23]

Understanding the power of this phenomenon, gay marriage opponents fought to prevent Judge Vaughn Walker from permitting the *Perry* trial to be broadcast on YouTube. Their stated objection was the potential for witness intimidation, but their real concern was probably the giant civics lesson that Judge Walker anticipated the trial would offer to the nation: gay and lesbian couples would have had an opportunity to introduce themselves to Americans as ordinary people who worked hard, raised children, and were committed to loving relationships that just happened to be with people of the same sex. Even gay activists who had opposed the filing of this federal lawsuit agreed that the more the issue of gay marriage was discussed in such forums, the better for their cause.[24]

The U.S. Supreme Court overturned Judge Walker's plan on procedural grounds—that he had not afforded adequate opportunity for public comment before changing court rules on the broadcasting of trials. Walker retired from the bench soon after rendering his verdict in *Perry*, and gay marriage opponents sought to compel him to return to the court the recordings of the trial that he had made for his own purposes. That order was rebuffed, and gay marriage attorney Ted Olson announced that he wanted the videos widely distributed, which he thought would change public attitudes toward gay marriage overnight. (The U.S. Court of Appeals for the Ninth Circuit recently ruled against making the videos public.) To the extent that gay marriage opponents need to quash public discussion of the issue to be successful, one wonders about their long-term prospects of success.[25]

Legislative debates on gay marriage have also illustrated the power of the coming-out phenomenon. These deliberations frequently have been "extraordinarily personal," with legislators "cast[ing] aside the often mundane rhetoric of lawmaking and delv[ing] into the most intimate details of their lives." When the Vermont house of representatives voted to legalize civil unions in 2000, its only openly gay member, William Lippert, spoke of reading the Bible with his minister father and learning to love thy neighbor as thyself. When he finished his speech, many of his colleagues were in tears.[26]

When the Massachusetts constitutional convention debated its response to *Goodridge*, the only openly lesbian member, Elizabeth Malia, gave a prominent speech, which was applauded loudly and explicitly referenced by several other lawmakers in their remarks. One of her colleagues observed that such a speech made it harder for other legislators, who loved and admired her, to support discrimination against her.[27]

During the Maine legislature's debates over gay marriage in the spring of 2009, freshman representative Terry K. Morrison surprised many of his colleagues by declaring that he was gay. In his speech, he explained how he and his partner had dreamed of getting married one day, but his partner had died before that day arrived. Several lawmakers later wrote him notes saying they were honored to be his friend.[28]

Gay marriage seems inevitable for a second, partially related reason: young people strongly support it. One study by political scientists found a gap of 44 percentage points between the oldest and youngest survey respondents in their attitudes toward gay marriage. One poll conducted in 2011 found that 65 percent of those between the ages of eighteen and twenty-nine favored the legalization of gay marriage, compared with just 30 percent of those sixty-five and above. That year, a Gallup poll found that 70 percent of those between the ages of eighteen and thirty-four supported gay marriage.[29]

The disparity between age groups in attitudes toward gay marriage is actually starker than that between red and blue states. Voters ages eighteen to twenty-nine in even the most conservative states, such as Alabama and Mississippi, are more likely to support gay marriage than are voters sixty-five and older in the most liberal states, such as Massachusetts and Vermont. By 2009, a majority of people between the ages of eighteen and twenty-nine supported gay marriage in thirty-eight states, including very conservative ones, such as Kansas, Idaho, and Wyoming.[30]

One study even found that among white evangelical Protestants, 44 percent of those between eighteen and twenty-nine supported the legalization of gay marriage, as compared with just 12 percent of those sixty-five and above. In 2011, Jim Daly, president of Focus on the Family, admitted that "among the 20- and 30-somethings 65% to 70%...favor same-sex marriage.... We've probably lost that [battle]."[31]

One reason for this enormous age-based disparity in views on gay marriage is that younger people are far more likely to know someone who is openly gay. One

2004 poll found that 68 percent of those thirty or under knew someone who was gay, as compared with only 26 percent of those seventy-five and up. Another 2009 study found that 58 percent of those ages eighteen to thirty-four reported having a family member or close friend who is gay, compared with just one in three of those sixty-five and above.[32]

In addition, younger people have grown up in an environment that is far more tolerant of homosexuality than was that of their parents. They read comic strips that have openly gay characters participating in same-sex marriages. They go to schools that have gay-straight alliances. And they live in a culture that features gay celebrities whose sexual orientation seems irrelevant to their popularity.[33]

Ellen DeGeneres has served as spokesperson for American Express and Cover Girl makeup, hosted the Emmys and the Oscars, and served as a judge on one of television's highest-rated programs, *American Idol*. Showing a video of her same-sex wedding on *Oprah*, along with a public display of "gushingly romantic affection" for her lesbian partner, Portia de Rossi, had no apparent detrimental impact on her popularity.[34]

Rachel Maddow is an open lesbian who hosts a popular evening political talk show on MSNBC. Wanda Sykes is another open lesbian who is a popular comedian and roasted President Obama at a recent White House correspondents' dinner. The easy popular acceptance of such openly gay celebrities marks an enormous cultural shift from only a decade ago.

Younger people are also far more likely to believe that a person's sexual orientation is immutable rather than chosen. Such a belief highly correlates with support for gay marriage.[35]

It is hard to imagine a scenario in which young people's support for gay marriage dissipates as they grow older. Tolerance of homosexuality does not appear to be a life cycle issue, on which attitudes change with age.[36]

Not only are younger Americans more supportive of gay marriage than their elders, but younger gay activists are more insistent than older ones about demanding it as a right. Younger activists have grown up in a social and political climate in which they are less fearful of violence and discrimination based on sexual orientation. They tend to be more self-confident and less inclined to be patient with incremental social change. For them, gay marriage is a right to which they feel entitled, not a dream that they dare to see realized. One poll of LGBT Americans found that younger people were 31 percentage points more likely to support the legalization of gay marriage than were senior citizens.[37]

A third reason to regard gay marriage as inevitable is that as the social and political environment becomes more gay-friendly, changes in attitudes and practices occur that make gay marriage harder to resist. This factor partially explains why the greatest increases in support for gay marriage in the last fifteen years have come in the states that already were the most supportive of gay rights.[38]

For example, as society becomes more accepting of homosexuality, opponents of gay marriage find it harder to argue that homosexuality is immoral without alienating moderates, thus depriving them of one of their principal arguments against gay marriage. Similarly, as more openly gay couples raise children, and as social scientists increasingly show that those children do not suffer from being raised by same-sex couples, gay marriage opponents will find it more difficult to argue that society benefits from denying marriage to such couples. As of the 2000 census, 34 percent of lesbian couples and 22 percent of gay couples were raising young children. Furthermore, as more states allow same-sex couples to marry, and as predictions that gay marriage will produce deleterious social consequences are proven wrong, gay marriage opponents in other states will be deprived of another of the conventional arguments against same-sex marriage.[39]

Fourth and finally, economic pressures are likely to build against states that resist gay marriage. Tourism officials and chambers of commerce have long opposed anti-gay ballot initiatives because of concerns about boycotts by tourists and consumers. Business corporations are increasingly adopting gay-friendly policies. Well over half of the Fortune 500 companies now offer health care benefits to same-sex partners of employees. Such gay-friendly corporations are starting to pressure state legislatures to legalize gay marriage, arguing that highly skilled employees are reluctant to live and work in states with regressive social policies. Moreover, estimates of lost revenue from same-sex couples who are forced to wed outside of their home states are considerable.[40]

In 2007, five of Indiana's largest employers spoke out against a proposed state constitutional amendment to ban gay marriage. A letter from the drug company Eli Lilly to the Speaker of the Indiana house expressed concern that the proposed amendment "sends an unwelcoming signal to current and future employees by making Indiana appear intolerant." The amendment was eventually killed in committee.[41]

In 2009, Google and other business interests filed a brief with the California supreme court urging it to invalidate Proposition 8. They argued that "employees deserve fundamental civil rights, and that when employees are harmed, businesses suffer." In 2009, the Greater Seattle Chamber of Commerce endorsed Washington's Everything but Marriage Act, observing that diversity and inclusiveness were core values of the business community. Microsoft donated $100,000 to the campaign to defend the measure against a voter initiative to overturn it. That same year, Harrah's Entertainment warned Nevada legislators that the state's tourism industry would lose the business of gays and lesbians if lawmakers failed to override the governor's expected veto of a civil unions bill. In 2009 in Vermont, business groups testified in favor of gay marriage at legislative hearings. Early in 2012, Microsoft, Nike, and several other large corporations came out in favor of gay marriage in Washington State. Lloyd Blankfein, chief executive officer of Goldman Sachs, recently made a video endorsing gay marriage for the Human Rights Campaign.[42]

Most large law firms no longer wish to be associated with litigation opposing gay marriage. In 2011, former solicitor general Paul Clement left his Atlanta law firm after it countermanded his agreement to represent the U.S. House of Representatives in defending the constitutionality of the Defense of Marriage Act in court.[43]

A study by statistician Nate Silver demonstrates just how inevitable same-sex marriage has become. Building a regression model based on all gay marriage referenda, Silver identifies the variables that seem to influence the outcomes: the year of the vote (that is, how distant from the present), the percentage of state residents identifying religion as an important part of their daily lives, the percentage of evangelicals, the median age of adults, and the state's general political leanings. Silver then projects those variables into the future and predicts the dates by which each state will have a popular majority in favor of gay marriage.[44]

The results are startling. Silver finds that by 2012 or 2013, a majority of people in a majority of states will support gay marriage. By 2016, only the states of the Deep South will still resist it. By 2024, even the last holdout, Mississippi, will have a majority in favor of gay marriage. Studies by other statisticians have yielded broadly similar findings.[45]

In recent years, even many conservatives have begun to acknowledge the inevitability of gay marriage. In March 2011, Albert Mohler, president of the Southern Baptist Theological Seminary, told Focus on the Family that "it is clear that something like same-sex marriage . . . is going to become normalized, legalized, and recognized in the culture." "It's time," Mohler said, "for Christians to start thinking about how we're going to deal with that." When New York adopted gay marriage in June 2011, one of Nevada's foremost conservative activists, Chuck Muth, urged that his state do so as well: "It's inevitable. It can and will be delayed, but not stopped." Even some Republican pollsters now admit—usually anonymously—that "it's only a matter of time."[46]

That a particular social reform may be inevitable does not mean that opponents will cease fighting it. White southerners continued to massively resist *Brown* long after most of them came to believe that school desegregation was inevitable. Although conceding that "you can't fight the Federal government and win," many whites in Alabama and Mississippi still insisted that "we'll never accept it voluntarily" and "they'll have to force it on us." As William Faulkner pointed out, Mississippi whites "will accept another civil war, knowing they're going to lose."[47]

People who believe that gay marriage contravenes God's will are not likely to stop fighting it simply because their prospects of success seem constantly to be diminishing. Moreover, because religious conservatives are both intensely opposed to gay marriage and highly mobilized politically, they are likely for the next several years to continue exerting significant influence over Republican politicians who need their support to win primary elections. Although the ultimate outcome of the contest over gay marriage no longer seems much in doubt, plenty of fighting remains to be done until that battle is won.[48]

Ultimately, the gay marriage debate is likely to be resolved for the nation through litigation (although the outcome of that litigation heavily depends on factors such as public opinion). However many states liberalize their laws to permit gay marriage, others will staunchly resist for at least another decade or so.[49]

The challenges to DOMA that won in federal district court in Boston are now before the First Circuit. In late February 2012, another federal district judge, in San Francisco, also struck down the section of DOMA denying federal recognition to same-sex marriages lawfully performed in the states. The appeal of Judge Walker's decision invalidating Proposition 8 in California was delayed while the Ninth Circuit certified to the California supreme court the question of whether, under California law, the official sponsors of an initiative have standing to defend its constitutionality in court when state officials decline to do so. In November 2011, the California high court answered in the affirmative. Then, in February 2012, a panel of the Ninth Circuit struck down Proposition 8, though on the narrow ground that the state could not take away by voter initiative marriage rights that had been conferred. Any of these cases could eventually end up before the U.S. Supreme Court.[50]

One can easily imagine a Court composed of liberal justices who probably sympathize with gay marriage and conservative justices who believe in states' rights agreeing to invalidate DOMA on the ground that the federal government should not be involved in defining marriage. What might one expect the Supreme Court to do with state laws that define marriage as the union of a man and a woman?

Trying to predict Supreme Court rulings is risky business, though informed speculation is possible. Had such a case reached the Court in or around 2004, it is possible that not a single justice would have ruled that the federal Constitution protects gay marriage. Even liberal justices such as Ruth Bader Ginsburg and Stephen Breyer, who probably sympathize with gay marriage as a policy matter, likely would have been wary of venturing too far in advance of public opinion and exacerbating a political backlash that might undermine the cause of gay marriage.[51]

Notably, Justice Ginsburg has repeatedly criticized *Roe v. Wade* on precisely this ground—that the Court intervened too quickly and too aggressively on the abortion issue, thus generating an enormous political backlash that undermined the cause of abortion reform in the long term. That this interpretation of *Roe*'s effect is controversial does not mean that the liberal justices do not accept it. The Supreme Court's unanimous refusal in 1997 to find a constitutional right to physician-assisted suicide seemed a conscious rejection of litigants' invitation to intervene early on another divisive issue of social reform.[52]

Whether the liberal justices would be equally wary today of intervening on gay marriage is a different question. Since 2004, several additional state courts have ruled in favor of gay marriage, and several legislatures have enacted it. National opinion polls now consistently show majority support for gay marriage, which seems to be gaining in popularity at a rate of several percentage points a year. In the last few years, even many Republican politicians have ceased attacking gay marriage, and a few have gone so far as to embrace it. A Supreme Court ruling in favor of gay marriage in 2012 or beyond would not generate the same explosive political backlash that such a decision would have ignited in 2004.

Predicting the votes of today's conservative justices on gay marriage seems more straightforward. Justice Antonin Scalia has publicly stated that the constitutional case for gay marriage is "absurd." In 2003, Justice Clarence Thomas voted to uphold a Texas ban on same-sex sodomy, although he did acknowledge that the law was "silly." If Thomas believes that the Constitution permits a state to criminalize same-sex sodomy, he certainly thinks that a state can ban same-sex marriage.[53]

Chief Justice John Roberts and Justice Samuel Alito have yet to express judicial opinions on gay rights issues. Given their religious backgrounds (they are conservative Catholics) and their generally conservative political ideologies, however, one may surmise that they are unlikely anytime soon to support gay marriage, either as a policy matter or as one of constitutional interpretation.

On nearly all important issues of constitutional law today, the U.S. Supreme Court divides 5 to 4 along predictable political lines. There are four consistent liberals and four consistent conservatives. Despite all of the talk of differing methodologies of constitutional interpretation—originalism versus living constitutionalism—the justices' political ideologies seem to predict their votes better than their professed interpretive methodologies do. This is true about abortion, affirmative action, school desegregation, gun control, campaign finance reform, the death penalty, school prayer, political gerrymandering, federalism, and civil liberties issues arising from the War on Terror.

Virtually every constitutional question today turns on the vote of Justice Anthony Kennedy, who is undoubtedly the most powerful justice in the history of the U.S. Supreme Court. Justice Kennedy has tended to vote with the liberals on some abortion issues, some death penalty issues, school prayer, and civil liberties issues arising from the War on Terror. On most other constitutional issues, he has tended to side with the conservatives. For as long as the current composition of the Court holds, gay marriage will likely turn on Justice Kennedy's vote. What might that vote be?[54]

One possibility is that Justice Kennedy follows the compromise path charted by the Vermont and New Jersey supreme courts and rules that the Constitution mandates at least civil unions for same-sex couples. On a number of constitutional issues—including the death penalty, political gerrymandering, government race consciousness, and abortion—Justice Kennedy has demonstrated an affinity for compromise positions.

Two-thirds of the country now supports civil unions. Even many staunch conservatives including Rush Limbaugh endorse them. In September 2011, New Hampshire Republicans had to agree to protect civil unions as the price of securing support from some caucus members in their effort to repeal the state's gay marriage law. A Supreme Court ruling in favor of civil unions for same-sex couples would not generate much backlash in 2012 or beyond.[55]

If Justice Kennedy were to rule on gay marriage itself, what might he decide? The outcome may depend on how the justice reconciles two of his proclivities, which seem to cut in opposite directions on gay marriage.

On one hand, Justice Kennedy has often taken dominant national norms, converted them into constitutional mandates, and then suppressed outlier state practices. His decisions barring the death penalty for minors and the mentally disabled, forbidding sentences of life in prison without the possibility of parole for juvenile offenders, and invalidating the Texas ban on same-sex sodomy all fit this description.[56]

On gay marriage, this propensity to use the Constitution only to suppress outliers would counsel restraint. Just eight states and the District of Columbia currently permit gay marriage. Intervening at this stage of a social reform movement would be somewhat analogous to *Roe v. Wade*, where the Court essentially took the laws deregulating abortion in four states and turned them into a constitutional command for the other forty-six. Justice Kennedy has given little indication that he favors using the Constitution in so aggressive a manner.[57]

On the other hand, Justice Kennedy authored the Court's only two decisions supporting gay rights—*Romer* (1996) and *Lawrence* (2003). He comes from a part of the country—northern California—that is overwhelmingly supportive of gay rights in general and gay marriage in particular. As a judge on the Ninth Circuit in 1980, he authored an opinion that was remarkably gay-friendly for its time, strongly implying that criminal prosecution of private consensual homosexual sodomy would be unconstitutional in the course of upholding the navy's policy of dismissing gay servicemen. Although Kennedy's opinion in *Lawrence* explicitly distinguished the issue of same-sex marriage from that of criminalizing same-sex sodomy, he embraced an interpretive methodology of living constitu-tionalism, which construes the open-ended language of the Constitution according to evolving social mores rather than the original understanding of its authors.[58]

Moreover, Kennedy's opinions frequently treat international norms as rele-vant to American constitutional interpretation. In recent years, gay marriage and civil unions have begun to spread from Western Europe and Canada to Australia and New Zealand, South Africa, and many cities and some countries in South America.[59]

In addition, the language of Justice Kennedy's opinion in *Lawrence* suggests that he may be especially attentive to his historical legacy. Whether judges should be in the business of predicting the future is debatable. As the majority of the New York court of appeals observed in rejecting gay marriage in 2006: "The dis-senters assert confidently that 'future generations' will agree with their view of this case. We do not predict what people will think generations from now, but we believe the present generation should have a chance to decide the issue through its elected representatives."[60]

Yet the handwriting on the wall is as clear as it ever gets on gay marriage. Many state legislators have explained their votes in favor of gay marriage on the ground that they wanted to be on the right side of history and to have their chil-dren be proud when looking back on their parent's legislative voting record.[61]

Judges authoring opinions in support of gay marriage have frequently invoked examples of courts being on the right side of history. Chief Justice Margaret Marshall, the author of *Goodridge*, has compared it to the Massachusetts court's decision in the 1790s in *Quock Walker*, which barred slavery in the common-wealth using the same "free and equal" provision of the state constitution that was invoked in *Goodridge*. The California supreme court's decision in favor of gay marriage proudly invoked that court's landmark ruling in 1948 in *Perez v. Lippold*, which invalidated the state's ban on interracial marriage twenty years before the U.S. Supreme Court reached the same result in *Loving v. Virginia*. In *Varnum*, the Iowa supreme court invoked its historic role in pioneering social reform, noting decisions that struck blows against slavery and racial segregation and in favor of women's rights long before such rulings became common at the federal level. Judges dissenting from state court decisions that have rejected a right to gay marriage have warned that future generations would look back at such rulings "with regret and even shame."[62]

In 1954, *Brown v. Board of Education* split the nation down the middle, but within two decades it had become an iconic decision. A Supreme Court ruling in favor of gay marriage in 2012 or 2013 would also split the country down the middle. Yet, given how quickly public opinion is evolving in favor of gay marriage, within a decade or two such a decision would probably also become iconic.

What justice would not be tempted to author the opinion that within a few short years likely would become known as the *Brown v. Board* of the gay rights movement? Justice Kennedy would have the option of writing that opinion if he wished to do so. When he votes with the liberals, he is the senior justice in the majority, which means he gets to assign the opinion.[63]

Whatever the Court may do in the short term—possibly including a refusal to grant review in a gay marriage case—eventually it is almost certain to rule in favor of gay marriage. Once public opinion has shifted overwhelmingly in favor and many more states have enacted gay marriage, the Court will constitutionalize the emerging consensus and suppress resisting outliers. That is simply how constitutional law works in the United States.[64]

Conclusion

Gay marriage supporters have often disagreed about strategy and tactics. Some have been incrementalists, favoring legislative reform and endorsing a gradual progression from domestic partnerships to civil unions to gay marriage. On this view, gradual reform minimizes backlash by enabling public opinion and politicians to grow comfortable with incremental change before being asked to digest more radical reform. Incrementalism also secures tangible benefits for same-sex couples at a time when marriage equality may not yet be politically feasible.[1]

Others have favored a more aggressive approach, advocating litigation even when public opinion was not likely to support gay marriage. These activists argue that any social change generates backlash, that asking for less produces less, and that pushing the envelope makes other reform proposals seem more moderate and palatable. Does the history of gay marriage litigation shed light on this debate?[2]

On one hand, gay marriage litigation has undeniably advanced the cause of gay rights in a number of ways. In 2012, it is hard to remember what a radical concept gay marriage was in 1990. Dramatic social change does not happen until people begin contemplating and discussing it. Litigation put gay marriage on the table. Newspapers were filled with letters to the editor debating gay marriage after *Baehr, Baker,* and *Goodridge.*[3]

Without such litigation to make the issue salient, it seems unlikely that more than 50 percent of Americans would support gay marriage in 2012. This salience-raising effect of litigation is different from the so-called educational effect of court decisions. Little evidence supports the notion that court rulings educate public opinion to agree with them. Americans did not change their views on school segregation because of *Brown,* abortion because of *Roe,* or the death penalty because of *Furman.* Yet even if court decisions do not educate, they do make issues salient and generate conversations about them.[4]

Victories in court can also raise the hopes and expectations of beneficiaries, convincing them that genuine social reform is possible. Even during the darkest days of Jim Crow, an occasional victory in court could "keep open the door of hope to the Negro," as one black leader observed in 1935. After one such litigation triumph in the 1940s, an NAACP official noted, "It is just such rifts in the dark clouds of prejudice which cause black folks to know that a better day is coming by and by."[5]

For many gays and lesbians, same-sex marriage did not seem like a realistic possibility until court decisions made it so. As pioneer gay rights litigator Mary Bonauto observed, *Goodridge* was a "beacon of hope."[6]

Court victories can change people's desires as well as their expectations. Whereas previously gays may have chosen not to desire marriage in order to avoid the pain of wishing for something that was beyond reach, after decisions such as *Goodridge*, marriage became more desirable because it seemed more attainable. The emotion and joy on display at the weddings inspired by *Goodridge*—"people were experiencing for the first time what it felt like to be equal"—led many same-sex couples to want to get married in a way they had never imagined they would before.[7]

Litigation victories were inspirational for the gay rights movement. As gay marriage pioneer Evan Wolfson explained, *Baehr* "unleashed a tremendous energy amongst gay and non-gay people on our side." Each victory in court sparked additional litigation elsewhere. The Hawaii litigation inspired lawsuits in Alaska and Vermont. Victory in Vermont inspired litigation in Massachusetts. The landmark decision in *Goodridge* fomented marriage litigation in several additional states.[8]

Litigation victories inspired not just additional lawsuits but more gay activism of every sort. Gays and lesbians who were touched by the same-sex weddings that followed *Goodridge* became more politically engaged. They made financial contributions to gay rights groups and engaged in legislative lobbying.[9]

Court rulings in favor of gay marriage mattered also because they changed the status quo. By contrast, Supreme Court decisions invalidating racial segregation in public education and forbidding organized prayer in public schools were widely defied for years, meaning that schools in the South remained racially segregated and organized prayer in public schools continued unabated.[10]

Yet gay marriage rulings met with little outright defiance. A few county clerks resigned rather than issue marriage licenses to gay couples, but same-sex marriages took place—and in significant numbers. Eighteen thousand same-sex couples married in California in the six months between the court's decision legalizing it and the passage of Proposition 8. By early 2009, twelve thousand same-sex couples had married in Massachusetts.[11]

Changing the status quo on gay marriage mattered because it influenced public opinion. Married gay couples put a public face on the issue, enabling Americans to see real people whose lives were affected by the law. Watching hundreds of gay couples standing in line for hours in the rain to get married showed

Eleven-year-old McKinley BarbouRoske reacts to Iowa court ruling, with her parents, Dawn and Jen BarbouRoske, and her six-year-old sister Bre, Apr. 3, 2009. (*Associated Press/Christopher Gannon*)

how much marriage meant to them. How many people may have reconsidered their views on gay marriage upon seeing the unadulterated joy on the face of an eleven-year-old girl, McKinley BarbouRoske, whose parents had just won their gay marriage case in the Iowa supreme court? Her photograph appeared on hundreds of news sites.[12]

Gay couples getting married also upended traditional stereotypes of homosexuals by presenting "an image of stable couples in search of lifetime commitments." One can only guess how many people have changed their attitudes toward gay marriage after experiencing gay married couples as good neighbors or as parents of well-adjusted children.[13]

Changing the status quo on gay marriage has mattered in another way as well. Gay marriage opponents have regularly predicted a doomsday scenario if gay marriage was legalized. Yet in states that have done so, little has changed. Marriage as an institution has not suffered in any obvious ways. Western civilization has not ended—at least not yet—as James Dobson and others have predicted that it would.[14]

In his findings of fact in *Perry*, Judge Walker highlighted the experience of Massachusetts, where five years of gay marriage had not seemed to affect heterosexual marriage. Well aware of this status-quo-shifting effect of court rulings in favor of gay marriage, opponents have desperately sought to delay the effective date of such decisions, hoping to overturn them by referendum before any actual marriages could take place and thereby build support for the institution.[15]

Although far from dispositive, evidence seems to confirm this status-quo-altering effect of court decisions in favor of gay marriage. Many Massachusetts legislators pointed to the gay marriages that took place beginning in May 2004 to explain the dramatic shift in legislative sentiment on the proposed state marriage amendment between 2004 and 2005. The rapidity with which public opinion has changed on gay marriage in Massachusetts has been extraordinary. In 2004, one survey found that Massachusettans opposed gay marriage by 44 percent to 42 percent. Four years later, they supported it by 59 percent to 37 percent.[16]

At the national level as well, the increase in support for gay marriage has happened so quickly in the years since *Goodridge* that its status-quo-altering effect seems difficult to deny. Backing for gay marriage increased by at least 10 percentage points in the five years after *Goodridge*. This is unusually rapid opinion change relative to most of the great moral controversies in American history.[17]

One other positive effect of gay marriage litigation from the perspective of the gay rights movement has been to "open up the middle" by making domestic partnerships and civil unions seem more moderate by comparison. As political scientist Thomas Keck has explained, "By pushing the policy envelope, ambitious litigation can clear space for legislative progress in its wake." To invoke an analogy, in the 1960s, Malcolm X's radical black nationalism was widely credited with making Martin Luther King Jr.'s nonviolent integrationism more palatable to many white Americans.[18]

Within just a few years, civil unions went from provoking a powerful political backlash in Vermont to becoming the fallback option for opponents of gay marriage. The Massachusetts legislature, which would not enact even domestic partnership benefits before *Goodridge*, quickly embraced civil unions after the decision. Support for civil unions among Americans increased dramatically between the middle of 2003 and the middle of 2005—a change that is hard to attribute to anything but the visibility that *Goodridge* provided to gay marriage. Even without direct judicial prompting, numerous states have enacted domestic partnership legislation and/or civil unions in the years since *Goodridge*. Today, more than two-thirds of Americans support civil unions.[19]

The dynamic behind this phenomenon of "opening up the middle" may operate in any of several different ways. First, psychologists have shown that people often display a cognitive bias in favor of intermediate positions. Gallup pollsters find that support for civil unions increases when respondents are first asked a question about gay marriage. Second, gay activists may use same-sex marriage litigation to provide political cover to friendly politicians, who otherwise would have been fearful to act; these politicians can explain their votes in favor of civil unions as an effort to head off a judicial mandate of gay marriage.[20]

Third, even legislators generally unsympathetic toward gay rights have occasionally endorsed compromise positions for fear that courts would otherwise impose something more extreme. Thus, some gay marriage opponents in the Massachusetts legislature supported a civil unions bill soon after *Goodridge* to test whether it would satisfy the court. (It did not.) Similarly, in 1997, some legislators in Hawaii combined a proposed constitutional amendment barring gay marriage with the most advanced domestic partnerships law in the nation, hoping to convince courts that the amendment had not been motivated by animus toward gays.[21]

Fourth and finally, embracing lesser protections for gay rights can be a means by which gay marriage opponents seek to ameliorate a reputation for homophobia. After the Mormon Church had played a prominent role in promoting the passage of Proposition 8 in California, it quietly posted on its website a statement clarifying that it had no objection to civil unions or legal protections for gay couples in areas such as health care, housing, and employment benefits. The Mormon Church had never before endorsed gay rights legislation.[22]

Similarly, it was no accident that the same day in 1996 that the U.S. Senate voted overwhelmingly in favor of DOMA, it also came within a single vote of passing the Employment Nondiscrimination Act. Gay rights groups have consciously sought to "guilt" legislators who voted to ban gay marriage into simultaneously supporting protection against other forms of discrimination against gays and lesbians.[23]

Although litigation has clearly furthered the cause of gay marriage in some ways, it has also plainly retarded it in others. Indeed, the political backlash ignited by *Baehr* and *Goodridge* has led some commentators to deem the gay marriage litigation campaign a "disaster." Gay rights activist and author John D'Emilio has gone so far as to blame such litigation for "a series of defeats that constitute the greatest calamity in the history of the gay and lesbian movement in the United States."[24]

Were it not for the *Baehr* litigation, DOMA probably would not exist. That law has imposed enormous costs on thousands of same-sex couples who have lawfully married in the several states that permit gay marriage but whose unions are not recognized by federal law. These costs are not just financial. Many immigrants have been deported because their same-sex marriages to U.S. citizens are not recognized by the federal government.

Before *Goodridge*, just three states had constitutional bans on gay marriage. Since the decision, the number of states with such prohibitions has increased to thirty. In these states, gay marriage will be harder to secure in the future because the legislature is barred from enacting it. Moreover, most of these state constitutional bans contain language that explicitly or implicitly forbids civil unions and even domestic partnerships. In such states, the gay marriage litigation that inspired passage of marriage amendments has cost gay couples the opportunity to secure some of the rights and benefits of marriage.

In fact, gay marriage litigation has probably cost same-sex couples not just the opportunity to secure domestic partnerships and civil unions but the reality of them. In state after state, voters have rejected gay marriage when they probably would have approved civil unions if given the opportunity. In 2009, Mainers rejected gay marriage by 53 percent to 47 percent, while polls showed that they favored either gay marriage or civil unions over no legal recognition for same-sex couples by 73.8 percent to 23 percent. Also in 2009, the New York legislature voted down gay marriage while polls showed that New Yorkers supported civil unions by 65 percent to 27 percent.[25]

By making gay marriage salient and reducing the appeal of civil unions to gay activists, same-sex marriage litigation has diverted attention from civil unions, which many state legislatures might otherwise have enacted in light of strong public support. Only twelve of the twenty-five states that have popular majorities in favor of civil unions have enacted them thus far. For years, then, thousands of same-sex couples in numerous states have been denied many of the rights and benefits of marriage that otherwise might have been attainable.[26]

More speculatively, gay marriage litigation may have delayed realization of other items on the gay rights agenda. Gay rights organizations have limited resources. Money and time spent defending against efforts to enact statutes and constitutional amendments banning gay marriage cannot be devoted to other issues. Might not the Employment Nondiscrimination Act have passed by now or "don't ask, don't tell" have been repealed sooner had gay marriage not become such a salient issue beginning in the 1990s?

Legal protection against discrimination in employment based on sexual orientation has been one of the top priorities of gay rights organizations since the 1970s. In the early 1990s, some gay activists were predicting that Congress would pass the Employment Nondiscrimination Act within a decade. Although 70 percent to 80 percent of Americans support that measure, Congress still has not enacted it. Litigation focused public attention on gay marriage at a time when gays could still be dismissed from their jobs because of their sexual orientation in a majority of states. "Don't ask, don't tell" was not repealed until 2010, despite several years' worth of polls showing that 75 percent of the country opposed it.[27]

The point is not simply that social reform organizations have finite resources. In addition, when litigation places the most controversial issue on a social reform agenda front and center, one effect can be to generate additional resistance to other items on the agenda that previously had been less controversial.

After *Brown v. Board of Education*, African Americans found it harder to vote in the Deep South, and progress on desegregating higher education, public transportation, and athletic competitions was stalled and then reversed. Once the Supreme Court invalidated racial segregation in public education, all other racial reforms became more controversial as well.[28]

In the same way, gay marriage litigation may have rendered more controversial other items on the gay rights agenda by making marriage seem like the inevitable end of the reform process. In 2004 in New Mexico, one leading gay activist worried that the issuance of gay marriage licenses by the Sandoval County clerk would jeopardize the recently enacted anti-discrimination law by rendering all gay rights reforms more controversial: "It is a threat to everything we have spent the past ten years fighting for in terms of equality."[29]

In 2009 in West Virginia, the heightened focus on gay marriage caused by the Iowa court's decision in *Varnum* appeared to kill the prospects of a bill to forbid discrimination based on sexual orientation in employment and housing. That bill had appeared likely to pass before public attention was diverted to gay marriage, which Republicans were able to use as a "scare tactic," according to one Democratic lawmaker.[30]

The cost of shifting public attention to gay marriage may have been even higher than missed opportunities to enact anti-discrimination laws in certain jurisdictions. In some cases, gay rights policies already in place have come under attack because they have received greater scrutiny in light of gay marriage litigation.

In 2000, the controversy over civil unions in Vermont brought public attention to the state Department of Education's funding of an organization called Outright Vermont, which worked in schools to foster understanding of, and sensitivity toward, issues confronting LGBT youth. That program had slipped under the public radar before *Baker*. However, after an election campaign dominated by the civil unions issue in which the Republican gubernatorial candidate had charged Outright Vermont with promoting a homosexual agenda in the schools, the state education department decided to terminate its funding.[31]

In 2004, after *Goodridge* and the West Coast weddings made gay marriage salient, the Christian Coalition in Oregon sent out seventy-five thousand voter guides opposing the reelection of Justice Rives Kistler of the state supreme court and denouncing him as "the only openly homosexual supreme court judge in the nation." Although his opponent, James Leuenberger, did not mention Kistler's sexual orientation, he did emphasize that he himself was a father of two children and a person of faith. Leuenberger also helped the Christian Coalition draft a state constitutional amendment to ban same-sex marriage and called into question the state supreme court's ability to rule impartially on pending gay marriage litigation. Kistler ultimately survived the challenge but won a much smaller share of the vote—about 60 percent—than is customary among Oregon appellate judges.[32]

In assessing the costs and benefits of gay marriage litigation, one must consider whether securing gay marriage in one state was worth the cost of gays not enjoying protection from job discrimination in another, of gay teens losing public funding for a support group, and of a gay justice possibly losing his seat on a state supreme court.[33]

In addition to impacting a variety of gay rights issues, same-sex marriage litigation has had broader political ramifications. Although such collateral political effects may not impact the gay rights agenda directly, they do so indirectly by influencing the fate of politicians who generally support gay rights.[34]

In 2004, the political backlash ignited by *Goodridge* almost certainly led to the defeat of a Democratic candidate for a U.S. Senate seat in Kentucky. That year in South Dakota, Tom Daschle became the first Senate party leader in fifty years to lose his seat, and gay marriage was an important factor. George W. Bush possibly would not have been reelected president in 2004 had it not been for *Goodridge*. President Bush's party opposed almost all aspects of the gay rights agenda. The judges he appointed during his second term in office—including the two justices he put on the U.S. Supreme Court—are unlikely candidates to support gay marriage anytime soon.

In Iowa, three supreme court justices lost their seats in 2010 because of their ruling in favor of gay marriage. They were the first Iowa justices in the fifty-year history of merit selection in that state to lose their retention elections. Their defeat influences how state judges everywhere think about gay marriage litigation—indeed, about any controversial litigation. The executive director of Lambda Legal described the Iowa campaign as "a warning shot across the bow of judges." Judicial rulings in favor of gay marriage elsewhere also have inspired attacks on judicial independence, although none has succeeded as they did in Iowa. The group responsible for removing the Iowa justices has expanded its agenda to target merit selection in other states.[35]

Thinking about gay marriage litigation in terms of its costs and benefits does not necessarily entail criticizing the lawyers who brought the cases that sparked political backlashes when they won. Lawyers have obligations to clients, not necessarily to causes. Gay couples seeking a constitutional right to marry are entitled to legal representation, regardless of whether gay rights strategists believe that the time is ripe for such litigation.[36]

More important, gay rights lawyers have been fully aware of the backlash potential of gay marriage litigation if commenced too far in advance of public opinion, and they have assiduously sought to minimize it. When Mary Bonauto, the chief plaintiffs' lawyer in *Goodridge*, began her job with the Gay and Lesbian Advocates and Defenders in 1990, she turned down requests to represent gay couples seeking to marry because she thought such litigation was premature.

At that time, Massachusetts did not offer even domestic partnerships to same-sex couples, and the right of gays to raise children was tenuous.[37]

The principal national gay rights organizations did not support the *Baehr* litigation in Hawaii in 1991. The plaintiffs in that case hired a local ACLU lawyer to represent them, and the national organizations only filed an amicus brief once the case was headed to the state supreme court, whether they liked it or not.[38]

In 1995, when local officials in Ithaca, New York, agreed to grant a marriage license to a same-sex couple, national gay rights organizations urged them to desist, fearing judicial and legislative backlash. One group advocating for gay and lesbian immigrants worried that the Ithaca couple's attempt to marry, even if supported by local politicians, "may backfire in a way which would make it doubly hard to ultimately win the right to marry in this state." This group believed that a "long term, deliberately paced approach which combines public education and grassroots organizing is most likely to yield lasting results."[39]

Gay rights organizations have been highly strategic in their decisions about when and where to file gay marriage lawsuits. They have litigated only in those jurisdictions with the most gay-friendly policies and judiciaries. Moreover, they have gone to court only after working to educate public opinion by holding informational meetings at which gay couples shared their stories. In Iowa, gay activists went so far as to invest money in state legislative races in 2006, seeking to defeat opponents of gay marriage in anticipation of the state supreme court's decision.[40]

When they have deemed the time or place not to be right, gay rights groups have discouraged same-sex couples from filing marriage litigation. Just days before the California supreme court's decision in favor of gay marriage became effective in 2008, nine major gay rights organizations asked same-sex couples not to sue the federal government or other states to force recognition of their California marriages, fearing adverse court decisions that might take years to overturn.[41]

Moreover, for nearly two decades, gay rights organizations have mostly succeeded at keeping marriage litigation out of the federal courts, operating on the assumption that they did not yet have the votes to win in the U.S. Supreme Court. Instead, they have proceeded state by state, and they have pressed claims only under state constitutions, which the U.S. Supreme Court generally does not have authority to interpret differently from how state courts have construed them.[42]

When gay rights lawyers initially challenged Proposition 8 after it passed, they relied only on a state-law argument—that the amendment was a constitutional "revision" that could not be enacted through a voter referendum. They did so because they wished to keep the case out of federal court. When GLAD finally entered federal court in a marriage case in 2009, it filed a narrow challenge to

DOMA, seeking to invalidate only the provision denying federal benefits to same-sex couples who were legally married under state law. GLAD did not yet challenge state laws barring gay marriage. When *Perry* was filed in 2009, the leading national gay rights organizations issued a joint statement condemning the decision by Boies and Olson to bring a federal court challenge when the odds of winning in the U.S. Supreme Court seemed slim.[43]

The point is that gay rights litigators have been plenty strategic; they have simply been unable to control gay marriage litigation. Generations ago, the NAACP was virtually a monopolist with regard to school desegregation litigation in the South. Most southern blacks could not afford to hire lawyers, few black lawyers practiced in the South, and white lawyers often refused to take civil rights cases. Moreover, only the NAACP could offer some modicum of protection from the economic and physical reprisals that often were directed at civil rights plaintiffs.[44]

Gay marriage litigation in today's world is very different. Same-sex couples wishing to marry generally can find a lawyer willing to bring their case, regardless of opposition from national gay rights groups. These organizations could not prevent same-sex marriage litigation in Hawaii in the early 1990s, and they could not keep it out of federal court in 2009. Once such lawsuits were filed, these groups had little choice but to pitch in and help, as the cases were going to proceed with or without their support.[45]

In the last forty years, extraordinary changes have taken place with regard to social attitudes and legal practices on issues involving homosexuality. In the 1960s, even the most optimistic gay activists would not have thought it possible to advance from the goal of ending police harassment of gay bars to achieving state recognition of gay marriage in only half a lifetime.[46]

For those actually living through a social reform movement and experiencing the defeats along with the victories, it can be difficult to maintain perspective on how transformative the changes have been and how positive the likely future trajectory of the movement remains. Gay marriage does not appear so inevitable when Maine becomes the thirty-first state to reject it in a referendum and the New York and New Jersey legislatures reject gay marriage bills soon thereafter. After referendum defeats such as those in California and Maine, one easily overlooks the powerful trend in favor of gay marriage reflected in the narrow margins of those defeats, and one takes little comfort from the observation that subsequent referenda in those states within just a few years almost certainly will yield positive outcomes. Taking the long view is especially difficult for young gay activists, who have grown up experiencing something close to equality and are more confident in their demands and less patient for change.[47]

Yet the changes have been extraordinary. Fifty years ago, every state criminalized same-sex sodomy; today it is a constitutional right. Thirty years ago, not a single state barred discrimination based on sexual orientation in employment or public accommodations; today more than twenty states have enacted such laws. Twenty years ago, no state was close to enacting gay marriage, many gays and lesbians thought they would not see it during their lifetimes, and most gay activists opposed filing lawsuits in pursuit of it. Even a dozen years ago, no state—indeed, no country—had enacted gay marriage, and Vermont's adoption of civil unions had generated such an enormous firestorm of resistance that some commentators wondered if any state ever would permit gay couples to marry. By contrast, in 2012, two-thirds of Americans, including Rush Limbaugh, support civil unions; about fifteen states have enacted either civil unions or gay marriage; and many gay activists now denounce civil unions as separate and unequal.[48]

The pace at which public opinion has shifted in favor of gay marriage is stunning. In 1990, no more than one in every four Americans supported same-sex marriage. In 2003–4, Americans still opposed it by a margin of two to one. By 2010–11, national polls consistently showed a majority of Americans in support. Moreover, the rate of change has accelerated from one or two percentage points a year to roughly four per year. At that rate, every state will have a majority in favor of gay marriage within a decade or so. Yet currently only eight states have enacted gay marriage.

Of course, predicting the future can be fraught with peril. When the Supreme Court invalidated abortion restrictions in *Roe v. Wade* (1973) and cast doubt upon the constitutionality of the death penalty in *Furman v. Georgia* (1972), the justices were probably imagining a future in which public opinion would have continued to shift in the same direction that the Court was pushing. The justices probably believed that abortion reform was about to sweep the country and that the death penalty was on the road to extinction. They likely saw themselves as providing a nudge forward to social reforms that they believed inevitable.[49]

Suffice it to say that on both occasions the justices' predictions proved mistaken. Over the next four decades, public opinion on abortion changed very little, while on the death penalty it shifted quickly and powerfully against the Court. Yet neither of those issues featured the enormous disparity in opinion based on age that exists on gay marriage.[50]

For reasons discussed earlier, gay marriage is probably inevitable in the United States—and fairly soon. On balance, litigation has probably advanced the cause of gay marriage more than it has retarded it. But such litigation has also probably impeded the realization of other objectives of the gay rights movement, and it has had significant collateral effects on politics. Because of the litigation, U.S. Senate candidates have lost their bids, state judges have lost their jobs, and the outcome of a presidential election may have been affected, which in turn has influenced the composition of the U.S. Supreme Court.

How gay marriage happens may be almost as important as that it happens. Perhaps the backlash potential of gay marriage litigation has been exhausted now that a slim majority of Americans support same-sex marriage. But perhaps it has not. *Brown v. Board of Education* and *Roe v. Wade* both produced dramatic political backlashes, even though opinion polls showed that half of the country supported those rulings when they were decided.

Opposition to gay marriage remains strong in many states and will continue to be so for several years. Powerful political constituencies not only continue to resist gay marriage, but they regard the issue as one of the most important in politics today. That opposition will eventually wither away. Until it does, however, it may continue to exercise influence over our politics. That influence may be greater or lesser, depending partly on how the path to gay marriage unfolds.[51]

ACKNOWLEDGMENTS

I first became interested in the topic of judicial decisions and political backlash twenty years ago when trying to figure out the effects of *Brown v. Board of Education*. Conventional wisdom holds that *Brown* inspired the civil rights movement, but it seemed to me that *Brown* also generated a potent political backlash in the South, both retarding racial progress on some issues and radicalizing southern politics.

While working on that project, which culminated in my book *From Jim Crow to Civil Rights: The Supreme Court and the Struggle for Racial Equality* (2004), it dawned on me that several other prominent Supreme Court decisions had also sparked powerful political backlashes. *Roe v. Wade* (1973) mobilized a right-to-life movement that previously had played little or no role in national politics. By threatening to invalidate the death penalty, *Furman v. Georgia* (1972) immediately generated additional support for capital punishment and inspired thirty-five states to enact new death penalty laws in the four years following the decision. *Miranda v. Arizona* (1966) helped elect Richard Nixon president in 1968 on a law-and-order platform. Even in the nineteenth century, pro-slavery rulings in *Prigg v. Pennsylvania* (1842) and *Dred Scott v. Sandford* (1857) seemed to rally popular support for abolitionists and the Republican party, respectively.

In the 1990s, I was vaguely aware that a 1993 decision of the Hawaii supreme court had strongly hinted that gay marriage was constitutionally protected and that this ruling had inspired dozens of states and Congress to pass laws "defending" traditional marriage. But it was the Massachusetts court's decision in *Goodridge* in 2003 that really got me thinking about gay marriage litigation and political backlash. As the 2004 election campaign unfolded, I worked on an article comparing the backlashes ignited by *Brown* and *Goodridge*. Ever since then, I have closely followed developments on gay rights generally and same-sex marriage specifically, largely through the efforts of Michelle Beecy, a reference librarian and good friend, who has kept me up to date with weekly Internet searches for news on these topics.

Because this project has been germinating so long, I have accumulated a lengthy list of debts, which I wish to acknowledge here. An army of research assistants, mostly law students from Virginia and Harvard, with a few from Cornell thrown in for good measure, have collected newspaper articles and consulted distant archives, enabling me to research more comprehensively than otherwise would have been possible. The list has grown so long that I fear I will forget to include everyone who has helped with the research. I am grateful to Daria Auerbach, Alex Bradshaw, Andrew Chan, Rachel Clark, Adrianne Clarke, Julia Copping, Jonathan Cox, Carrie DeCell, Steven Dunst, Samantha Fang, Michael Firestone, Amanda Frye, Matt Greenfield, Sarah Hack, Katie Hansen, Zsaleh Harivandi, Kelsey Israel-Trummel, Elizabeth Kim, Jessica King, Bryan Koch, Lindsay Kosan, Kevin Lake, Kostya Lantsman, Kevin Lewis, Brandie Lustbader, Jamie McFarlin, Joelle Milov, Lynette Miner, Asieh Nariman, Juhyun Park, Rio Pierce, Amanda Rice, Erika Rickard, Andrew Rubenstein, Yoni Schencker, Joseph Scherban, Jenn Schultz, Alexa Shasteen, Brett Stark, Carol Szurkowski, Sarah Teich, Ben Tettlebaum, Amanda Vaughn, Heather Whitney, and Seth Wiener.

Several friends read the entire manuscript and provided scores of helpful comments and suggestions: Marco Basile, Michelle Beecy, Risa Goluboff, Tarun Chhabra, and Chris Schmidt. My editor at Oxford University Press, Dave McBride, also suggested helpful improvements to the manuscript. Other friends and colleagues helped refine my thinking about backlash with comments on workshop papers presented along the way: Tomiko Brown-Nagin, Neal Devins, Julie Kobich, Daryl Levinson, Liz Magill, Richard McAdams, Jim Ryan, Mike Seidman, Bill Stuntz, and David Strauss. I also have benefited from comments offered by faculty members who attended workshops I gave on backlash at the law schools of Arizona, Boston University, Chicago, Harvard, Marquette, Missouri, Northeastern, Northwestern, NYU, Oklahoma, Oxford, Stanford, Toronto, UCLA, USC, Villanova, Virginia, Washington and Lee, William and Mary, and Yale. Three anonymous reviewers for Oxford University Press also provided helpful comments on my prospectus for this book. Dean Martha Minow of Harvard Law School supplied moral and other support.

I have been fortunate over the years to have the help of splendid faculty assistants, who have cheerfully transcribed my dictation, organized my research assistants, and generally made my life easier: Sylvia Baldwin, Phyllis Harris, and Kimberly O'Hagan.

Two reference librarians have helped me in ways too numerous to count, without ever turning down one of my hundreds of requests. June Casey at

Harvard Law School has met all of my reference needs for the past four years and almost single-handedly illustrated this volume. This book would not have been possible without the help of Michelle Beecy, who not only read the entire manuscript and provided detailed comments but also has kept me apprised of developments on gay rights and same-sex marriage for the last eight years. In addition, Kent Olson of the University of Virginia Law School Library was a great help during the early stages of this project.

With all of this assistance, I should have written a much better book.

One of the beauties of writing history is that the subject matter does not change, though our perspectives on it surely do. One of the great hazards of writing a history of a topic as timely as gay marriage is that the subject matter changes—at present, often on a daily basis. I am humbled and more than a bit intimidated knowing that what I wrote about gay marriage litigation and political backlash in 2005 is not the same as what I think about it in 2012, and that what I have written about it in this book may not accurately reflect my thinking on the subject a few years down the road.

I hope that this account of the history of gay marriage litigation is accurate and complete as of the day I turn this manuscript over to the publisher, February 27, 2012. In just the last two weeks, legislatures in Washington State, New Jersey, and Maryland have passed gay marriage bills (though Governor Chris Christie has vetoed the measure in New Jersey). From my vantage point today, it appears likely that North Carolina voters will pass a constitutional amendment barring gay marriage in May. Minnesotans may do the same in November, though that contest is too close to call with any confidence. Voters in Maine this fall will get a second chance to make their state the first to embrace gay marriage by referendum. Voters in Washington and Maryland are also likely to be asked to affirm or reject their legislatures' recent enactments of gay marriage, and opinion polls in both states suggest close contests, with gay marriage proponents possibly having the edge. It looks unlikely to me that President Obama will change his position and endorse gay marriage before the presidential election in November.

I could well be mistaken in any or all of these predictions. Forecasting the future is more difficult than recounting the past, and I am just a humble legal historian, not a soothsayer. I have chosen not to update this account of same-sex marriage developments in the months between submitting the manuscript to the publisher and the book's publication date. Even were I to do so, fast-changing events would quickly overtake my account of developments in the first half of 2012.

Yet whatever happens in the next few months, I hope the basic thrust of my narrative remains accurate: Gay marriage is inevitable in the United States.

Litigation to accomplish it has advanced the movement in many ways and retarded it in others. That litigation has also had unpredictable and significant effects on our politics. Court decisions that strongly contravene public opinion frequently produce political backlashes. The American political system is too responsive to public opinion for judges to have the final word on issues of great public controversy.

Michael Klarman
Cambridge, Massachusetts
February 27, 2012

ABBREVIATIONS USED IN THE NOTES

538	fivethirtyeight.com
AAN	*Aberdeen American News* (South Dakota)
AAS	*Austin American-Statesman* (Texas)
ACLU	American Civil Liberties Union
ADG	*Arkansas Democrat-Gazette*
ADN	*Anchorage Daily News*
ai	americanindependent.com
AJ	*Albuquerque Journal*
AJC	*Atlanta Journal Constitution*
AL	*Argus Leader* (Sioux Falls, South Dakota)
AP	Associated Press
AT	*Albuquerque Tribune*
au	anglicansunited.com
BDC	*Boulder Daily Camera*
bdh	browndailyherald.com (Providence, Rhode Island)
bdn	bangordailynews.com
BFP	*Burlington Free Press* (Vermont)
BG	*Boston Globe*
bh	bostonherald.com
BN	*Buffalo News*
BS	*Baltimore Sun*
bs	baltimoresun.com
CC	*Christian Century*
CD	*Columbus Dispatch*
CDT	*Columbia Daily Tribune* (Missouri)
CE	*Cincinnati Enquirer*
CG	*Charleston Gazette* (West Virginia)

ci	coloradoindependent.com
CM	*Concord Monitor* (New Hampshire)
cm	concordmonitor.com
co	concurringopinions.com
cp	christianpost.com
CPD	*Cleveland Plain Dealer*
CSM	*Christian Science Monitor*
csm	csmonitor.com
CT	*Chicago Tribune*
ct	chicagotribune.com
DFP	*Detroit Free Press*
dk	dailykos.com
DMN	*Dallas Morning News*
DMR	*Des Moines Register*
dmr	desmoinesregister.com
DN	*Deseret News* (Salt Lake City)
DP	*Denver Post*
dp	denverpost.com
du	democraticunderground.com
ESPA	Empire State Pride Agenda
EW	*Entertainment Weekly*
FK Papers	Frank Kameny Papers
fn	foxnews.com
gcn	gaycitynews.com
gnb	gaynewsblog.net
HA	*Honolulu Advertiser*
HC	*Houston Chronicle*
hp	huffingtonpost.com
HRC	Human Rights Campaign Records
HSB	*Honolulu Star Bulletin*
ii	iowaindependent.com
IS	*Idaho Statesman*
KCS	*Kansas City Star*
KJ&MS	*Kennebec Journal and Morning Sentinel* (Augusta, Maine)
kns	keennewsservice.com
KP	*Kentucky Post*
LAT	*Los Angeles Times*
latb	latimesblogs.latimes.com
LAW	*Los Angeles Weekly*
LCJ	*Louisville Courier-Journal*
LHL	*Lexington Herald-Leader*

LVRJ	*Las Vegas Review-Journal*
lvs	lasvegassun.com
mi	minnesotaindependent.com
MJS	*Milwaukee Journal Sentinel*
mm	michellemalkin.com
MSNY	Mattachine Society, Inc., of New York Records
MT	*Minneapolis Tribune*
NGLTF	National Gay and Lesbian Task Force Records
npr	npr.org
NRO	nationalreview.com
nt	nashuatelegraph.com (New Hampshire)
nydn	nydailynews.com
NYS	*New York Sun*
NYT	*New York Times*
nyt	nytimes.com
NYTM	*New York Times Magazine*
ola	onlineathens.com (Athens, Georgia)
OT	*Oakland Tribune*
otb	outsidethebeltway.com
otm	ontopmag.com
OWH	*Omaha World-Herald*
PDN	*Philadelphia Daily News*
pew	pewresearch.org
PI	*Philadelphia Inquirer*
PJ	*Providence Journal* (Rhode Island)
PN	*Patriot-News* (Harrisburg, Pennsylvania)
PPG	*Pittsburgh Post-Gazette*
PPH	*Portland Press Herald* (Maine)
pwn	patchworknation.org
RCJ	*Rapid City Journal* (South Dakota)
rcp	realclearpolitics.com
rd	religiondispatches.com
RMN	*Rocky Mountain News* (Denver, Colorado)
sa	socialistalternative.org
scj	siouxcityjournal.com (South Dakota)
SFC	*San Francisco Chronicle*
SFNM	*Santa Fe New Mexican*
SJ	*Statesman Journal* (Salem, Oregon)
SJMN	*San Jose Mercury News*
SL	*Star Ledger* (Newark, New Jersey)
SLT	*Salt Lake Tribune*

SPI	*Seattle Post-Intelligencer*
spi	seattlepi.com
ST	*Star Tribune* (Minneapolis)
st	seattletimes.nwsource.com
sw	socialistworker.org
tch	tri-cityherald.com (Washington State)
tdb	thedailybeast.com
TNR	*The New Republic*
TO	*The Oklahoman*
tp	thinkprogress.org
tpm	talkingpointsmemo.com
TRG	*The Register-Guard* (Eugene, Oregon)
USAT	*USA Today*
USN&WR	*U.S. News & World Report*
VV	*Village Voice*
WB	*Washington Blade*
wb	washingtonblade.com
wcp	washingtoncitypaper.com
WCT	*Windy City Times* (Chicago)
wct	windycitymediagroup.com
we	washingtonexaminer.com
wi	washingtonindependent.com
wm	washingtonmonthly.com
WO	*Williston Observer* (Vermont)
WP	*Washington Post*
wp	washingtonpost.com
ws	weeklystandard.com
WT	*Washington Times*
wt	washingtontimes.com

NOTES

Introduction

1. *Griswold v. Connecticut*, 381 U.S. 479 (1965); *Lawrence v. Texas*, 539 U.S. 558 (2003).
2. Klarman, 310–11; Luks and Salamone, 91 fig. 4.3; *NYT*, Jan. 28, 1973, 45.
3. Gash and Gonzales, 69 fig. 3.2; Hanson, 187 fig. 8.1.
4. Klarman, 450, 452–53; D'Emilio, "Lessons," 12.
5. Klarman, 452; Andersen, 212; Banner, 239.
6. Klarman, 385–442; Graham, 9, 284; Banner, ch.10; Epstein and Kobylka, 89–90, 207, 232–33, 235, 252.

Chapter 1

1. D'Emilio, "Courts," 45; Andersen, 60, n. 3; Cain, 137.
2. Cain, 89, 143; Chauncey, 9–10; D'Emilio, *Sexual Politics*, 49.
3. D'Emilio, *Sexual Politics*, 50–51.
4. Ibid., 50, 121, 182–84, 206; Chauncey, 8.
5. Anonymous letter, Jan. 19, 1959, ACLU, box 1127, folder 14; D'Emilio, *Sexual Politics*, 15, 49; Cain, 57–59, 144.
6. D'Emilio, *Sexual Politics*, 47, 124.
7. Chauncey, 7–8; Cain, 79–81, 83–86.
8. Cain, 82–84.
9. D'Emilio, *Sexual Politics*, 41–43.
10. Cain, 103, 105; Chauncey, 6, 21.
11. D'Emilio, "Courts," 46; Francis Martin Ruland to ACLU, May 5, 1958, ACLU, box 1127, folder 11; Kenneth F. Beall to ACLU, Jan. 15, 1958, ibid., folder 13.
12. D'Emilio, *Sexual Politics*, 47–48.
13. Ibid., 44–45; Edward N. Heghinian to Alan Reitman, Nov. 28, 1951, ACLU, box 1127, folder 1.
14. Franklin Kameny to Ralph Temple, Feb. 4, 1968, FK Papers; D'Emilio, *Sexual Politics*, 45; Barbara Scammell to the ACLU, Feb. 15, 1951, ACLU, box 1127, folder 1.
15. D'Emilio, "Courts," 46; Chauncey, 11.
16. Cain, 56–57; Rimmerman, *Identity*, 53–54; Walker, 312; policy statement, Jan. 7, 1957, ACLU, box 1127, folder 7; Spencer Coxe to E. A. Dioguardi, May 11, 1962, ACLU, box 1127, folder 16.

17. Herbert Levy to June Fusca, Apr. 4, 1951, ACLU, box 1127, folder 1; June Fusca to Herbert Monte Levy, April 23, 1951, ACLU, box 1127, folder 1; minutes of Due Process Committee, Dec. 18, 1963, ACLU, box 983, folder 3.

18. Reitman to Dioguardi, May 10, 1962, ACLU, box 1127, folder 16; minutes of board meeting, Dec. 13, 1965, ACLU, box 1127, folder 18.

19. D'Emilio, *Sexual Politics*, 58, 64, 115–16, 123–24.

20. Steve Sgromolo to NY Mattachine Society, May 20, 1965, NYMS, reel 28, box 3, folder 28; Dorr to Marc Williams, July 9, 1971, NYMS, reel 10, box 4, folder 34; D'Emilio, *Sexual Politics*, 115–16.

21. D'Emilio, *Sexual Politics*, 120–21.

22. Klarman, 163; D'Emilio, *Sexual Politics*, 53, 57, 65, 124; Altman, 142–43.

23. D'Emilio, *Sexual Politics*, 66, 125.

24. Ibid., 82–83, 149; *VV*, Oct. 11, 1962, 20.

25. D'Emilio, *Sexual Politics*, 124–25, 149–50, 153; Chauncey, 28.

26. Klarman, 373–74, 377–80; D'Emilio, *Sexual Politics*, 149–50, 165–66.

27. D'Emilio, *Sexual Politics*, 134, 244–45, 260; Chauncey, 34.

28. D'Emilio, *Sexual Politics*, 129, 147–48; letter to editor (from Mattachine Society to *People Today*), March 5, 1959, NYMS, reel 11, box 4, folder 4.

29. D'Emilio, *Sexual Politics*, 19, 130–31.

30. Ibid., 132–33.

31. Ibid., 135, 137.

32. Ibid., 137, 148.

33. Ibid., 138–39; *NYT*, Dec. 17, 1963, 1; *Newsweek*, Dec. 30, 1963, 42; *Time*, Jan. 21, 1966, 41.

34. D'Emilio, *Sexual Politics*, 159; *Newsweek*, July 30, 1962, 48; *NYT*, July 16, 1962, 35, 36.

35. D'Emilio, *Sexual Politics*, 159–60.

36. Ibid., 209–10, 216; Duberman, 172.

37. D'Emilio, *Sexual Politics*, 144–46, 211–14; Cain, 136; *Newsweek*, Jan. 2, 1967, 28, 30; *Time*, July 14, 1967, 30.

38. D'Emilio, *Sexual Politics*, 156, 206–7, 212–13; Andersen, 22; Walker, 312.

39. D'Emilio, *Sexual Politics*, 212–13; Cain, 68; Dick Leitsch to Tom Hendrix, June 25, 1969, NYMS, reel 11, box 4, folder 11.

40. D'Emilio, *Sexual Politics*, 141–43, 211, 216–17.

41. Ibid., 143, 217.

42. Ibid., 193–95, 200, 214–15.

43. Ibid., 173, 191, 197–99.

44. Ibid., 150, 223, 243.

45. Ibid., 161, 244.

46. Ibid., 152–53, 162, 199; Chauncey, 29; Frank Kameny to Don Sorenson, May 31, 1965, FK Papers; Kameny to Robert Sloane, July 23, 1965, FK Papers; Kameny to Mattachine Midwest, July 2, 1968, FK Papers.

47. D'Emilio, *Sexual Politics*, 154, 164–65; *Time*, Oct. 31, 1969, 56.

48. D'Emilio, *Sexual Politics*, 174, 216, 227; Duberman, 172; memorandum from Franklin Kameny to Eastern Homophile Organizations, NYMS, reel 10, box 3, folder 26.

49. Transcript of 1965 conference, 21–22, Legal Panel: Homosexuality and the Law—A Prognosis, NYMS, reel 11, box 4, folder 1; D'Emilio, *Sexual Politics*, 197, 211.

50. Cain, 80–81, 84–86; D'Emilio, *Sexual Politics*, 202–3, 208.

51. Cain, 108–9; *Norton v. Macey*, 417 F. 2d 1161 (D.C. Cir. 1969); D'Emilio, *Sexual Politics*, 213–14; *Newsweek*, June 13, 1966, 24; *NYT*, Jan. 7, 1967, 1.

52. D'Emilio, *Sexual Politics*, 203, 208; *Newsweek*, Oct. 27, 1969, 76; *Time*, Oct. 31, 1969, 56.

53. D'Emilio, *Sexual Politics*, 70, 201–3, 207–8; Chauncey, 35–36; Kameny to Mattachine Midwest, May 18, 1968, FK Papers; *Newsweek*, Oct. 27, 1969, 76.

54. *Time*, Oct. 31, 1969, 61.

55. D'Emilio, *Sexual Politics*, 146; Andersen, 60.

56. Cain, 58, 146.

57. Chauncey, 36; Valerie Taylor to Frank Kameny, Oct. 23, 1969, FK Papers.

58. *Time*, Oct. 10, 1969, 22; William Farnum to Leitsch, Jan. 26, 1965, NYMS, reel 11, box 4, folder 8.

59. *CD*, May 31, 1969, 3; Central Ohio Mattachine Society to Paul Brown, June 3, 1969, FK Papers.

60. D'Emilio, *Sexual Politics*, 208.

61. John Doe to ACLU, May 8, 1969, ACLU, box 1127, folder 27; Alan Reitman to John Doe, May 15, 1969, ibid.

62. D'Emilio, *Sexual Politics*, 162, 211; *Boutellier vs. INS*, 387 U.S. 118 (1967).

63. D'Emilio, *Sexual Politics*, 219; D'Emilio, "Courts," 46.

64. D'Emilio, *Sexual Politics*, 146–47, 165, 204–5, 218–19, 242, 246.

Chapter 2

1. D'Emilio, *Sexual Politics*, 231–32; Cain, 90; Duberman, 181–90.

2. Andersen, 24; Duberman, 190–91.

3. *VV*, July 3, 1969, 1; D'Emilio, *Sexual Politics*, 232; Duberman, 195–202; *Newsweek*, Oct. 27, 1969, 76; *NYT*, June 29, 1969, 33.

4. *NYT*, June 30, 1969, 22; July 3, 1969, 19; *VV*, July 3, 1969, 1; Andersen, 23–24; Duberman, 202–11; Altman, 126–27.

5. D'Emilio, *Sexual Politics*, 232; *VV*, July 3, 1969, 1.

6. D'Emilio, *Sexual Politics*, 232–33, 260; Rimmerman, *Identity*, 24; Altman, 127.

7. D'Emilio, *Sexual Politics*, 225–26; Chauncey, 30; Altman, 128.

8. *NYT*, Aug. 30, 1970, 49; Aug. 30, 1970, 28; D'Emilio, *Sexual Politics*, 234; Altman, 118–19.

9. D'Emilio, *Sexual Politics*, 235; Altman, 119, 142.

10. D'Emilio, *Sexual Politics*, 235; Rimmerman, *Identity*, 24.

11. D'Emilio, *Sexual Politics*, 235; Chauncey, 32; Eskridge, *Equality*, 4.

12. D'Emilio, *Sexual Politics*, 237–238; *NYT*, June 29, 1970, 1; Andersen, 24; *LAT*, Nov. 11, 1976, H1.

13. Andersen, 19; NGTF, "Brief Summary"; "An End to Ignorance Campaign," n.d., NGLTF, box 2, folder 57; NGTF Interim Board of Directors' meeting minutes, Dec. 1, 1974, NGLTF, box 2, folder 53; Media Director's report, Feb. 12, 1976, NGLTF, box 2, folder 56; memo from Ginny Vida to Co-Executive Directors, Feb. 10, 1978, NGLTF, box 2, folder 66; NGTF to "Dear Friend," n.d. (probably 1981 or 1982), HRC, box 5, folder 43.

14. Chauncey, 88–89; Pascoe, 91–92; Murdoch and Price, 164–66, 168; *NYT*, Jan. 7, 1973, 55; Coyle; Cain, 160–61, 165; Andersen, 175; *Baker v. Nelson*, 291 Minn. 310 (1971).

15. *Jones v. Hallahan*, 501 S.W.2d 588 (Ky. 1973); *Singer v. Hara*, 522 P.2d 1187 (Wash. Ct. App. 1974); *Anonymous v. Anonymous*, 325 N.Y.S. 982 (N.Y. Sup. Ct. 1971); *M.T. v. J.T.*, 355 A.2d 204 (N.J. Super. Ct. App. Div. 1976); *DeSanto v. Barnsley*, 476 A.2d 952 (Pa. Sup. Ct. 1984); *Adams v. Howerton*, 486 F. Supp. 1119 (C.D. Cal. 1980), *aff'd*, 673 F.2d 1036 (9th Cir. 1982); *Sullivan v. INS*, 772 F. 2d 609 (9th Cir. 1985); Cain, 161–65.

16. Chauncey, 90; Pascoe, 92.

17. Eskridge, *Equality*, 7–9; *Baker*, 191 N.W.2d at 187; *Singer*, 522 P.2d at 1191–92, 1195; Pascoe, 100–101.

18. Cain, 111–13, 160–61; *Look*, Jan. 26, 1971; *McConnell v. Anderson*, 316 F. Supp. 809, 814 (D. Minn. 1970), *rev'd*, *McConnell v. Anderson*, 451 F.2d 193, 196 (8th Cir. 1971); *MT*, Oct. 20, 1971; *NYT*, Jan. 7, 1973, 55.

19. *Singer v. U.S. Civil Service Commission*, 530 F.2d 247 (9th Cir. 1976); Murdoch and Price, 189–93.

20. Pascoe, 92–93; *Baker,* 191 N.W.2d at 186; *LCJ,* Nov. 12, 1970, A14; Chauncey, 91; Murdoch and Price, 171.
21. findlaw.com, Oct. 23, 2009.
22. Andersen, 212–13; *NYT,* Oct. 28, 1986, A20.
23. 118 *Cong. Rec.* 9331 (1972); Gallagher and Bull, 11; Pascoe, 95, 97, 100; Cain, 257; Chauncey, 145–47; Eskridge, *Equality,* 8.
24. Lofton and Haider-Markel, 315; Rom, 26; Eskridge, *Equality,* 9–12.
25. *NYT,* Apr. 27, 1975, 49; *BFP,* Aug. 30, 2009, A1; Chauncey, 90.
26. *NYT,* Apr. 27, 1975, 4; *DP,* March 27, 1975, 19.
27. *BDC,* March 27, 1975; March 28, 1975, 2; Cain, 163.
28. *BDC,* March 30, 1975, 10.
29. *BDC,* Apr. 25, 1975, 3; *NYT,* Apr. 27, 1975, 49; *DP,* Apr. 22, 1975, 3; Murdoch and Price, 220–21.
30. *NYT,* Apr. 27, 1975, 49; *DP,* May 8, 1975, 21; *BDC,* Apr. 15, 1975, 1.
31. *DP,* Apr. 10, 1975, 3; Apr. 25, 1975, 21; Apr. 26, 1975, 3; *BDC,* Apr. 25, 1975, 3; Apr. 26, 1975, 1; *NYT,* Apr. 27, 1975, 49; Eskridge, *Equality,* 6.
32. Eskridge, *Equality,* 10–11; *LAT,* Aug. 12, 1977, B33; Apr. 22, 1977, B20; Chauncey, 91; Pascoe, 87, 95, 101,
33. Chauncey, 88, 93–94; D'Emilio, "Courts," 48; Cain, 158–59; Tim Mayhew, "Position Statement on Marriage," Dec. 5, 1971, Tim Mayhew Collection on Gay Rights, box 10, folder 8, University of Washington Libraries.
34. Eskridge, *Equality,* 4–5; D'Emilio, "Courts," 47.
35. Chauncey, 87, 91–92; Cain, 158, D'Emilio, "Courts," 48.
36. *NYT,* Feb. 22, 1981, § 1, 42; Apr. 27, 1989, B1; Cain, 165–67.
37. Chauncey, 94; press release of ACLU of Southern California, 1973, FK Papers.
38. *NYT,* Dec. 16, 1973, 1; Apr. 9, 1974, 12; July 4, 1975, 45; July 10, 1975, 8; D'Emilio, *Sexual Politics,* 238; Chauncey, 36–38; Eskridge, *Equality,* 6; Andersen, 63; Cain, 137–42; D'Emilio, "Courts," 47.
39. Cain, 78.
40. Shilts, 69–80, 169–85; Gallagher and Bull, 19; *BG,* March 3, 1974, B18; July 8, 1974, 1; Sept. 11, 1974, B21; Nov. 6, 1974, 11; Activities at the Executive Level, n.d. (probably 1982 or 1983), HRC, box 4, folder 32; *LAT,* July 7, 1975, B3.
41. D'Emilio, "Courts," 47.
42. Andersen, 35, 247 n. 12; Chauncey, 38; Cain, 204; *CT,* Aug. 22, 1976, 14; Memo from Co-Executive Directors to the Board of Directors, June 1978, NGLTF, box 2, folder 30.
43. *LAT,* July 7, 1975, B3; *CT,* Aug. 22, 1976, 14.
44. Activities at the Executive Level, n.d. (probably 1982 or 1983), HRC, box 4, folder 32.
45. *CT,* Aug. 22, 1976, 14; *WP,* June 16, 1976, A1; Dec. 21, 1979, A8; *NYT,* March 28, 1977, 56; Gallagher and Bull, 17; Statement of Kay Whitlock, Dec. 19, 1979, NGLTF, box 2, folder 52.
46. *NYT,* June 24, 1980, 13; NGTF board members to "Dear Friend," Nov. 1980, NGLTF, box 2, folder 52.
47. NGTF, "Brief Summary"; Andersen, 247 n. 15; Cahill, *Same-Sex Marriage,* 67; *NYT,* June 25, 1980, A1; *WP,* Aug. 13, 1980, A15; Aug. 15, 1980, A7.
48. *WP,* Aug. 31, 1980, A1; *NYT,* Nov. 1, 1980, 25.
49. Gay Rights National Lobby, "Does Support for Gay Civil Rights Spell Political Suicide?—A Close Look at Some Long-Held Myths," May 1, 1980, HRC, box 4, folder 21; *NYT,* Nov. 1, 1980, 25.
50. Cain, 94–99; Andersen, 68–72; Garrow, 621; *NYT,* Dec. 19, 1980, B2.
51. *Florida Board of Bar Examiners v. N.R.S.,* 403 So.2d 1315 (Fla. 1981); *Saal v. Middendorf,* 427 F. Supp. 192 (N.D. Cal. 1977), *rev'd, Beller v. Middendorf,* 632 F.2d 788 (9th Cir. 1980); *Lesbian/Gay Freedom Day Committee, Inc. v. INS,* 541 F. Supp. 569 (N.D. Cal. 1982); NGTF, "Brief Summary."

52. *Acanfora v. Board of Educ. of Montgomery County*, 359 F. Supp. 843 (D. Md. 1973), *aff'd*, 491 F.2d 498 (4th Cir. 1974); *Gayer v. Schlesinger*, 490 F.2d 740 (D.C. Cir. 1973).

53. *LAT*, Nov. 11, 1976, H1; NGTF, Interim Board of Directors' meeting minutes, Dec. 1, 1974, NGLTF, box 2, folder 53; Media Director's Report, Feb. 12, 1976, NGLTF, box 2, folder 56; Memo from Ginny Vida to Co-Executive Directors, Feb. 10, 1978, NGLTF, box 2, folder 66; *CT*, Aug. 22, 1976, 14; Franklin Kameny to Jay Murley, Dec. 17, 1972, FK Papers; Chauncey, 38.

54. Chauncey, 37; *LAT*, July 7, 1975, B3; *NYT*, May 31, 1977, 14; "You're Fired" (1980), 4, HRC, box 4, folder 20; Gay Rights National Lobby, "A Long and Growing List of Organizations and Religious Denominations Support Civil Rights for Gay People," 1981, HRC, box 4, folder 20.

55. Gay Rights National Lobby, "If Your Constituents Ask About Your Support of Justice for Gays," 1980, HRC, box 4, folder 20; NGTF, "Brief Summary"; Cain, 116–17; Chauncey, 34–35.

56. D'Emilio, "Courts," 47.

57. Wald and Scher, 85; Herman, 4–5, 61–62.

58. *NYT*, Jan. 17, 1977, A14; May 10, 1977, 18; Wald and Scher, 85.

59. *NYT*, May 10, 1977, 18; June 5, 1977, 22; Andersen, 35.

60. *NYT*, May 10, 1977, 18; June 9, 1977, 1.

61. *NYT*, May 10, 1977, 18; June 5, 1977, 22.

62. *NYT*, June 5, 1977, 22; June 12, 1977, 152; Dec. 28, 1977, 14; Dec. 2, 1998, A1.

63. Pascoe, 101; *BG*, June 1, 1977, 2.

64. *NYT*, June 19, 1977, 35; "An End to Ignorance Campaign," n.d., NGLTF, box 2, folder 57.

65. *NYT*, June 9, 1977, 1; June 17, 1977, A12; June 27, 1977, 20.

66. Andersen, 35; *NYT*, Apr. 27, 1975, 49; *DP*, March 20, 1974, 63; May 8, 1974, 2; Aug. 29, 1974, 34.

67. *NYT*, March 26, 1977, 13; May 10, 1977, 18; June 8, 1977, 1; June 9, 1977, 1.

68. Andersen, 35; *NYT*, June 8, 1977, 1; June 9, 1977, 21; *WP*, June 17, 1977, A25.

69. Cahill, "Anti–Gay Marriage Movement," 165; *NYT*, Apr. 30, 1978, E8; May 28, 1978, E16; *MT*, Apr. 26, 1978, 1A; *WP*, Nov. 1978, A7.

70. *Advocate*, Nov. 15, 1978, 7; Shilts, 242.

71. Cain, 127; Gallagher and Bull, 18; Andersen, 144 table 11; Shilts, 221–51; "Prop. 6 Is Trounced," 1978, NGLTF, box 153, folder 35.

72. Chauncey, 45–46; Andersen, 143–74; Smith, "Politics of Same-Sex Marriage," 227; *NYT*, May 28, 1978, E16.

73. Bruce Voeller and Jean O'Leary to think tank participants, Jan. 3, 1978, ACLU, box 1127, folder 32; agenda from NGTF conference on public referenda on civil rights, Jan. 12, 1978, ACLU, box 1127, folder 32; Memo from Co-Executive Directors to Board of Directors, June 1978, NGLTF, box 2, folder 30; Memo from Pokey Anderson and Steve Endean to executive committee, Feb. 2, 1978, NGLTF, box 2, folder 66.

74. D'Emilio, *Sexual Politics*, 247; *NYT*, June 5, 1977, 23; Chauncey, 46.

75. Cain, 117–22; *Beller v. Mittendorf*, 632 F.2d 788 (9th Cir. 1980); *Dronenburg v. Zech*, 741 F.2d 1388 (D.C. Cir. 1984); NGTF, "Brief Summary"; NGTF board members to "Dear Friend," Nov. 1980, NGLTF, box 2, folder 52; Andersen, 36.

76. Cain, 105, 113–17; *McConnell v. Anderson*, 451 F.2d 193 (8th Cir. 1971); *Singer v. Civil Service Commission*, 530 F.2d 247 (9th Cir. 1976); *Gaylord v. Tacoma Sch. Dist. No. 10*, 559 P. 2d 1340 (Wash. 1977); *Rowland v. Mad River Local Sch. Dist.*, 730 F.2d 444 (6th Cir. 1984); *NYT*, Oct. 4, 1977, 24.

77. *LAT*, May 13, 1975, C3; May 8, 1975, B3.

78. *NYT*, March 30, 1976, 17, 65; Cain, 141; Murdoch and Price, 182–85; *Doe v. Commonwealth's Attorney*, 403 F. Supp. 1199, 1202 (E.D. Va. 1975); *LAT*, March 30, 1976, B1; Garrow, 621–22; Andersen, 65–68.

79. *NYT*, March 30, 1976, 17; Andersen, 4, 31–34, 39; Cain, 146–51, 170; D'Emilio, "Courts," 43.

80. *BG*, May 8, 1985, B21; May 9, 1985, B1; May 24, 1985, B1; May 25, 1985, B1.

81. Garrow, 622; Report from Co–Executive Directors to the Board, n.d., NGLTF, box 2, folder 24; Gallagher and Bull, 12, 69; *BG*, March 3, 1974, B18.

82. Cain, 61; Andersen, 28; "Austin Housing Ordinance."

83. NGTF to Fred Silverman, Sept. 6, 1977, NGLTF, box 2, folder 52; Ginny Vida to Richard Gitter, Sept. 20, 1977, NGLTF, box 2, folder 52.

84. *WP*, Sept. 20, 1971, B1; July 3, 1972, C1; Oct. 15, 1976, B1; *RMN*, Nov. 4, 1976; Jean O'Leary and Bruce Voeller to Aryek [*sic*] Neier, Dec. 3, 1976, ACLU, box 1127, folder 31.

85. *NYT*, Aug. 20, 1980, B22.

86. *NYT*, Aug. 17, 1980, 1; Aug. 20, 1980, B22.

87. NYT, Aug. 17, 1980, 1.

88. *NYT*, Aug. 20, 1980, B22.

89. *NYT*, May 27, 1980, B9; Aug. 20, 1980, B22.

90. *NYT*, July 13, 1980, 1; July 16, 1980, 1; Aug. 20, 1980, B22.

91. *NYT*, Aug. 20, 1980, B22; Aug. 21, 1980, 9; Aug. 23, 1980, 8; Sept. 25, 1980, A27; *Newsweek*, Sept. 15, 1980, 36.

92. Gallagher and Bull, 20, 21; *NYT*, Oct. 4, 1980, 9.

93. Cahill, "Anti–Gay Marriage Movement," 181–82 n. 21; *NYT*, Oct. 30, 1980, B14; *WP*, Oct. 31, 1980, A5; Busch, 106, 127.

94. NGTF, "Brief Summary"; Cahill, "Anti–Gay Marriage Movement," 181–82 n. 21; Gallagher and Bull, 21–22; *NYT*, Apr. 7, 1981, A16; Apr. 9, 1981, A22; May 19, 1981, C3.

95. *NYT*, Feb. 26, 1982, D16; June 21, 1982, A16.

96. Andersen, 36; *NYT*, Nov. 19, 1981, A31; *WP*, Feb. 4, 1987, A16; July 22, 1981, C3; Sept. 10, 1981, C9; Oct. 1, 1981, B1; Oct. 2, 1981, A1; *NYT*, Apr. 9, 1993, A14.

97. *NYT*, Feb. 15, 1981, § 1, 28; Brian Chandler Thompson to John McDermott, Dec. 1, 1983, FK Papers.

98. "Austin Housing Ordinance"; NGTF to "Dear Friend," n.d. (probably 1981 or 1982), HRC, box 5, folder 43; Joe Easley to Barbara Gittings, Aug. 30, 1982, HRC, box 5, folder 43; NGTF, "Brief Summary"; *NYT*, Nov. 19, 1981, A31; Jan. 18, 1982, A17; Gallagher and Bull, 21.

99. Chauncey, 40–41; Cahill, *Same-Sex Marriage*, 68; *NYT*, June 17, 1983, A1; Feb. 24, 1985, § 1, 33; Jan. 10, 1986, A14; Jan. 20, 1987, C11; Nov. 19, 1989, E5; Gallagher and Bull, 26.

100. *NYT*, June 17, 1983, A1; Jan. 21, 1986, B4; Andersen, 42–44, 78–79; Gallagher and Bull, 52; *People v. 49 W. 12 Tenants Corp.*, No. 43604/83 (N.Y. Sup. Ct. Oct. 17, 1983).

101. Chauncey, 41; Andersen, 42–43; *WSJ*, Apr. 22, 1986, 64; Gallagher and Bull, 78–79.

102. Chauncey, 43; *NYT*, Jan. 21, 1986, B4; Apr. 24, 1987, A12; Oct. 10, 1987, 1; *CT*, March 18, 1987, § 2, 3; June 21, 1987, § 2, 1.

103. Chauncey, 40–41; Andersen, 42–43; *WP*, Oct. 25, 1987, C8.

104. *NYT*, June 17, 1983, A1; July 5, 1986, 32; Chauncey, 96.

105. *NYT*, Jan. 21, 1986, B4; May 10, 1987, 36; Oct. 10, 1987, 1; Apr. 3, 1995, A12; Memo from Tim Drake to staff, Oct. 24, 1991, NGLTF, box 2, folder 34; Chauncey, 45; Andersen, 33–34; *BG*, Sept. 21, 1985, Metro, 21; Sept. 24, 1985, B1; Cahill, "Anti–Gay Marriage Movement," 181–82 n. 21; *BFP*, May 4, 1999, 3B.

106. Andersen, 38, table 2; Gay Rights National Lobby fund-raising letter to Chicago Resource Center, March 23, 1983, HRC, box 54, folder 21; Gay Rights National Lobby to John Glenn, July 1, 1983, HRC, box 4, folder 36; Gay Rights National Lobby draft press release, "Mayors Endorse GRNL's AIDS Agenda," n.d. (probably 1983), HRC, box 4, folder 36; "Recent Accomplishments, NGLTF," n.d. (probably 1985 or 1986), NGLTF, box 1, folder 18; *NYT*, Jan. 21, 1986, B4.

107. *WP*, June 26, 1986, A17; Aug. 26, 1986, A4; Nov. 6, 1986, A51; *NYT*, Sept. 11, 1986, A27; *LAT*, Nov. 6, 1986, A24; *WSJ*, Apr. l, 1986, 64.

108. Andersen, 32–34.

109. Andersen, 68–72, 85; Cain, 64.

110. Andersen, 42–43, 78–81; *NYT*, Jan. 21, 1986, B4; *State v. Walsh*, 713 S.W.2d 508, 512 (Mo. 1986); *WP*, July 2, 1986, A8; *LAT*, July 7, 1986, B5.

111. Cain, 174, 177; Andersen, 87; Murdoch and Price, 285.

112. Greenhouse, 150; *WP*, July 13, 1986, A1; Garrow, 660; Jeffries, 515; Murdoch and Price, 307–8.

113. Garrow, 660; Jeffries, 521; Murdoch and Price, 23, 313–14.

114. *Bowers v. Hardwick*, 478 U.S. at 186, 194, 197 (Burger, C.J., concurring), 197–98 (Powell, J., concurring); Brigham, 98; Jeffries, 530; Murdoch and Price, 317–20, 338.

115. Cain, 179, 183–84; *LAT*, July 1, 1986, A1; *WP*, July 2, 1986, A1; Gerstmann, 219.

116. *NYT*, July 2, 1986, A30; *LAT*, July 2, 1986, D4; *AJC*, July 4, 1986, 18A; Andersen, 94.

117. Andersen, 73–74, 92–94.

118. Andersen, 92–94; "What We Want: The Gay Agenda," n.d. (probably 1996), NGLTF, box 293, folder 2; *Padula v Webster*, 822 F.2d 97 (D.C. Cir. 1987); *Shahar v. Bowers*, 114 F.3d 1097 (11th Cir. 1997); Cain, 187.

119. *Ben-Shalom v. Marsh*, 881 F.2d 454 (7th Cir. 1989); *High Tech Gays v. Def. Indus. Sec. Clearance Office*, 895 F.2d 563 (9th Cir. 1990); *Equality Foundation of Greater Cincinnati v. City of Cincinnati*, 54 F.3d 261 (6th Cir. 1995); *In re opinion of the Justices*, 530 A.2d 21 (N.H. 1987).

120. Cain, 179–80.

121. Andersen, 94, 117–18; Cain, 257; *NYT*, July 5, 1986, 32.

122. *NYT*, July 5, 1986, 32; Andersen, 44; Chauncey, 43.

123. *WP*, Aug. 26, 1986, A4.

124. Andersen, 40, 46, 95; Cain, 64, 257; *NYT*, May 3, 1987, 43; May 8, 1987, 43.

125. *NYT*, Oct. 10, 1987, 1; Oct. 12, 1987, A1; Oct. 14, 1987, B8; Andersen, 44–45; Chauncey, 43; *WP*, Oct. 13, 1987, B1; Oct. 14, 1987, A1; Murdoch and Price, 333.

126. Chauncey, 119; Andersen, 118–19.

127. *NYT*, Jan. 21, 1986, B4; June 17, 1983, A1; Gallagher and Bull, 28–29; *LAT*, May 20, 1990, A3; Schmalz, 29.

128. *WSJ*, Apr. 22, 1986, 64; Schmalz, 29.

129. *WSJ*, Apr. 22, 1986, 64; Schmalz, 29; Chauncey, 41, 44; *WP*, Aug. 26, 1986, A4; *NYT*, Oct. 10, 1987, 1; *LAT*, May 20, 1990, 3.

130. Chauncey, 41–42, 44; Gallagher and Bull, 29; Chambers, 185.

131. Chauncey, 43–44; Gallagher and Bull, 29–30; Schmalz, 29.

132. Cain, 64; *NYT*, May 3, 1987, 43; Andersen, 44, 45 table 3; *WP*, Aug. 26, 1986, A4.

133. *NYT*, Jan. 21, 1986, B4; Oct. 10, 1987, 1; *WP*, Aug. 26, 1986, A4; Gallagher and Bull, 28.

134. *WP*, Aug. 26, 1986, A4; Gallagher and Bull, 28–29, 69; *NYT*, Oct. 14, 1988, A12; Nov. 19, 1989, E5; Chauncey, 111–13; Chambers, 199.

135. Andersen, 112–14.

136. *NYT*, Dec. 10, 2008, A23.

137. Cain, 126, 150, 189–90; *NGTF v. Bd. of Educ. of Oklahoma City*, 729 F.2d 1270 (10th Cir. 1984); *Watkins v. United States Army*, 847 F.2d 1329, 1349 (9th Cir. 1988), 875 F.2d 669, 731 (9th Cir. 1989); *High Tech Gays v. Def. Indus. Sec. Clearance Office*, 668 F. Supp. 1361, 1368 (N.D. Cal. 1987).

138. *WSJ*, Apr. 22, 1986, 64.

139. Schmalz, 42; *CT*, Apr. 28, 1987, §2, 1; *Fortune*, Dec. 16, 1991, 41.

140. Andersen, 36, 45 table 3; Cain, 63; *NYT*, Oct. 10, 1987, 1.

141. NGTF press release, "U.S. Mayors' Conference Endorses Gay/Lesbian Rights," June 19, 1984, HRC, box 5, folder 43; *NYT*, Sept. 2, 1984, § 1, 26; March 21, 1986, A1; Dec. 22, 1988, A18; *WP*, May 24, 1988, 3.

142. *BG*, Nov. 19, 1989, § 2, 33; Oct. 24, 1989, § 2, 19; Pinello, 34; *NYT*, Apr. 4, 1993, § 1, 16; Eskridge, *Equality*, 45; Activities at the Executive Level, n.d. (probably 1982 or 1983), HRC, box 4, folder 32; Gallagher and Bull, 40.

143. *NYT*, Oct. 10, 1987, 1.

144. Gallagher and Bull, 79–80; *LAT*, May 20, 1990, 3; Memo from Tim Drake to Staff, Oct. 24, 1991, NGLTF, box 2, folder 34; *BG*, Oct. 21, 1991, B1.

145. *NYT*, May 10, 1987, 36; *BG*, May 25, 1987, B1; Nov. 5, 1987, B45; Jan. 20, 1988, B17.

146. *NYT*, Nov. 8, 1987, 40; Dec. 3, 1987, B16; Apr. 9, 1988, 10; Apr. 13, 1988, A25; Gallagher and Bull, 33; Charles, 170.

147. Schmalz, 29; *NYT*, Aug. 20, 1992, A1.

148. Andersen, 51; Chauncey, 49; Gallagher and Bull, 71–77; Schmalz, 42.

149. Gallagher and Bull, 69, 129; *BG*, Oct. 31, 1991, B22; Schmalz, 20; *NYT*, Apr. 7, 1992, A24.

150. *LAT*, May 19, 1992, A24; Schmalz, 42; Gallagher and Bull, 78; Rimmerman, *Identity*, 64–65.

151. Gallagher and Bull, 85; *NYT*, Aug. 20, 1992, A1.

152. *NYT*, July 6, 1992, A1; Gallagher and Bull, 87.

153. *NYT*, May 26, 1992, A17; Aug. 18, 1992, 8; Aug. 20, 1992, A1, A27.

154. Cahill, "Anti–Gay Marriage Movement," 168–69; Gallagher and Bull, 78–79, 81, 93, 188; *NYT*, Aug. 23, 1992, A26.

155. *NYT*, Aug. 20, 1992, A1.

156. *NYT*, Nov. 5, 1992, B8; Gallagher and Bull, 95–96, 125.

157. Andersen, 51–52; Gallagher and Bull, 86, 161.

158. Rom, 11 fig.1.1; Chauncey, 150; Gallagher and Bull, 202.

159. *BG*, Oct. 15, 1989, A30; Wilcox et al., "Public Opinion," 227–28; Schacter, "Backlash," 1193; *Newsweek*, May 24, 1993, 69.

160. Eskridge, *Equality*, 13; Chambers, 183; *NYT*, Dec. 10, 1982, A17; *SFC*, Dec. 8, 1982, 1; Dec. 10, 1982, 1; *LAT*, Nov. 24, 1982, A3.

161. *SFC*, Nov. 8, 1990, A17; Chambers, 183, 201; Eskridge, *Same-Sex Marriage*, 59; *NYT*, Jan. 8, 1993, A1; Oct. 31, 1993, B1.

162. Gallagher and Bull, 194–95; *AAS*, May 9, 1994, A1; May 8, 1994, A1.

163. *NYT*, Aug. 12, 1993, A16; *AJC*, Aug. 11, 1993, A1; July 30, 1993, B1; Aug. 10, 1993, A22; Keck, 158; *BG*, Sept. 24, 1992, B34; *LAT*, Aug. 28, 1994, M4; D'Emilio, "Courts," 58; Pinello, 34–35; Chambers, 201.

164. *Braschi v. Stahl Assocs. Co.*, 543 N.E.2d 49 (N.Y. 1989); *NYT*, July 7, 1989, A1; Dec. 18, 1991, A26; Eskridge, *Equality*, 87; Chauncey, 103; Cain, 273; Chambers, 194–97; *In re Guardianship of Kowalski*, 478 N.W.2d 790 (Minn. Ct. App. 1991).

165. Gallagher and Bull, 190–91; Chauncey, 116; D'Emilio, "Courts," 52; Rosenberg, 410; *Fortune*, Dec. 16, 1991, 42; *SFC*, Dec. 9, 1992, D6; Dec. 23, 1992, A8; *CT*, Dec. 22, 1992, 3.

166. Andersen, 149, 152; *NYT*, Nov. 6, 1994, 30; Jan. 12, 1994, A17.

167. Andersen, 51; Schmalz, 20, 29; *WP*, May 14, 1996, A6; *NYT*, Aug. 20, 1992, A1.

168. Gallagher and Bull, 131–36, 149; Rimmerman, *Identity*, 67; *NYT*, Jan. 13, 1993, A1; Jan. 23, 1993, A1; Jan. 26, 1993, A1; Jan. 27, 1993, A1; *AJC*, Jan. 12, 1993, A1.

169. *NYT*, Jan. 25, 1993, A1; Jan. 26, 1993, A1; Jan. 27, 1993, A1; Jan. 28, 1993, A1; Gallagher and Bull, 142–44.

170. *NYT*, Jan 27, 1993, A1; Jan. 28, 1993, A16; Feb. 1, 1993, A14; Feb. 7, 1993, A26.

171. *NYT*, Jan. 26, 1993, A1; Jan. 28, 1993, A1; Jan. 29, 1993, A1; Jan. 30, 1993, A1; May 12, 1993, A1; May 20, 1993, B10; May 28, 1993, A1.

172. Gallagher and Bull, 147, 155–56; Rimmerman, *Identity*, 67–69; *NYT*, May 12, 1993, A1; May 19, 1993, A14; July 14, 1993, A1; July 18, 1993, § 4, 18; July 20, 1993, A16; July 21, 1993, A14.

173. *SFC*, June 1, 1993, A5.

Chapter 3

1. Andersen, 177; Pinello, 24–25; Cain, 257–59; Tom Selles to Walter Mondale, May 24, 1983, HRC, box 4, folder 36; Stephen Endean to John Glenn, July 1, 1983, ibid.; Egan and Sherrill, "Marriage," 229.
2. Stoddard, 17; D'Emilio, "Courts," 52; John D'Emilio, "The Marriage Debate," n.d., NGLTF, box 293, folder 2; Wilcox et al., "Public Opinion," 216.
3. NGLTF Strategic Plan, March 11, 1991, NGLTF, box 2, folder 33; press release, "Major Gay and Lesbian Conference Set for Minneapolis," Apr. 12, 1990, NGLTF, box 2, folder 32; Minutes of Board of Directors' Meeting, Jan 27, 1991, ESPA, folder 1.36.
4. Ettelbrick, 20; Brownworth; Chauncey, 120; Cain, 257; Eskridge, *Same-Sex Marriage*, 53–54.
5. Ettelbrick, 20–26; Chauncey, 121; *SFC*, June 1, 1993, A5.
6. Stoddard, 13–19; Eskridge, *Same-Sex Marriage*, 51–52, 62–74, 80–85.
7. Stoddard, 13–19; Cain, 257–58; Chauncey, 121; Sullivan.
8. Chauncey, 3, 95–111; Chambers, 184–85; D'Emilio, "Courts," 49.
9. Chauncey, 98–102, 105–6; D'Emilio, "Courts," 49; Chambers, 184–85, 187, 193–94; *Newsweek*, May 24, 1993, 69; "What We Want: The Gay Agenda," n.d. (probably 1996), NGLTF, box 293, folder 2; Eskridge, *Same-Sex Marriage*, 58.
10. Charles, 6, 16–20.
11. Charles, 24, 29–30, 111, 114, 117–18, 133, 142–43, 179.
12. *In re Guardianship of Kowalski*, 478 N.W.2d 790, 797 (Minn. App. 1991); D'Emilio, "Courts," 49; Chauncey, 111–16; Charles, 7, 13, 110, 121, 144–47, 170, 172, 186–87, 198, 245–47, 252–53; *NYT*, Aug. 7, 1988, A26; Feb. 8, 1989, D25; Dec. 18, 1991, A26.
13. D'Emilio, "Courts," 50; Eskridge, *Equality*, 15–16; Chauncey, 105–10; *Advocate*, Nov. 30, 1993, 40–47; Gallagher and Bull, 223–24.
14. Chauncey, 105–6; Cain, 152.
15. NGLTF Strategic Plan, March 11, 1991, NGLTF, box 2, folder 33; Chauncey, 107; *Advocate*, Nov. 30, 1993, 43.
16. Gallagher and Bull, 216; Chauncey, 111.
17. D'Emilio, "Courts," 50; Chauncey, 95; Egan and Sherrill, "Marriage," 231–32; Eskridge, *Equality*, 2–3.
18. Chauncey, 59–66; D'Emilio, *Sexual Politics*, 248; Rom, 8; Wax, 1102.
19. Rom, 9–10; Chauncey, 59–60, 147, 152; Eskridge, *Equality*, x–xi.
20. Chauncey, 119, 124; *WP*, Oct. 11, 1987, B1; Pinello, 24–25; *BG*, Nov. 23, 2003, A1.
21. Wax, 1066–97; Chauncey, 153; Pinello, 169–71; Gallagher; Shorto.
22. *Loving v. Virginia*, 388 U.S. 1 (1967); *Zablocki v. Redhail*, 434 U.S. 374 (1978); *Turner v. Safley*, 482 U.S. 78 (1987).
23. Pinello, 25–26; Eskridge, *Equality*, 16–17; Cain, 259–60; *HSB*, Nov. 25, 1990, A1; Dec. 18, 1990, A1; Dec. 19, 1990, A10.
24. *WP*, Jan. 20, 1995, C6; *HSB*, Dec. 18, 1990, A4.
25. *Advocate*, July 23, 1996, 24.
26. *HA*, Nov. 9, 1998, A1; Andersen, 178; Gallagher and Bull, 198, 203; Pinello, 25; Eskridge, *Equality*, 16–17; *Advocate*, June 15, 1993, 24–27.
27. O'Connor and Yanus, 293, 296; Pinello, 26.
28. *Baehr v. Lewin*, 74 Haw. 530 (1993); Stouffer, 17.
29. Gallagher and Bull, 204; Hull, 211–12.
30. Rom, 26; Andersen, 63, 251 n. 8; Cain, 259; Lewis, 196; *HA*, Sept. 11, 1996, A1.
31. *HA*, May 7, 1993, A7; Dec. 4, 1996, 1; Gallagher and Bull, 205–6; *BG*, Nov. 23, 2003, A1; Eskridge, *Equality*, 40; *Advocate*, June 15, 1993, 26; Andersen, 194.
32. Eskridge, *Equality*, 3, 26; *HA*, May 7, 1993, A1; Gallagher and Bull, 206.
33. *HA*, May 7, 1993, A1; May 8, 1993, A2; Gallagher and Bull, 205–6; Rom, 27.
34. *Advocate*, May 17, 1994, 24–26; Pascoe, 105–6; *HA*, Apr. 13, 1994, A9; *NYT*, June 24, 1994, A18.

35. *HA*, Aug. 25, 1996, A2.
36. Eskridge, *Equality*, 22–23; Andersen, 178–79; Pascoe, 106; *NYT*, Dec. 11, 1995, A18; *HA*, Aug. 25, 1996, A1.
37. *NYT*, May 7, 1993, A14; *WP*, May 7, 1993, A7; *LAT*, May 7, 1993, A3; *CPD*, May 18, 1993, 5B; *CT*, May 9, 1993, 27; *DMN*, May 7, 1993, 1A; *Advocate*, July 26, 1994, 5; *Newsweek*, May 24, 1993, 69; *USN&WR*, May 24, 1993, 19; *SLT*, May 17, 1993, A4.
38. *Newsweek*, May 17, 1993, 62; Eskridge, *Equality*, 26–27; Schacter, "Backlash," 1203–4.
39. *DN*, July 18, 1993, A2.
40. *NYT*, March 3, 1995, B7; *SLT*, Feb. 9, 1995, B1; March 3, 1995, A1; March 17, 1995, C1.
41. *AL*, Feb. 3, 1995, 4A; *NYT*, March 15, 1995, A18; *ADN*, March 10, 1995, A1.
42. *DMR*, Feb. 1, 1996, A1; *SFC*, Jan. 25, 1996, A13; Jan. 30, 1996, A1; *LAT*, Apr. 10, 1996, A5.
43. *Manhattan Spirit*, June 28, 1996, 12; *LAT*, Apr. 2, 1996, B6; Apr. 10, 1996, A5; *SFC*, March 23, 1996, A1; March 26, 1996, A1.
44. *LAT*, Apr. 10, 1996, A5; Rimmerman, "Presidency," 276; Cahill, *Same-Sex Marriage*, 81; *WP*, May 23, 1996, A14; *Advocate*, July 23, 1996, 22.
45. *LAT*, Apr. 10, 1996, A5; Rimmerman, "Presidency," 275; Wald and Clover, 121; *WP*, May 23, 1996, A14; *DMR*, Feb. 1, 1996, A1; *PI*, May 14, 1996, B2; *CT*, March 29, 1996, 1.
46. Rosenberg, 357 table 13.1; *PDN*, Oct. 2, 1996, 7; *PPG*, Oct. 2, 1996, B6; *CT*, Apr. 25, 1996, 3; Apr. 26, 1996, 8.
47. *NYT*, Nov. 10, 1994, B11; May 22, 1996, A17; Sept. 5, 1997, A20; Gallagher and Bull, 199.
48. Lofton and Haider-Markel, 320–23; *NYT*, Sept. 6, 1996, A24; *LAT*, Oct. 15, 1999, A3; Jan. 29, 2000, A19; *BFP*, Feb. 21, 1999, 10B; Oct. 21, 2000, 3A; *OWH*, Nov. 4, 2000, 51; Eskridge, *Equality*, 27–28; Rosenberg, 357 table 13.1.
49. *LAT*, Sept. 12, 1994, A1; Sept. 13, 1994, A3.
50. *PI*, June 8, 1996, A1; June 16, 1996, E8; June 23, 1996, B1.
51. Gallagher and Bull, 229–30; *NYT*, Nov. 4, 1994, A35; Nov. 7, 1994, B9; Nov. 12, 1994, A10.
52. Gallagher and Bull, 249.
53. Gallagher & Bull, 248, 251–54; *NYT*, Aug. 27, 1995, A1.
54. *DMR*, Feb. 10, 1996, A1.
55. Cahill, "Anti–Gay Marriage Movement," 169; Rimmerman, "Presidency," 276; *NYT*, March 6, 1996, A13; *DMR*, Feb. 9, 1996, 3M; Feb. 11, 1996, A1; Andersen, 180.
56. *NYT*, March 6, 1996, A13; May 9, 1999, B15.
57. 142 Cong. Rec. H7270 (July 11, 1996) (Scott McInnis, R-Colo.; Bob Barr, R-Ga.; Steve Largent, R-Okla.); 142 Cong. Rec. S10100 (Sept. 10, 1996) (Trent Lott, R-Miss.).
58. 142 Cong. Rec. H7270 (July 11, 1996) (Steve Largent, R-Okla.); 142 Cong. Rec. H7482 (July 12, 1996) (Bob Dornan, R-Calif.; Bob Barr, R-Ga.); Cahill, *Same-Sex Marriage*, 6–7.
59. 142 Cong. Rec. S10100 (Sept. 10, 1996) (Robert Byrd, D-W.Va.).
60. 142 Cong. Rec. H7270 (July 11, 1996) (Patricia Schroeder, D-Colo.; Barney Frank, D-Mass.; Jerrold Nadler, D-N.Y.).
61. 142 Cong. Rec. H7270 (July 11, 1996) (Carolyn Maloney, D-N.Y.); 142 Cong. Rec. . S10100 (Sept. 10, 1996) (Edward Kennedy, D-Mass.); *WP*, May 23, 1996, A14; June 13, 1996, A8; *NYT*, May 22, 1996, A17.
62. *NYT*, May 16, 1996, B9; May 23, 1996, A1; May 30, 1996, A19.
63. Gallagher and Bull, 262; *NYT*, May 16, 1996, B9.
64. *LAT*, May 21, 1996, A21; May 23, 1996, A15; *NYT*, May 16, 1996, B9; May 23, 1996, A1; May 24, 1996, A14; *WP*, May 24, 1996, A1.
65. Rimmerman, "Presidency," 277–78; *NYT*, May 23, 1996, A1; *LAT*, May 23, 1996, A15; *Advocate*, July 23, 1996, 26.
66. *NYT*, June 7, 1996, A12; *LAT*, June 8, 1996, A12; June 10, 1996, 1; *SFC*, June 11, 1996, A26.

67. Eskridge, *Equality*, 39; Rom, 18; *NYT*, July 13, 1996, A1; Sept. 11, 1996, A1.
68. *NYT*, May 23, 1996, A1; July 13, 1996, 1.
69. *NYT*, Sept. 21, 1996, A8; Rimmerman, "Presidency," 277; Cahill, "Anti–Gay Marriage Movement," 183 n. 24.
70. *HA*, Aug. 25, 1996, A2.
71. *HA*, Sept. 22, 1996, A3.
72. *HA*, Sept. 11, 1996, A1; Hull, 213–14.
73. *HA*, Sept. 15, 1996, A2; Sept. 19, 1996, A23; Sept. 22, 1996, A3; Nov. 1, 1996, E4.
74. *HA*, Oct. 29, 1996, A1; Oct. 30, 1996, A7; Nov. 4, 1996, A1.
75. *HA*, Nov. 7, 1996, A1, A14; Dec. 8, 1996, A21; Dec. 12, 1999, A1.
76. *Baehr v. Miike*, CIV. No. 91-1394, 1996 WL 694235 (Haw. Cir. Ct. Dec. 3, 1996); Eskridge, *Equality*, 22; *HA*, Dec. 4, 1996, 1.
77. Tony Varona and Anthony Miranda to Elizabeth Birch, July 20, 1998, HRC, box 54, folder 18; 1998 Anti-Marriage Bills Status Report, May 11, 1998, HRC, box 1, folder 25; *HA*, Dec. 4, 1996, A1; Dec. 5, 1996, A1; Jan. 12, 1997, A1; Sept. 18, 1998, A1.
78. *HA*, Jan. 12, 1997, A1, B2; Jan. 16, 1997, A1; Jan. 18, 1997, A1.
79. *HA*, Jan. 24, 1997, C1; Jan. 25, 1997, A1; March 20, 1997, B4; Dec. 12, 1999, A1.
80. *HA*, Apr. 1, 1997, A1; Apr. 12, 1997, A1; Apr. 13, 1997, A1; Apr. 17, 1997, A1; Eskridge, *Equality*, 25; *NYT*, July 10, 1997, B7.
81. *HA*, Apr. 17, 1997, A1; Apr. 18, 1997, A1; May 2, 1997, A15; Nov. 5, 2008, A1.
82. *HA*, Sept. 10, 1998, B1; Oct. 24, 1998, A1; *WP*, May 29, 2009, A3; Hull, 214.
83. *HA*, Oct. 1, 1998, B1; Oct. 15, 1998, A10; Oct. 18, 1998, B3; Oct. 19, 1998, C6; Hull, 216.
84. *HA*, Sept. 18, 1998, A1; Oct. 1, 1998, A5; Oct. 4, 1998, A16; Oct. 8, 1998, A1, A6; Oct. 9, 1998, A14; Oct. 18, 1998, A16, B3; Hull, 215.
85. *HA*, Nov. 5, 1998, A1; Dec. 10, 1999, A1; *NYT*, Dec. 10, 1999, A28; Andersen, 189.
86. O'Connor and Yakus, 300; Eskridge, *Equality*, 17–18; Andersen, 53, 181; *HA*, Nov. 5, 1998, A1.
87. *ADN*, Aug. 5, 1995, E1; Feb. 28, 1998, A1; Andersen, 183, 197–98.
88. *ADN*, March 10, 1995, A1; Aug. 5, 1995, E1; Feb. 28, 1998, A1; March 3, 1998, C1; Andersen, 183, 263 n. 22; *Brause v. Bureau of Vital Statistics*, No. 3AN-95-6562 CI, 1998 WL 88743 (Alaska Super. Ct. Feb. 27, 1998).
89. *ADN*, June 6, 1998, D1; Tony Varona and Anthony Miranda to Elizabeth Birch, July 20, 1998, HRC, box 54, folder 18.
90. Andersen, 191; *ADN*, Apr. 16, 1998, B1; Apr. 17, 1998, A1; May 12, 1998, A1.
91. *ADN*, Sept. 8, 1998, B1; Sept. 13, 1998, A12; Oct. 3, 1998, A1; Oct. 7, 1998, B1.
92. *ADN*, Aug. 29, 1998, B7; Sept. 13, 1998, A1; Oct. 18, 1998, H4.
93. *ADN*, Sept. 13, 1998, A12; Oct. 18, 1998, H4.
94. *ADN*, Oct. 30, 1998, D4.
95. *ADN*, Sept. 24, 1999, B2.
96. For internal roundtable discussion, "'Plan B': 'Post-Breakdown' Options if the Hawaii Constitutional Amendment Is Adopted," Sept. 26, 1998, HRC, box 1, folder 25.
97. Andersen, 153; Gallagher and Bull, 100–5; Herman, 139–48; Murdoch and Price, 452; Zwier, 200; *RMN*, Oct. 13, 1992, 8.
98. Gallagher and Bull, 40, 111–12, 115; Andersen, 155–56; Murdoch and Price, 454–55.
99. Gallagher and Bull, 119; *RMN*, Oct. 18, 1992, 12; *NYT*, Nov. 8, 1992, A38; *CE*, June 20, 2004, A1; July 28, 2004, C1.
100. *Evans v. Romer*, 882 P.2d 1335 (Colo. 1994); *Equality Foundation of Greater Cincinnati v. City of Cincinnati*, 54 F.3d 261 (6th Cir. 1995); *NYT*, May 20, 1995, A10.
101. *Romer v. Evans*, 517 U.S. 620, 632–33 (1996); ibid., 636 (Scalia, J., dissenting).
102. *NYT*, May 21, 1996, A21; *LAT*, May 21, 1996, A1.
103. *NYT*, Jan. 12, 1994, A17; May 21, 1996, A21; Keck, 157; memo from Tim Drake to staff, Oct. 24, 1991, NGLTF, box 2, folder 34; Andersen, 143–46; Chauncey, 45–46.

104. *NYT*, May 21, 1996, A21; Nov. 14, 1994, B9; *Oregonian*, Nov. 10, 1994, C9; Nov. 12, 1994, B1; *IS*, Nov. 9, 1994, 1A; *PPH*, Nov. 9, 1995, 1A; Gallagher and Bull, 242, 260.
105. *NYT*, May 21, 1996, A1; May 26, 1996, WK4; *LAT*, May 21, 1996, A1.
106. *NYT*, May 26, 1996, WK4.
107. Andersen, 116 fig. 4; Wilcox, "Same-Sex Marriage," 223–24 fig. 9.1; AEI Studies, 3.
108. Wilcox et al., "Public Opinion," 225; Egan, Persily, and Wallsten, 236; *BFP*, Apr. 23, 1999, 14A.
109. Yang, 10.
110. Andersen, 46; Dick Dadey letter, Aug. 20, 1997, ESPA, folder 2.18; Chauncey, 48.
111. Chauncey, 51; *NYT*, Nov. 14, 1994, B9; Dick Dadey memo summarizing 1994, Nov. 19, 1994, ESPA, file 2.6.
112. *NYT*, Sept. 13, 1999, A14; Sept. 17, 1999, A16; Oct. 3, 1999, A30; Oct. 28, 1999, A1; Dec. 28, 1999, A1; May 1, 2000, A14; Chauncey, 52.
113. Memorandum from the Tarrance Group and Lake Sosin Snell and Associates to HRC, Apr. 14, 1997, HRC, box 2, folder 1; Andersen, 54, 257 n. 15; *NYT*, Dec. 2, 1998, A1; Eskridge, *Gaylaw*, 356–60 app. B; Chauncey, 52.
114. *NYT*, Sept. 11, 1996, A1; Aug. 2, 1998, WK3; May 29, 1998, A1; HRC press release, Apr. 24, 1997, HRC, box 2, folder 1; Andersen, 116.
115. *NYT*, Oct. 13, 1998, A1; Oct. 21, 1998, A1; email from Sean Lyons or Stephen Cuevas to HRC, Oct. 19, 1998, HRC, box 2, folder 25; email from Charles Brossmann to Elizabeth Birch, Oct. 12, 1998, HRC, box 2, folder 25; Stephen Brown to Elizabeth Birch, Oct. 15, 1998, HRC, box 2, folder 25; Keck, 172–73; Chauncey, 56; *BFP*, March 21, 1999, 6A; July 23, 1999, 7A; Oct. 30, 1999, 8A.
116. Keck, 171; Cain, 236–37, 252 nn. 10–11, 273–74 n. 23; Chauncey, 150; Andersen, 116.
117. Pinello, 51.
118. Andersen, 208; Cain, 150, 248–49; Gay and Lesbian Parents Coalition International, "Adoption and Sexual Orientation," July 1996, HRC, box 2, folder 1.
119. Chauncey, 52; Rom, 12 fig. 1.2; *BFP*, June 25, 2000, 1E; Rosenberg, 410–11.
120. *NYT*, March 30, 2000, A1; *WP*, July 2, 2000, A3.
121. Chauncey, 52–54; *Time*, Apr. 14, 1997, 81; *NYT*, March 5, 1993, A1.
122. Andersen, 265 n. 47; Chauncey, 54; *Time*, Apr. 14, 1997, 80; *Advocate*, Feb. 18, 1997, 30.
123. Chauncey, 54; *EW*, May 8, 1998, 26; *Time*, Apr. 14, 1997, 80.
124. *BFP*, Feb. 28, 1999, 5D; March 16, 1999, 3C; Chauncey, 54; Wilcox et al., "Public Opinion," 236–37.
125. Chauncey, 48; Wilcox et al., "Public Opinion," 225; Egan et al., 237.
126. *NYT*, Jan. 21, 1996, A12; May 28, 1996, A12; Chauncey, 49.
127. Wilcox et al., "Public Opinion," 227; Pew Research Center Study, Oct. 6, 2010; Andersen, 201.

Chapter 4

1. Eskridge, *Equality*, 45; Rom, 28; Keck, 177; *In re B.L.V.B.*, 160 Vt. 368 (1993); Andersen, 185; Eskridge, *Same-Sex Marriage*, 59; *NYT*, June 13, 1994, A13.
2. *BFP*, July 9, 1999, 1B.
3. *BG*, Nov. 23, 2003, A1; *BFP*, Apr. 12, 2009, A1; Eskridge, *Equality*, 46–47; Andersen, 197; Tony Varona and Anthony Miranda to Elizabeth Birch, July 20, 1998, HRC, box 54, folder 18.
4. Andersen, 184.
5. Eskridge, *Equality*, 51; *BFP*, Jan. 28, 1999, 1B; Apr. 17, 1999, 14A.
6. *State v. Baker*, 170 Vt. 194 (1999); Eskridge, *Equality*, 52–53; Tony Varona and Anthony Miranda to Elizabeth Birch, July 20, 1998, HRC, box 54, folder 18.
7. *Baker*, 170 Vt. at 197–98, 225–26, 227; *BFP*, Dec. 26, 1999, 4E.

8. *BFP*, Dec. 26, 1999, 4E; *Brigham v. State*, 692 A.2d 384 (Vt. 1997).

9. *LAT*, Oct. 3, 1999, A24.

10. Chauncey, 129.

11. *BFP*, Dec. 21, 1999, 1A, 10A; Jan. 3, 2000, 1A; Jan. 27, 2000, 1A.

12. *BFP*, Dec. 24, 1999, 1A; Dec. 26, 1999, 1B; Jan. 14, 2000, 3B; March 21, 2000, 5E; Andersen, 191.

13. *BFP*, Dec. 21, 1999, 1A; Jan. 4, 2000, 1A; Jan. 6, 2000, 3B; Jan. 20, 2000, 1B.

14. *BFP*, Jan. 27, 2000, 1A; Jan. 30, 2000, 6E; Feb. 26, 2000, 1A; March 22, 2000, 1B; Eskridge, *Equality*, 56, 73–75.

15. *BFP*, Jan. 16, 2000, 6E; Jan. 20, 2000, 1B; Jan. 21, 2000, 3B; Jan. 26, 2000, 1A; Jan. 30, 2000, 6E; Jan. 31, 2000, 3D; Feb. 2, 2000, 6A; Feb. 3, 2000, 1B; March 25, 2000, 1A; May 17, 2000, 1A.

16. *BFP*, Jan. 30, 2000, 6E; March 23, 2000, 1B; Eskridge, *Equality*, 146–47.

17. *BFP*, Jan. 29, 2000, 5B; Feb. 1, 2000, 3B; Feb. 4, 2000, 3B; Feb. 8, 2000, 3B; March 2, 2000, 1A; Apr. 12, 2000, 1B; Apr. 16, 2000, 1B; Apr. 20, 2000, 13A; Apr. 21, 2000, 1B.

18. *BFP*, Feb. 8, 2000, 3B; Feb. 10, 2000, 1A; Feb. 11, 2000, 1A; March 2, 2000, 1A; March 18, 2000, 1A; March 23, 2000, 1B.

19. *BFP*, Feb. 10, 2000, 1A; Feb. 24, 2000, 1A; March 8, 2000, 1A; March 9, 2000, 1A; March 10, 2000, 3B; March 14, 2000, 1B; March 15, 2000, 1A.

20. *BFP*, Apr. 2, 2000, 1A; March 10, 2000, 3B; May 17, 2000, 1A.

21. *BFP*, March 16, 2000, 1A; March 17, 2000, 1A; March 19, 2000, 1A; March 29, 2000, 9A; Apr. 23, 2000, 6E.

22. *BFP*, Apr. 19, 2000, 1A; Apr. 20, 2000, 1A; Apr. 23, 2000, 6E; Apr. 27, 2000, 1A; Andersen, 186.

23. *BFP*, Apr. 20, 2000, 1A; Apr. 26, 2000, 1A; May 10, 2000, 1A.

24. *BFP*, May 16, 2000, 9A; June 10, 2000, 3B; July 2, 2000, 1A.

25. *BFP*, May 1, 2000, 3B; May 6, 2000, 1B; May 17, 2000, 1A; Sept. 1, 2000, 1A.

26. *BFP*, Apr. 27, 2000, 1D; Sept. 1, 2000, 1A; Sept. 3, 2000, 1A.

27. *BFP*, July 2, 2000, 1A; Aug. 3, 2000, 13A; Aug. 5, 2000, 1A; Aug. 20, 2000, 1A; Sept. 2, 2000, 1B; Sept. 10, 2000, 1A.

28. *BFP*, Apr. 2, 2000, 4A; May 26, 2000, 1B; July 18, 2000, 1A; Aug. 27, 2000, 1A; Nov. 3, 2000, 1B.

29. *BFP*, July 18, 2000, 1A; Sept. 10, 2000, 1A; Sept. 17, 2000, 1A; Nov. 2, 2000, 1B.

30. *BFP*, Sept. 10, 2000, 1A; Sept. 13, 2000, 1A, 8A; Sept. 14, 2000, 1A; Sept. 17, 2000, 1A, 8E; *NYT*, Sept. 14, 2000, A24; Eskridge, *Equality*, 81.

31. *BFP*, April 2, 2000, 6E; June 2, 2000, 1B; Sept. 2, 2000, 1B; Sept. 16, 2000, 1A; Eskridge, *Equality*, 70, 81–82.

32. *BFP*, Aug. 22, 2000, 3B; Aug. 24, 2000, 1A; Aug. 27, 2000, 6E; Sept. 2, 2000, 1A.

33. *BG*, Dec. 4, 2003, B21; *BFP*, Oct. 12, 2000, 1B; Oct. 15, 2000, 8E.

34. *BFP*, Oct. 12, 2000, 1B; Oct. 15, 2000, 1B; Oct. 16, 2000, 3B; Oct. 20, 2000, 1B; Oct. 22, 2000, 8E.

35. *BFP*, Oct. 15, 2000, 1B; Oct. 24, 2000, 1A; Nov. 3, 2000, 1A.

36. *BFP*, Oct. 15, 2000, 1B; Oct. 20, 2000, 1B; Oct. 29, 2000, 1A; Nov. 8, 2000, 1A.

37. *BFP*, Oct. 20, 2000, 4B; Oct. 24, 2000, 1A; Nov. 2, 2000, 5B; Dec. 3, 2000, 1A.

38. *BFP*, Nov. 8, 2000, 1A; Keck, 162.

39. *BFP*, Nov. 8, 2000, 6A; Nov. 9, 2004, A1, A15; Dec. 16, 2000, 1B; Dec. 17, 2000, 13B.

40. Eskridge, *Equality*, 150–51; Amestoy, 1264–66; Rom, 19–20; Andersen, 191; *BFP*, March 2, 2000, 1A.

41. *BFP*, Dec. 16, 2000, 1B; Apr. 12, 2009, A1; Rom, 20; AP, June 27, 2002; Apr. 27, 2003.

42. *BFP*, Apr. 10, 2000, 1A; Dec. 27, 1999, 4A.

43. *NYT*, Dec. 28, 1999, A22; *BFP*, Dec. 21, 1999, 7A; Apr. 7, 2000, 1A; Oct. 13, 2000, 10A; Eskridge, *Equality*, 71–72; Cahill, "Anti-Gay Marriage Movement," 169–70.

44. *BFP*, Apr. 30, 2000, 1A, 8A; May 1, 2000, 1A; *NYT*, March 2, 2000, A24; May 1, 2000, A14.

45. *BFP*, Apr. 10, 2000, 6A; *LAT*, May 4, 2000, 13A.

46. Andersen, 187; *LAT*, Sept. 12, 1999, B17; Feb. 11, 2000, A3; *BFP*, Apr. 10, 2000, 6A; Lofton and Haider-Markel, 322.

47. *LAT*, Oct. 15, 1999, A3; Nov. 24, 1999, A1; March 8, 2000, 1A.

48. *LAT*, Oct. 3, 1999, A24; Dec. 22, 1999, B1; Jan. 3, 2000, A3; Jan. 29, 2000, A19; March 8, 2000, A23.

49. *LAT*, March 8, 2000, A23; March 9, 2000, A3.

50. *OWH*, Sept. 17, 2000, 1; Oct. 15, 2000, 27A; Oct. 16, 2000, 1; *BFP*, Oct. 21, 2000, 3A.

51. *BFP*, Oct. 21, 2000, 3A; *OWH*, Oct. 1, 2000, 8B; Oct. 11, 2000, 2; Oct. 15, 2000, 1A; Oct. 20, 2000, 19; Oct. 31, 2000, 12.

52. *OWH*, Sept. 17, 2000, 1; Lofton and Haider-Markel, 318, 322–23.

53. Andersen, 98.

54. *Commonwealth v. Wasson*, 842 S.W.2d 487, 501 (Ky. 1992); Cain, 236–37, 242, 252 nn. 10–11; Andersen, 98–106, 105 table 9; Eskridge, *Gaylaw*, 168; *WP*, Feb. 4, 1987, A16.

55. *Lawrence v. Texas*, 539 U.S. 558, 572 (2003).

56. Andersen, 120–21.

57. *NYT*, June 27, 2003, A20; D'Emilio, "Lessons," 8; Cain, 243; Andersen, 129.

58. *Lawrence*, 539 U.S. at 562, 582 (O'Connor, J., concurring), 605 (Thomas, J., dissenting); Andersen, 136.

59. *Public Opinion Online* (May 20, 2003), accession no. 0429847; Rom, 10; *NYTM*, Sept. 7, 2003, 50; *NYT*, July 8, 2003, B2; Lund and McGinnis, 1556; Sunstein, "Lawrence," 27; D'Emilio, "Courts," 57–58.

60. Andersen, 118–19; Egan, Persily, and Wallsten, 240–42; Lund and McGinnis, 1556; Sunstein, "Lawrence," 27; *Lawrence*, 539 U.S. at 566, 578.

61. *Lawrence*, 539 U.S. at 585 (O'Connor, J., concurring).

62. *Lawrence*, 539 U.S. at 605 (Scalia, J., dissenting); Pinello, 105; Rimmerman, "Presidency," 280; Cahill, *Same-Sex Marriage*, 3; D'Emilio, "Lessons," 4.

63. *Halpern v. Toronto*, 2003 WL 34950 (Ontario Ct. App.); *WP*, June 12, 2003, A25; *NYT*, June 18, 2003, A1; June 21, 2003, B8; June 24, 2003, A24; June 28, 2003, A2, B4; *BG*, March 5, 2003, A1; *NYS*, Sept. 23, 2003, 1.

64. *NYT*, July 2, 2003, A22; *NYTM*, Sept. 7, 2003, 48; *Time*, July 7, 2003, 38; Cahill, "Anti-Gay Marriage Movement," 171, 183 n.26; *BG*, Sept. 28, 2003, A1.

65. Rimmerman, "Presidency," 280, 282–84; *NYT*, July 2, 2003, A22; Lucas, 251.

66. Egan, Persily, and Wallsten, 240–41, 250; Egan and Persily.

Chapter 5

1. *TNR*, Dec. 22, 2003, 19; Andersen, 219–20; Pinello, 34–35; *Adoption of Tammy*, 416 Mass. 205 (1993); *E.N.O. v. L.M.M.*, 429 Mass. 824 (1999).

2. *BG*, Sept. 6, 2001, B3; Nov. 23, 2003, A1; Andersen, 54, 220–21; *NYT*, June 26, 2002, B5.

3. *BG*, July 25, 2001, B2; Sept. 6, 2001, B3; Nov. 23, 2003, A1; Pinello, 35–36.

4. Pinello, 36–37.

5. *BG*, Dec. 21, 2001, B10; Apr. 25, 2002, B1; June 20, 2002, A1.

6. *BG*, May 2, 2002, B8; June 20, 2002, A1; Pinello, 36–37.

7. *BG*, July 16, 2002, B1; July 18, 2002, A1.

8. Pinello, 37, 40; *BG*, July 25, 2001, B2; July 16, 2002, B1; July 18, 2002, A1; Sept. 15, 2002, B4; Nov. 23, 2003, A1.

9. *BG*, June 22, 2002, A1; Oct. 16, 2002, A1; Oct. 20, 2002, B4; Nov. 20, 2003, B10.

10. *Goodridge v. Dep't of Public Health*, 798 N.E.2d 941, 949, 968, 970 (Mass. 2003); *BG*, Nov. 19, 2003, A1; Feb. 5, 2004, A1.

11. *BG*, Nov. 19, 2003, B6; Nov. 22, 2003, B1; Dec. 1, 2003, B4; Dec. 16, 2003, B5; Jan. 17, 2004, A1.

12. *BG,* June 22, 2002, A1; Oct. 16, 2002, A1; Nov. 19, 2003, A1; Nov. 20, 2003, B10.
13. Andersen, 225–26.
14. *BG,* Nov. 19, 2003, A1; Nov. 20, 2003, A1; Nov. 21, 2003, A1; Nov. 22, 2003, B1; Dec. 5, 2003, A1; Jan. 5, 2004, A1; *Economist,* Nov. 22, 2003, 29.
15. *BG,* Dec. 1, 2003, B1; Dec. 12, 2003, B8.
16. *Opinions of the Justices to the Senate,* 802 N.E.2d 565, 571 (Mass. 2004); Pinello, 44–45; Andersen, 222; Egan and Sherrill, "Marriage," 230.
17. *BG,* Nov. 19, 2003, A1; Nov. 23, 2003, A1; Dec. 13, 2003, A1.
18. *BG,* Jan. 8, 2004, B1; Jan. 17, 2004, A1; Feb. 22, 2004, A1.
19. *BG,* Jan. 17, 2004, A1; Feb. 2, 2004, B2; Feb. 5, 2004, A15; Feb. 6, 2004, A26; Feb. 22, 2004, A1.
20. *BG,* Jan. 26, 2004, B1; Feb. 8, 2004, B1; Feb. 11, 2004, B6.
21. *BG,* Jan. 27, 2004, A1; Jan. 30, 2004, A1.
22. *BG,* Feb. 5, 2004, A1; Feb. 6, 2004, A19; Feb. 7, 2004, A11; Feb. 9, 2004, B6; Feb. 14, 2004, A1; March 12, 2004, A1.
23. *BG,* Feb. 12, 2004, A1; Pinello, 47–49, 51.
24. Pinello, 52–53; *BG,* Feb. 9, 2004, A1; Feb. 11, 2004, B6.
25. *BG,* Feb. 5, 2004, A19; Feb. 10, 2004, A1; Feb. 11, 2004, A23.
26. *BG,* Feb. 11, 2004, A1.
27. *BG,* Feb. 9, 2004, A1; Feb. 12, 2004, A1, B6, B7; Feb. 14, 2004, B4, B5.
28. *BG,* Feb. 13, 2004, A1, B8.
29. *BG,* Feb. 21, 2004, B1.
30. *BG,* March 3, 2004, B6; March 9, 2004, A1; March 10, 2004, B5; March 30, 2004, A1, A6; Pinello, 56.
31. Andersen, 220, 225; *BG,* March 30, 2004, A6.
32. *BG,* March 30, 2004, A1, A8; Oct. 28, 2004, GW1.
33. Pinello, 68–69; *BG,* Feb. 11, 2004, A23; March 26, 2004, B1; Nov. 3, 2004, B8; thebostonpilot.com, March 26, 2004.
34. *BG,* Feb. 28, 2004, B1; March 4, 2004, B1; March 12, 2004, B6; Nov. 3, 2004, B8.
35. *BG,* Nov. 3, 2004, B8; Pinello, 69.
36. *BG,* Sept. 15, 2004, B4; Sept. 26, 2004, B1; Pinello, 69–70.
37. Pinello, 71; *BG,* Sept. 28, 2004, A1.
38. *BG,* Sept. 28, 2004, A1; Nov. 5, 2004, B1.
39. *BG,* Sept. 26, 2004, B1; Oct. 17, 2004, GS15; Oct. 24, 2004, B1; Nov. 3, 2004, B8; Nov. 7, 2004, CW5.
40. Pinello, 70; Andersen, 229; *BG,* Nov. 3, 2004, B8; Nov. 5, 2004, B1; Nov. 9, 2004, A15.
41. Pinello, 183; *BG,* March 17, 2005, B1; March 20, 2005, CW6; Sept. 8, 2005, A1.
42. Pinello, 70; Keck, 162; *BG,* May 15, 2005, B7; Sept. 8, 2005, A1.
43. *BG,* Aug. 26, 2005, B1; Aug. 30, 2005, B1; Sept. 7, 2005, B1; Sept. 8, 2005, A28; Sept. 12, 2005, B1.
44. *BG,* Sept. 7, 2005, B1; Sept. 12, 2005, B1; Sept. 14, 2005, B1; Sept. 15, 2005, A1; Pinello, 71.
45. *BG,* Sept. 15, 2005, A1.
46. Pinello, 72; Andersen, 230–32; *BG,* Aug. 30, 2005, B1; Sept. 30, 2005, B4.
47. *BG,* Dec. 28, 2006, 1A; Jan. 3, 2007, 1A; June 15, 2007, 1A; Rosenberg, 349–50.
48. dk, Oct. 4, 2011; *BG,* Jan. 14, 2010, A15.
49. D'Emilio, "Courts," 52–53; Wilcox et al., "Public Opinion," 218; O'Connor and Yanus, 293.
50. Rosenberg, 402–3; Pew Research Center, news releases, Feb. 27, 2004, July 21, 2004, Aug. 24, 2004.
51. Lofton and Haider-Markel, 319 table 13.1.
52. 538, Apr. 9, 2009; Egan, Persily, and Wallsten, 242; *NYT,* Apr. 12, 2009, WK1.
53. Wilcox et al., "Public Opinion," 216; kns, June 27, 2010.

54. *NYT*, Feb. 5, 2004, A6; Feb. 25, 2004, A1; Feb. 29, 2004, § 4, 14.

55. *Nation*, July 5, 2005, 33; *NYT*, Nov. 20, 2003, A29.

56. *BG*, Nov. 19, 2003, A1; Nov. 20, 2003, A23; *NYT*, Nov. 20, 2003, A29; Jan. 21, 2004, A18; Pinello, 75.

57. Pinello, 73–76; *SFC*, Feb. 13, 2004, A1; Feb. 15, 2004, A1.

58. Pinello, 76–77; *SFC*, Feb. 15, 2004, A1.

59. *SFC*, Feb. 13, 2004, A1; Feb. 18, 2004, A1; Feb. 21, 2004, A1; Feb. 23, 2004, A1.

60. Pinello, 80–81; *SFC*, Feb. 14, 2004, A1; Feb. 15, 2004, A17.

61. Pinello, 84–85.

62. *SFC*, Feb. 14, 2004, A1; Feb. 19, 2004, A2; Feb. 21, 2004, A1; March 12, 2004, A19; Pinello, 87, 90; *Lockyer v. City and County of San Francisco*, 95 P.3d 459 (Cal. 2004).

63. *AJ*, Feb. 24, 2004, A1; AP, Apr. 8, 2004; Reuters, Feb. 20, 2004; *AT*, June 15, 2004, 1.

64. *WP*, Feb. 22, 2004, A13; Reuters, Feb. 21, 2004; AP, Feb. 20, 2004.

65. *AJ*, Feb. 21, 2004, A1; March 9, 2004, B1; AP, March 21, 2004.

66. AP, March 23, 2004; June 5, 2004; *AT*, March 23, 2004, A1; *AJ*, March 30, 2004, A1; Apr. 24, 2004, A10; June 2, 2004, B1; Pinello, 16.

67. Pinello, 103–7.

68. Pinello, 111–12; *SPI*, March 4, 2004, A1.

69. *Oregonian*, Sept. 11, 2004, B1; Pinello, 19, 115–16.

70. Pinello, 143.

71. *NYT*, March 4, 2004, B4; Pinello, 144–45.

72. *NYT*, March 3, 2004, B4.

73. Pinello, 146; *BN*, Feb. 5, 2005, A1; *NYT*, Feb. 27, 2004, B2; Feb. 28, 2004, A1, A2; March 4, 2004, A1; March 7, 2004, A30; March 14, 2004, A36.

74. Pinello, 19; *NYT*, March 9, 2004, B1, B5; March 11, 2004, B5.

75. Pinello, 19; *BG*, May 17, 2004, A1.

76. Rimmerman, "Presidency," 284; Pinello, 20; *NYT*, Feb. 25, 2004, A1; *LAT*, Feb. 25, 2004, A1.

77. *CPD*, Sept. 20, 2004, A1; Pinello, 178; *LAT*, Apr. 11, 2004, A1; Lewis, 195; Smidt and Penning, 115.

78. Rozell and Das Gupta, 17; Campbell and Robinson, 135; Wilcox et al., "Public Opinion," 221; *NYT*, Feb. 8, 2004, A1; *Nation*, July 5, 2004, 33.

79. Wilcox et al., "Saving Marriage," 59.

80. Lucas, 259; Rimmerman, "Presidency," 284; Lofton and Haider-Markel, 334; *KCS*, Aug. 5, 2004, B1; *Economist*, Nov. 22, 2003, 29.

81. Lucas, 243–44.

82. *SPI*, Sept. 1, 2004, A11; *Newsweek*, June 28, 2004, 8.

83. *Time*, July 26, 2004, 78; *LAT*, July 15, 2004, A1.

84. *LAT*, July 15, 2004, A1; *CC*, Aug. 10, 2004, 10; Rimmerman, "Presidency," 285–86; Pinello, 20; Rosenberg, 366–67; *NYT*, Oct. 1, 2004, A14.

85. NPR, "Gay Marriage and Civil Unions," Dec. 24, 2003; Cahill, "Anti–Gay Marriage Movement," 158; Lofton and Haider-Markel, 335; Wald and Glover, 123–24; Keck, 163; Schacter, "Backlash," 1205–6; Lucas, 268; *CPD*, Sept. 20, 2004, A1; *KCS*, Aug. 5, 2004, B1.

86. *CE*, Nov. 3, 2004, A10; Pinello, 102 table 5.1; Andersen, 232–33; *LAT*, June 29, 2008, A1.

87. *KCS*, July 17, 2004, B2; July 23, 2004, A1; July 30, 2004, B4.

88. *KCS*, Aug. 4, 2004, A1; Aug. 5, 2004, B1; *NYT*, Aug. 4, 2004, A13; Aug. 5, 2004, A17; Andersen, 233–34, table 14; Pinello, 102; Rosenberg, 364.

89. *BG*, Feb. 6, 2004, A1; *CE*, Feb. 7, 2004, 1B; Oct. 10, 2004, E1; Green, 81.

90. *NYT*, Nov. 26, 2004, A28.

91. *CE*, July 11, 2004, C1; Oct. 10, 2004, E1; Campbell and Robinson, 147–48; Green, "Ohio," 83; *BG*, Nov. 7, 2004, B1.

92. *CE*, Oct. 26, 2004, B5; July 21, 2004, C1; Sept. 14, 2004, C1; Green, "Ohio," 85; Djupe, Neiheisel, and Sokhey, 77.

93. *CE*, July 20, 2004, C2; Aug. 18, 2004, B2; Oct. 9, 2004, B1; Djupe, Neiheisel, and Sokhey, 77, 79.

94. *CE*, July 20, 2004, C2; Oct. 9, 2004, B1; Oct. 14, 2004, C1; Oct. 26, 2004, B5; Green, "Ohio," 88.

95. *Oregonian*, Oct. 8, 2004, A6, M2.

96. Pinello, 119–21, 128; Wilcox et al., "Saving Marriage," 64.

97. Pinello, 124–28, 132; *Oregonian*, Oct. 20, 2004, D12.

98. *Oregonian*, Sept. 1, 2004, C10; Nov. 4, 2004, D4; *NYT*, Sept. 28, 2004, A14; *WP*, July 3, 2006, B2; Pinello, 102, 131.

99. Keck, 168; D'Emilio, "Courts," 60; Rosenberg, 368.

100. Pinello, 102, table 5.1, 177–78; Segura, 189; Cahill, "Anti–Gay Marriage Movement," 168; Keck, 168; Andersen, 234; *State v. Burk*, No. CR 462510, 2005 WL 786212 (Ohio C.P. Mar. 23, 2005).

101. Lucas, 264–65; Rosenberg, 375–76.

102. Lucas, 264–65; *CT*, Oct. 22, 2004, 5.

103. Lucas, 256–57.

104. *ADG*, Oct. 27, 2004.

105. *ADG*, Nov. 4, 2004; politico.com, Nov. 24, 2009.

106. *TO*, Oct. 23, 2004, 10A.

107. *TO*, Oct. 27, 2004, 8A; Nov. 3, 2004, 6A; *BG*, Nov. 7, 2004, B1.

108. *LHL*, May 9, 2004, A1.

109. *LHL*, Oct. 30, 2004, A1, B4; *KP*, Oct. 30, 2004, A12; Lucas, 257.

110. *LCJ*, Oct. 30, 2004, A1; *NYT*, Nov. 4, 2004, P4.

111. *NYT*, Nov. 4, 2004, P4; *BG*, Nov. 7, 2004, B1; *LCJ*, Nov. 4, 2004, A1; Nov. 7, 2004, A1.

112. *Newsweek*, July 26, 2004, 34; *RCJ*, Oct. 28, 2004; July 9, 2004; *AL*, Oct. 5, 2004, 1B.

113. *AAN*, July 14, 2004; Rosenberg, 374.

114. *NYT*, Jan. 1, 2005, A10.

115. Lucas, 261–63; *BG*, Nov. 19, 2003, B11; Feb. 26, 2004, A1; Nov. 7, 2004, B1; *Economist*, Nov. 22, 2003, 30; *SFC*, Dec. 2, 2003, A1; worldmag.com, Dec. 6, 2003.

116. *BG*, Nov. 7, 2004, B1; *NYT*, Aug. 4, 2004, A14; *Newsweek*, June 28, 2004, 8; *New Statesman*, July 26, 2004, 13; *Time*, July 26, 2004, 78.

117. Lewis, 195; *NYT*, Nov. 6, 2004, A19.

118. *CE*, Oct. 30, 2004, A1; Green, "Ohio," 88, 90–92; Cahill, "Anti–Gay Marriage Movement," 178; Rom, 1; Lewis, 197–98; Wilcox et al., "Saving Marriage," 68; *TNR*, Nov. 22, 2004, 11; Rozell and Das Gupta, 17–18.

119. Donovan et al.; Rosenberg, 380–81; Campbell and Monson, 23–27; Djupe, Neiheisel, and Sokhey, 97–98; Green, "Ohio," 90; *WP*, Nov. 5, 2004, A3; *BS*, Oct. 16, 2004, 1A; Nov. 7, 2004, 1A.

120. *CPD*, Nov. 7, 2004, A20; Wilcox et al., "Saving Marriage," 63; Djupe, Neiheisel, and Sokhey, 86–87.

121. *CPD*, Nov. 16, 2004, B9; Nov. 7, 2004, A20.

122. *NYT*, Nov. 4, 2004, P4; *BG*, Nov. 4, 2004, A15; *BS*, Nov. 4, 2004, 1A; Nov. 7, 2004, 1A; *WP*, Nov. 4, 2004, A1; Rosenberg, 378–81; Djupe, Neiheisel, and Sokhey, 77.

123. *BG*, Nov. 7, 2004, B1; *CPD*, Sept. 20, 2004, A1; Nov. 4, 2004, A1; *WP*, Nov. 4, 2004, A1; Rosenberg, 380.

124. Compare Rosenberg, 369–71; Donovan et al.; Smith, Desantis, and Kassel; Rozell and Das Gupta, 13–14; Green, "Ohio," 81, 90–92; Campbell and Monson; and Lewis, 197–98; with Jackman; Hillygus and Shields; Burden; Ansolabehere and Stewart; Sherrill; Klein.

125. *NR*, Nov. 22, 2004, 11; *LAT*, Nov. 6, 2004, E1; Segura, 189.

126. *BG*, Nov. 14, 2004, A25; Dec. 13, 2004, A1; *NYT*, Nov. 12, 2004, A16; Nov. 14, 2004, A30; Dec. 9, 2004, A1; *CSM*, Nov. 29, 2004, 1; *DMN*, Nov. 16, 2004, 11A; *LAT*, Nov. 10, 2004, B11; *SFC*, Nov. 21, 2004, B5.

127. Segura, 189–90; *BG*, Nov. 14, 2004, A25; Jan. 16, 2005, A1; *WP*, Jan. 11, 2005, B6; Nov. 4, 2004, A39.
128. Segura, 189; Rimmerman, "Presidency," 287.
129. *LAT*, Nov. 8, 2004, A13; *NYT*, Dec. 24, 2004, A1; Jan. 1, 2005, A10; *WP*, Jan. 17, 2005, A3.
130. *LAT*, Nov. 10, 2004, B11; Andersen, 235.
131. *CE*, Nov. 4, 2004, B8; *LAW*, Dec. 24, 2004, A20; *CSM*, Nov. 29, 2004, 1.
132. Wilcox et al., "Public Opinion," 226 table 9.2, 227–28; Keck, 166.
133. Pinello, 161; Segura, 192; Campbell and Robinson, 148; *BG*, Feb. 15, 2004, D11; *TNR*, Nov. 22, 2004, 11; *LAT*, March 14, 2004, A35; *NYT*, March 23, 2004, A21.
134. Andersen, 236; gallup.com, July 22, 2003; Schacter, "Sexual Orientation," 869–70.
135. *WT*, Nov. 9, 2004, A3; *NYT*, Nov. 9, 2005, A24; Nov. 9, 2006, P16; *CSM*, Apr. 7, 2005, 2.
136. *WP*, Jan. 14, 2006, B1; Jan. 26, 2006, A1; Apr. 11, 2006, B5; May 18, 2006, B1; July 18, 2006, A4; Oct. 23, 2006, B2.
137. ws, Dec. 8, 2008; *WP*, Nov. 8, 2006, A46; *NYT*, Nov. 6, 2008, A1.
138. *NYT*, June 4, 2006, A30.
139. Rimmerman, "Presidency," 284; *WP*, June 11, 2006, C3; *NYT*, June 6, 2006, A19; June 8, 2006, A20; July 19, 2006, A17.
140. Keck, 164; Andersen, 237–38; *NYT*, June 26, 2002, B5; Apr. 8, 2004, B4; *SPI*, March 9, 2004, A1; Apr. 2, 2004, B1; *BS*, Nov. 17, 2004, 1B.
141. Andersen, 238; *SPI*, Aug. 5, 2004, A1, B8; Sept. 8, 2004, A1; *NYT*, March 7, 2004, WK12; Feb. 5, 2005, 1; *WP*, Jan. 26, 2006, A1; *SFC*, March 15, 2005, A1; *Oregonian*, Sept. 11, 2004, B1; *BS*, Jan. 22, 2006, 22A.
142. *Hernandez v. Robles*, 855 N.E.2d 1 (N.Y. 2006); *Andersen v. King County*, 138 P.3d 963 (Wash. 2006); *Lewis v. Harris*, 908 A.2d 196 (N.J. 2006); *Conaway v. Deane*, 932 A.2d 571 (Md. 2007); *Perdue v. O'Kelley*, 632 S.E.2d 110 (Ga. 2006); *Citizens for Equal Protection v. Bruning*, 455 F.3d 859 (8th Cir. 2006).
143. *SPI*, July 27, 2006, A15.
144. *SPI*, July 27, 2006, A15; Sept. 11, 2006, B1; *NYT*, July 7, 2006, B7; *BS*, Feb. 24, 2006, 5B.
145. D'Emilio, "Courts," 60; *BS*, July 28, 2006, A1; *NYT*, Feb. 16, 2006, B8; Oct. 23, 2006, B1; *BN*, July 7, 2006, A1; *Hernandez v. Robles*, 7 N.Y.3d 338 (N.Y. 2006); *Lewis v. Harris*, 908 A.2d 196, 223 (N.J. 2006).
146. *NYT*, Oct. 26, 2006, B9; *Lewis v. Harris*, 908 A.2d at 222, 226 (Poritz, J., concurring and dissenting).
147. *NYT*, Nov. 3, 2006, B4.
148. *NYT*, Oct. 26, 2006, A1, B8, B9; *SL*, Oct. 26, 2006, 1.
149. *NYT*, Oct. 26, 2006, A1, B1, B8; Keck, 164.
150. *WP*, Oct. 27, 2006, A7; *NYT*, Oct. 27, 2006, A1; Oct. 28, 2006, A14; *DMR*, Oct. 27, 2006, 1A.
151. *WP*, Oct. 26, 2006, A24; Oct. 27, 2006, B6; Oct, 28, 2006, B1; *PN*, Oct. 29, 2006, A1; *NYT*, Oct. 27, 2006, A1.
152. *SPI*, July 27, 2006, A1.
153. *BS*, Sept. 19, 2007, A1; D'Emilio, "Courts," 45; *NYT*, July 7, 2006, A1; Rom, 15–16; coloradodaily.com, May 12, 2009.

Chapter 6

1. *BS*, Dec. 7, 2006, 1A; Nov. 20, 2007, 1A; Rom, 12; ola, June 1, 2009.
2. Keck, 174 table 6.
3. *NYT*, Nov. 8, 2007, A1; Rosenberg, 357 table 13.1.
4. Egan, Persily, and Wallsten, 250–51; Persily and Egan; pewresearch.org, Oct. 6, 2010; gallup.com, May 27, 2009; cbsnews.com, June 15, 2008.

5. *BS*, Feb. 15, 2008, B1.

6. *LAT*, May 16, 2008, A1; Nov. 19, 2008, A1; *In re Marriage Cases*, 183 P.3d 384 (Cal. 2008).

7. *Kerrigan v. Comm'r of Pub. Health*, 957 A.2d 407 (Conn. 2008).

8. Rom, 20–21; *LAT*, Sept. 7, 2005, A1; Sept. 8, 2005, A1; Sept. 30, 2005, B3.

9. Rom, 20–22; Pinello, 90–91; *LAT*, May 18, 2008, A1.

10. nhregister.com, Dec. 17, 2008.

11. Schacter, "Backlash," 1191–92; samesexmarriageadvocate.blogspot.com, Feb. 11, 2009.

12. *LAT*, May 16, 2008, A20; June 3, 2008, B1.

13. *Perry v. Schwarzenegger*, 704 F. Supp. 2d 921, 955 (N.D. Cal. 2010); *LAT*, June 26, 2008, A1.

14. *LAT*, Nov. 6, 2008, A1; *PPH*, Sept. 24, 2009, B1; Schubert and Flint, 45; Feldblum.

15. Schubert and Flint, 47; *SFC*, Oct. 11, 2008, A1; Oct. 14, 2008, A1.

16. *SFC*, Nov. 10, 2008, B5; *LAT*, Nov. 6, 2008, A1; *WP*, Nov. 7, 2008, A3; AP, Nov. 6, 2009; Chauncey, 150–51; Andersen, 35, 155; Gallagher and Bull, 40.

17. *SLT*, May 3, 2009; *LAT*, June 16, 2008, B1; Segura, 190.

18. Talbot, 48; sfbg.com, June 2, 2009; *LAT*, Nov. 6, 2008, A28; Nov. 11, 2008, A18; *SFC*, Oct. 14, 2008, A1; Schubert and Flint, 47.

19. *SFC*, Feb. 3, 2009, B1; Feb. 4, 2009, B5; *LAT*, June 29, 2008, A1; edgeboston.com, June 9, 2010; *SLT*, May 3, 2009; *WB*, Nov. 2, 2008; christianexaminer.com, Nov. 2008; rd, Jan. 31, 2010.

20. *SFC*, Nov. 10, 2008, B5; *LAT*, June 16, 2008, B1; Schubert and Flint, 45.

21. *SFC*, Jan. 18, 2010, A1; articles.latimes.com, Nov. 6, 2008; ocregister.com, Nov. 14, 2008; *WP*, Nov. 7, 2008, A3; memorandum.com, Nov. 6, 2008; *OT*, Jan. 6, 2009; blackpolitics-ontheweb.com, Aug. 14, 2009; Egan and Sherrill, "Proposition 8," 9–12.

22. *LAT*, Nov. 10, 2008, A19; Nov. 19, 2008, A1; wavenewspapers.com, May 23, 2009.

23. law.com, Nov. 6, 2008; *LAT*, Nov. 19, 2008, A1.

24. *OT*, Jan. 6, 2009; *WP*, Jan. 15, 2009, A19; Keck, 165; catholiccitizens.org, Nov. 6, 2008; Egan and Sherrill, "Proposition 8," 3 table 1.

25. sw, Aug. 12, 2009; *LAT*, Nov. 13, 2008, A1; *NYT*, Dec. 10, 2008, A23; *WP*, Nov. 24, 2008, A17; *USAT*, Nov. 14, 2008, 3A.

26. sa, Sept. 9, 2009; *LAT*, Nov. 11, 2008, A18; sfgate.com, Nov. 15, 2008; sltrib.com, Nov. 13, 2008; *NYT*, Nov. 16, 2008, A25; Dec. 10, 2008, A23.

27. *SFC*, Nov. 16, 2008, A1; *Seattle Times*, Nov. 16, 2008, B2.

28. sw, Aug. 12, 2009; *NYT*, Dec. 10, 2008, A23; sa, Sept. 9, 2009.

29. Talbot, 49; sw, Aug. 12, 2009.

30. *SLT*, Nov. 8, 2008; sltrib.com, Nov. 13, 2008; sfgate.com, Nov. 15, 2008.

31. otm, Aug. 16, 2009; drivingequality.com, Aug. 15, 2009; boston.com, Aug. 16, 2009.

32. *Examiner Today*, Aug. 15, 2009; examiner.com, Nov. 16, 2009.

33. sfgate, Nov. 15, 2008; *LAT*, Nov. 13, 2008, A1; *SFC*, Nov. 23, 2008, G9.

34. swingstateproject.com, Sept. 3, 2009.

35. *WP*, Nov. 5, 2008, A37; Nov. 11, 2008, A19; Apr. 29, 2009, A4.

36. *WP*, Nov. 5, 2008, A37; *NYT*, Nov. 6, 2008, P1.

37. sfbaytimes.com, Feb. 5, 2009; *PPH*, Jan. 14, 2009, A1; *Economist*, Apr. 8, 2009, 31.

38. *WP*, Apr. 15, 2009, A1; *DMR*, Dec. 7, 2008, 1A.

39. *Varnum v. Brien*, 763 N.W.2d 862, 897–904 (Iowa 2009).

40. *Varnum*, 763 N.W.2d at 877, 904–6, 907 n. 33.

41. time.com, Apr. 4, 2009; *WP*, Apr. 15, 2009, A1; wb, Apr. 3, 2009.

42. time.com, Apr. 4, 2009; wb, Apr. 3, 2009; *WP*, Apr. 4, 2009, A3; *NYT*, Apr. 5, 2009, A16; *DMR*, Apr. 4, 2009, 1A; *ST*, Apr. 25, 2009, 1A.

43. *CSM*, Apr. 6, 2009, 2; blog.lib.umn.edu, Apr. 4, 2009; *DMR*, Apr. 4, 2009, 1A.

44. time.com, Apr. 4, 2009.

45. *DMR*, Apr. 4, 2010, 1A, 4A; fn.com, Apr. 7, 2009; ii, May 29, 2009; dmr, Apr. 9, 2009.

46. *DMR*, Apr. 4, 2009, 1A; Apr. 28, 2009, 11A.

47. *DMR*, Apr. 8, 2009, 1A.

48. *DMR*, Apr. 15, 2009, 12A; Apr. 23, 2009, 1A; Apr. 28, 2009, 13A; May 3, 2009, 1A.

49. Lax and Phillips, 373 table 1; wcax.com, Nov. 18, 2008; *BFP*, Jan. 5, 2009, A1; March 18, 2009, A6.

50. *BFP*, Jan. 5, 2009, A1; Jan. 25, 2009, D1; March 6, 2009, A1; Nov. 5, 2009, A1.

51. edgeboston.com, July 27, 2009; *BFP*, March 17, 2009, A1; March 19, 2009, A1; March 24, 2009, A6.

52. *BFP*, March 26, 2009, A8; Apr. 3, 2009, A1; Apr. 4, 2009, A1; Apr. 8, 2009, A1; *WO*, Apr. 9, 2009; cbsnews.com, Apr. 9, 2009; *NYT*, Apr. 8, 2009, A1.

53. *NHUL*, March 18, 2009, 2; March 27, 2009, 8; May 8, 2009, 6.

54. *NHUL*, Apr. 16, 2009, 1; Apr. 30, 2009, 1; May 7, 2009, 1; May 13, 2009, 8; May 15, 2009, 5; May 18, 2009, 7; June 4, 2009, 1; July 23, 2009, 2; *NYT*, March 26, 2009, A17; *WP*, Apr. 4, 2009, A3; NRO, June 18, 2009.

55. *PPH*, Apr. 22, 2009, A1; Apr. 23, 2009, A1.

56. *PPH*, Apr. 25, 2009, A5; May 1, 2009, A1; May 6, 2009, A1; May 7, 2009, A1; Nov. 8, 2009, A10; wsj, Apr. 30, 2009.

57. politico.com, May 1, 2009; *LAT*, May 3, 2009, A39; *NYT*, May 15, 2009, A16; *WP*, Apr. 10, 2009, A4; May 16, 2009, B2; *NHUL*, May 6, 2009, 7.

58. poconorecord, Apr. 11, 2009; *NHUL*, May 15, 2009, 1.

59. *NYT*, Apr. 8, 2009, A1; andrewgelman.com, June 8, 2009; religionnews.com, June 8, 2009; usatoday.com, May 8, 2009; *PJ*, May 9, 2009, 1.

60. *PDN*, May 19, 2009, 3; examiner.com, June 26, 2009; *WP*, May 27, 2009, A1; *NYT*, Dec. 3, 2009, A40; *PI*, Dec. 10, 2008, B1.

61. *PDN*, May 19, 2009, 3; moremonmouthmusings.blogspot.com, Sept. 29, 2009; governing.com, Aug. 25, 2009.

62. *NYT*, Nov. 6, 2008, A27; Dec. 11, 2008, A43; Jan. 7, 2009, A23.

63. *NYT*, Dec. 17, 2002, B8.

64. *NYT*, Apr. 9, 2009, A22; Apr. 17, 2009, A1; May 13, 2009, A24; tpm, Apr. 20, 2009; nydailynews.com, May 14, 2009; nymag.com, May 13, 2009.

65. *NYT*, Apr. 27, 2009, A16.

66. *NYT*, Apr. 9, 2009, A22; Apr. 15, 2009, A20; Apr. 18, 2009, A17; Apr. 27, 2009, A16; May 10, 2009, A13; Nov. 10, 2009, A1.

67. *NYT*, Apr. 27, 2009, A17; May 10, 2009, A13; May 13, 2009, A24; May 18, 2009, A17; nomblog.com, Aug. 19, 2009.

68. *NYT*, Apr. 17, 2009, A1, A28; May 10, 2009, A13; May 12, 2009, A1; hp, Apr. 16, 2009.

69. *NYT*, May 10, 2009, A13; May 18, 2009, A17; June 4, 2009, A28; *Newsday*, June 4, 2009, A28.

70. *NYT*, June 9, 2009, A1; June 10, 2009, A23; June 13, 2009, A1; June 14, 2009, A1.

71. *NYT*, June 16, 2009, A1; June 29, 2009, A15; July 11, 2009, A13.

72. andrewgelman.com, June 11, 2009; seattlepi.com, Apr. 15, 2009; komonews.com, May 18, 2009; katu.com, May 18, 2009.

73. *LVRJ*, March 28, 2009, 1B; Apr. 15, 2009, 1A; Apr. 22, 2009, 1A; May 16, 2009, 1B; May 26, 2009, 1A; May 31, 2009, 1A; June 1, 2009, 1A; *DP*, Feb. 17, 2009, B4; Apr. 10, 2009, B1.

74. *MJS*, July 2, 2009, B1.

75. *WP*, Apr. 9, 2009, B1; Apr. 12, 2009, C1; Apr. 13, 2009, B1; wp, May 5, 2009.

76. *WP*, May 5, 2009, B1; sroblog.com, May 17, 2009; wcp, Sept. 10, 2009.

77. *DFP*, June 7, 2009, 8; examiner.com, June 26, 2009.

78. time.com, Apr. 4, 2009; rd, Apr. 7, 2009; *LAT*, May 7, 2009, A1; *WP*, May 27, 2009, A1; sw, June 2, 2009.

79. *LAT*, May 7, 2009, A1.

80. sw, Aug. 12, 2009; mercurynews.com, May 29, 2009; May 31, 2009; *LAT*, Dec. 1, 2009, A4; *NYT*, July 27, 2009, A11.

81. sw, Aug. 12, 2009; advocate.com, June 3, 2009; sa, Sept. 9, 2009.
82. *SJMN*, May 30, 2009, 1; sfgate.com, July 14, 2009; sw, Aug. 12, 2009.
83. pwn, Apr. 8, 2009; Cole, 12; co, Apr. 30, 2009; *WP*, Apr. 8, 2009, A1; *BG*, Apr. 17, 2009, A15; herald-mail.com, May 10, 2009; ola, June 2, 2009.
84. cbsnews.com, May 26, 2009; *NYT*, Apr. 12, 2009, WK1; *WP*, May 5, 2009, B1.
85. pew, June 4, 2009.
86. pew, June 4, 2009; fn, Apr. 20, 2009; mm, Apr. 22, 2009.
87. cp, May 3, 2009; latimesblogs.com, Sept. 18, 2009.
88. hp, Apr. 23, 2009; *WP*, May 17, 2009, 1; *LAT*, May 16, 2009, A1; July 11, 2009, A3; wm, May 6, 2009; *NYT*, July 16, 2009, A20.
89. *NYT*, Apr. 19, 2009, WK10; abcnews.go.com, Apr. 22, 2009; edgechicago.com, Apr. 28, 2009; slate.com, May 20, 2009.
90. *NYT*, Apr. 29, 2009, A15.
91. usnews.com, Apr. 7, 2009.
92. politico.com, Apr. 26, 2009; sltrib.com, May 2, 2009; hp, June 1, 2009; July 2, 2009; *NYT*, Apr. 29, 2009, A15; abcnews.go.com, Apr. 19, 2009; Apr. 22, 2009; abc4.com, Feb. 10, 2009.
93. abcnews.go.com, Apr. 22, 2009; politico.com, Apr. 26, 2009; *NYT*, Apr. 29, 2009, A15; gallup.com, May 27, 2009.
94. *CT*, May 26, 2011, C19; spi, Oct. 7, 2009.
95. sltrib.com, May 2, 2009; abcnews.go.com, May 14, 2009.
96. hp, Jan. 23, 2009; Oct. 27, 2009; *NYT*, March 24, 2009, A24; June 24, 2009, A22; *WP*, May 17, 2009, A1; politico.com, July 14, 2009.
97. latb, May 26, 2009.
98. topics.time.com, June 4, 2009.
99. advocate.com, May 26, 2009; *WP*, June 14, 2010, A1; Talbot, 44.
100. *SFC*, Aug. 9, 2009, C1.
101. *NYT*, May 28, 2009, A1; Oct. 27, 2009, A14; Talbot, 47; writ.news.findlaw.com, May 29, 2009; slate.com, May 29, 2009; kns, June 27, 2010.
102. scotusblog.com, May 27, 2009; topics.time.com, June 4, 2009; slate.com, Jan. 8, 2010; Talbot, 44, 51.
103. *LAT*, June 18, 2009, A4; *SFC*, June 13, 2009, B4.
104. lawdork.net, Aug. 19, 2009; slate.com, Jan. 8, 2010.
105. *BG*, March 3, 2009, B1; July 7, 2009, B1; July 9, 2009, B1; blogs.abcnews.com, June 12, 2009; sovo.com, July 17, 2009; baywindows.com, July 21, 2009.
106. wb, Nov. 2, 2008; detnews.com, June 3, 2009.
107. npr.org, June 29, 2009.
108. tch, May 27, 2009; cnsnews.com, March 16, 2009; npr.com, June 29, 2009; salon.com, June 19, 2009; newsweek.com, Oct. 26, 2009; rcp, June 9, 2009; *WCT*, June 24, 2009; csm, June 17, 2009.
109. seattletimes.nwsource.com, Aug. 27, 2009.
110. *NYT*, May 7, 2009, A1; salon.com, Apr. 7, 2009; detnews.com, June 3, 2009; nymag.com, May 19, 2009.
111. *NYT*, May 7, 2009, A1; May 24, 2009, WK8; nymag.com, May 19, 2009; rcp, June 9, 2009; detnews.com, June 3, 2009; *WP*, May 2, 2009, A15; rcp, June 9, 2009.
112. politicalticker.blogs.cnn.com, June 17, 2009; americablog.com, June 14, 2009; *LAT*, June 17, 2009, A1.
113. transcripts.cnn.com, June 12, 2009; slog.thestranger.com, June 12, 2009; latimesblogs.latimes.com, June 14, 2009; otm, June 15, 2009.
114. wct, June 24, 2009; treehugger.com, June 26, 2009; *NYT*, June 28, 2009, A1.
115. *NYT*, June 30, 2009, A1; *LAT*, June 30, 2009, A10; npr.org, June 30, 2009.
116. 365gay.com, June 29, 2009.

117. *NYT*, May 7, 2009, A1; csm, May 6, 2009; msnbc.msn.com, June 2, 2009; towleroad.com, June 4, 2009.

118. *NYT*, June 28, 2009, A1; npr.org, June 29, 2009.

Chapter 7

1. wallstrip.cbsnews.com, June 18, 2009.

2. *NYT*, Apr. 9, 2009, A22; politico.com, Apr. 8, 2009.

3. *DMR*, Sept. 21, 2009, 1A; christiantelegraph.com, July 15, 2009.

4. timesrepublican.com, Apr. 28, 2009; ii, Apr. 30, 2009; rcp, June 4, 2009; *DMR*, Sept. 21, 2009, 1A.

5. ii, Apr. 4, 2009; politico.com, Apr. 26, 2009; whotv.com, Apr. 13, 2009; ct, Apr. 22, 2009; kribnews.com, Apr. 24, 2009; dmr.com, Apr. 27, 2009.

6. stormlakepilottribune, July 27, 2009; otm, Aug. 17, 2009.

7. advocate.com, Aug. 16, 2009; ii, Aug. 13, 2009; *DMR*, Aug. 23, 2009, A1; heartlandconnection.com, Apr. 24, 2009; lgbtqnation.com, Aug. 15, 2009.

8. *DMR*, Aug. 28, 2009, 4; Sept. 2, 2009, 3; Sept. 3, 2009, 1; ii, Aug. 21, 2009; au, Aug. 31, 2009.

9. *PPH*, Apr. 22, 2009, A1; May 15, 2009, A1; au, July 31, 2009; *NYT*, Sept. 3, 2009, A16.

10. *PPH*, June 18, 2009, A1; Sept. 11, 2009, B1; Sept. 16, 2009, A10; Sept. 24, 2009, B1; Oct. 10, 2009, A1; Oct. 17, 2009, A1; Oct. 27, 2009, B1; hp, July 14, 2009; sunjournal.com, Sept. 12, 2009.

11. *PPH*, June 21, 2009, A5; Oct. 6, 2009, A1; Nov. 3, 2009, A1; Nov. 4, 2009, A1; Dec. 17, 2009, A1; politico.com, Nov. 3, 2009; salon.com, Nov. 4, 2009.

12. salon.com, Nov. 4, 2009; kjonline.com, Oct. 19, 2009; *PPH*, Oct. 16, 2009, A1; Oct. 17, 2009, A1; Oct. 26, 2009, B1; hp, Nov. 4, 2009; politico.com, Nov. 3, 2009.

13. 538, Oct. 1, 2009; *NYT*, Nov. 2, 2009, A18; *PPH*, Sept. 19, 2009, B1; Oct. 27, 2009, A1.

14. *PPH*, Nov. 4, 2009, A1; Nov. 5, 2009, A1; Nov. 8, 2009, A10; *NYT*, Nov. 5, 2009, A25.

15. *NYT*, Nov. 5, 2009, A25; *LAT*, Nov. 5, 2009, A34.

16. downeast.com, Nov. 6, 2009; *PPH*, Nov. 5, 2009, A12; prawfsblaug.blogs.com, Nov. 6, 2009; examiner.com, Dec. 21, 2009.

17. heraldnet.com, May 5, 2009; spi, May 5, 2009; *LAT*, June 8, 2009, A11; thenewstribune.com, May 18, 2009; spi, Oct. 13, 2009.

18. spi, Sept. 10, 2009; Oct. 16, 2009; Oct. 19, 2009; Oct. 20, 2009.

19. spi, May 5, 2009; 538, Apr. 3, 2009.

20. politicsandsociety.usc.edu, Nov. 13, 2009; *LAT*, Dec. 1, 2009, A4; *NYT*, Dec. 3, 2009, A40; afer.org, Nov. 4, 2009.

21. *NYT*, Nov. 2, 2009, A20; Nov. 5, 2009, A25; Nov. 9, 2009, A18; Dec. 3, 2009, A1; catholicexchange.com, Oct. 23, 2009.

22. *NYT*, Nov. 6, 2009, A24; Nov. 11, 2009, A25; Dec. 3, 2009, A1; Dec. 4, 2009, A28.

23. *NYT*, Dec. 3, 2009, A1, A42; Dec. 6, 2009, WK2; du, Apr. 20, 2009.

24. *NYT*, Nov. 5, 2009, A25; Jan. 5, 2010, A16; Jan. 7, 2010, A30; Jan. 8, 2010, A18; otm, Oct. 8, 2009; nj.com, Oct. 25, 2009; nowpublic.com, Oct. 10, 2009.

25. *NYT*, Nov. 24, 2009, A29; blog.nj.com, Nov. 5, 2009.

26. *NYT*, Nov. 24, 2009, A29; Dec. 8, 2009, A30; Jan. 5, 2010, A16; tpm, Nov. 30, 2009; nj.com, Nov. 8, 2009.

27. blog.nj.com, Nov. 30, 2009; tpm, Nov. 30, 2009; *NYT*, Jan. 8, 2010, A18; nj.com, Dec. 9, 2009.

28. *NYT*, Dec. 3, 2009, A40; Jan. 8, 2010, A18; nj.com, Dec. 8, 2009; nbcny.com, March 17, 2010; queerty.com, July 26, 2010; southbrunswick.patch.com, Nov. 23, 2011.

29. *NYT*, Nov. 13, 2009, A17; Dec. 3, 2009, A40; *WP*, Dec. 16, 2009, A1.

30. *WP*, Nov. 18, 2009, B3; Jan. 15, 2010, B2; Feb. 5, 2010, B2; March 4, 2010, A4.

31. *NHUL*, Nov. 5, 2009, 1; Jan. 5, 2010, 1; Jan. 15, 2010, 3; March 8, 2010, 1; *WCT*, Jan. 5, 2010.
32. *NHUL*, Feb. 18, 2010, 1; Apr. 20, 2010, 9; eagletribune.com, Apr. 4, 2010.
33. cm, Apr. 17, 2010.
34. *CM*, Jan. 2, 2011, 1; boston.com, Jan. 13, 2011; *BG*, Feb. 18, 2011, B1; kns.com, Jan. 31, 2011; *NHUL*, Jan. 22, 2011, 3.
35. *BG*, Feb. 18, 2011, A1; nt, Sept. 15, 2011; csm, Sept. 18, 2011.
36. therevealer.org, March 8, 2011; *DMR*, Apr. 10, 2009, 1A; Jan. 13, 2010, A6; Feb. 11, 2010, B6; lifesite.net, Jan. 13, 2010.
37. *DMR*, Apr. 9, 2010, A11; May 27, 2010, A1; June 3, 2010, A1; June 7, 2010, A5.
38. *DMR*, Jan. 13, 2010, B1; Feb. 11, 2010, B6; Apr. 8, 2010, B1; thefreelibrary.com, Feb. 3, 2010.
39. *DMR*, March 10, 2010, B3; Apr. 8, 2010, B1; May 27, 2010, A1.
40. *DMR*, May 21, 2010, A7; May 27, 2010, A1.
41. dmr, June 6, 2010; *DMR*, June 9, 2010, A11; June 10, 2010, A1; mi, July 9, 2010.
42. *DMR*, Oct. 4, 2010, A1.
43. *DMR*, Oct. 4, 2010, A1; Nov. 4, 2010, A7; dmr, Oct. 31, 2010.
44. qctimes.com, Nov. 4, 2009; *DMR*, Sept. 28, 2010, B2; Oct. 1, 2010, B1; Oct. 11, 2010, A1; Oct. 29, 2010, B1; tp, Aug. 27, 2010; prospect.org, Sept. 19, 2011; Bartrum, 1048–49.
45. *DMR*, Oct. 7, 2010; Oct. 20, 2010, B5; dmr, Oct. 25, 2010.
46. stateline.org, Sept. 10, 2010; prospect.org, Sept. 19, 2011.
47. *DMR*, Oct. 4, 2010, A1; Oct. 19, 2010, B1.
48. *DMR*, Sept. 8, 2010, B2; Sept. 28, 2010, B2; Oct. 20, 2010, B1.
49. *DMR*, Oct. 4, 2010, A1; ii, Nov. 18, 2010; Bartrum, 1048; prospect.org, Sept. 19, 2011.
50. *DMR*, Oct. 4, 2010, A1; Nov. 4, 2010, A7.
51. *DMR*, Nov. 4, 2010, A1, A7; gayapolis.com, Nov. 14, 2010; Bartrum, 1049–50.
52. *DMR*, Oct. 4, 2010, A1; Nov. 3, 2010, A1; Nov. 4, 2010, A7; hp, Nov. 5, 2010.
53. wb, Feb. 2, 2011; scj, Feb. 2, 2011.
54. *DMR*, Sept. 17, 2011, A6; globegazette.com, Oct. 17, 2011; hp, Nov. 9, 2011.
55. ames.patch.com, Jan. 18, 2012; 538, June 29, 2011; tp, Nov. 25, 2011; thonline.com, Jan. 8, 2012.
56. startribune.com, June 4, 2009; *LAT*, March 3, 2011, A1.
57. *DMR*, May 3, 2009, 1; caucuses.desmoinesregister.com, June 26, 2011; otb, March 12, 2011.
58. politico.com, Apr. 26, 2009; *DMR*, May 3, 2009, 1; ct, Apr. 22, 2009; *LAT*, March 3, 2011, A1; foxnews.com, Nov. 24, 2011; wb, Jan. 8, 2012.
59. boston.com, Aug. 30, 2011; tpm, Jan. 2, 2012; nyt, Dec. 28, 2011; newyorker.com, Dec. 16, 2011.
60. nyt, Dec. 28, 2011; otm, Dec. 16, 2011; buzzfeed.com, Jan. 15, 2012; hp, Jan. 14, 2012; wp, Jan. 20, 2012, A5.

Chapter 8

1. *NYT*, Nov. 8, 2009, WK7; Dec. 3, 2009, A40; Dec. 12, 2009, A11; *HC*, Dec. 6, 2009, A1; afj.org.
2. gallup.com, May 25, 2010; nbcnewyork.com, July 9, 2010; france24.com, July 28, 2010.
3. lifesitenews.com, July 30, 2010; hp, Aug. 12, 2010.
4. *NYT*, Jan. 31, 2010, WK1; Feb. 2, 2010, A26; wi, March 24, 2010; tdb, July 27, 2009.
5. humanevents.com, July 28, 2010; rcp, June 9, 2009; tdb, July 27, 2010; gallup.com, May 27, 2009.
6. tdb, Feb. 16, 2010; humanevents.com, July 28, 2010; *NYT*, Feb. 1, 2010, A1; foxnews.com, Feb. 2, 2010.
7. *NYT*, May 28, 2010, A1; politico.com, Sept. 21, 2010.

8. cbsnews.com, Aug. 5, 2010; slate.com, Sept. 4, 2010.

9. hp, Sept. 24, 2010; gov.exec.com, Oct. 15, 2011.

10. politico.com, Oct. 27, 2010; cnn.com, Dec. 22, 2010; wb, Jan. 24, 2011.

11. articles.sfgate.com, Aug. 16, 2009; Feb. 9, 2010.

12. *SFC*, Jan. 11, 2010, A12; Jan. 13, 2010, C1; Jan. 14, 2010, C1.

13. *LAT*, Jan. 13, 2010, A8; Jan. 15, 2010, A13; *SFC*, Jan. 13, 2010, C1; Jan. 16, 2010, C3; Jan. 21, 2010, C3; Jan. 29, 2010, A1; *Perry*, 704 F. Supp. 2d at 932–44.

14. *SFC*, Jan. 12, 2010, A1; Jan. 18, 2010, A1; Jan. 22, 2010, C9.

15. slate.com, Aug. 4, 2010; *SFC*, Jan 22, 2010, C9; Jan. 27, 2010, C1; Jan. 28, 2010, C3; *NYT*, March 23, 2010, A14.

16. volokh.com, Aug. 4, 2010; *Perry*, 704 F. 2d at 991–1004.

17. unitedliberty.org, Aug. 5, 2010.

18. sfgate.com, Feb. 7, 2010; advocate.com, Sept. 29, 2010; hp, Aug. 8, 2010; slate.com, June 13, 2011; csm, June 14, 2011; *Perry v. Brown*, 2012 WL 308539 (9th Cir. Feb. 1, 2012).

19. *Massachusetts v. U.S. Dep't of Health & Human Services*, 698 F. Supp. 2d 234 (D. Mass. 2010); *Gill v. Office of Personnel Management*, 699 F. Supp. 2d 374 (D. Mass. 2010); slate.com, July 9, 2010.

20. syracuse.com, Nov. 9, 2010; *NYT*, Feb. 27, 2011, WK5; hp, Feb. 23, 2011; politico.com, Feb. 23, 2011.

21. politico.com, Feb. 23, 2011; dk, Feb. 28, 2011; npr.org, March 1, 2011; politicsdaily, Feb. 25, 2011; abcnews.com, Apr. 18, 2011; wm, Feb. 25, 2011; tdb, March 5, 2011.

22. politico.com, Feb. 23, 2011; March 1, 2011.

23. wb, March 17, 2011; cp, March 17, 2011; wp, March 18, 2011; gallup.com, May 20, 2011; americanprogress.com, June 16, 2011.

24. gcn, March 24, 2011; lgbtqnation.com, Aug. 23, 2011; talkleft.com, June 14, 2011.

25. advocate.com, June 20, 2011; July 3, 2011; *WP*, Aug. 19, 2011, A5; *SFC*, Nov. 11, 2011, A10; Jan. 5, 2012, A1.

26. wb, Jan. 6, 2011; nymag.com, Jan. 12, 2011.

27. *WP*, May 11, 2010, B1; Feb. 9, 2011, B4; csm, Feb. 24, 2010; wp, Jan. 6, 2011; blogs.cnn.com, Jan. 12, 2011; wb, Feb. 24, 2011.

28. wb, March 24, 2011; *WP*, March 9, 2011, B1.

29. theroot.com, March 4, 2011.

30. *WP*, March 7, 2011, B1; March 12, 2011, A4; cbn.com, March 14, 2011; we, March 11, 2011.

31. *WP*, March 15, 2011, A20.

32. *NYT*, June 30, 2011, A16; advocate.com, July 2, 2011; nyt, June 29, 2011; bdh, Sept. 8, 2011.

33. politico.com, Dec. 14, 2010; quinnipiac.edu, Jan. 27, 2011; *NYT*, Jan. 6, 2011, A1.

34. cnn.com, June 16, 2011; *NYT*, June 26, 2011, A1.

35. *LAT*, June 22, 2011, A15.

36. *NYT*, June 24, 2011, A20; June 25, 2011, A1.

37. wsj.com, June 27, 2011.

38. nyt, Jan. 18, 2012.

39. queerty.com, June 3, 2011; dp, Jan. 3, 2012.

40. cnn.com, June 27, 2011; politico.com, July 2, 2011.

41. *NYT*, July 3, 2011, A14; cityroom.blogs.nyt.com, Sept. 7, 2011; nyt.com, Sept. 16, 2011.

Chapter 9

1. Klarman, 364–65, 463; Persily, 9; Keck, 158.

2. Rosenberg, 387 table 13.3; *HA*, May 7, 1993, A1; *WP*, May 7, 1993, A10; Dec. 4, 1996, A1; *NYT*, May 7, 1993, A14; Dec. 4, 1996, A1; Andersen, 200–1; O'Connor and Yanus, 293 table 12.1; *PPG*, Sept. 10, 1996, A1; *LAT*, Dec. 4, 1996, A1; *BFP*, Dec. 26, 1999, 1B; Dec. 26, 2000, 1A.

3. O'Connor and Yanus, 293 table 12.1; Wilcox et al., "Saving Marriage," 58–59; Rom, 25 fig. 1.3; Rosenberg, 384 table 13.2; *BG,* Nov. 23, 2003, A1.

4. *World Magazine,* Dec. 6, 2003, 21; *Time,* Feb. 16, 2004, 56.

5. Klarman, 364–65; *NYT,* March 2, 2004, B1; March 4, 2004, A1; Pinello, 146.

6. *NYT,* March 6, 2004, A1; Feb. 6, 2005, B1; Feb. 7, 2005, B3; *SFNM,* May 22, 2004, A1.

7. Klarman, 238–39, 254, 265, 455–56; Eskridge, *Equality,* 234–35 and table E1; Wilcox et al., "Public Opinion," 226–29; *Newsweek,* June 30, 1997, 51; *Advocate,* July 23, 1996, 26.

8. *Advocate,* July 23, 1996, 26; Klarman, 310, 321.

9. Klarman, 391–92, 463–64.

10. Egan and Sherrill, "Marriage," 231; *Newsweek,* June 27, 1994, 46; Wilcox et al., "Public Opinion," 216.

11. Eskridge, *Equality,* 115–16, 121; Waaldijk; Rayside, 343–44; *CT,* Apr. 14, 2009, C1.

12. Fontana and Braman; Schacter, "Sexual Orientation," 870–71.

13. Gallagher and Bull, 202; *HA,* Sept. 18, 1998, A1; andrewgelman.com, June 11, 2009.

14. Pinello, 40–41, 44–45, 183; Eskridge, *Equality,* 232–34; *BG,* June 22, 2002, A1; blog.lib. umn.edu, Apr. 4, 2009.

15. Wilcox et al., "Saving Marriage," 60; *WSJ,* Aug. 3, 2009, A11; heritage.org, Aug. 4, 2010; ct, Apr. 22, 2009; *NYT,* Nov. 20, 2003, A29; Dec. 21, 2003, A1; Feb. 29, 2004, § 4, 13.

16. *WP,* Apr. 15, 2009, A1; wp, Apr. 7, 2009; NRO, June 18, 2009; religionnews.com, June 8, 2009.

17. Keck, 180–81; Andersen, 149; Pinello, 93–95; Schacter, "Backlash," 1218–19; Schacter, "Sexual Orientation," 878–79; americanprospect.com, Nov. 12, 2009; *TNR,* June 11, 2008, 12.

18. D'Emilio, *Sexual Politics,* 247; *NYT,* June 5, 1977, 23; *KJ&MS,* May 10, 2009.

19. Klarman, 5–6, 448–50; Friedman.

20. Rom, 22–23; Klarman, 450.

21. upi.com, Aug. 11, 2010; Klarman, 6, 309–10, 450–51.

22. *WP,* June 22, 1970, C2; *NYT,* Jan. 28, 1973, 45; Hanson, 190; Persily, 7.

23. *Public Opinion Online,* Aug. 22, 2000; *SFC,* Nov. 10, 2008, B5.

24. Smidt and Penning, 118–19; *Perry v. Schwarzenegger,* 704 F. Supp. 2d 921, 952, 985 (N.D. Cal. 2010); *SFC,* Nov. 10, 2008, B5; nydn, May 14, 2009.

25. *BFP,* Jan. 28, 1999, 1B; Egan, Persily, and Wallsten, 247.

26. *LAT,* Nov. 19, 2008, A1; time.com, Apr. 4, 2009; theatlantic.com, July 14, 2010.

27. Gerstmann, 217.

28. rd, Aug. 6, 2010; bdn, July 14, 2010; *Varnum v. Brien,* 763 N.W.2d 862, 904 (Iowa 2009).

29. Gerstmann, 218; *NYT,* Aug. 5, 2010, A26.

30. *NYT,* Oct. 27, 2009, A14.

31. Gerstmann, 219.

32. Klarman, 365–66.

33. *WSJ,* Apr. 22, 1986, 64; *NYT,* Jan. 28, 1993, A1; Feb. 1, 1993, A14; March 5, 1993, A14.

34. *Nation,* July 5, 2004, 33; *Newsweek,* May 17, 2004, 43; Pew Research Center, news release, Feb. 27, 2004; Egan, Persily, and Wallsten, 245.

35. salon.com, March 27, 2011; Wilcox et al., "Saving Marriage," 59–60.

36. *BG,* Nov. 7, 2004, D11; wi, Nov. 4, 2011.

37. Gallagher and Bull, 15–16, 239; Rom, 16; Chauncey, 45–46, 147; *NYT,* Feb. 1, 1993, A14; Klarman, 374.

38. "Austin Housing Ordinance"; wb, Nov. 2, 2008; ws, Dec. 8, 2008.

39. Andersen, 199–202; Egan and Sherrill, "Marriage," 229–30; Rimmerman, "Presidency," 274–75.

40. Klarman, 352–53, 368.

41. Ibid., 368–69.

42. *BFP,* July 25, 2000, 5A; Dec. 17, 2000, 13B; ch. 5 in this book.

43. Lucas, 250; *SFC*, Feb. 19, 2004, A2; *NYT*, Feb. 27, 2004, A24; Nov. 5, 2004, A18; *BG*, Nov. 7, 2004, B1; *Time*, Feb. 16, 2004, 56; *Newsweek*, March 1, 2004, 42; Wilcox et al., "Public Opinion," 229–30.

44. *Newsweek International*, March 1, 2004, 42.

45. *Newsweek*, March 1, 2004, 42; *SFC*, Feb. 19, 2004, A1, A2; Dec. 21, 2004, A1; *NYT*, Feb. 25, 2004, A1; Nov. 5, 2004, A18; *LAT*, March 14, 2004, A35.

46. *BG*, Nov. 7, 2004, B1; *SPI*, Nov. 14, 2004, F1; Rimmerman, "Presidency," 284.

47. *HSB*, Nov. 25, 1990, A1; Schacter, "Backlash," 1220–21; Chauncey, 122–23; John D'Emilio, "The Marriage Debate," NGLTF, box 293, folder 2.

48. *Advocate*, Nov. 30, 1993, 41; Gallagher and Bull, 214.

49. Andersen, 52–53; Pinello, 26–28; Eskridge, *Equality*, 45.

50. *NYT*, June 7, 1996, A12; Andersen, 52–53; D'Emilio, "Courts," 53; *PI*, June 30, 1996, D1.

51. Andersen, 53, 197–98, 202; John D'Emilio, "The Marriage Debate," NGLTF, box 293, folder 2; Lucas, 250; *NYT*, June 7, 1996, A12; *PI*, May 14, 1996, B2; May 29, 1996, 6; *ADN*, Oct. 18, 1998, H3, H4; 142 Cong. Rec. H7270 (July 11, 1996) (Bob Barr, R–Ga.); 142 Cong. Rec. S10100 (Sep. 10, 1996) (Trent Lott, R–Miss.).

52. *KCS*, July 17, 2004, B7; *CE*, Sept. 14, 2004, C1.

53. *HA*, Dec. 10, 1996, A12; *NYT*, June 7, 1996, A12; *WP*, May 23, 1996, A14.

54. *NYT*, June 7, 1996, A12; *WP*, June 16, 1996, C1.

55. *NYT*, June 7, 1996, A12; *WP*, June 16, 1996, C1; *HA*, Dec. 10, 1996, A12; *PI*, June 30, 1996, D1; Chauncey, 127.

56. *WP*, June 16, 1996, C1; June 13, 1996, A8; *Advocate*, July 23, 1996, 27.

57. Dick Dadey to board of directors, July 24, 1991, ESPA, file 4.10; 1993 public policy agenda, ESPA, file 1.1; Dadey to board of directors, July 29, 1993, ESPA, file 1.9; *NYT*, Feb. 2, 1993, B1.

58. Earl Plante to staff, Apr. 29, 1996, ESPA, file 1.34; Paula Ettelbrick to Dick Dadey, July 31, 1996, ESPA, file 1.35.

59. Egan and Sherrill, "Marriage," 230; Shaiko, 91; Pinello, 184–85.

60. *BG*, Nov. 19, 2003, A1; *WP*, Feb. 22, 2004, A13; Egan and Sherrill, "Marriage," 231; Keck, 157–58; Pinello, 7–8, 13, 82–84, 184–85; Chauncey, 137–38.

61. *SPI*, March 9, 2004, A1; Apr. 2, 2004, B1; *NYT*, March 5, 2004, A19; *LAT*, Apr. 21, 2004, A1; Keck, 164; O'Connor and Yanus, 303.

62. Wilcox et al., "Public Opinion," 226 table 9.2; andrewgelman.com, Jan. 22, 2009; Rosenberg, 408–9; Egan and Sherrill, "Marriage," 229–30.

63. hp, July 17, 2009; theroot.com, Jan. 25, 2011; *WB*, Jan. 3, 1997; *CE*, June 20, 2004, A1.

64. gallup.com, May 15, 2003; May 27, 2009; Egan, Persily, and Wallsten, 254; freep.com, June 7, 2009; csm, Apr. 6, 2009.

65. pewresearch.org, July 11, 2007; *WP*, June 11, 2006, C3; *LAT*, Apr. 11, 2004, A1; *BS*, Nov. 9, 2004, 15A; theledger.com, May 2, 2009.

66. *WP*, Jan. 26, 2006, T12; *PPH*, Apr. 22, 2009, A1; quinnipiac.edu, May 14, 2009.

67. *LAT*, March 21, 2004, A1; *PPH*, Apr. 22, 2009, A8; *BG*, March 14, 2004, A1; Pinello, 8, 140, 188; Chauncey, 140–41.

68. *BG*, Apr. 21, 2005, A1; Andersen, 237.

69. Cahill, "Anti–Gay Marriage Movement," 166; Wilcox et al., "Saving Marriage," 59.

70. *LAT*, Aug. 31, 1991, A27; Sept. 30, 1991, A1; Oct. 1, 1991, B1; Gallagher and Bull, 64–66, 78–79, 84.

71. Cahill, "Anti–Gay Marriage Movement," 161, 169; foxnews.com, Apr. 30, 2009; rolling-stone.com, Feb. 2, 2012.

72. Cahill, "Anti–Gay Marriage Movement," 159–60, 163.

73. news.change.org, Apr. 18, 2010.

74. Pinello, 161; *NYT*, Feb. 8, 2004, A1.

75. *SFC*, Nov. 24, 2008, B1; mi, July 9, 2010; politico.com, Apr. 26, 2009; rd, Apr. 7, 2009.

76. Rom, 16; Segura, 190.
77. *WP*, June 10, 1998, A11; *NYT*, June 29, 1998, A1; Dec. 29, 1999, A22; *LAT*, Feb. 11, 2000, A3; Cahill, "Anti–Gay Marriage Movement," 170.
78. tp, Jan. 8, 2012; *NYT*, Feb. 1, 1993, A14; Schmalz, 20; *Oregonian*, Oct. 4, 1992, D1; Nov. 1, 1992, A1; Chauncey, 51; Pinello, 103–4; Gallagher and Bull, 44, 60.

Chapter 10

1. Wald and Glover, 115, 121; Schacter, "Backlash," 1205–6; *WP*, July 24, 2006, A9.
2. Zwier, 192–204.
3. *BG*, Nov. 19, 2003, A1; Lucas, 248; Cahill, "Anti–Gay Marriage Movement," 177–78; Wald and Glover, 121.
4. *NYT*, Feb. 25, 2004, A1; *Newsweek*, Dec. 1, 2003, 34; *Economist*, Nov. 22, 2003, 29.
5. Gallagher and Bull, 68; Shorto, 38; *Nation*, July 5, 2004, 34–35; *Newsweek*, May 17, 2004, 43; *NYT*, Feb. 8, 2004, A1; *Economist*, Nov. 22, 2003, 29; Nov. 13, 2004, 28; Rozell and Das Gupta, 13; Wilcox et al., "Saving Marriage," 56.
6. *Nation*, July 5, 2004, 33; Wilcox et al., "Saving Marriage," 62, 65.
7. *CE*, Sept. 14, 2004, C1; *NYT*, Aug. 28, 2004, A10.
8. *CE*, Sept. 14, 2004, C1; *NYT*, March 3, 2004, A11; *AJC*, Nov. 4, 2004, 1D.
9. thetimesnews.com, Aug. 30, 2011.
10. *Nation*, July 5, 2004, 33; *Newsweek*, June 28, 2004, 8; quinnipiac.edu, July 17, 2008; *Economist*, Nov. 22, 2003, 30; Soper and Fetzer, 216–17, 227.
11. *WP*, Oct. 17, 2006, A1; KESQ.com, June 20, 2009.
12. *Newsweek*, Dec. 1, 2003, 34; worldmag.com, Dec. 6, 2003.
13. *SPI*, March 9, 2004, A1; Aug. 5, 2004, A11; npr.org, Dec. 26, 2003; worldmag.com, Dec. 6, 2003; *Nation*, March 15, 2004, 14; *Time*, Feb. 16, 2004, 56.
14. *BG*, Nov. 7, 2004, B1; *PPG*, Nov. 6, 2004, A16.
15. *NYT*, March 4, 2004, A22, A29; March 10, 2004, A24; npr.org, Dec. 26, 2003; *CPD*, Nov. 16, 2004, B9; Sept. 20, 2004, A1; Lucas, 262–63.
16. *WP*, Oct. 2, 2006, B1.
17. Eskridge, *Equality*, 10; Cahill, "Anti–Gay Marriage Movement," 168–169.
18. Klarman, 365–66.
19. Ibid., 398–99, 405–6, 407, 419.
20. Ibid., 423.
21. Ibid., 420.
22. Ibid., 398–99, 426–28.
23. Ibid., 421–42.
24. *Advocate*, Aug. 23, 1994, 20–21; *PPH*, Nov. 8, 2009, A10.
25. *Oregonian*, Nov. 3, 2004, A1; *KCS*, Aug. 4, 2004, A1; Aug. 5, 2004, B1; *PPH*, Nov. 5, 2009, A7.
26. Rayside, 354; Smith, "Politics of Same-Sex Marriage," 227.
27. Paula Ettelbrick to public policy committee, June 12, 1995, ESPA, file 2.7; *NYT*, July 27, 1995, B1.
28. *DMR*, Feb. 1, 1996, A1; *BG*, Nov. 19, 2003, B7; Nov. 20, 2003, B11; Nov. 22, 2003, B1; Nov. 25, 2003, B5.
29. Pinello, 74, 77; *SFC*, Feb. 22, 2004, A1; Apr. 5, 2004, A1.
30. Pinello, 75–78; *SFC*, Feb. 15, 2004, A1.
31. *SFC*, Feb. 13, 2004, A1; Feb. 14, 2004, A1; Feb. 20, 2004, A1; Feb. 22, 2004, A1; March 14, 2004, B1.
32. *SFC*, Feb. 22, 2004, A1; Feb. 29, 2004, A1; Aug. 13, 2004, A15; *Newsweek*, Aug. 2, 2004, 48.
33. Pinello, 78; *LAT*, May 16, 2008, A19.
34. Klarman, 414.

35. *NYT*, Feb. 29, 2004, A30; March 1, 2004, B4; March 4, 2004, B6; March 10, 2004, B5; Pinello, 145.

36. *NYT*, March 1, 2004, B4; Feb. 7, 2005, B3.

37. *SPI*, March 9, 2004, A1; March 8, 2004, A1.

38. *SPI*, March 4, 2004, A11; March 8, 2004, A1.

39. *SFC*, Feb. 22, 2004, A1; March 27, 2004, A1; *Time*, Feb. 16, 2004, 56; *Newsweek*, March 1, 2004, 42; *NYT*, Feb. 27, 2004, A24; *AT*, Feb. 25, 2004, A1.

40. *NYT*, Nov. 7, 2004, D5; Nov. 10, 2004, A20; *LAT*, Nov. 6, 2004, E1; *SFC*, Nov. 8, 2004, B6; *DMN*, Nov. 16, 2004, 11A.

Chapter 11

1. wt, Jan. 23, 2012; crookstontimes.com, Jan. 24, 2012.

2. tpm, June 2, 2011; otm, Nov. 12, 2011; ci, Jan. 5, 2012; 538, June 29, 2011.

3. ai, Nov. 6, 2011; charlotteobserver.com, Sept. 13, 2011.

4. politico.com, Sept. 13, 2011; 538, June 29, 2011; tp, Dec. 9, 2011; otm, Nov. 5, 2011; charlotteobserver.com, Jan. 31, 2012.

5. bh, July 4, 2011; nt, Sept. 15, 2011; thedartmouth.com, Nov. 4, 2011; cm, Jan. 29, 2012.

6. 538, June 29, 2011; nt, Dec. 28, 2011; hp, Jan. 5, 2012; kns, Nov. 3, 2011.

7. AP, Feb. 2, 2012; seattletimes.com, Feb. 2, 2012; Feb. 14, 2012; columbian.com, Jan. 7, 2012.

8. nj.com, Jan. 8, 2012, Jan. 19, 2012; kns, Nov. 3, 2011; lgbtqnation.com, Jan. 13, 2012; dailyrecord.com, Feb. 4, 2012; hp, Feb. 3, 2012; articles.philly.com, Feb. 10, 2012; *NYT*, Feb. 17, 2012, A1; bh, Feb. 17, 2012.

9. yahoo.com, Nov. 28, 2011; bs, Nov. 1, 2011; Jan. 1, 2012; Jan. 4, 2012; Feb. 7, 2012; nyt, Oct. 31, 2011; Feb. 16, 2012; wp, Jan. 17, 2012; Jan. 31, 2012; gazette.net, Jan. 6, 2012.

10. ct, Feb. 16, 2012.

11. scrippsnews.com, Nov. 23, 2011; sfgate.com, Jan. 17, 2012; advocate.com, Feb. 24, 2012.

12. 538, June 29, 2011.

13. 538, Apr. 3, 2009; andrewgelman.com, June 11, 2009; advocate.com, Dec. 23, 2011; otm, Dec. 11, 2011.

14. lifesitenews.com, June 21, 2011; articles.cnn.com, June 21, 2011; *NYT*, June 19, 2011, A1; hp, Nov. 16, 2011.

15. newyorker.com, Dec. 19, 2011; articles.cnn.com, June 21, 2011; thestranger.com, Dec. 20, 2011.

16. forbes.com, Apr. 29, 2009; onlineathens, June 2, 2009; *NYT*, June 19, 2003, A24; examiner.com, Aug. 12, 2010; *CDT*, Sept. 18, 2011, E9; gallup.com, May 11, 2011; abcnews.go.com, March 18, 2011; otm, Jan. 26, 2011.

17. 538, Aug. 12, 2010; Apr. 20, 2011; June 29, 2011; hp, March 5, 2011; slate.com, May 20, 2009; abcnews.go.com, March 18, 2011.

18. forbes.com, Apr. 29, 2009; *NYT*, June 28, 2009, A1; Chauncey, 34, 47–48; Eskridge, *Equality*, 115–17; andrewgelman.com, June 11, 2009.

19. Pinello, 18; *WP*, Oct. 14, 1987, A1; Stephen Endean to Frank Scheuern, March 17, 1982, HRC, box 5, folder 47.

20. wsj.com, May 5, 2009; *LAT*, Apr. 11, 2004, A1; forbes.com, Apr. 29, 2009; ii, May 29, 2009; Chauncey, 151.

21. Jeffries, 521; Murdoch and Price, 273; *BG*, Nov. 19, 1987, B33.

22. Chauncey, 48; freep.com, June 7, 2009.

23. Wilcox et al., "Public Opinion," 237; wsj.com, May 5, 2009.

24. cp, Jan. 7, 2010; *SFC*, Jan. 13, 2010, C1; slate.com, Jan. 8, 2010.

25. *SFC*, Jan. 14, 2010, C1; metroweekly.com, June 16, 2011; *Perry v. Brown*, 2012 WL 308539 (9th Cir. Feb. 1, 2012).

26. msnbc.msn.com, March 6, 2011; *NYT*, Dec. 3, 2009, A41; *BFP*, March 17, 2000, 1A; Rom, 19.

27. *BG*, Feb. 15, 2004, B6.
28. Linda Hersey, "Legislator's Story a Key Moment for Gay Marriage," May 12, 2009; pressherald.com, May 5, 2009; *PPH*, May 6, 2009, A1.
29. Egan, Persily, and Wallsten, 247; americanprogress.org, June 16, 2011; gallup.com, May 20, 2011.
30. thesocietypages.org, Nov. 5, 2009; news.columbia.edu, July 28, 2009.
31. publicreligion.org, Aug. 29, 2011; *CT*, May 26, 2011, C19.
32. Wilcox et al., "Public Opinion," 237; cnn.com, May 4, 2009.
33. perezhilton.com.
34. *NYT*, Apr. 4, 2010, AR1; Nov. 15, 2009, WK1; Sept. 21, 2008, ST2; Talbot, 42.
35. Haider-Markel and Joslyn, 234.
36. Talbot, 42.
37. st, June 27, 2009; Egan and Sherrill, "Marriage," 231.
38. andrewgelman.com, June 11, 2009.
39. Keck, 159–60; Pinello, 156; Gerstmann, 218; Eskridge, *Equality*, 118; articles.cnn.com, June 28, 2009; voices.washingtonpost.com, June 28, 2010; *LAT*, May 16, 2008, A1.
40. Gallagher and Bull, 246; *CE*, Sept. 30, 2004, D1; *CE*, Oct. 24, 2004, E2; nyt, June 30, 2010; ola, June 2, 2009; *BS*, Nov. 29, 2007, B1; timesunion.com, June 18, 2011.
41. ola, June 1, 2009.
42. ola, June 2, 2009; spi, Sept. 15, 2009; Oct. 6, 2009; *LVRJ*, May 21, 2009, 1B; *BFP*, March 18, 2009, 1A; theatlantic, Jan. 19, 2012; *NYT*, Feb. 6, 2012, B1.
43. abovethelaw.com, Apr. 25, 2011.
44. 538, Apr. 3, 2009; Oct. 1, 2009; June 29, 2011.
45. Egan and Persily.
46. politicsdaily.com, March 5, 2011; lvs, July 4, 2011; politico.com, Dec. 9, 2009.
47. Klarman, 419.
48. *AJC*, Aug. 12, 1993, A12; ct, May 26, 2011.
49. bloomberg.com, June 30, 2011.
50. volokh.com, Jan. 4, 2011; hp, Nov. 28, 2011; *Perry v. Brown*, 2012 WL 308539 (9th Cir. Feb. 1, 2012); sfgate.com, Feb. 23, 2012.
51. *NYT*, Oct. 29, 2006, § 4, 3.
52. *NYT*, Apr. 12, 2009, WK1; Oct. 27, 2009, A14; *WSJ*, Aug. 3, 2009, A11; Ginsburg, 1206; *Washington v. Glucksberg*, 521 U.S. 702 (1997).
53. prawfsblawg.blog, Oct. 29, 2009; *Lawrence v. Texas*, 539 U.S. 558, 605 (2003) (Thomas, J., dissenting).
54. uncpressblog.com, Nov. 8, 2010.
55. ct, May 26, 2011; cm, Sept. 18, 2011.
56. *Roper v. Simmons*, 543 U.S. 551 (2005); *Lawrence v. Texas*, 539 U.S. 558 (2003); *Atkins v. Virginia*, 536 U.S. 304 (2002); *Graham v. Florida*, 130 S. Ct. 2011 (2010).
57. cbsnews.com, Apr. 9, 2009; slate.com, Jan. 8, 2010; aei.org, Apr. 13, 2009; wbur.org, July 16, 2010.
58. *Beller v. Middendorf*, 632 F.2d 788, 810 (9th Cir. 1980); Murdoch and Price, 210–11; latimes.com, Feb. 8, 2012; guardian.co.uk, Feb. 8, 2012.
59. voanews, Nov. 14, 2009; news.bbc.co.uk, Apr. 2, 2009; wikipedia.org; sdgln.com, Dec. 24, 2011.
60. Bickel, 99, 173–74; *Hernandez v. Robles*, 855 N.E.2d 1, 12 (N.Y. 2006).
61. *LAT*, Sept. 7, 2005, A1; *BFP*, March 19, 2000, 1A.
62. *Legal Affairs*, May/June 2004, 30; *In re Marriage Cases*, 183 P.3d 384, 399 (Cal. 2008); *Varnum v. Brien*, 763 N.W.2d 862, 877 (Iowa 2009); *Andersen v. King County*, 138 P.3d 963, 1040 (Wash. 2006); *Hernandez v. Robles*, 855 N.E.2d 1, 34 (N.Y. 2006) (Kaye, C.J., dissenting); roomfordebate.blogs.nytimes, Apr. 3, 2009.
63. forbes.com, Apr. 29, 2009.
64. Klarman, 453–54.

Conclusion

1. *CT*, Apr. 14, 2009, 1A; Waaldijk, 440–41; Eskridge, *Equality*, 155–56; Cole, 16; Sunstein, "Foreword," 97; Eskridge, "Pluralism," 1324–27; Rosen, "Immodest Proposal"; Rosen, "Prop 8."
2. Keck, 159, 181; Schacter, "Sexual Orientation."
3. *HA*, Dec. 11, 1999, A1; May 8, 1993, A2; *BFP*, Apr. 20, 2000, 1A; *OWH*, Oct. 25, 2000, 14.
4. Schacter, "Backlash," 1220; Keck, 158; Andersen, 179, 197; Chauncey, 126; volokh.com, May 25, 2009; Gash and Gonzales, 64–65, 77; Murakami, 33; Luks and Salamone, 81; Persily, 10–12; Klarman, 464.
5. Klarman, 167.
6. Pinello, 183–85, 187, 193; Keck, 157–58; Eskridge, *Equality*, 45.
7. Pinello, 82–84, 139–40.
8. Chauncey, 125; Keck, 158; Andersen, 53–54, 237; Eskridge, *Equality*, 45; *BG*, Nov. 23, 2003, A1.
9. Pinello, 190.
10. Klarman, 344–63; Gash and Gonzales, 63–64; Powe, 362–63.
11. Keck, 163–64; Andersen, 232; advocate.com, June 3, 2009; gnb, Apr. 26, 2009.
12. Pinello, 79–80, 92, 105; *TNR*, June 11, 2008, 12; tch, May 27, 2009.
13. *HA*, Dec. 10, 1996, A12; tch, May 27, 2009.
14. Keck, 159–60; hp, Sept. 3, 2009.
15. *Perry v. Schwarzenegger*, 704 F. Supp. 2d 921, 972 (N.D. Cal. 2010); *LAT*, June 17, 2008, A14.
16. Schacter, "Backlash," 1219–21; Egan and Persily; Andersen, 229; Cole, 16; Pinello, 71, 182–83; independent.co.uk, July 11, 2009; *BG*, Sept. 28, 2004, B1; Nov. 3, 2004, B8; gnb, Apr. 26, 2009.
17. Cole, 12; 538, Apr. 9, 2009; Aug. 12, 2010; June 29, 2011; *NYT*, Apr. 12, 2009, WK1.
18. Keck, 159, 170–71; Andersen, 237, 239; Rosenberg, 351–52, 406–7; *HA*, Dec. 10, 1996, A12.
19. *NYT*, Nov. 6, 2004, A15; Nov. 30, 2004, A20; *BG*, Dec. 5, 2003, A1; Pinello, 182; Egan, Persily, and Wallsten, 253–54; Wilcox et al., "Public Opinion," 228; Schacter, "Backlash," 1189–90; Andersen, 236; Keck, 171, 174.
20. Wilcox et al., "Public Opinion," 228; Egan, Persily, and Wallsten, 254; Keck, 159, 170.
21. *BG*, Nov. 1, 2003, A1; Nov. 2, 2003, B3; *BG*, Dec. 11, 2003, A1; *HA*, Jan. 18, 1997, A1; Nov. 23, 1998, A8; *NYT*, July 10, 1997, B7.
22. sltrib.com, May 3, 2009; examiner.com, Nov. 16, 2009.
23. *NYT*, Sept. 11, 1996, A1; *WP*, June 13, 1996, A8; conference call minutes, Apr. 8, 1997, NGLTF, box 135, folder 2.
24. D'Emilio, "Courts," 45, 61; Rosenberg, 416–17; Cole, 12; Rosen, "Disputations"; Rimmerman, "Presidency," 275–77.
25. *PPH*, Apr. 22, 2009, A1; quinnipiac.edu, May 14, 2009.
26. Lax and Phillips, 373 table 1.
27. Notes on meeting of board of directors of GRNL, Dec. 4–5, 1976, HRC, box 5, folder 28; "What We Want: The Gay Agenda," n.d. (probably 1996), NGLTF, box 293, folder 2; Schmalz, 53; columbiamissourian.com, July 30, 2009; Wilcox et al., "Public Opinion," 226 table 9.2; andrewgelman.com, Jan. 22, 2009.
28. Klarman, 392–94.
29. *AT*, Feb. 25, 2004, A1.
30. *CG*, Apr. 8, 2009, 1C.
31. *BFP*, Oct. 13, 2000, 1A; Dec. 7, 2000, 1A.
32. *Newsweek*, May 17, 2004, 43; kgw.com, March 21, 2004; *TRG*, Apr. 21, 2004, A12; May 17, 2004, B1; *SJ*, May 3, 2004, 1C; May 20, 2004, 2A.

33. hp, July 17, 2009.

34. salon, May 27, 2009.

35. hp, Nov. 5, 2010; *ADN*, March 8, 1998, F2; March 29, 1998, A1; *BFP*, Feb. 11, 2000, 6B.

36. Keck, 176, 182–83; Olson, 53.

37. Egan and Sherrill, "Marriage," 229; *BG*, Nov. 23, 2003, A1; Chauncey, 124.

38. Keck, 176.

39. *NYT*, July 27, 1995, B1; Lavi S. Soloway and Dana Gordon to ESPA, Aug. 2, 1995, ESPA, file 1.39.

40. Egan and Sherrill, "Marriage," 229; Chauncey, 129–30; Andersen, 214–15; *NYT*, June 26, 2002, B5; Oct. 26, 2006, B1; *WP*, Apr. 15, 2009, A1; *BG*, Nov. 23, 2003, A1; *DMR*, May 30, 2010, B1; Green, "Growing Power"; Green, "'They Won't Know.'"

41. ct, Apr. 14, 2009; trib.com, Sept. 16, 2010; Anderson, 187; Keck, 178; Lambda Legal, *A Historic Victory* (2000); *LAT*, June 11, 2008, B3.

42. Talbot, 40; Cole, 16; baywindows.com, July 23, 2009.

43. *Strauss v. Horton*, 207 P.3d 48, 60 (Cal. 2009); baywindows.com, July 23, 2009; Talbot, 50.

44. Andersen, 239; Klarman, 351–52, 460–61.

45. *WP*, Nov. 14, 2004, B4; *BG*, Dec. 13, 2004, A1; slate.com, Jan. 8, 2010; Andersen, 178; Pinello, 25–26.

46. Chauncey, 166; Cain, 287; *SPI*, March 7, 2005, B1.

47. sfgate.com, Dec. 16, 2009; politico.com, Dec. 9, 2009; st, June 27, 2009; advocate.com, July 27, 2009; abcnews.go.com, Dec. 16, 2009; theatlantic.com, Nov. 4, 2009.

48. Eskridge, *Equality*, 118–19, 157; Wilcox et al., "Public Opinion," 228; forbes.com, Apr. 29, 2009; abcnews.go.com, Dec. 16, 2009; *BG*, Feb. 15, 2004, D1; *BFP*, Feb. 6, 2009, A1; ct, Apr. 14, 2009.

49. Jeffries, 352, 413–14.

50. NRO, Dec. 9, 2009; 538, Apr. 9, 2009; Persily, 8–9.

51. andrewgelman.com, June 11, 2009.

BIBLIOGRAPHY

Archival Collections

American Civil Liberties Union Records, Princeton University, Mudd Manuscript Library, Princeton, New Jersey.

Empire State Pride Agenda Records, Collection #7630, Human Sexuality Collection, Division of Rare and Manuscript Collections, Cornell University Library, Ithaca, New York.

Frank Kameny Papers, Library of Congress, Washington, DC.

Human Rights Campaign Records, Collection #7712, Human Sexuality Collection, Division of Rare and Manuscript Collections, Cornell University Library, Ithaca, New York.

Mattachine Society, Inc. of New York Records, New York Public Library, Humanities and Social Sciences Library, Manuscripts and Archives Division.

National Gay and Lesbian Task Force Records, Collection #7301, Human Sexuality Collection, Division of Rare and Manuscript Collections, Cornell University Library, Ithaca, New York.

Scholarly Books, Articles, and Frequently Cited Archival Documents

AEI Studies in Public Opinion. "Attitudes About Homosexuality and Gay Marriage." Compiled by Karlyn Bowman and Adam Foster. June 3, 2008.

Altman, Dennis. *Homosexual: Oppression and Liberation*. New York: New York University Press, 1971.

Amestoy, Jeffrey L. "Foreword: State Constitutional Law Lecture: Pragmatic Constitutionalism—Reflections on State Constitutional Theory and Same-Sex Marriage Claims." *Rutgers Law Journal* 35 (Summer 2004): 1249–66.

Andersen, Ellen Ann. *Out of the Closets and into the Courts: Legal Opportunity Structure and Gay Rights Litigation*. Ann Arbor: University of Michigan Press, 2005.

Ansolabehere, Stephen, and Charles Stewart III. "Truth in Numbers: Moral Values and the Gay-Marriage Backlash Did Not Help Bush." *Boston Review*, Feb./Mar. 2005.

"Austin Housing Ordinance: First Victory over Moral Majority, Opinion by Jim Olinger, Feb. 3, 1982." HRC, box 4, folder 32.

Banner, Stuart. *The Death Penalty: An American History*. Cambridge, MA: Harvard University Press, 2002.

Bartrum, Ian. "Constitutional Rights and Judicial Independence: Lessons from Iowa." *Washington University Law Review* 88 (2011): 1047–54.

Bickel, Alexander M. *The Supreme Court and the Idea of Progress*. New York: Harper and Row, 1970.

Brewer, Paul R. "The Shifting Foundations of Public Opinion About Gay Rights." *Journal of Politics* 65 (Nov. 2003): 1208–20.

Brigham, John. "Some Thoughts on Institutional Life and 'The Rest of the Closet.'" In *The Future of Gay Rights in America*, edited by H. N. Hirsch, 95–106. New York: Routledge, 2005.

Brownworth, Victoria. "The Matrimonial Noose." *The Advocate*, Oct. 19, 1993, 80.

Burden, Barry C. "An Alternative Account of the 2004 Election." *Forum* 2 (2004): 1–10.

Busch, Andrew. *Reagan's Victory: The Presidential Election of 1980 and the Rise of the Right.* Lawrence: University Press of Kansas, 2005.

Cahill, Sean. *Same-Sex Marriage in the United States: Focus on the Facts.* Lanham, MD: Lexington Books, 2004.

———. "The Anti-Gay Marriage Movement." In *The Politics of Same-Sex Marriage*, edited by Craig R. Rimmerman and Clyde Wilcox, 155–91. Chicago: University of Chicago Press, 2007.

Cain, Patricia A. *Rainbow Rights: The Role of Lawyers and Courts in the Lesbian and Gay Civil Rights Movement.* Boulder, CO: Westview Press, 2000.

Campbell, David E., and J. Quin Monson. "The Religion Card: Gay Marriage and the 2004 Presidential Election." *Public Opinion Quarterly* 72 (Fall 2008): 399–419.

Campbell, David C., and Carin Robinson. "Religious Coalitions For and Against Gay Marriage: The Culture War Rages On." In *The Politics of Same Sex-Marriage*, edited by Craig R. Rimmerman and Clyde Wilcox, 131–54. Chicago: University of Chicago Press, 2007.

Chambers, David L. "Tales of Two Cities: AIDS and the Legal Recognition of Domestic Partnerships in San Francisco and New York." *Law and Sexuality* 2 (Summer 1992): 181–208.

Charles, Casey. *The Sharon Kowalski Case: Lesbian and Gay Rights on Trial.* Lawrence: University Press of Kansas, 2003.

Chauncey, George. *Why Marriage? The History Shaping Today's Debate over Gay Equality.* New York: Basic Books, 2004.

Cole, David. "The Same-Sex Future." *New York Review of Books*, July 2, 2009, 12–16.

Coyle, Marcia. "The First Case, 40 Years On." *National Law Journal*, Aug. 23, 2010.

D'Emilio, John. *Sexual Politics, Sexual Communities: The Making of a Homosexual Minority in the United States, 1940–1970.* Chicago: University of Chicago Press, 1998.

———. "Some Lessons from *Lawrence*." In *The Future of Gay Rights in America*, edited by H. N. Hirsch, 3–14. New York: Routledge, 2005.

———. "Will the Courts Set Us Free? Reflections on the Campaign for Same-Sex Marriage." In *The Politics of Same-Sex Marriage*, edited by Craig R. Rimmerman and Clyde Wilcox, 39–64. Chicago: University of Chicago Press, 2007.

Djupe, Paul A., Jacob R. Neiheisel, and Anand Edward Sokhey. "Clergy and Controversy: A Study of Clergy and Gay Rights in Columbus, Ohio." In *Religious Interests in Community Conflict: Beyond the Culture Wars*, edited by Paul A. Djupe and Laura R. Olson, 73–100. Waco, TX: Baylor University Press, 2007.

Donovan, Todd, Caroline Tolbert, Daniel Smith, and Janine Parry. "Did Gay Marriage Elect George W. Bush?" Paper presented at the Western Political Science Association Annual Meeting in Austin, Texas, Jan. 2005.

Duberman, Martin. *Stonewall*. New York: Penguin Group, 1993.

Egan, Patrick J., and Nathaniel Persily. "Court Decisions and Trends in Support for Same-Sex Marriage. *Polling Report*, Aug. 17, 2009.

Egan, Patrick J., Nathaniel Persily, and Kevin Wallsten. "Gay Rights." In *Public Opinion and Constitutional Controversy*, edited by Nathaniel Persily, Jack Citrin and Patrick J. Egan, 234–66. New York: Oxford University Press, 2008.

Egan, Patrick J., and Kenneth Sherrill. "California's Proposition 8: What Happened, and What Does the Future Hold?" Policy Institute of the National Gay and Lesbian Task Force, Jan. 2009.

———. "Marriage and the Shifting Priorities of a New Generation of Lesbians and Gays." *PS: Political Science and Politics* 38 (Apr. 2005): 229–32.

Epstein, Lee, and Joseph F. Kobylka. *The Supreme Court and Legal Change: Abortion and the Death Penalty.* Chapel Hill: University of North Carolina Press, 1992.

Eskridge, William N., Jr. *The Case for Same-Sex Marriage: From Sexual Liberty to Civilized Commitment.* New York: Free Press, 1996.

————. *Equality Practice: Civil Unions and the Future of Gay Rights.* New York: Routledge, 2002.

————. *Gaylaw: Challenging the Apartheid of the Closet.* Cambridge, MA: Harvard University Press, 1999.

————. "Pluralism and Distrust: How Courts Can Support Democracy by Lowering the Stakes of Politics." *Yale Law Journal* 114 (Apr. 2005): 1279–328.

Ettelbrick, Paula L. "Since When Is Marriage a Path to Liberation?" In *Lesbian and Gay Marriage: Private Commitments, Public Ceremonies,* edited by Suzanne Sherman, 20–26. Philadelphia: Temple University Press, 1992.

Feldblum, Chai. "The Selling of Proposition 8." *Gay and Lesbian Review* 16 (Jan./Feb. 2009): 34–36.

Fontana, David, and Donald Braman. "Judicial Backlash or Just Backlash? Evidence from a National Experiment." *Columbia Law Review* 112 (2012).

Friedman, Barry. *The Will of the People: How Public Opinion Has Influenced the Supreme Court and Shaped the Meaning of the Constitution.* New York: Farrar, Straus and Giroux, 2009.

Gallagher, John, and Chris Bull. *Perfect Enemies: The Religious Right, the Gay Movement, and the Politics of the 1990s.* New York: Crown Publishers, 1996.

Gallagher, Maggie. "What Marriage Is For." *Weekly Standard,* Aug. 4–11, 2003, 22–25.

Garrow, David J. *Liberty and Sexuality: The Right to Privacy and the Making of Roe v. Wade.* New York: Macmillan, 1994.

Gash, Alison, and Angelo Gonzales. "School Prayer." In *Public Opinion and Constitutional Controversy,* edited by Nathaniel Persily, Jack Citrin, and Patrick J. Egan, 62–79. New York: Oxford University Press, 2008.

Gerstmann, Evan. "Litigating Same-Sex Marriage: Might the Courts Actually Be Bastions of Rationality?" *PS: Political Science and Politics* 38 (Apr. 2005): 217–20.

Ginsburg, Ruth Bader. "Speaking in a Judicial Voice." *New York University Law Review* 67 (Dec. 1992): 1185–209.

Graham, Fred P. *The Self-Inflicted Wound.* New York: Macmillan, 1970.

Green, John C. "Ohio: The Bible and the Buckeye State." In *The Values Campaign? The Christian Right and the 2004 Elections,* edited by John C. Green, Mark J. Rozell, and Clyde Wilcox, 79–97. Washington, DC: Georgetown University Press, 2006.

Green, John C., Mark J. Rozell, and Clyde Wilcox, eds. *The Christian Right in American Politics: Marching to the Millennium.* Washington, DC: Georgetown University Press, 2003.

————. *The Values Campaign? The Christian Right and the 2004 Elections.* Washington, DC: Georgetown University Press, 2006.

Green, Joshua. "The Growing Power of the Gay Rights Movement." *Atlantic,* Dec. 14, 2010. Available online at www.theatlantic.com/politics/archive/2010/12.

————. "They Won't Know What Hit Them." *Atlantic,* Mar. 2007, 76.

Greenhouse, Linda. *Becoming Justice Blackmun: Harry Blackmun's Supreme Court Journey.* New York: Times Books, 2005.

Haider-Markel, Donald, and Mark R. Joslyn. "Attributions and the Regulation of Marriage: Considering the Parallels Between Race and Homosexuality." *PS: Political Science and Politics* 38 (Apr. 2005): 233–39.

Hanson, Peter. "Flag Burning." In *Public Opinion and Constitutional Controversy,* edited by Nathaniel Persily, Jack Citrin and Patrick J. Egan, 184–208. New York: Oxford University Press, 2008.

Herman, Didi. *The Antigay Agenda: Orthodox Vision and the Christian Right.* Chicago: University of Chicago Press, 1997.

Hillygus, D. Sunshine, and Todd G. Shields. "Moral Issues and Voter Decision Making in the 2004 Presidential Election." *PS: Political Science and Politics* 38 (Apr. 2005): 201–09.

Hull, Kathleen E. "The Political Limits of the Rights Frame: The Case of Same-Sex Marriage in Hawaii." *Sociological Perspectives* 44 (Summer 2001): 207–32.

Jackman, Simon. "Same-Sex Marriage Ballot Initiatives and Conservative Mobilization in the 2004 Election." PowerPoint presentation, Nov. 9, 2004.

Jeffries, John C., Jr. *Justice Lewis F. Powell, Jr.* New York: C. Scribner's Sons, 1994.

Keck, Thomas M. "Beyond Backlash: Assessing the Impact of Judicial Decisions on LGBT Rights." *Law and Society Review* 43 (Mar. 2009): 151–85.

Klarman, Michael J. *From Jim Crow to Civil Rights: The Supreme Court and the Struggle for Racial Equality.* New York: Oxford University Press, 2004.

Klein, Ethel D. "The Anti-Gay Backlash?" In *The Future of Gay Rights in America*, edited by H. N. Hirsch, 81–93. New York: Routledge, 2005.

Lax, Jeffrey R., and Justin H. Phillips. "Gay Rights in the States: Public Opinion and Policy Responsiveness." *American Political Science Review* 103 (Aug. 2009): 367–86.

Lewis, Gregory B. "Same-Sex Marriage and the 2004 Presidential Election." *PS: Political Science and Politics* 38 (Apr. 2005): 195–99.

Liu, Frederick, and Stephen Macedo. "The Federal Marriage Amendment and the Strange Evolution of the Conservative Case against Gay Marriage." *PS: Political Science and Politics* 38 (Apr. 2005): 211–15.

Lofton, Katie, and Donald P. Haider-Markel. "The Politics of Same-Sex Marriage Versus the Politics of Gay Civil Rights: A Comparison of Public Opinion and State Voting Patterns." In *The Politics of Same-Sex Marriage*, edited by Craig A. Rimmerman and Clyde Wilcox, 313–340. Chicago: University of Chicago Press, 2007.

Lucas, DeWayne L. "Same-Sex Marriage in the 2004 Election." In *The Politics of Same-Sex Marriage*, edited by Craig A. Rimmerman and Clyde Wilcox, 243–271. Chicago: University of Chicago Press, 2007.

Luks, Samantha, and Michael Salamone. "Abortion." In *Public Opinion and Constitutional Controversy*, edited by Nathaniel Persily, Jack Citrin and Patrick J. Egan, 80–107. New York: Oxford University Press, 2008.

Lund, Nelson, and John O. McGinnis. "*Lawrence v. Texas* and Judicial Hubris." *Michigan Law Review* 102 (June 2004): 1555–1614.

Murakami, Michael. "Desegregation." In *Public Opinion and Constitutional Controversy*, edited by Nathaniel Persily, Jack Citrin, and Patrick J. Egan, 18–40. New York: Oxford University Press, 2008.

Murdoch, Joyce, and Deb Price. *Courting Justice: Gay Men and Lesbians v. the Supreme Court.* New York: Basic Books, 2001.

National Public Radio. "Gay Marriage and Civil Unions." Dec. 26, 2003. Available online at www.greenbergresearch.com/articles/1268/861_NPR%20Poll%20-%20Gay%20Marriage%20 (Graphs).pdf.

NGTF. "A Brief Summary of Recent Achievements (1979–1982)." National Gay and Lesbian Task Force Records, Collection #7301, box 1, folder 16. Human Sexuality Collection, Division of Rare and Manuscript Collections, Cornell University Library, Ithaca, New York.

O'Connor, Karen, and Alixandra B. Yanus. "Til Death—or the Supreme Court—Do Us Part: Litigating Gay Marriage." In *The Politics of Same-Sex Marriage*, edited by Craig A. Rimmerman and Clyde Wilcox, 291–311. Chicago: University of Chicago Press, 2007.

Olson, Theodore B. "The Conservative Case for Gay Marriage." *Newsweek*, Jan. 18, 2010: 48–54.

Pascoe, Peggy. "Sex, Gender, and Same-Sex Marriage." In *Is Academic Feminism Dead?: Theory in Practice*, edited by the Social Justice Group at the Center for Advanced Feminist Studies, University of Minnesota, 86–129. New York: New York University Press, 2000.

Persily, Nathaniel. "Introduction." In *Public Opinion and Constitutional Controversy*, edited by Nathaniel Persily, Jack Citrin, and Patrick J. Egan, 3–17. New York: Oxford University Press, 2008.

Persily, Nathaniel, Jack Citrin, and Patrick J. Egan, eds. *Public Opinion and Constitutional Controversy.* New York: Oxford University Press, 2008.

Pinello, Daniel R. *America's Struggle for Same-Sex Marriage.* New York: Cambridge University Press, 2006.

Powe, Lucas A., Jr. *The Warren Court and American Politics*. Cambridge, MA: Harvard University Press, 2000.

Rayside, David. "The United States in Comparative Context." In *The Politics of Same-Sex Marriage*, edited by Craig A. Rimmerman and Clyde Wilcox, 341–64. Chicago: University of Chicago Press, 2007.

Rimmerman, Craig A. *From Identity to Politics: The Lesbian and Gay Movements in the United States*. Philadelphia: Temple University Press, 2002.

———. "The Presidency, Congress, and Same-Sex Marriage." In *The Politics of Same-Sex Marriage*, edited by Craig A. Rimmerman and Clyde Wilcox, 273–90. Chicago: University of Chicago Press, 2007.

Rimmerman, Craig A., and Clyde Wilcox, eds. *The Politics of Same-Sex Marriage*. Chicago: University of Chicago Press, 2007.

Rom, Mark Carl. "Introduction: The Politics of Same-Sex Marriage." In *The Politics of Same-Sex Marriage*, edited by Craig A. Rimmerman and Clyde Wilcox, 1–38. Chicago: University of Chicago Press, 2007.

Rosen, Jeffrey. "Disputations: Learning from Prop. 8." *New Republic*, Nov. 6, 2008. Available online at www.tnr.com/article/politics/disputations-learning-prop-8.

———. "Immodest Proposal." *New Republic*, Dec. 22, 2003, 19–21.

Rosenberg, Gerald N. *The Hollow Hope: Can Courts Bring About Social Change?* 2nd ed. Chicago: University of Chicago Press, 2008.

Rozell, Mark J., and Debasree Das Gupta. "The 'Values Vote'? Moral Issues and the 2004 Elections." In *The Values Campaign? The Christian Right and the 2004 Elections*, edited by John C. Green, Mark J. Rozell and Clyde Wilcox, 11–21. Washington, DC: Georgetown University Press, 2006.

Schacter, Jane S. "Courts and the Politics of Backlash: Marriage Equality Litigation, Then and Now." *Southern California Law Review* 82 (Sept. 2009): 1153–223.

———. "Sexual Orientation, Social Change, and the Courts." *Drake Law Review* 54 (2005–6): 861–93.

Schmalz, Jeffrey. "Gay Politics Goes Mainstream." *New York Times Magazine*, Oct. 11, 1992, 18.

Schubert, Frank, and Jeff Flint. "Passing Prop 8." *Politics (Campaigns and Elections)* 30 (Feb. 2009): 44–47.

Segura, Gary M. "A Symposium on the Politics of Same-Sex Marriage—An Introduction and Commentary." *PS: Political Science and Politics* 38 (Apr. 2005): 189–93.

Shaiko, Ronald G. "Same-Sex Marriage, LGBT Organizations, and the Lack of Spirited Political Engagement." In *The Politics of Same-Sex Marriage*, edited by Craig A. Rimmerman and Clyde Wilcox, 85–103. Chicago: University of Chicago Press, 2007.

Sherrill, Kenneth. "Same-Sex Marriage, Civil Unions, and the 2004 Presidential Vote." In *The Future of Gay Rights in America*, edited by H. N. Hirsch, 37–45. New York: Routledge, 2005.

Shilts, Randy. *The Mayor of Castro Street: The Life and Times of Harvey Milk*. New York: St. Martin's Press, 1982.

Shorto, Russell. "What's Their Real Problem with Gay Marriage? It's the Gay Part." *New York Times Magazine*, June 19, 2005, 34.

Smidt, Corwin E., and James M. Penning. "The Christian Right's Mixed Success in Michigan." In *The Christian Right in American Politics: Marching to the Millennium*, edited by John C. Green, Mark J. Rozell, and Clyde Wilcox, 101–20. Washington, DC: Georgetown University Press, 2003.

Smith, Daniel A., Matthew DeSantis, and Jason Kassel. "Same-Sex Marriage Ballot Measures and the 2004 Presidential Election." *State and Local Government Review* 38 (2006): 78–91.

Smith, Miriam. "The Politics of Same-Sex Marriage in Canada and the United States." *PS: Political Science and Politics* 38 (Apr. 2005): 225–28.

Soper, J. Christopher, and Joel S. Fetzer. "The Christian Right in California: Dimming Fortunes in the Golden State." In *The Christian Right in American Politics: Marching to the Millennium*, edited by John C. Green, Mark J. Rozell, and Clyde Wilcox, 209–30. Washington, DC: Georgetown University Press, 2003.

Stoddard, Thomas B. "Why Gay People Should Seek the Right to Marry." In *Lesbian and Gay Marriage: Private Commitments, Public Ceremonies*, edited by Suzanne Sherman, 13–19. Philadelphia: Temple University Press, 1992.

Stouffer, Robert. "Another View of Same-Gender Marriage." *Island Lifestyle*, Jan. 1994, 15–17.

Sullivan, Andrew. "Here Comes the Groom." *New Republic*, Aug. 28, 1989, 20–22.

Sunstein, Cass R. "Foreword: Leaving Things Undecided." *Harvard Law Review* 110 (1996–97): 4–101.

———. "What Did Lawrence Hold? Of Autonomy, Desuetude, Sexuality, and Marriage." *Supreme Court Review*, 2003, 27–74.

Talbot, Margaret. "A Risky Proposal." *New Yorker*, Jan. 18, 2010, 40–51.

Waaldijk, Kees. "Small Change: How the Road to Same-Sex Marriage Got Paved in the Netherlands." In *Legal Recognition of Same-Sex Partnerships: A Study of National, European and International Law*, edited by Robert Wintemute and Mads Andenæs, 437–64. Portland, OR: Hart, 2001.

Wald, Kenneth D., and Graham B. Glover. "Theological Perspectives on Gay Unions: The Uneasy Marriage of Religion and Politics." In *The Politics of Same-Sex Marriage*, edited by Craig A. Rimmerman and Clyde Wilcox, 105–29. Chicago: University of Chicago Press, 2007.

Wald, Kenneth D., and Richard K. Scher. "'A Necessary Annoyance'? The Christian Right and the Development of Republican Party Politics in Florida." In *The Christian Right in American Politics: Marching to the Millennium*, edited by John C. Green, Mark J. Rozell, and Clyde Wilcox, 79–100. Washington, DC: Georgetown University Press, 2003.

Walker, Samuel. *In Defense of American Liberties: A History of the ACLU*. New York: Oxford University Press, 1990.

Wax, Amy L. "The Conservative's Dilemma: Traditional Institutions, Social Change, and Same-Sex Marriage." *San Diego Law Review* 42 (2005): 1059–103.

Wilcox, Clyde, Paul R. Brewer, Shauna Shames, and Celinda Lake. "If I Bend This Far I Will Break? Public Opinion About Same-Sex Marriage." In *The Politics of Same-Sex Marriage*, edited by Craig A. Rimmerman and Clyde Wilcox, 215–42. Chicago: University of Chicago Press, 2007.

Wilcox, Clyde, Linda M. Merolla, and David Beer. "Saving Marriage by Banning Marriage: The Christian Right Finds a New Issue in 2004." In *The Values Campaign? The Christian Right and the 2004 Elections*, edited by John C. Green, Mark J. Rozell, and Clyde Wilcox, 56–76. Washington, DC: Georgetown University Press, 2006.

Yang, Alan. "From Wrongs to Rights: 1973 to 1999." Policy Institute of the National Gay and Lesbian Task Force, 1999. Available online at www.thetaskforce.org/downloads/reports/reports/1999FromWrongsToRights.pdf.

Zwier, Robert. "The Christian Right and the Cultural Divide in Colorado." In *The Christian Right in American Politics: Marching to the Millennium*, edited by John C. Green, Mark J. Rozell, and Clyde Wilcox, 187–207. Washington, DC: Georgetown University Press, 2003.

INDEX

Note: Page numbers in *italics* refer to illustrations.

Achtenberg, Roberta, 44
adoption of children
    and Dade County ordinance, 28
    laws barring, 35, 38, 72, 84, 122
    in Massachusetts, 89
    public opinion on, 51, 72, 114
    Republican opposition to, 44
adoptions, adult, 22, 28
The Advocate, 18, 25, 59, 176, 177
African Americans
    civil rights of, 166–67, 172, 174, 186–87
    and *Goodridge* decision, 92
    and Maryland gay marriage bill, 162–63, 195
    mobilizing effect of gay marriage on, 184–85
    opposition to gay marriage among, 105, 123,
        133, 162, 184–85
    and presidential election of 2004, 112
    and Proposition 8, 123
    and slavery analogy, 132
    in Washington, D.C., 133
age and attitudes, 70, 84, 123, 136, 170–71,
    199–200
AIDS. *See* HIV and AIDS epidemic
Alabama, 72
Alaska, xxi, 41, 58, 66–68, 169
Alito, Samuel, 114, 204
American Civil Liberties Union (ACLU)
    on abolition of marriage, 22
    and *Baehr* case, 55, 216
    and *Bowers* litigation, 36
    on employment discrimination, 14, 25
    and gay rights litigation, 25
    Lesbian and Gay Rights Project, 38–39
    and McConnell-Baker marriage, 19
    and *Perry* litigation, 138
    policies of, 10, 20
    priorities of, 22–23
    and referenda, 29
    and USPS entrapment practices, 13
American Family Association, 152, 153–54, 160
Amestoy, Jeff, 81

Anderson, John, 25
Angelo, Jeff, 164
Arizona, 20, 59, 71, 89, 115, 122
Arkansas, 109, 122
Armey, Dick, 60
attitudes toward homosexuality. *See* public opinion
attorneys
    gay attorneys, 14, 25
    in gay marriage cases, 215–17

Bachmann, Michele, 155
backlashes
    and agenda-setting effect of gay marriage,
        176–80
    and AIDS epidemic, 34–35
    attempts to avoid, 7–8
    against *Baehr* ruling, xxi, 56, 66, 168, 178
    Bryant's Dade County campaign, 26–29
    against Colorado's gay rights ordinances, 68
    and court rulings, xx, xxi, 166–68, 172, 174–76
    against gay wedding ceremonies, 175–76,
        189, 192
    and geographic segmentation, 186–92
    against *Goodridge* ruling, 95–98, 106, 114,
        116–17, 168, 174–76, 212, 215
    and incrementalism strategy, 208
    and intensity of supporters' commitment,
        172–74
    against justices, xxi, 116–17, 123, 151–54,
        152, 215
    and legislatures, 167–69
    against Maine's gay marriage legislation,
        144–46
    and mobilizing effect of gay marriage, 183–86
    potential for, 219
    and public opinion, 166–69, 172, 186
    and religious conservatives, 180–82
    against *Varnum* ruling, 143, 151–54
    against Vermont's civil union legislation,
        80–83, 84, 218

Baehr v. Lewin, 55–59
  and backlash, xxi, 56, 66, 168, 178
  and Defense of Marriage Act, 61, 212
  and gay rights organizations, 176, 216, 217
  and gays' attitudes toward marriage, 176
  impact of victory on gay rights activists, 209
  media coverage of, 165
  and public opinion, 66, 168
  reciprocal-beneficiaries law, 65
  ruling on, 63–66
Baker, Jack, 18, 19
Baldacci, John, 129
Balliett, Amy, 124
BarbouRoske, McKinley, *210*, 210
Barr, Bob, 61, 176–77
Barry, Marion, 133
Basha, Eddie, 59
Bauer, Gary
  and *Baker* case, 83, 182
  and *Brause* case, 67
  and congressional races, 109, 111
  as Reagan appointee, 33
  and Republican primaries, 60, 155
  and *Romer* case, 69
Beck, Glenn, 156
Birmingham, Thomas, 90
Blackmun, Harry, 36
Blackwell, Ken, 112–13, 177, 184
Blankenhorn, David, 159
Bloomberg, Michael, 131–32, 147, 164, 166, 191
Boehner, John, 157, 161
Boies, David, 137–39, *138*, 217
Bonauto, Mary, 52, 209, 215
Bottoms, Sharon, 51
Bowers v. Hardwick, 36–39, 41, 72, 138, 197
Bradley, Bill, 71, 84
Branstad, Terry, 150–51, 153, 181
Brause v. Bureau of Vital Statistics, 66–68
Breyer, Stephen, 203
Briggs, John, 21–22, 29
Brown, Jerry, 23, 24, 134, 139
Brown, Scott, 95, 97
Brown, Willie, 58, 62
Brown v. Board of Education, xx, 167, 172, 174,
  186–87, 190, 202, 213–14
Bryant, Anita, 26–29, *27*, 68, 169
Buchanan, Pat, 44, 61, 83, 160
Buckley, William, 34
Bunning, Jim, 110
Burger, Warren, 37
Burgmeier, Stephen, 144
Burlington Free Press, 77, 79, 80, 82–83
Burress, Phil, 106, 184
Bush, George H. W., 32, 43, 44, 60, 158, 180
Bush, George W.
  on civil unions, 103, 114, 181
  and federal marriage amendment, 88, 111,
    114, 115–16, 175, 189
  gay marriage position of, 87–88
  judicial appointments of, 114, 215
  on New Jersey court decision, 118
  and presidential elections, 99, 103, 105–6,
    107, 110, 111–13, 215

Cady, Mark, 171
California
  adult adoptions in, 22
  African American constituency of, 184
  and AIDS epidemic, 35–36
  and *Baehr* case, 65–66
  court justices in, 123
  defense-of-marriage bills in, 59
  domestic partnerships in, 45, 77, 120
  employment policies in, 24
  gay marriage bill in, 129, 178
  gay marriage litigation in, 120, 137–39
  gay marriages in, 99–100, 120, 209
  gay officeholders in, 71
  opposition to gay marriage in, 98, 121–22
  Proposition 22, 84, 120
  public opinion in, 120, 123
  sodomy laws in, 21–22, 30
  teaching positions in, 29
  See also Proposition 8; San Francisco
Canada, 87
Carson, Brad, 109
Carter, Jimmy, 24–25, 32, 34, 142
Catholic Church
  and amendment to define marriage, 87
  and *Baehr* case, 56, 65–66
  and censorship of homosexuality, 9
  and domestic partnerships and civil unions,
    45, 79–80
  financial support from, 84, 85, 145
  and *Goodridge* case, 91, 92, 93–94, 95, 96, 97
  and health care benefits in Philadelphia, 60
  and Maine's Amendment 1, 145
  and New Jersey gay marriage bill, 148
  and New York gay marriage bill, 163
  organizational strength of, 174
  and Proposition 8, 121
  and Proposition 22, 84
  and Rhode Island, 130
  and *Varnum* case, 127
  and Washington, D.C., gay marriage law, 149
celebrities, 25–26, 200
censorship of homosexuality, 8–9
Chafee, Lincoln, 44, 163
Chang, Kevin, 63, 64, 65, 66
Cheney, Dick, 136, 139
Chicago, 14, 17, 20
children
  and *Baehr* arguments, 63, 64
  and Bryant's campaign, 27, 28
  and child-predator argument, 27, 29, 51, 122,
    159, 197
  court rulings on, 120
  and *Perry* challenge, 159, 160
  prevalence of gay families, 201
  and public education, 121
  and stability-in-marriage argument, 172
  See also adoption of children; parental rights
    and abilities
Christian Coalition, 45, 60–61, 214
Christie, Chris, 148, 195
Ciampa, Vincent, 95
Civil Rights Act (1964), 24, 71

civil rights movement, 7, 8, 15, 174, 186–87
civil unions and domestic partnerships
    advocates of, 83–84, 91
    and benefits for partners, 41, 45, 77, 78
    and Bush, 103, 181
    campaigns for, 51
    and Clinton, 71
    and Democrats, 185
    effect of gay marriage debate on, 59, 89, 213
    and *Goodridge* decision, 91–92, 93–94,
        179–80
    laws barring, 84–85
    and marriage amendments of states, 108
    media coverage of rulings, 165
    and Mormon Church, 212
    and Obama, 142
    and Ohio amendment campaign, 107
    opponents of, 78–83
    outside the U.S., 167
    political exploitation of, 186
    and priorities of gay rights movement, 23
    public opinion on, 80, 82, 92, 114, 179–80,
        205, 211, 218
    recognition of, 45–46
    and state legislatures, 98
    states' enactments of, 119, 218
    Varnum ruling on, 127
    wedding ceremonies for, 58, 188
    See also specific states
Clement, Paul, 161, 202
Clinton, Bill
    appointments of, 71
    and Defense of Marriage Act, 62, 63
    on discrimination in federal agencies, 71
    election of 1988, 43–44
    gay marriage position of, 46, 137, 171, 186
    and gays in the military, 43–44, 46–47, 60,
        140, 168, 169
    Republican efforts to demonize, 186
    and Shepard's murder, 72
Clinton, Hillary, 139
Coburn, Tom, 109
Colorado
    acceptance of gays in, 74
    constitutional amendment in, 68–70
    designated-beneficiary agreements in, 133
    gay rights ordinances in, 28, 46, 62, 68–70
    marriage licenses issued in, 20–21
    public opinion in, 196
    Republican gay marriage supporters in, 164
Columbia University, 10, 12
"coming out," 17–18, 197
Connecticut, 72, 115, 116, 120, 121
corporations, 26, 41, 46, 72, 119, 201–2
Corzine, Jon, 130, 137, 147, 148
courts and court rulings
    and backlashes, 166–68, 172, 174–76
    and elite bias of judges, 170–71
    gay-friendly rulings of, 46
    and gay marriage spring, 120
    and implementation of rulings, 174–76
    media coverage of rulings, 165–66
    and NOM's candidate pledge, 155

    political exploitation of, 186
    and political repercussions, 116–17, 123
    and position clarifications, 166
    and public opinion, xix–xx, xxi–xxii, 20,
        169–70, 186
    rejections of gay marriage in, 116–18
    retaliation against judges, xxi, 151–54,
        152, 215
    and sodomy laws, 72, 85
    See also litigation in same-sex marriages;
        specific states
Culver, Chet, 127–28
Cuomo, Mario, 71, 147

Dade County, Florida, 26–29, 68
Daly, Jim, 199
Dannemeyer, William, 34
Daschle, Tom, 110–11, 215
Davis, Gray, 84
Dean, Howard, 77–82, 111, 137
Defense of Marriage Act (DOMA), 61–63
    and *Baehr* case, 61, 212
    calls for repeal of, 137
    challenges to, 139, 160–61, 203, 217
    constitutionality of, 98, 161, 162
    court rulings on, 162
    and Kerry, 111
    and law firms, 202
    and NOM's candidate pledge, 155
    and Obama, 126, 140, 141, 142, 157, 161
    partial invalidation of, 160–61, 203
    public opinion on, 161
defense-of-marriage laws and amendments
    advent of, 59
    and Democrats, 185
    and gay rights agenda, 177, 178
    pursued in Massachusetts, 89
    in response to *Baehr*, 58, 66, 188
    in response to *Baker*, 84
    in response to *Brause*, 67–68
    in response to *Goodridge*, 106–7
    See also marriage amendments of states
DeGeneres, Ellen, 200
Delaware, 163
D'Emilio, John, 118, 212
Democrats and Democratic Party
    and *Baker* case, 78–79, 80, 81, 82
    and *Brause* case, 68
    on civil unions and domestic partnerships,
        133, 185
    and congressional races of 2004, 108–11
    and Defense of Marriage Act, 61–62, 63
    and defense-of-marriage bills, 59
    and Dukakis, 42
    and federal marriage amendment, 105, 185
    gay constituency of, 104–5
    gay rights plank in, 24
    and gays in the military, 46–47
    and *Goodridge* case, 117, 185
    and New Jersey gay marriage bill, 148
    and New York gay marriage bill, 131–32,
        147–48

Democrats and Democratic Party (*continued*)
    and presidential elections, 32, 42–44, 111–13
    support for gay marriage, 87, 93, 96, 120, 137, 185
    and *Varnum* case, 127–28
    wedge effect of gay marriage on, 105, 183,
        184–85, 186
Diaz, Ruben, 131, 132, 164
DiMasi, Salvatore, 95, 96, 97
Dinkins, David, 45
Dobson, James
    and Bush's judicial nominees, 114
    and congressional races of 2004, 111
    dire declarations of, 87, 109, 184, 210
    on fight against gay marriage, 98
    and Republican primaries, 60
Dolan, Timothy, 163
Dole, Robert, 47, 60, 61, 62
domestic partnerships. *See* civil unions and
        domestic partnerships
"don't ask, don't tell" policy. *See* military service
        of gays
Douglas, James, 83, 128–29
Duane, Tom, 58, 132
Due Process Clause, 53–54, 86
Dukakis, Michael, 30, 42–43
Dunlap, Victoria, 100–101, 101
Dwyer, Ruth, 81–82

educational settings
    activism in, 12
    and AIDS epidemic, 34, 35
    desegregation of, 166, 167
    domestic-partnership recognition in, 46
    employment discrimination in, 19, 29, 30,
        34, 41
    and fear of gay agenda, 27, 81, 108, 121–22
    and oppositional strategies, 121–22, 145
    and Proposition 8, 121
    student organizations in, 10, 25, 34
Eisenhower, Dwight, 5
Emanuel, Rahm, 195
Empire State Pride Agenda (ESPA), 48, 71,
        177–78
employment discrimination
    and AIDS epidemic, 34, 35, 40
    and benefits for partners, 72
    court decisions on, 13, 25, 38
    effect of gay marriage debate on, xxi
    Employment Nondiscrimination Act, 119,
        126, 140, 179, 212, 213
    in federal government, 4–5, 10, 12, 19
    legislation on, 42, 119, 218
    and Mormon Church, 125
    ordinances addressing, 23
    and organizational membership, 6
    policy changes regarding, 26
    prevalence of, 14, 30
    priority of, 22, 213
    public opinion on, 71, 179
    in public school positions, 23
    and repercussions for litigants, 19
Episcopal Church, 136

Equal Protection Clause, 54–55, 86, 160, 171
Equal Rights Amendment (ERA), 20, 29, 31,
        32, 56
Establishment Clause, 126–27, 171
Ettelbrick, Paula, 178

Falwell, Jerry, 32, 34, 44, 87
Family Protection Act, 34
Family Research Council
    and *Brause* case, 67
    on civil unions, 115
    on consequences of gay marriage, 92
    and federal marriage amendment, 114
    and *Goodridge* case, 92, 98
    and Mormon Church, 125
    on Obama, 181
    and Prejean, 135
    and Proposition 8, 125
    retaliation against *Varnum* judges, 152
family values movement, 32
Faubus, Orval, 187, 190
Federal Bureau of Investigation (FBI), 4, 38
federal marriage amendment
    and Bush, 87–88, 99, 103, 111, 114, 115–16,
        175, 189
    congressional debate and votes on, 105, 115–16
    and congressional races of 2004, 108–11
    and Democrats, 105, 185
    and *Goodridge* case, 106
    and *Lawrence* case, 87–88
    and NOM's candidate pledge, 155
    Olson's opposition to, 138
    and presidential election of 2004, 111–13
    and Republicans, 105
    See also marriage amendments of states
Feinstein, Dianne, 45, 192
feminist movement, 17, 20, 22, 31, 49
film portrayals of homosexuality, 9
Finneran, Thomas, 91, 93, 94, 95
First Amendment, 33
Florida
    adoptions in, 28
    Bryant's campaign in, 26–29
    on employment discrimination, 25
    gay marriage litigation in, 116
    gay officeholders in, 156
    marriage amendment in, 28, 122
    police harassment in, 14
Florida State University, 5
Focus on the Family, 68, 111, 114, 184
Fourteenth Amendment, 53–55, 86
Frank, Barney
    Armey's slur, 60
    and Defense of Marriage Act, 62, 141
    on difficulty of gay marriage issue, 167
    on Log Cabin Republicans, 42
    on marriages in San Francisco, 99
    and Sciortino, 95
Freedom to Marry Task Force, 75–76, 164
Free Exercise Clause, 129–30
Fried, Charles, 161
Frum, David, 83, 164

Gallagher, Maggie, 127, 146, 155
Garland, Judy, 16
Gates, Robert, 157
Gay and Lesbian Advocates and Defenders
    (GLAD), 52, 89, 139, 215, 216–17
gay bars, xx, 3–4, 6, 10, 12–14, 17, 23
gay individuals, contact with, 39, 73, 197–98
gay rights movement
    and AIDS epidemic, 39–41
    and *Bowers* ruling, 38
    effect of gay marriage debate on, xxi, 176–80,
        213–14, 218–19
    and gay population estimates, 197
    militancy in, 11–12, 40
    priorities of, xx, 48, 213
    progress in, 41
    and Republican Party, 183
gay rights organizations
    activism of, 18
    agenda of, 176–80
    and *Baehr* case, 55, 176, 216, 217
    consequences for associating with, 6
    effect of gay marriage activism on, 213
    and Family Protection Act, 34
    founding of, 6–7
    funding issues of, 31
    and *Goodridge* backlash, 95
    growth of, 11, 18, 70–71
    legal victories of, 12–13
    and *Perry* litigation, 138, 139, 217
    priorities of, 22–23, 48, 213
    reaction to Proposition 8, 124–25
    and Shepard's murder, 72
    size of, 15
    strategic approach of, 216–17
    student organizations, 25
George, Ronald, 171
Georgia, 14, 38, 45, 116, 156, 184
Gibbs, Robert, 142, 158
Gingrich, Newt, 152–55, 161
Ginsburg, Ruth Bader, 203–4
Giuliani, Rudy, 136
Goodman, Ellen, 135, 177
Goodridge v. Department of Public Health
    agenda-setting effect of, 177–80
    amendment proposals, 93–94, 96, 97
    and backlash, 95–96, 97, 98, 106, 114,
        116–17, 168, 174–76, 212, 215
    and civil unions, 91–92, 93–94, 179–80
    and Democrats, 117, 185
    gay marriages following, 103, 174–76, 209
    impact of, on gay marriage trends, 98, 116, 209
    media coverage of, 165–66
    opposition to, 89–90, 91, 92, 93, 97–99
    and presidential election of 2004, 111,
        113, 114
    public opinion on, 92, 187–88
    ruling, 90–91, 165
    support for, 92–93
Gore, Al, 71, 84, 112
Gramm, Phil, 60
Gregoire, Christine, 185, 194
Griswold v. Connecticut, 6, 10, 36

Gronstal, Mike, 154
Gunderson, Steve, 63

Hardwick, Michael, 38, 39
Harkin, Tom, 31, 137
hate crimes laws, 72, 119, 126, 142
Hawaii
    civil unions and domestic partnerships in, 77, 163
    and Defense of Marriage Act, 61
    gay marriage litigation in (see *Baehr v. Lewin*)
    opposition to gay marriage in, 98, 168
    public opinion in, 56, 65, 66, 168, 169, 196
    sodomy law of, 56
HIV and AIDS epidemic
    advent of, 34–35
    casualties of, 35, 39, 49
    and gay rights movement, 39–41
    and legal status of partners, xx, 49–50
    and public awareness, 39
    and public opinion, 39–41
    and religious conservatives, 34, 180
    research and treatment funding for, 39, 40, 43
    and sodomy laws, 36
    and visa restrictions, 140
Holt, Jim, 109
Hoover, J. Edgar, 34
hospital visitation. *See* legal benefits of marriage
housing discrimination. *See* legal benefits of
    marriage
Hudson, Rock, 35, 39
Human Rights Campaign
    and AIDS epidemic, 40
    and Clinton, 44, 62
    and Defense of Marriage Act, 62
    and electoral defeats of 2004, 113
    fundraising of, 41
    leadership of, 95
    and New York gay marriage bill, 163
    on opposition to same-sex marriage, 68
    on support for gay marriage, 196
    on viability of gay rights campaigns, 25
Huntsman, Jon, Jr., 136, 155, 181

Idaho, 69, 114
Illinois, 14, 24, 59, 109, 163, 195
immigrants and immigration, 10, 12, 15, 24–25,
    30, 161–62, 212
incrementalism strategy, 208
Indiana, 89, 201
inevitability of gay marriage
    and economic pressures, 201–2
    and knowledge of gay individuals, 197–200
    and *Lawrence* case, 87
    and recent progress, 193–96
    and social/political environment, 200–201
    statistical modeling on, 202
    and support of young people, 199–200
    and trends in support for gay marriage,
        196–97
inheritance rights. *See* legal benefits of marriage
interracial marriage, 166, 167

Iowa
   backlash in, 143, 150–51
   and Bush's reelection, 112
   gay marriage litigation in, 116, 126–28, *210*, 214
   marriage amendment sought in, 154
   presidential primaries in, 60–61, 154–55
   public opinion in, 154, 168, 169
   Republican supporters of gay marriage in, 164
   retaliation against judges, xxi, 151–54, *152*, 215

Jackson, Jesse, 42
Jacques, Cheryl, 95, 97, 113
Jewish constituents, 72, 92, 164

Kameny, Franklin, 12
Keck, Thomas, 211
Kendell, Kate, 134
Kennedy, Anthony, 70, 86, 139, 204–7
Kennedy, Edward, 24
Kentucky, 19, 20, 85, 110
Kerrigan v. Commissioner of Public Health, 120, 121
Kerry, John, 63, 93, 111, 112, 171, 185
Keyes, Alan, 61, 83, 109
King, Steven, 144, 151
kiss-in demonstrations, 125
Kistler, Rives, 214
Koop, Everett, 33
Kowalski, Sharon, 50, *50*
Kramer, Larry, 41

Lambda Legal
   agenda of, 176
   and AIDS epidemic, 35, 40
   and *Baehr* case, 176
   and *Bowers* case, 36–38
   early years of, 18
   and gay marriage litigation, 55, 57, 89
   income of, 31, 40, 41, 70–71
   and *Lawrence* case, 87
   and *Perry* case, 138
   and *Romer* ruling, 69
   and sodomy laws, 36
Land, Richard, 118
Langbehn, Janice, 181
LaRouche, Lyndon H., 35–36
Latinos, 130–31, 132
Lawrence v. Texas, 85–88, 138, 139, 160, 205–6
Lees, Brian, 95, 96
legal benefits of marriage
   absence of, 49, 50
   and adult adoptions, 22
   and AIDS epidemic, 34
   Branstad on, 150
   and child custody, 51, 89
   and corporate America, 41
   and Defense of Marriage Act, 61
   for domestic partners, 45, 59, 77, 120,
      132, 133
   effect of gay marriage on, 213
   in Hawaii's reciprocal-beneficiaries act, 65

and incrementalism strategy, 208
and Mormon Church, 212
and Obama, 181
public opinion on, 45, 114, 179
and religious conservatives, 181
Leuenberger, James, 214
Lewis, John, 195
libertarians, 10, 31, 52–53
Limbaugh, Rush, 156, 205, 218
Lincoln, Blanche, 109
Lindsay, John, 4, 13
Lippert, William, 199
litigation in same-sex marriages
   in the 1970s and 80s, 18–20
   benefits of, 208–12, 218
   in California (see *Perry v. Schwarzenegger*)
   consequences of, xxi, 212–15, 218–19
   constitutional arguments, 19, 53–54
   courts' rejection of, 19
   educational effect of, 208
   following *Goodridge*, 116
   in Hawaii (see *Baehr v. Lewin*)
   in Iowa (see *Varnum v. Brien*)
   and law firms, 202
   in Massachusetts (see *Goodridge v. Department
      of Public Health*)
   media coverage of, 20
   state-court emphasis of, 216
   strategic advantages of, 208–11
   in Vermont (see *State v. Baker*)
Log Cabin Republicans, 42, 44, 60
Los Angeles, 12, 23, 125
Los Angeles Times, 37, 58–59, 146
Lott, Trent, 182
Loving v. Virginia, 19, 206
Lugar, Richard, 44, 61
Lynch, John, 129, 130, 149–50, 194

Maddow, Rachel, 200
Maine
   Amendment 1, 144–46, 147, 188, 217
   backlash in, 144–46
   domestic partnerships in, 115
   gay marriage bill in, 195
   gay marriage enacted in, 126, 129
   gay officeholders in, 199
   public opinion in, 129, 146, 169, 180, 195, 213
Malia, Elizabeth, 199
marriage amendments of states
   arguments for, 115
   and Democrats, 105
   effect on civil unions and domestic
      partnerships, 108
   and legal benefits, 212–13
   and religious groups, 106–8
   and Republicans, 105, 184, 185–86
   in response to *Baker*, 84–85
   in response to *Goodridge*, 105, 106, 212
   in swing states, 184
   trends in, 115, 126
   See also federal marriage amendment; *specific states*
Marshall, Margaret, 171, 206

Maryland, 115, 116, 117, 162–63, 195
Massachusetts
    and AIDS epidemic, 35
    civil unions in, 90, 91–92, 211
    discrimination policies in, 42
    enthusiasm for gay marriage in, 188–89
    foster-parents policies in, 30
    gay marriage litigation in, xxi, 87
    gay marriages in, 103, *104*
    gay officeholders in, 42, 199
    marriage amendment in, 89–90, 92
    opposition to gay marriage in, 168
    political influence in, 23
    public opinion in, 92, 94, 119–20, 168, 169
    reaction to Proposition 8 in, 124
    See also *Goodridge v. Department of Public
        Health*
Mattachine Society, 6–8, 10, 11, 12, 13, 17
Maynard, Keith, *175*
McCarthyism, 4–5, 8, 11
McConnell, James Michael, 18, 19
McCurry, Mike, 62, 63
McLaughlin, Chip, 175
media
    coverage of AIDS epidemic, 40
    coverage of court cases, 20, 165–66
    coverage of gay marriages, 175–76, 191
    expanded coverage of gay issues, 9
    gay personalities in, 73
    stereotypes promoted by, 31
mental health field, 10, 11, 15, 23
Metropolitan Community Churches, 22, 23
Michigan
    discrimination policies in, 23, 24, 156
    marriage amendment in, 106, 184
    public opinion in, 133
    and religiosity of voters, 170
    sodomy laws in, 85
militant gay rights activism, 11–12
military service of gays
    ban on, 5–6, 12, 29
    and *Bowers* ruling, 38
    and Clinton, 43–44, 46–47, 60, 140, 168, 169
    court decisions on, 25, 41
    "don't ask, don't tell" policy, 46–47, 71, 126,
        140, 142, 156–57
    media coverage of, 26
    and Obama, 126, 140, 142, 156–58, *158*
    public opinion on, 71, 114, 157, 173, 178–79
    repeal of ban on, 157–58, *158*
Milk, Harvey, 23, 38
Minnesota
    anti-discrimination ordinance in, 23, 29
    gay marriage litigation in, 19–20
    Kowalski guardianship case in, 46, 50
    marriage amendment in, 193
    marriage licenses in, 18
    public opinion in, 193
Mississippi, 84, 106, 202
Missouri, 37, 106, 188
Mohler, Albert, 202
Mongiardo, Daniel, 110

Moral Majority, 31–34, 174
Mormon Church
    and anti-discrimination ordinance, 125
    and *Baehr* case, 56, 65–66
    and *Brause* case, 67
    financial support from, 67, 84, 85, 122, 145
    and gay rights, 212
    and Maine's Amendment 1, 145
    organizational strength of, 174
    and Proposition 8, 121, 122, 125, 212
    and Proposition 22, 84
Morrison, Terry K., 199
Moscone, George, 29

National Association for the Advancement of
        Colored People (NAACP), 6, 12, 31, 174,
        187, 209, 217
National Center for Lesbian Rights, 134, 177
National Gay Task Force (later the National Gay
        and Lesbian Task Force)
    and AIDS epidemic, 35
    and *Bowers* ruling, 38
    budget of, 41
    and Defense of Marriage Act, 62
    early years of, 18
    and electoral defeats of 2004, 113
    Families Project of, 51
    and Leadership Conference on Civil Rights, 31
    and media portrayal of gays, 26
    priorities of, 48
    reaction to Dade County defeat, 28
    on *Romer* ruling, 69
National March on Washington for Lesbian and
        Gay Rights, 39, 42, 52, 83
National Organization for Marriage (NOM)
    and Burgmeier campaign, 144
    and Maine's Amendment 1, 145
    and Minnesota campaign, 193
    and New Hampshire's gay marriage repeal bill, 149
    and New Jersey's gay marriage bill, 148
    presidential candidates' pledge, 155
    and Proposition 8, 160
    retaliation against Republican supporters, 164
    television advertisements of, 143, 193
    and *Varnum* case, 127, 152, 153
Nebraska, 59, 84–85, 98
Nevada, 98, 109, 133, 196
New Hampshire
    adoption ban in, 35, 38
    civil unions in, 119, 128, 129
    gay marriage enacted in, 126, 129
    gay marriage repeal bill, 149–50, 194
    presidential primaries in, 155
    public opinion in, 129, 149–50, 194
New Jersey
    civil unions in, 117, 118, 119, 130, 186
    congressional races in, 118
    gay marriage bill in, 126, 148, 194–95, 217
    gay marriage litigation in, 87, 89, 116, 117
    marriage licenses issued in, 103
    public opinion in, 130, 195

New Mexico, 100–101, *101*, 112, 166, 214
Newsom, Gavin, 99, 134, *189*, 189–90, 192
New York (state)
　adult adoptions in, 22
　backlash anticipated in, 216
　gay candidates and officeholders in, 71
　gay marriage bill in, 126, 130–32, 147–48,
　　163, 217
　gay marriage litigation in, 116, 117
　gay marriages in, 102, *102*, 166, 190–91
　opposition to gay marriage in, 131
　parental rights policies in, 41
　public opinion in, 131, 180
　and religiosity of voters, 170
　sodomy laws in, 13–14
New York City
　AIDS epidemic in, 40
　and *Bowers* ruling, 38
　domestic partnerships in, 45
　and employment discrimination, 14, 24
　gay activism in, 9, 12, 17
　gay bars in, 4, 12–13, 16
　inheritance laws in, 46
　Mattachine Society of, 8, 10, 11, 14, 17
　ordinance barring discrimination in, 41
　police harassment in, 3, 4, 12–13, 14
　reaction to Bryant's campaign in, 27, 28
　reaction to Proposition 8 in, 124, 125
　wedding ceremonies in, 58
New York Times
　on *Baehr* litigation, 57
　on *Bowers* ruling, 37
　on Bryant's campaign, 28–29
　on election of 1992, 43
　on gay marriage in New York, 131, 147
　on gay nightlife, 9
　on Maine's Amendment 1, 146
Nickels, Greg, 191
Noble, Elaine, 23
North American Conference of Homophile
　Organizations, 11, 177
North Carolina, 156, 193–94
North Dakota, 111, 114

Obama, Barack
　and Defense of Marriage Act, 126, 140, 141,
　　142, 157, 161
　and gay community, 139–42, 161
　gay marriage position of, 126, 140, 142,
　　157–58, 196
　gay rights support of, 126, 140
　and gays in the military, 126, 140, 142,
　　156–58, *158*
　on hospital visitation rights, 181
　judicial appointments of, 135–36, 156
　and Proposition 8, 123
　and Senate race of 2004, 109
O'Connor, Sandra Day, 38, 70, 86–87, 153
Ohio
　and *Bowers* ruling, 38
　gay-rights amendment repeal in, 69, 114
　marriage amendment in, 106–7, 108, 112, 184
　and presidential election of 2004, 112, 113
　Republican strategies in, 184
　violence against gays in, 14
Oklahoma, 109, 179
Olson, Ted, 136, 137–39, *138*, 198, 217
O'Malley, Martin, 195
opposition to gay marriage
　among African Americans, 105, 123, 133, 162,
　　184–85
　arguments for, 53, 54–55, 121–22, 171–72
　and education levels, 170
　intensity of conviction in, 98, 172–74,
　　185, 219
　and judges' pro-gay decisions, 117
　and religiosity, 123, 145, 162, 170
　of Republicans, 59, 137, 184, 186
　statistics on, 59, 97–98, 119, 135
　See also backlashes; marriage amendments of
　　states
ordinances for gay rights, 18, 23, 26–29, 41, 46,
　68–69
Oregon
　anti-discrimination ordinances in, 29
　civil unions and domestic partnerships in,
　　115, 119
　gay marriage litigation in, 116
　gay marriages in, 101–2, 178, 189
　gay officeholders in, 71, 214
　marriage amendment in, 106, 107–8, 184, 188
　public opinion in, 196
　religious conservatives in, 182

Palmer, Richard, 171
parental rights and abilities
　and AIDS epidemic, 34, 35
　arguments against, 30, 53, 55
　and *Baker* backlash, 84
　and *Bowers* ruling, 38
　court rulings on, 41, 120
　and custody cases, 3, 14, 23, 36, 40, 41,
　　51, 72
　and Dukakis, 42
　and legal recognition of relationships, 51
　and *Perry* case, 159
　public opinion on, 51
　Republican Party on, 44
　social science evidence on, 52
　and sodomy laws, 36
　See also adoption of children
Parents, Families and Friends of Lesbians and
　Gays, 71, 198
Paterson, David, 131–32
pathology model of homosexuality, 6, 10, 12,
　15, 23
Paul, Ron, 155
Pence, Mike, 157
Pennsylvania, 24, 59–60, 118, 133–34
Perez v. Lippold, 206
Perkins, Tony, 87, 92, 98, 111
Perry, Rick, 155

Perry v. Schwarzenegger
  and defeat of gay marriage in Maine, 147
  in federal courts, 195–96
  filing of, 137–39
  and gay rights organizations, 139, 217
  ruling on, 160
  trial of, 158–60, 172
  and YouTube broadcast of case, 159, 198
Persily, Nate, 117
Philadelphia, 12, 59
police
  and gay bars, xx, 3, 4, 6, 10, 12–13, 16, 217
    (*see also* Stonewall)
  and organizational membership, 6
  police brutality, 12
  police harassment, 3–4, 11, 12–13,
    14, 23
polygamy, 67, 92, 159
popular culture, 25–26, 200
Powell, Colin, 46–47
Powell, Lewis, 36–37, 197
Prejean, Carrie, 135
prisoners, gay, 23, 25, 54
Proposition 8, 121–25
  challenge to (see *Perry v. Schwarzenegger*)
  corporate response to, 201
  predictions for, 135, 196
  reactions to, *124*, 124–25
  and referendum proposals, 134, 147
  and religious constituents, 170, 171,181, 212
  state-law argument against, 216
  struck down, 157, 160, 203
Protestants and Protestant churches, 72–73, 78,
    104, 127, 136, 199
public office, gays in, 23, 41, 42, 71, 114, 156
public opinion
  on adoption of children, 51, 72, 114
  and AIDS epidemic, 35
  and backlashes, 166–69, 172, 186
  and *Bowers* ruling, 39
  on Bush's gay marriage position, 105–6
  changes in, 8, 218
  on civil unions, 80, 82, 92, 114, 133, 179–80,
    205, 211
  and court rulings, xix–xx, xxi–xxii, 20, 169–70,
    186, 218
  on Defense of Marriage Act, 161
  demographic differences in, 51, 70, 123, 136,
    170–71, 187–88
  effect of coming out on, 197
  on employment discrimination, 71, 179
  and familiarity with gays, 51
  on federal marriage amendment, 103–4
  on gay marriage, 52, 59, 74, 97–98, 115, 119,
    121, 128, 132–37, 143, 161, 218
  and gay marriage spring, 135, 136–37, 148
  on gay officeholders, 156
  on gay rights issues, 178–79
  geographic segmentation of, 186–92
  on *Goodridge* decision, 92, 187–88
  intermediaries' influence on, 8
  and knowledge of gay individuals, 39, 73, 197–98

  and *Lawrence* case, 88
  on legal benefits, 45, 114, 179
  on legalization of gay relations, 86
  and legislatures, 167–68, 169–70
  and litigation victories, 209–10, *210*
  on military service of gays, 71, 114, 157, 173,
    178–79
  on morality of homosexuality, 31, 45, 70, 85,
    98, 156, 170, 198
  on parental rights, 51
  and religious conservatives, 182
  on religious exemptions, 130
  trends in, 156
  on *Varnum* ruling in Iowa, 127

Raspberry, William, 28
Reagan, Ronald, 29, 31–33, 35, 41
reciprocal-beneficiaries law, 65
Reich, Robert, 90
Reilly, Thomas, 91, 94
religion and religiosity
  as basis for opponents' arguments, 53, 171
  court decisions based on, xix, 20
  and intensity of conviction, 173–74
  and opposition to gay marriage, 123, 145,
    162, 170
  of young people, 199
religious groups and organizations
  and *Baehr* case, 56, 65–66
  and Bush, 99, 103
  changing attitudes in, 11, 26, 72–73
  Christian Coalition, 45, 60–61
  and congressional races of 2004, 111
  financial support from, 67, 84, 85, 122, 145
  fundamentalists, 20, 26
  and gays in the military, 46
  and *Goodridge* case, 91, 92, 98–99
  and *Lawrence* litigation in Texas, 86, 87
  and Maine's Amendment 1, 145
  and marriage amendments, 106–8
  and Maryland gay marriage bill, 162–63
  mobilizing effect of gay marriage on, 183–86
  Moral Majority, 31–34, 174
  and Ohio amendment campaign, 106–7
  organizational strength of, 174
  and Prejean controversy, 135
  and presidential election of 1980, 31–33
  and presidential election of 2004,
    112–13, 114
  and Proposition 8, 121, 122, 123
  and public opinion, 180–82
  religious exemptions, 129–30
  religious right, 26–29, 33, 60, 176, 180,
    182, 184
  and Republican Party, 104, 154, 183–84, 203
  retaliation against judges by, 152, 153
  and sodomy laws, 30
  support for gay marriage by, 78, 119, 136
  unifying effect of gay marriage on, 180–82
  and *Varnum* case, 126–27
Rendell, Ed, 59–60

Republicans and Republican Party
  and AIDS epidemic, 34–35
  and Alaska's *Brause* litigation, 67
  attitudes among, 41, 44, 136–37
  and congressional races of 2004, 108–11
  and Defense of Marriage Act, 61–63, 161
  and "don't ask, don't tell" repeal, 157
  and federal marriage amendment, 104, 105,
    115–16
  and gay marriage spring, 136–37
  gay marriage supporters among, 164
  gay members of, 42, 44, 60
  and gays in the military, 47
  and inevitability of gay marriage, 202
  and Iowa's *Varnum* litigation, 127–28,
    143–44, 151–54
  and judges, 171
  and marriage amendments of states, 185–86,
    193–94
  mobilizing effect of gay marriage on, 183–86
  and New Hampshire's gay marriage bill, 129
  and New Mexican marriage licenses, 100
  and New York gay marriage bill, 131, 132
  opposition to gay marriage of, 59, 137, 184, 186
  opposition to gay rights of, 137
  and presidential election of 1980, 32
  and presidential election of 2004, 111–13
  and presidential election of 2008, 126
  and presidential primaries of 2012, 154–55
  and religious conservatives, 183–84, 203
  religious constituency of, 104, 154
  and Texas' *Lawrence* litigation, 87–88
  unifying effect of gay marriage on, 180–82
  and Vermont's *Baker* litigation, 78–79, 80–81,
    82, 83, 128–29
Respect for Marriage Act, 162
rhetoric, extremes in, 186–87
Rhode Island, 126, 130, 163
Rich, Frank, 62
Roberts, John, 114, 204
Roberts, Rod, 150–51, 152
Robertson, Pat, 34, 60–61, 182
Robison, James, 33
Roe v. Wade, xx, 203–4, 205, 218
Romer v. Evans, 68–70, 139, 159, 205
Romney, Mitt, 91, 93–97, 154–55
Rorex, Clela, 21
Rove, Karl, 106, 114, 183–84, 186, 192

Safire, William, 28–29
San Francisco
  attitudes toward homosexuality in, 11
  and Clinton, 62
  courts and justices in, 120
  domestic partnerships in, 45
  employment policies in, 24
  gay bars in, 23
  gay marriage litigation in, 137–39
  gay marriages in, 99–100, 175–76, 178,
    189–90, 191
  gay rights organizations in, 11

police harassment in, 3, 11, 14
political activism in, 23
reaction to Bryant's campaign in, 27, 28
reaction to Proposition 8 in, 124
wedding ceremonies in, 58, 188
Santorum, Rick, 105, 118, 153, 155
Savage, Dan, 141
Scalia, Antonin, 69, 87, 204
Schmidt, Steve, 136, 139
Schumer, Charles, 137, 147
Schwarzenegger, Arnold, 99, 120,
  129, 139
Sciortino, Carl, 95
Shapp, Milton, 24
Shepard, Matthew, 72, 84
Silver, Nate, 145, 196, 202
Sims, Ron, 191
Socarides, Richard, 127, 140, 141, 161
sodomy and sodomy laws
  and AIDS epidemic, 40
  and *Bowers* case, 36–39, 41, 72, 138, 197
  considered a crime, 3, 13–14, 30
  constitutional challenges to, 23, 30, 36–39
  as a constitutional right, 218
  court decisions on, xix, 25, 30, 72, 204
  and discriminatory practices, 14, 36
  early policy statements on, 6, 10
  and *Lawrence* case, 85–88, 138, 139, 160,
    205–6
  outside the U.S., 167
  priority of, 22–23
  public opinion on, 35, 45
  and religious conservatives, 180
  repeals and invalidation of sodomy laws,
    21–22, 23, 56, 72, 85
  and threat of backlashes, 7–8
South Carolina, 115
South Dakota, 58, 72, 110–11
Spitzer, Eliot, 102, 103, 166
Starr, Ken, 168
state courts. *See* courts and court rulings
state legislatures, 194
  Bush on, 103
  and civil unions, 163, 213
  compromise positions of, 212
  corporate pressure on, 201
  and defense-of-marriage acts, 59
  and gay marriage bills, 98, 115, 169, 194
  and laws defining marriage, 21–22
  and legislative races, 63–64
  motivations of, 206
  and public opinion, 59, 115, 196
  and Republicans, 193
  and sodomy laws, 85
  See also marriage amendments of states;
    specific states
State v. Baker, 75–79, 81, 83, 94, 165, 182
Stoddard, Tom, 37, 48, 70
Stonewall, 16–17, 18, 140, 141–42
support for gay marriage
  arguments of advocates, 52–54
  of Democrats, 87, 93, 96, 120, 137, 185

intensity of conviction in, 172–74
statistics on, 97–98, 119, 135, 143
trends in, 156, 196–97
of young people, 199–200
Sykes, Wanda, 200

Tam, William, 159
Tauro, Joseph, 160–61, 171
Tennessee, 115
Ternus, Marsha, 153
Texas
domestic partnerships in, 45
gay officeholders in, 114, 156
housing discrimination in, 34
Lawrence case, 85–88, 138, 139, 160, 205–6
reaction to Bryant's campaign in, 28
sodomy law in, 86, 204, 205
Thomas, Clarence, 86, 204
Thune, John, 110–11, 136
Tribe, Laurence, 91

United States Postal Service (USPS), 7, 13
U.S. Civil Service Commission, 5, 10, 12, 23, 30
U.S. Congress, 30, 47
U.S. Supreme Court
backlash against rulings of, xx
and *Baehr* case, 65, 66
and *Bowers* case, 36–39, 72, 138, 197
Bush's appointments to, 114, 215
on censorship of homosexuality, 8–9
on Colorado amendment, 68–70
and constitutional arguments, 53–54
early appeals to, 20
and future of gay marriage, 203–7
and *Lawrence* case, 86–87
media coverage of rulings, 165
Obama's appointments to, 135–36
and *Perry* case, 138–39, 159, 198
and public opinion, xix–xx, xxi–xxii, 218
and rigorous judicial scrutiny, 54
on sodomy laws, xix, 25, 30, 36–39, 72
Utah, 58, 72, 124, 125

Vander Plaats, Bob, 128, 144, 150–55
Varnum v. Brien, 126, 143–44, 151–54, 214
Vermont
backlash in, 80–83, 84, 218
civil unions in, xxi, 77–84, 114, 128–29, 214, 218
corporate testimony in, 201
and crimes with anti-gay motive, 42
gay marriage bill in, 126, 201
gay marriage enacted in, 128–29

gay marriage litigation in, 75–79, 81, 83, 94, 165, 182
gay officeholders in, 199
public opinion in, 128, 169, 171
reaction to developments in, 84, 89
requests for licenses in, 20
violence against gays, 14, 35, 42, 72, 84
Virginia
African American constituents of, 184
congressional races in, 118
custody cases in, 30, 51
marriage amendment in, 115, 186
support for civil unions in, 180
Von Hoffman, Nicholas, 31
vulnerability of same-sex relationships, 49–51

Walker, Vaughn, 139, 158–60, 171, 172, 198, 203
Warren, Rick, 136, 140–41
Washington, D.C.
anti-discrimination ordinances in, 23
and employment discrimination, 14, 24
gay marriage legalized in, 133, 148–49
gay marriage litigation in, 55
Mattachine Society of, 12, 13
police harassment in, 3, 13, 14
political influence of gay community in, 25
recognition of gay marriages, 133
sodomy laws in, 33
Washington Blade, 47, 109, 127
Washington Post, 28, 59, 115, 126
Washington State
and AIDS epidemic, 36
anti-discrimination ordinances in, 23
attitudes toward marriage in, 22
civil unions and domestic partnerships in, 119, 132–33
and congressional races of 2004, 109
equal rights amendment in, 19
Everything but Marriage Act, 132–33, 146–47, 201
gay marriage bill in, 194
gay marriage litigation in, 19, 116
judges targeted in, 117
Weld, William, 42, 91
Weprin, David, 164
West, Jason, 102, 166, 190–91
West Virginia, 214
White, Byron, 37, 38
Wicker, Randy, 9–10
Wilson, Pete, 42, 59, 180
Wirthlin, Richard, 184
Wisconsin, 35, 45, 109, 115, 133
Wolfson, Evan, 55, 57, 164, 177, 209

young people, 199–200

CPSIA information can be obtained
at www.ICGtesting.com
Printed in the USA
BVHW042001161222
654425BV00002B/28